OXFORD ENGLISH DRAMA

Ge~~neral Editor~~ ~~MICHAEL CORDNER~~

Associate General  GINS

'TIS

JOHN FORD began his literary career as an occasional poet and pamphleteer before becoming a dramatist who wrote six plays in various collaborative combinations with Middleton, Rowley, Webster, and Dekker. Later he was sole author of eleven plays, three of which were subsequently lost, but *'Tis Pity She's a Whore*, *The Broken Heart*, and *Perkin Warbeck* eventually became famous. This edition sets his earliest surviving drama, *The Lover's Melancholy*, alongside his best-known work.

Ford may have been born just before his baptism on 12 April 1586, the only date known. A 'John Ford Devon gent.' matriculated as a member of Exeter College, Oxford, on 26 March 1601, and there is a record of John Ford entering the Middle Temple in November 1602, but no indication of him ever being called to the bar. It is possible that Ford remained in law chambers all his working life, perhaps managing property for the gentry. It is supposed that he returned to settle in Devon just before the Civil War and died there later. His death could have taken place at any time after 1639, when he published his last play and then disappeared from public view.

MARION LOMAX is the author of *Stage Images and Traditions: Shakespeare to Ford* (Cambridge University Press, 1987). *The Peep-show Girl* (Bloodaxe, 1989), a libretto, *Beyond Men and Dreams*, commissioned by the Royal Opera House Garden Venture (performed 1991), and numerous articles on early drama, poetry, and feminist literary theory. She has also edited *The Rover* by Aphra Behn (New Mermaids, 1995).

MICHAEL CORDNER is Ken Dixon Professor of Drama at the University of York. He has edited editions of George Farquhar's *The Beaux' Stratagem*, the *Complete Plays* of Sir George Etherege, and *Four Comedies* of Sir John Vanbrugh. His editions include *Four Restoration Marriage Comedies* and he is completing a book on *The Comedy of Marriage 1660–1737*.

PETER HOLLAND is McMeel Family Professor in Shakespeare Studies at the University of Notre Dame.

MARTIN WIGGINS is a Fellow of the Shakespeare Institute and Lecturer in English at the University of Birmingham.

OXFORD ENGLISH DRAMA

J. M. Barrie
Peter Pan and Other Plays

Aphra Behn
The Rover and Other Plays

George Farquhar
The Recruiting Officer and Other Plays

John Ford
'Tis Pity She's a Whore and Other Plays

Ben Jonson
The Alchemist and Other Plays

Ben Jonson
The Devil is an Ass and Other Plays

Christopher Marlowe
Doctor Faustus and Other Plays

John Marston
The Malcontent and Other Plays

Thomas Middleton
Women Beware Women and Other Plays

*A Mad World, My Masters and
Other Plays*

Richard Brinsley Sheridan
*The School for Scandal and
Other Plays*

J. M. Synge
*The Playboy of the Western World and
Other Plays*

John Vanbrugh
The Relapse and Other Plays

John Webster
*The Duchess of Malfi and
Other Plays*

Oscar Wilde
*The Importance of Being Earnest and
Other Plays*

William Wycherley
The Country Wife and Other Plays

Court Masques
ed. David Lindley

Eighteenth-Century Women Dramatists
ed. Melinda Finberg

Four Jacobean Sex Tragedies
ed. Martin Wiggins

Four Restoration Marriage Plays
ed. Michael Cordner

Four Revenge Tragedies
ed. Katharine Maus

*London Assurance and Other Victorian
Comedies*
ed. Klaus Stierstorfer

*The Roaring Girl and Other City
Comedies*
ed. James Knowles and Eugenen
Giddens

*She Stoops to Conquer and Other
Comedies*
ed. Nigel Wood

OXFORD WORLD'S CLASSICS

JOHN FORD

The Lover's Melancholy
The Broken Heart
'Tis Pity She's a Whore
Perkin Warbeck

Edited with an Introduction and Notes by
MARION LOMAX

OXFORD
UNIVERSITY PRESS

OXFORD
UNIVERSITY PRESS

Great Clarendon Street, Oxford OX2 6DP

Oxford University Press is a department of the University of Oxford.
It furthers the University's objective of excellence in research, scholarship,
and education by publishing worldwide in

Oxford New York

Athens Auckland Bangkok Bogotá Buenos Aires Cape Town
Chennai Dar es Salaam Delhi Florence Hong Kong Istanbul Karachi
Kolkata Kuala Lumpur Madrid Melbourne Mexico City Mumbai Nairobi
Paris São Paulo Shanghai Singapore Taipei Tokyo Toronto Warsaw

with associated companies in Berlin Ibadan

Oxford is a registered trade mark of Oxford University Press
in the UK and in certain other countries

Published in the United States
by Oxford University Press Inc., New York

© Marion Lomax 1995

First published as a World's Classics paperback 1995
Reissued as an Oxford World's Classics paperback 1998
Reissued 2008

British Library Cataloguing in Publication Data

Data available

Library of Congress Cataloging in Publication Data

Ford, John, 1586–c.1640.
'Tis Pity She's a Whore / John Ford; edited by Marion Lomax.
p. cm.—(Oxford world's classics)
I. Lomax, Marion. II. Series.
PR2524.T5 1995 822'.3—dc20 94–47318

ISBN 978-0-19-955386-0

4

Printed in Great Britain by
Clays Ltd, St Ives plc

CONTENTS

ACKNOWLEDGEMENTS

I am particularly indebted to Michael Cordner for being an extremely patient General Editor and to Martin Wiggins for his scrupulous attentions as associate General Editor: additional thanks go to Susie Casement and Helen Gray of Oxford University Press.

I am also grateful to Michael Neill for helping to make material on Ford available to me in the early stages of this work and for generously giving his time to discuss Ford with me. Thanks are due to G. R. Proudfoot for his helpful suggestions on *The Broken Heart* 2.3.31–2; to Sergio Mazzarelli for his modernization of the Italian passages in *'Tis Pity She's a Whore*; to Lisa Hopkins who kindly provided me with her work prior to its publication and supplied helpful references on Ford's life; to members of the University of London's Centre for English Studies conference, 'Editing Renaissance Dramatic Texts' (1994), who provided useful feedback; to past and present colleagues at Strawberry Hill, for their friendship and encouragement (particularly Janet Clare and David Worrall); and to the staff of the British Library (especially those in the North Library).

Above all, I would like to thank my husband Michael, who travelled the length of the country with me to see Ford's plays in action and, throughout the years of this project, gave me more help than I can ever acknowledge here.

M.L.

St Mary's University College,
a College of the University of Surrey

INTRODUCTION

John Ford began his literary career as an occasional poet and pamphleteer before becoming a dramatist who wrote in various collaborative combinations with Middleton, Rowley, Webster, and Dekker. Later he was sole author of eleven plays (having already been co-author of six). Three of his own eleven plays were subsequently lost, but three others, *'Tis Pity She's a Whore*, *The Broken Heart*, and *Perkin Warbeck*, eventually became famous. This edition sets his earliest surviving independent drama, *The Lover's Melancholy*,[1] alongside his best-known work.

Ford's life presents scholars of his writings with a challenge. We don't know when he was born or where and when he died: his birth may have been close to his baptism in April 1586,[2] but his death could have taken place at any time after 1639 when he published his last play and then disappeared from the public view. He may or may not have been the 'John Ford Devon gent.' who matriculated as a member of Exeter College, Oxford, on 26 March 1601, and while there is a record of him entering the Middle Temple in November 1602, there is no indication of him ever being called to the bar. It is possible that he remained in law chambers all his working life, perhaps managing property for the gentry. When he left and where he went is still unclear, but the popular view supposes that he returned to settle in his native Devon just before the Civil War and died there later.

Lately we have experienced a revival of interest in the work of the man who, according to Charles Lamb, was 'of the first order of poets'.[3] Ford's plays have now been subjected to literary theory and feminist scrutiny. His family, friends, patrons, and possible religious sympathies (which have always seemed ambiguous) have been researched with new vigour by Lisa Hopkins,[4] who has uncovered some hitherto unnoticed Catholic associations, providing welcome

---

[1] *The Lover's Melancholy* was his first independent play to be published, although it may not have been the first written.

[2] See Anthony Telford Moore, 'The Date of John Ford's Baptism', *Notes and Queries*, 239 (1994), 70–1, for a revised date of 12 April instead of 17 April, as was formerly believed.

[3] Charles Lamb, *Works*, ed. C. Kent (London, n.d.), 582.

[4] Lisa Hopkins, *John Ford's Political Theatre* (Manchester, 1994).

additional information on one of the most elusive biographical subjects since Shakespeare. Perhaps best of all, there has been an increase in the number of performances of his plays.

Ford's work is accessible and invites us to take issue with it. His own attitude to his characters is often ambiguous, so that whether he is a moralist or a decadent libertine, an unequivocal supporter of patriarchy or a challenger of gender restrictions, is still a matter of opinion. Ford was expert in the creation of defeated women who possessed great strength of will. Annabella, Hippolita, Penthea, Calantha, and Katherine Gordon rank among the most dramatically powerful female characters on the post-Shakespearian stage, at a time when women's roles were still exclusively played by male actors.

He is not Shakespeare; we are under no pressure to idolize him or be in awe of the range of his achievements. Like John Webster and Thomas Middleton, he tantalizes with apparent echoes of, or allusions to, other Renaissance dramas (including some of Shakespeare's best-known plays), which is not a sign of slavish dependence but a way of stressing the different contexts and perspectives of his own work— and those contexts and perspectives often owe their fascination to their very perverseness. Ford's life may give us the impression of having been shadowy and relatively uneventful, but the same cannot be said of his best plays. Ronald Huebert is not the only critic to have thought that a 'poet who chooses witchcraft, melancholy, masochism, misogyny, and incest as major themes must have a taste for the bizarre'.[5] A closer look at some of the transformations which Ford engineers is revealing.

The Lover's Melancholy

Ford wrote *The Lover's Melancholy* for the King's Men (previously Shakespeare's Company). It was licensed for performance in November 1628 and published in 1629. Apart from a moment of dubious fame when Charles Macklin attributed the play to Shakespeare and staged it as part of a Drury Lane advertising stunt in 1748,[6] there is no record of a production after its original performances at the Globe and Blackfriars, even though there is evidence that a performance may have been planned just after the Restoration.[7]

---

[5] Ronald Huebert, *John Ford: Baroque English Dramatist* (Montreal and London, 1977), 1.
[6] *The Lover's Melancholy*, ed. R. F. Hill (Manchester, 1985), 32.
[7] Ibid. 33.

Set in Cyprus, a place well known for its worship of Venus, goddess of love, this romantic tragicomedy is indebted to Robert Burton's *The Anatomy of Melancholy*,[8] to the *Prolusiones Academicae, Oratoriae, Historicae, Poeticae* of Famiamus Strada (a Jesuit imitating the Latin poetry of Claudian), and to the works of Renaissance dramatists such as Daniel, Fletcher, Massinger, Marston, and Shakespeare, combining elements of the latter's earlier love comedies with aspects of his late plays.

The debt to Burton, which is acknowledged by Ford in a marginal note, is evident throughout. *The Anatomy of Melancholy* was first published in 1621. In Burton's view a whole society could be in a state of melancholy due to the disposition of its ruler, and this might result in general social decline, religious corruption, or even a reign of tyranny. When considering the condition of an individual, although Burton acknowledges that melancholy *can* have a physical cause, he is more likely to see it as the result of a person indulging in uncontrolled passions, and to regard the cure as spiritual rather than medical, often being drawn from Christian or Stoic philosophy. The familiar struggle between reason and passion which is so obvious in Ford's later work, *'Tis Pity She's a Whore*, is at the heart of Burton's treatise—and also, as its title implies, at the core of *The Lover's Melancholy*.

The plot is set in motion, as Ford's plots so often are, by a man who is subject to forbidden sexual desires. In this case Prince Palador's father, Agenor, failed to control his passion for Eroclea, the woman intended for his son. He is prone to what Burton terms 'heroical love' and suffers a violent passion associated with degenerate lust, while Palador is an innocent victim of love melancholy and belongs to a type frequently found elsewhere in Ford's plays, which Ian Robson has labelled 'the dispossessed lover'.[9] Before the play begins Eroclea has fled in male disguise, leaving a distraught father, Meleander. Agenor's death has brought the unhappy prince to power, so now both individual and state are under the influence of the lover's melancholy and only the restoration of the heroine to her female self, her father, and her intended husband, can bring about a cure.

At this level it is a drama of separation and reunion like so many of the Shakespearian plays which it evokes. Yet if a case is to be made

---

[8] T. C. Faulkner, N. K. Kiessling, and R. L. Blair edited volumes 1 and 2 of Burton's text (Oxford, 1989–90). A further volume of text and two of commentary (J. B. Borough with M. Dodsworth) are in preparation.

[9] Ian Robson, *The Moral World of John Ford's Drama* (Salzburg, 1983), 4.

for a twentieth-century production there must be evidence that it has all the ingredients of a workable piece of theatre and is not merely a collage of old plays held together by Burtonian ideas. The play's power lies in its symmetrical structure, its reworking of old motifs and familiar themes, its humour, and perhaps also the new possibilities it offers for gender-based interpretation.

The oldest motif—boy actor playing girl playing boy—recalls particularly Beaumont and Fletcher's *Philaster* and Shakespeare's *As You Like It*, *Twelfth Night*, and *Cymbeline*. In three of these works, though in different ways, the disguised woman becomes embroiled in a love intrigue with a fellow female. At first it seems that *The Lover's Melancholy* is merely following the familiar pattern, but this ignores Ford's inclination to take expressions of passion (by women as well as men) beyond expected boundaries. Here the original staging would have had even more resonance due to the additional cross-dressing of the male actors.

In Act 3, scene 2 Eroclea, disguised as a male, is accosted by not one woman, but two—both Thamasta and her maid, Kala. The verbally expressed doubts and accompanying actions of Kala, directed at the supposed youth's lack of virility (when she is rejected), must originally have occasioned some humour at the expense of the boy player taking Eroclea's part ('The thing is sure a gelding', 3.2.11). More laughter would have arisen at Kala's own expense when she declared herself desperate to lose her virginity to a boy who, the audience knows, is meant to be representing another woman in disguise. However, Kala, too, would originally have been played by a male, so the joke would again rebound on the boy actor who declared, 'My maidenhead will shortly grow so stale | That 'twill be mouldy . . .' (3.2.18–19). In the modern theatre, where women usually play women, the humour will lack this dimension, but it could be said to gain by the removal of the male impersonations which, at such moments, hover between mockery of the adolescent male (neither fully man nor woman) and a grotesque caricature (by a male) of female lust.

Mistaken sexual identity is a source of humour but it is also unsettling. Kala's 'receive | A secret that will, as you are a man, | Startle your reason' (3.2.23–5) is soon matched in the next part of the scene by the disguised Eroclea's 'Lady, take a secret' (160) which precedes her revelation to Thamasta that she is 'as you are . . . of the self-same sex' (161–2). At this point the comedy dissolves into an exploration of sexual confusion which might make the audience as uneasy as it has made Thamasta, who continues to declare herself in love with Eroclea, even when she knows that the latter is female. A few seconds later, with the arrival of Menaphon and Kala, her obsessive sexual jealousy for a woman is set against that of Menaphon, who sees the disguised Eroclea as his rival, but does not realize the full import of the situation. Shakespeare never explored sexual orientation quite like this.

If we are in any doubt that comedy is intended to spring from Ford's characters' cross-dressing we have only to remember that this scene is preceded by Act 3, scene 1 in which Grilla, Cuculus's supposed female page (who is in fact a youth), rehearses the parts of Kala, Cleophila, and Thamasta in the play to be performed for Palador, and successfully mimics each woman in turn from maid to mistress. Yet, as in scene 2, the comedy is not solely at the expense of women; here, most of it is directed at the ridiculous figure cut by Cuculus and, through her new roles, Grilla makes the most of every opportunity to abuse him.

Cuculus is closest to Malvolio in Shakespeare's *Twelfth Night*. He is a pedantic organizer of amateur dramatics, an ageing man flaunting his virility at Grilla, and one who is convinced he is observing the height of fashion as to his dress and his daring, innovative choice of a female page. The joke is against him on several counts. By taking his instructions for characterization to extremes, Grilla uses the role of the haughty princess as an excuse to ignore Cuculus and his fussing ('Thus I walk by, hear and mind you not', 3.1.50), his youthful clothes are ridiculous, his cross-garters out of date, and the female page he believes he is impressing with his sexual prowess is a disguised man.

Apart from these opportunities to invoke laughter, *The Lover's Melancholy* also has moments where an audience may be moved to experience other emotions. Eroclea's reunion with her father lacks the emotional depth of Cordelia's return to Lear, but is not without power, and while Ford may not rival Shakespeare's final achievements in his late plays, at times he proves himself a worthy descendant of the same tradition.

In Act 4, scene 3 Eroclea's gentle disclosure of herself to Palador, and her reaffirmation of their earlier vows, first meet with brutal rejection as he accuses her of being a male impostor seeking safety in an assumed female form. The reserved and prudish Palador, although a prince, may seem less deserving of her than she of him, but when he does acknowledge Eroclea it would be churlish to belittle the deepest expression of his feelings which, for a moment at least, recalls the words spoken by Posthumus to Imogen at the climax of *Cymbeline*. In these lines, as in several others in this play, Ford shows us a glimpse of the poetic potential he would realize in his works which followed:

> Come home, home to my heart, thou banished peace! . . .
> Eroclea, I am thine; O, let me seize thee
> As my inheritance. Hymen shall now
> Set all his torches burning to give light
> Throughout this land, new-settled in thy welcome.
>
> (4.3.136–43)

The Broken Heart

Andrew Gurr suggests that *The Broken Heart* was written in 1629.[10] Licensed for the press on 28 March 1633, it was printed the same year. Like *The Lover's Melancholy* it was written for the King's Company, to be performed at Blackfriars and the Globe, but after its original performances there is no record of a production until William Poel's truncated version at St George's Hall, London, on 11 June 1898. The play was revived in 1904 (Royalty Theatre, London), 1959 (Queen's University Dramatic Society at Belfast and Stratford-upon-Avon), 1962 (Chichester), twice in 1988 (Leicester Haymarket and Bulmershe College, Reading University), and at least twice in 1994 (RSC at the Swan Theatre, Stratford, and at the Lyric Studio, Hammersmith). In 1955, 1956, and 1970 it was adapted for radio and, in 1967, for French television, but the success of its most recent theatre performances suggests that we are only now experiencing its full power on the stage.

There is no major source for *The Broken Heart*: some of the Spartan details can be traced to Plutarch and there are associations with Sidney's *Arcadia*. The prologue suggests a source from life rather than fiction, but asserts that there is no intention to satirize 'place or persons', which has led some critics to look for classical parallels while others have argued for contemporary links, considering the play influenced by and sympathetic to the circumstances of Penelope Devereux.[11] *The Broken Heart* has its own life, perhaps springing from, but ultimately independent of, speculative sources.

---

[10] Andrew Gurr, 'Singing Through the Chatter: Ford and Contemporary Theatrical Fashion', in Michael Neill (ed.), *John Ford: Critical Re-Visions* (Cambridge, 1988), 93.

[11] In 'Stella and *The Broken Heart*', *PMLA* 17 (1909), 274–85, Stuart P. Sherman explores the Devereux case in detail, while Keith Sturgess, in *Jacobean Private Theatre* (London, 1987), 139, notes the similarities between Orgilus' death and that of the stoical Seneca, suggesting that *this* may be the 'truth' alluded to in the prologue.

The play was first likened to the French tragedy of Corneille and his contemporaries by Edmund Gosse in a programme note to Poel's 1898 production. Gosse commented on the 'rigidity' and 'devotion to dramatic discipline'[12] which made Ford's approach more in line with the French dramas that were to follow soon after him than with the English tradition that had gone before. Ford seems always to have been slightly out of line. He is often included within the ranks of Shakespeare and his contemporaries, yet is chronologically distanced from many of them, writing in the late 1620s and early 1630s in the run up to the Civil War and the closure of the playhouses in 1642. When the theatres opened again in 1660 women actors were on the Restoration stage, women playwrights were about to write for it, and the old drama had been replaced by the new. Ford is not truly 'Shakespearian', nor is he a premature Restoration dramatist: it is more helpful to regard him as a Caroline dramatist writing in a transitional period—looking back respectfully to earlier traditions and conventions, but also looking forward in his questioning of their applicability to the new dramatic age.[13]

In *The Broken Heart* he does this within a particularly rigid, unified design and through stylized characters. If, as Clifford Leech claimed, *The Lover's Melancholy* is 'a play almost devoid of incident',[14] then *The Broken Heart*, although it does not lack action, often gives us the impression that this takes place in slow motion against a muted background of tension. The Spartan setting is associated with the stoic endurance in the face of adversity which concerned Ford in early prose works such as *The Golden Mean* and *A Line of Life*. First impressions of *The Broken Heart* suggest that both men and women are tested to their limits in this respect, but further examination reveals certain differences in the way suffering is meted out and coped with by the sexes, and if we are to find more in these characters than dramatic stereotypes, we could begin to look for some degree of psychological plausibility here.

If we consider Orgilus' hopeless situation at the play's opening, it seems that men as well as women can be victims. When Penthea's brother overrules their dead father's decision to marry her to Orgilus

[12] Edmund Gosse, in *Chambers' Cyclopaedia of English Literature*, 3 vols. (London, 1901), i. 481–2.

[13] See Muriel Bradbrook, *Themes and Conventions of Elizabethan Tragedy*, 2nd edn. (Cambridge, 1952); Martin Butler, *Theatre and Crisis 1632–1642* (Cambridge, 1984); and Marion Lomax, *Stage Images and Traditions: Shakespeare to Ford* (Cambridge, 1987).

[14] Clifford Leech, *John Ford* (London, 1964), 17.

and gives her, instead, to the richer, socially superior, older, and jealous Bassanes (whom she does not love), it could be inflated ambition for the family good on Ithocles' part, or an example of male rivalry (because it is suggested that Orgilus and Ithocles have an unspecified long-standing feud), or it might have more to do with a topic which was to take centre stage in *'Tis Pity She's a Whore*—incestuous desires and related sexual jealousy.

Like Ferdinand and the Duchess of Malfi in Webster's play, Ithocles and Penthea are twins, and the same repressed incestuous feelings may be behind the possessive behaviour of both brothers. Is it religious scruple or personal jealousy when Ferdinand forbids his young widowed sister to marry again? 'Do not you ask the reason' (1.1.257)[15] he tells Bosola. Does Ithocles sacrifice Penthea to Bassanes because at this stage in his life he resembles Ferdinand and would be jealous of a younger, passionate man like Orgilus? Whatever the answers, incest is never more than a wild accusation by Bassanes in *The Broken Heart* and, as such, is used to demonstrate his insecurity rather than provide a motive for Ithocles; but a comparison with *The Duchess of Malfi* is useful in other respects.[16]

The difference between the two plays is most apparent in the different attitudes of their heroines. The duchess rejects patriarchy and pits herself against her brothers' authority, refusing to live her life according to their terms: she chooses to dispose of her body as she desires. The possession and control of women's bodies is central to both plays, and men use the patriarchal elements of law and religion to try to achieve this. Penthea is trapped because marriage is sacred to her even though she is married against her desires—and she will not abuse the institution. Nor will she go against her brother's ruling, even though she feels it to be unjust. She cannot rebel, not because she lacks the spirit to do so, but because she acknowledges the power of laws and of popular censure.

Penthea's situation is also complicated by the all-too-common phenomenon whereby a woman responds to a violation of her body with feelings of guilt—even though it occurred through no fault of her own. In *The Broken Heart* men try to exert control over women's bodies and women finally wrest this power from them, but often only to reserve the right to destroy themselves. Penthea's self-starvation

---

[15] John Webster, *The Duchess of Malfi*, ed. John Russell Brown (Manchester, 1976).
[16] Ford wrote commendatory verses for *The Duchess of Malfi*: links with *Love's Sacrifice* are pointed out by Martin Butler, and with *'Tis Pity She's a Whore* by Michael Neill in *John Ford: Critical Re-Visions*, 214 ff. and 169 ff.

resembles an early case of *anorexia nervosa*. Her mind takes charge of the body which is possessed against her will by Bassanes and, ironically, through her own actions she destroys the fertility which might have been her salvation. Menstruation ceases and she sees her ambition to become a mother thwarted. In isolation, denied even the companionship and love of dependent children, she literally begins to fade away. In exerting control over her own body Penthea begins to destroy both it and her mind, descending first into madness like Ophelia.[17]

After Penthea's death Calantha's body becomes the focal point in the final dance, and is in her control in one sense because she represses her feelings when told of each new calamity—but she, too, only uses her power over her body to destroy it. Euphrania, Chrystalla, and Philema are fulfilled women who survive; the unfulfilled respond with self-destruction. In this Calantha wields additional power because, by the end of the play, her body is also that of the head of state, yet she cannot separate her private self from her public person. She is admired by Bassanes for her masculine spirit in meeting the tragic news so stoically, but he is mistaken; her final response is particularly female. In this play men do not wish to self-destruct, nor are they able to destroy themselves without help when death is unavoidable—as Orgilus finds when he requests that he be his own executioner. The women's minds are the stronger, yet the extent of their emotional suffering seems greater. Calantha is not a weak character but, like Penthea, she can neither control her passions nor repress them sufficiently to continue living.

Both women also possess a strong sense of loyalty to and responsibility for men, which also makes their self-sacrifices inevitable. Penthea puts Orgilus' reputation and the legitimacy of his children before her own happiness. *He* is willing to take her out of the marriage she detests and run away with her, but *she* refuses to go on the grounds that he deserves better than second-hand goods. She places herself in a corner because she cannot compromise, yet has no future without him. Calantha is similarly trapped: she refuses to survive without Ithocles, a man to whom Penthea is also bound in loyalty. Like Annabella in *'Tis Pity*, Penthea's final thoughts, before madness overtakes her, are not for herself but for her brother, the man who wronged her most.

---

[17] See also Lisa Hopkins, 'Silence and the Language of the Body: Women in the Plays of John Ford', *Elizabethan Theatre XIV: Proceedings of the 14th Waterloo Conference on Elizabethan Theatre* (in press).

It would be too simplistic to view characters as male stereotypes oppressing female stereotypes: Ford's treatment of gender is more sophisticated than this. The situations of his characters are all-the-more poignant because they often reach a degree of mutual understanding when it is too late for them to benefit from it. Orgilus is typically protective of his sister for personal reasons and for the sake of the family honour, but he is also sensitive to her needs because of his own experience. His role of the pining lover is an essentially passive part, and even Ithocles, the active, daring warrior, becomes a pining lover eventually, and through this understands Penthea's plight and wins her aid in his own cause.

The men learn from the women, though the women usually take their leads from the men, and through the women we learn about the men. In some performances the characters of Lemophil, Groneas, Chrystalla, and Philema are either omitted or their parts severely reduced. Yet to do this denies the play some of its brief, but effective moments of humour which arise when male stereotypes of women are exposed to scrutiny. These scenes also show that men have not only created images for women but also for themselves, and sometimes, as in 'Tis Pity, they fail to live up to the latter.

'Tis Pity She's a Whore

Ford's most famous play was printed in 1633 and probably written about three years earlier.[18] It was first performed by the Queen's Men under Christopher Beeston's management at the Phoenix private theatre (known as the Cockpit) in Drury Lane, and there were other stagings later in the century, one of which was viewed by Samuel Pepys in 1661. It was adapted by Maeterlinck (Paris, 1894), performed in London by the Phoenix Society (1923), and by the Arts Theatre Club (1934), before Donald Wolfit produced it at both Cambridge and London in 1940. Since the mid-twentieth century it has been Ford's most performed play; the Actors' Company and the National Theatre's touring company offered it in 1972, Giuseppe Patroni Griffi filmed it in 1973, and Roland Joffé directed a version for BBC TV in 1980. One of the most celebrated productions occurred at The Other Place, Stratford-upon-Avon, in 1977 when Ron Daniels directed it for the RSC. Philip Prowse, who had directed the play ten years earlier, revived it at the Citizens Theatre, Glasgow,

---

[18] Andrew Gurr, 'Singing Through the Chatter', 93.

in February and March 1988. Almost simultaneously, Alan Ayckbourn directed 'Tis Pity on the National Theatre's Olivier stage, and both productions demonstrated different challenges for performance. If, like Ayckbourn, a director stresses the lovers' innocence, then the obsessive, defiant element of their passion may be diminished. If he or she concentrates on portraying distortion and obsession (like Prowse), there is a risk of setting main plot at odds with sub-plot. In Prowse's version Donado doubled as the Cardinal and his nephew, Bergetto, was played as a speechless idiot, so all comedy was cut. In the 1991/2 RSC season David Leveaux successfully took a middle course at the Swan in Stratford and the Pit in London.

No single source has been found for the plot. Ford may have borrowed and adapted a number of ideas from a wide range of texts, including Thomas Heywood's Gunaikeion, which is itself based on classical stories, Beaumont and Fletcher's A King and No King, Francis Quarles's Argalus and Parthenia (which has links with Sidney's Arcadia), Chapman's Bussy D'Ambois, Nash's Pierce Penniless, Middleton's Women Beware Women, and most strikingly, Shakespeare's Romeo and Juliet and Othello, Webster's The Duchess of Malfi, and Whetstone's Heptameron of Civil Discourses.[19] There is even a possible French source in François de Rosset's Les Histoires Tragiques de Nostre Temps (Paris, 1615). Ford may have used some or all of these as starting-points, but the transformations they undergo are crucial.

Ford's Parma has an undercurrent of violence running just below its respectable surface. When this violence erupts the play is clearly seen as a revenge drama with a difference. Giovanni and Annabella are portrayed as trapped victims rather than evil, immoral creatures, and the revenge which individual characters try to take on each other is set against the revenge which society wreaks on them for daring to defy its central tenets. Justice cannot be relied upon—especially if you are a woman or a character of lower rank.

The Church, in the form of the Cardinal, represents the law and gives those of noble birth preferential treatment. Defending the murderer, Grimaldi, the Cardinal argues, 'He is no common man, but nobly born; | Of princes' blood, though you, Sir Florio, | Thought him too mean a husband for your daughter' (3.9.55–7). One reading suggests that Florio, the merchant, is mocked with a title he does not

---

[19] Most of these sources are well documented, but Martin Wiggins recently remarked on the similarity of the Friar's description of Hell (3.6.8 ff.) to a passage in Pierce Penniless. This list is not exhaustive.

possess in order to suggest that he is behaving presumptuously; this is the Cardinal's revenge for the slighting of his favourite.

Yet the characters who are wronged in this incident, Florio and Donado, in turn, make unfair judgements on others who are considered even more inferior. When Hippolita attempts to murder Soranzo in revenge for his treatment of her and, instead, Vasques murders Hippolita by a trick, everyone present supports him even though she is a wronged, disturbed woman, perhaps to the point of being mentally unbalanced. No attempt is made to see the situation from her point of view: although a noblewoman, her fate is decreed by a servant and he is applauded by the rest of the largely male onlookers who declare, 'Wonderful justice!' (4.1.86).

In *'Tis Pity* women associated with dangerous sexual passions are controlled through the mutilation of their bodies. Here, Vasques burns Hippolita's body internally with the poison she intended for Soranzo; later he causes Putana's eyes to be put out and threatens to slit her nose, and the Cardinal finally has her burnt.[20] Even Giovanni carves up his beloved sister to extract her heart. Only Philotis remains physically intact, and she survives by locking her body and her sexuality away in a convent.

Within the play, while both men and women are guilty, women are blamed most. When Donado replies, ' 'Tis most just' to the Cardinal's death sentence on Putana, he speaks for the assembly in this echo of the unofficial public sentence on Hippolita. Unlike her prototype, the nurse who advocates bigamy to Shakespeare's Juliet, and is condemned by her mistress for so doing, Putana has received Annabella's blessing for condoning and encouraging the latter's incestuous relationship with her brother. The Cardinal's words, 'for example's sake',[21] suggest that women are scapegoats as society and the Church take revenge for deviancy. Giovanni instigated the affair, but it is Annabella, the woman who slighted the Cardinal by rejecting the murderer Grimaldi, shamed the immoral Soranzo, and scandalized society by daring to love the best of an unsuitable bunch of suitors, who receives the Cardinal's final condemnation, although there is no indication that the audience is encouraged to agree with him.

We may not wish to sympathize with incest, but we are forced to evaluate the evils within this society in such a way that the incestuous relationship emerges as an inevitable response to an inward-looking

---

[20] See *'Tis Pity*, note to 5.6.129. [21] Ibid. 5.6.131.

world where most values are distorted and strictures are rigidly applied to keep everyone in the places their sex or social position decrees. Characters from the merchant class, like the lively Annabella and the educated high-flyer, Giovanni, are exceptional.

In this play intelligent, passionate women of any class who try to be independent and achieve personal happiness are invariably forced into the position of trying to manipulate men who then bring the full force of the patriarchal system against them. Similarly, young men who come back from university set to challenge theological dogma and those whose authority depends on it, break away from their guardian friars and become a threat to nobles and cardinals. Such characters resist integration and are driven to try to achieve, by unusual means, what they might have been expected to attain as a normal matter of course—a mutually loving heterosexual relationship.

This aspect was forcibly stressed in David Leveaux's production when Giovanni (Jonathan Cullen) did not recoil in horror at Putana's news of Annabella's pregnancy (as is usually the case), but delivered, 'With child? How dost thou know't?' (3.3.9) as excited questions which showed his delight and immediately identified him as a proud, would-be father. For Giovanni, the incestuous aspect of the relationship is only a problem because of society's attitude. To him, it offers the most desirable of situations— a union with his sister who, he argues, is 'one flesh' with him.

Annabella is his female other: he thinks of her as an extension of himself, not someone in her own right. Richard Marienstras[22] points out that when they exchange their incestuous vows Annabella swears by 'our mother's dust', acknowledging that they are separate people, but Giovanni says 'my mother's dust', as if their mother was his alone and both offspring had only one identity—his. His sister, then, enables him to have the purest and most complete union of all—a spiritual and physical union with himself.

In this play men generally try to preserve their fantasies by applying the conventions of romantic love poetry and believing that they can control their destinies, while women learn that they will never be allowed to control their own lives and insist on being realistic, meeting the men's romantic notions with suspicion or mockery. In this they are rejecting manipulation by men, who are

[22] Richard Marienstras, *New Perspectives on the Shakespearean World*, tr. J. Lloyd (Cambridge and Paris, 1985), 195.

trying to make them conform to images of womanhood which are male creations, and with which they do not identify.

Parma's patriarchal society has not equipped its men to see women in any way other than in sexual terms—or as extensions of the male ego, as in Giovanni's case. The sexually inexperienced are just as unenlightened as the experienced: until he meets Philotis, who panders to his ego and is therefore viable as a permanent fixture, Bergetto can see no point in marriage; he presumes that those who want a woman can always purchase one indiscriminately for half-a-crown. (He seems as unsure of their purpose as he is of their price, half-a-crown being rather more than the usual rate.) The worldly Soranzo, on the other hand, fits women into a number of extreme sexual stereotypes—the lustful temptress, the pure virgin, and the adulterous whore.

Although women appear aware of the way men attempt to manipulate them through these stereotypes, they are ultimately trapped by them because, unlike the men who refuse to see themselves as culpable, the women do not believe themselves superior, are easily persuaded that they are sinful, and reproach themselves. Though Hippolita seems to challenge this when she takes her revenge, she accepts that she will be damned for her actions. Annabella, for all her spirited replies to Soranzo, eventually repents and puts herself under the Friar's control and, it could be argued, she does this not for her own, but for Giovanni's safety. As *The Broken Heart* shows, women are often unselfish to the point of self-sacrifice.

Annabella shares Giovanni's feelings that their love is natural, but cannot reject the religious teachings which say otherwise, while Giovanni manages to counter theological rulings about incest and rejects any notion of Hell because it suits him to do so. Similarly, Soranzo carefully twists religious arguments to make threats against Hippolita and exonerate his own behaviour. As in *The Broken Heart*, men assume the authority to challenge laws, but women, lacking the academic education which invites reasoning and intellectual challenge, are so thoroughly conditioned that they cannot do this, no matter how hard they try.

Maintaining a semblance of respectability is crucial for their status and survival in society. How could Annabella challenge a friar who put the sham of respectability above all else in counselling her to marry Soranzo, although he knew she was carrying Giovanni's child, when she knew that the future of her brother, her father, and herself depended on doing just that? Giovanni is stronger, but more foolhardy. The play shows that even a man like this can become a victim of the gendering which led him to believe that, as a man, he might actually succeed in controlling his own life.

Perkin Warbeck

This play was entered in the Stationers' Register on 24 February 1634 and may have been written two years before, although an argument has been made for an even earlier date in the last years of James I's reign.[23] *Perkin Warbeck* was first performed at the Phoenix for the Queen's Company. Nothing is then heard of it until 19 December 1745, when it was probably cut and adapted for a Hanoverian audience at Goodman's Fields Theatre, where it was revived to encourage anti-Jacobite feeling after the Young Pretender's rebellion. A manuscript, probably based on the play's 1714 reprint and assumed to be the prompt copy for this performance, is in the Bodleian Library (Rawl. poet. 122). Its only other revivals have taken place in this century, most notably the RSC's production at The Other Place in 1975, directed by Barry Kyle and John Barton. The play was also broadcast by BBC radio several times between 1969 and 1977.

Ford's historical details appear to come mainly from two sources: Francis Bacon's *History of the Reign of King Henry VII* (1622) and Thomas Gainsford's *The True and Wonderfull History of Perkin Warbeck* (1618). He may also have referred to Edward Hall's *The Union of the two Noble and Illustre Families of Lancaster and York* (1548) and William Warner's *Albion's England* (1586), but this is not certain. Ford rearranged the chronology of some events, compressed time intervals, and developed his characters inventively, demonstrating that he was not a slave to his sources. Significant additions emerge in relation to Huntly, Daliell (who is totally fictional), Katherine, and perhaps most interestingly, Perkin and Henry. Ford wrote *Perkin Warbeck* (so he claimed in his prologue) at a time when such dramas were unfashionable; it challenges not only this popular view of the genre, but also our expectations based on familiar earlier histories such as those of Shakespeare, particularly *Richard II*.

T. S. Eliot considered the play 'almost flawless',[24] and Roger Warren has claimed that '*Perkin Warbeck* alone of Ford's plays has

[23] Andrew Gurr, 'Singing Through the Chatter', 93 and *Perkin Warbeck*, ed. Peter Ure (Manchester, 1968), pp. xxviii–xxxv.
[24] T. S. Eliot, *Selected Essays*, 2nd edn. (London, 1934), 201.

been revived with complete success in the modern theatre'.[25] He gives a detailed account of Kyle and Barton's much-acclaimed RSC production, showing how it followed and drew on allusions to Barton's *Richard II* which had been performed at the Royal Shakespeare Theatre in the previous season.

Unlike Richard II, Perkin is a player-king who has no more than theatrical authenticity, yet in his play Ford refuses to allow the pretence to slip for a moment and successfully creates Perkin's charismatic personality out of it. In the source material Perkin confesses that he is the impostor, John Osbeck, but there is no such confession in Ford's play, and Perkin's unwavering belief in his right to be king becomes a strength. Richard II, however legitimate his claim, shows up badly in comparison. Once again Ford manages to create sympathy for a character who is challenging the *status quo*, and we are disinclined to judge him harshly. Set against the egocentric Richard, as he was by Kyle and Barton, Perkin is the more attractive figure, putting concern for his loyal supporters and the ordinary, innocent people before care for himself. He also, even without a kingdom, plays the king amazingly well and is a worthy contrast to both Henry VII and James of Scotland: after all, as Peter Ure asked in his Revels edition of the play: 'how are we, in the theatre, to distinguish between the man who plays the king and the man who plays the man who plays the king?'[26]

Perkin's behaviour is linked to that of Henry VII in Act 3, scene 1, when the King of England is merciful to the common people in the Cornish uprising and punishes only the leaders. However, this is also a demonstration of Henry's Machiavellian tactics to win popular support; Perkin never appears so calculating, nor so interested in the material aspects of power. Roger Warren draws attention to the way Kyle and Barton's production emphasized Henry's belief that 'money gives soul to action' (3.1.29), portraying him as a man who feared Stanley's betrayal partly because he held 'the keys and secrets' of Henry's treasury (1.3.108), and as a king who was extremely careful about his income and expenditure because his success depended upon its good management—whether shown by his determination not to reduce unpopular taxation (3.1.27–9) or by his shrewd payment of Hialas (3.3.45).[27]

[25] Roger Warren, 'Ford in Performance', in *John Ford: Critical Re-Visions*, 27.
[26] *Perkin Warbeck*, ed. Peter Ure (Manchester, 1968), p. lx.
[27] Roger Warren, 'Ford in Performance', 23.

The associations with Shakespeare's histories, *Richard II*, *Henry IV*, *Richard III*, and *Henry VIII* cannot be ignored: the play's construction, as well as its focus on the psychology of the central character, link it with *Richard II*, while the emphasis on the protagonist's actorly qualities draw it closer to *Richard III* and *Henry IV*. The burden of responsibility which weighs heavily on Ford's Henry VII, and the pressures springing from a largely *de facto* claim to the succession, link him with Shakespeare's Henry IV. The powerful scene of king confronting traitor evokes similar situations in *Richard III* and *Henry VIII*.

Yet for all this, Ford's drama is not merely an attempt to revive the history genre in the same old way. Probably the most striking difference is the key role allocated to Katherine Gordon, a woman to be pitied but, more importantly, a female figure to be admired and one who, as Lisa Hopkins has shown, achieves an 'enviable' position at the end of the play 'in the terms of the usual fates of Ford's heroines' because 'her husband has publicly and unambiguously transferred her to the guardianship of a man who can honourably and with propriety exercise the role of her protector . . . she has a proper and clearly demarcated place within patriarchal society'.[28]

Aspects of gender in *Perkin Warbeck* have come to the fore of late, although to read Roger Warren's otherwise excellent account of the production at Stratford it would appear that there wasn't a woman in this play which Clifford Leech termed 'predominantly masculine'.[29] Yet at the centre of the drama only the two legitimate kings stand alone: as tragedy mounts, Perkin shares this with his wife Katherine, a genuine princess who supports her husband's dubious claim loyally. Jean Howard's essay, ' "Effeminately Dolent": Gender and Legitimacy in Ford's *Perkin Warbeck*', finds this association of the female with a bid for illegitimate power significant: like the weak passivity of Richard II, it serves to distance Perkin from legitimate power which traditionally is strongly masculine. Like many of Ford's women, Perkin gains our respect through his 'nobility . . . through passive suffering'[30] and Howard successfully argues that by 'feminizing both Perkin and the history genre, Ford shows how a patriarchal, absolutist culture unthinks itself'.[31]

---

[28] Lisa Hopkins, 'Silence and the Language of the Body'.
[29] Clifford Leech, *John Ford*, 28.
[30] Jean Howard, ' "Effeminately Dolent": Gender and Legitimacy in Ford's *Perkin Warbeck*', in *John Ford: Critical Re-Visions*, 275.
[31] Ibid. 264.

This play is a long way from *The Lover's Melancholy*, yet it could be argued that there is a recognizable progression. In his early comedy Ford explored sexual passion and gendering largely for comic effect; in the more sensational *The Broken Heart* and *'Tis Pity* they were at the heart of the tragedy; and in *Perkin Warbeck* (where the most sensational aspect is Perkin's claim to be king), passion becomes political and gender is explored in relation to ideologies of power. Ford has more to offer than you might, at first, think.

NOTE ON THE TEXTS

The main copy-texts for all four plays are the original Quarto versions. Where there are differences between the corrected and uncorrected texts, the corrected version has been preferred. I owe a large debt of gratitude to editors of Ford, particularly Donald K. Anderson, N. W. Bawcutt, Havelock Ellis, Colin Gibson, R. F. Hill, Derek Roper, T. J. B. Spencer, Keith Sturgess, and Peter Ure; however, lack of space does not allow a complete textual history, and emendations proposed by previous editors, but not adopted here, have not all been listed. Act divisions follow the Quarto, but additional scene divisions have been made where necessary.

The term *'Dramatis Personae'* does not appear in the Quartos which give, instead, 'The names of such as acted', 'The Speakers' Names', 'The Actors' Names', or 'The Persons Presented'. These have been replaced and regularized by 'The Persons of the Play'. In all cases the Quarto order placed male characters first, but male and female roles have now been integrated and, in keeping with the listing of characters according to groupings within the drama in *Perkin Warbeck*, characters in the other plays have been arranged in a similar fashion (for example, by main-plot and sub-plot).

Wherever possible, punctuation follows the Quarto, but some minor alterations have been made to aid delivery of the lines and major changes are noted. Seventeenth-century practices such as the breaking of rules of concord, for example, *LM* 4.3.88, 'The incense of my love-desires are flamed' and the use of the genitive 'his' (for example, *PW* 1.3.41, 'Charles his court') have been preserved, with notes where necessary. Where there is an existing editorial precedent for changing the Quarto's lineation or allocation to verse or prose to aid delivery, such changes have not been noted. Speech-headings have been regularized according to the same principle, for example, 'Menander' (*LM* Quarto) becomes 'Meleander'; 'Prince' (ditto) becomes 'Palador'.

The Quartos' italics are retained for songs and, sometimes, for particular emphasis, but not all instances of italics and capitalization are noted.

The Quarto texts have been followed for Ford's colloquial terms such as ' 'a', 'y'are', 'w'are', 'd'ee', and so on, and these feature in the

Glossary; but the Quartos' 'thou't' has become 'thou'lt', and 'wu't', 'wilt', for greater clarity. Accents are occasionally provided where this aids delivery of the verse, but no notes are given on seventeenth-century pronunciation which would not normally be used in modern productions, for example, 'girl' is not given two syllables.

Where the Quartos' positioning of stage directions occurred earlier due to differences in the original conditions of staging, such as the need to cross a long stage, or where the positioning occurs erroneously *after* associated stage-business has been mentioned, small adjustments have been made and not noted. With the exception of 'Exit' and 'Exeunt', the stage directions have been Anglicized.

Spelling has been modernized, and when the modern form differs substantially, for example, at *Perkin Warbeck* 3.4.51, where the Quarto's 'conster' has become 'construe', such changes are noted. Proper names and the passages in Italian have also been modernized (except where metre demanded otherwise in the case of the former). Where the omission of syllables is necessary for scansion, the Quartos' contractions have been upheld; but where there is now no difference in the pronunciation of the words, with or without the apostrophe, the full forms are given, for example, *LM* 1.1.69, 'mean'st' is retained for the ten-syllable line, but *LM* 1.1.155, 'sigh'd' becomes 'sighed'.

SELECT BIBLIOGRAPHY

There are two major bibliographies of Ford's works: Kenneth Tucker's *A Bibliography of Writings By and About John Ford and Cyril Tourneur* (Boston, Mass., 1977), and an earlier compilation, *John Ford: A Concise Bibliography* (New York; Elizabethan Bibliography no. 20, 1941), by S. A. Tannenbaum. Bibliographies can also be found in many of the other books mentioned here, as well as in *The Annual Bibliography of English Language and Literature*, the Modern Language Association bibliographies, and the British Library computerized catalogue. Volume 21 (Winter 1991) of *English Literary Renaissance* (pp. 102–17) includes a survey by Reid Barbour, 'Recent Studies in John Ford (1977–1989)'.

In the nineteenth century there were editions of Ford by Henry Weber: *Dramatic Works of John Ford*, 2 vols. (Edinburgh, 1811); William Gifford: *Dramatic Works*, 2 vols. (London, 1827); Hartley Coleridge: *Dramatic Works of Massinger and Ford* (London, 1839); Alexander Dyce and Gifford: *Works*, 3 vols. (London, 1869; rev. A. H. Bullen, 1895); and Havelock Ellis: *Ford: Five Plays* (London, 1888).

The most modern collected editions of *The Broken Heart*, *'Tis Pity*, and *Perkin Warbeck* have been edited by Keith Sturgess: *John Ford: Three Plays* (Harmondsworth, 1970) and Colin Gibson: *The Selected Plays of John Ford* (Cambridge, 1986). Individual editions of some of these plays have existed since the late nineteenth century, but the most helpful are those in the Revels, Regents Renaissance Drama, and New Mermaid series (the latter does not include *Perkin Warbeck*). There is a Revels edition of *The Lover's Melancholy*, ed. R. F. Hill (Manchester University Press, 1985). Ford also produced non-dramatic works, which range from commendatory verses (to Henry Cockeram's *The English Dictionary* and a large number of contemporary poetic and dramatic works) to poems and prose pamphlets: all are included in *The Nondramatic Works of John Ford*, ed. L. E. Stock, Gilles D. Monsarrat, Judith M. Kennedy, and Dennis Danielson (Binghamton, New York, 1991).

Several anthologies of seventeenth-century drama contain plays by Ford. Russell A. Fraser and Norman Rabkin's *Drama of the English Renaissance* (New York and London, 1976) contains *The Broken Heart*, *'Tis Pity*, and *Perkin Warbeck*.

Early critics of Ford polarized into two camps: A. C. Swinburne and Havelock Ellis followed the lead of Charles Lamb in his *Specimens of English Dramatic Poets Who Lived About the Time of Shakespeare* (London, 1808), who valued Ford both as poet and dramatist, and as a prophet of modern times, while his more negative critics (such as William Gifford and Hartley Coleridge) looked to William Hazlitt (*Lectures Chiefly on the Dramatic*

Literature of the Age of Elizabeth, London; Bell, 1820), who thought the plays were largely 'exercises of style and effusions of wire-drawn sentiment', with 'an artificial elaborateness' as their general characteristic (p. 180). Havelock Ellis's response was to see Ford as a rebel and a questioner, an analyst of his characters' psychologies—particularly his women characters. Yet Una Ellis-Fermor, in *The Jacobean Drama: An Interpretation* (London, 1936) regarded Ford as an upholder of the traditional virtues of 'courage, continence, and chivalry' and an advocator of stasis (p. 246).

Although he admired some of it, T. S. Eliot, in *Selected Essays*, 2nd edn. (London, 1934), generally viewed Ford's work as 'poetry and drama of the surface' (p. 196). Others questioned Ford's writing on moral rather than aesthetic grounds. Gerard Langbaine, *An Account of the English Dramatic Poets* (Oxford, 1691) and Adolphus Ward, *History of English Dramatic Literature* (London, 1899) suggested that Ford's apparently sympathetic attitude to incest and the other moral ambiguities in his plays cast doubt on his own moral integrity. Charges of decadence (for example, Stuart P. Sherman, 'Forde's Contribution to the Decadence of the Drama', in Bang's *Materialien*, vol. 23 (Louvain, 1908), pp. vii–xix) followed this line of criticism.

The view of Ford as immoral or potentially anarchic was countered by Irving Ribner's argument that Ford sought a moral order, but was unsuccessful in his quest: *Jacobean Tragedy: The Quest for Moral Order* (London, 1962); while Mark Stavig's notion of Ford as a liberal thinker does not prevent him from viewing the dramatist primarily as a strong defender of traditional values and a champion of reason over depraved worldly passions: *John Ford and the Traditional Moral Order* (Madison and London, 1968). For Robert Ornstein, *The Moral Vision of Jacobean Tragedy* (Madison, 1960), Ford's aristocratic and Neoplatonic values are the starting-point for his testing of the traditional moral order. Not all later criticism focuses on the moral perspective: Ronald Huebert, *John Ford: Baroque English Dramatist* (Montreal and London, 1977), concentrates solely on Ford's work in relation to the European baroque movement and subordinates moral issues to aesthetic considerations.

More recently Ian Robson, *The Moral World of John Ford's Drama* (Salzburg, 1983), suggests that Ford should be considered in relation to 'corporate morality', and concludes that Ford does not offer solutions to the dilemmas he explores in his plays because these problems 'admit of no settlement' (p. 6), leaving us with a playwright whose moral purpose seems to be to highlight the shortcomings of society as a whole, rather than condemn individuals within it.

How progressive was John Ford? Havelock Ellis set the trend for considering Ford 'the most modern of the tribe to whom he belonged' (*John Ford: Five Plays* (London, Viztelly, 1888), p. xvi), and George F. Sensabaugh related this modernity to the idea of individualism and a belief in scientific determinism: *The Tragic Muse of John Ford* (Stanford, Conn., 1944). Florence Ali, *Opposing Absolutes: Conviction and Convention in John Ford's Plays* (Salzburg, 1974) also drew attention to the questioning implied in the plays' paradoxes, and a reassessment of Ford's attitude to change or 'process' can be found in Reid Barbour's 'John Ford and Resolve', *Studies in Philology*, 86: 3 (Summer 1989), 341–66, where he argues that 'Ford's tragedy becomes critical, if not "radical" or "oppositional", in countenancing the need for process' (p. 349). Barbour links Ford to 'a seventeenth-century prose genre which directly addresses the dynamics of self in terms of fixity and change' (p. 342) and, referring to Stephen Greenblatt's *Renaissance Self-Fashioning* (Chicago, 1980), Thelma Greenfield's 'The Language of Process in Ford's *The Broken Heart*' (*PMLA* 87 (1972), 397–405), and Roger Burbridge's 'The Moral Vision of Ford's *The Broken Heart*' (*SEL* 10 (1970), 397–407), as well as to other works mentioned in this review, argues that the stoic suffering in Ford's plays is the price his characters pay for trying to refashion the self and resist stasis.

Behind this conclusion is a long history of critical studies which have tended to take a more conventional approach to Ford's relationship with stoicism. Such works range from Samuel A. Caldwell's 'John Ford and Seventeenth-Century Stoicism' (Ph.D. dissertation, Harvard University, 1968) to the more recent work of Gilles D. Monsarrat, *Light From the Porch: Stoicism and English Renaissance Literature* (Paris, 1984), on which Barbour draws.

Barbour's attempt to relate the stoicism of Ford's characters to social psychology needs to be put into a wider context because many critics have commented on Ford's ability to write psychological drama, though opinions on the exact nature of this vary. One line of criticism developed in relation to Ford's use of Burton's *Anatomy of Melancholy* was led by S. Blaine Ewing, *Burtonian Melancholy in the Plays of John Ford* (Princeton, NJ, 1940). Ewing's approach reduced the plays to case studies of melancholic subjects, and M. E. Cochnower, in R. Shafer (ed.), *Seventeenth Century Studies* (Princeton, NJ, 1933) thought Ford was 'interested in the mind' but was 'not successful in individual characterization' because his characters 'gain truth through reflection from type' (p. 164). A more rewarding line of enquiry was offered by H. J. Oliver in *The Problem of John Ford* (Melbourne, London, and New York, 1955), who did not view Ford's concentration on mental states solely in relation to his reading of Burton but saw it as breaking new ground in psychological drama. Clifford Leech, in *John Ford and the Drama of his Time* (London, 1957), also acknowledged Ford's capacity for psychological analysis as being more than a dependence on Burton, and R. J. Kaufmann's 'Ford's Tragic Perspective', *Texas Studies in Language and Literature*, 1 (1960), 522–37, went so far as to argue that Ford's psychological insights were the distinguishing features of his plays. William Dyer's, 'Holding/Withholding Environments: A Psychoanalytic Approach to Ford's *The Broken Heart*', *English Literary Renaissance*, 21 (1991), 401–24, is one of the latest pieces in this line of criticism.

Recent criticism of Ford's work includes Rowland Wymer's *Webster and Ford* (London, 1994), and challenging pieces can also be found in two collections of essays, edited by D. K. Anderson and Michael Neill, respectively. These contain many gender-based studies, such as D. M. Bergeron's 'Brother–sister relationships in Ford's 1633 plays' (in *Concord in Discord: The Plays of John Ford 1586–1986*, ed. D. K. Anderson (New York, 1986), 195–219), Thelma Greenfield's 'John Ford's Tragedy: The Challenge of Re-engagement' (ibid. 1–26), Sharon Hamilton's 'The Broken Heart: Language Suited to a Divided Mind' (ibid. 171–93), and Jean Howard's ' "Effeminately Dolent": Gender and Legitimacy in Ford's *Perkin Warbeck*' (in *John Ford: Critical Re-Visions*, ed. Michael Neill (Cambridge, 1988), 261–80).

Other stimulating essays include those by Verna Foster and Kathleen McLuskie (' *'Tis Pity She's a Whore* as City Tragedy' and 'Language and Matter With a Fit of Mirth: Dramatic Construction in the Plays of John Ford', ibid. 181–200 and 97–128), an exploration of the iconographical context by Michael Neill (' "What Strange Riddle's This?": Deciphering *'Tis Pity She's a Whore*', ibid. 153–80), and there are several important studies relating to staging and performance (Alan C. Dessen, ' *'Tis Pity She's a Whore*: Modern Productions and the Scholar', in *Concord and Discord*, 87–108; Andrew Gurr, 'Singing Through the Chatter: Ford and Contemporary Theatrical Fashion', in *Critical Re-Visions*', 81–96; Richard Madelaine, ' "Sensationalism" and "Melodrama" in Ford's plays', ibid. 29–54; and Roger Warren, 'Ford in Performance', ibid. 11–28). Michael Scott also considers performance aspects of Ford's plays in his *Renaissance Drama and a Modern Audience* (London, 1982).

Additional full-length studies of Ford's works include Joan M. Sargeaunt, *John Ford* (Oxford, 1935); D. K. Anderson, *John Ford* (New York, 1972); Orbison Tucker, *The Tragic Vision of John Ford* (Salzburg, 1974); Dorothy Farr, *John Ford and the Caroline Theatre* (London, 1979); and Dale B. J. Randall, 'Theatres of Greatness': A Missionary View of Ford's Perkin Warbeck', English Literary Studies Monograph, no. 37 (University of Victoria, 1986).

Some works which place Ford's plays in a comparative contemporary context are M. C. Bradbrook, *Themes and Conventions of Elizabethan Tragedy*, 2nd edn. (Cambridge, 1952); Cyrus Hoy, 'Ignorance in Knowledge: Marlowe's Faustus and Ford's Giovanni', *Modern Philology*, 57 (1960), 145–54; David L. Frost, *The School of Shakespeare: The Influence of Shakespeare on English Drama 1600–42* (Cambridge, 1968); A. C. Kirsch, *Jacobean Dramatic Perspectives* (Charlottesville, Va., 1972); Ann J. Abadie, 'The Dramatic Kinship of John Ford and Ben Jonson' (Ph.D. dissertation, University of Mississippi Press, 1973); M. Axton and R. Williams (eds.), *English Drama: Forms and Development* (Cambridge, 1977); T. Logan and D. S. Smith (eds.), *Later Jacobean and Caroline Dramatists* (Lincoln, Nebr., 1978); my *Stage Images and Traditions: Shakespeare to Ford* (Cambridge, 1987), and Ira Clark, *Professional Playwrights: Massinger, Ford, Shirley, and Brome* (Lexington, 1992).

Other useful articles and essays include D. K. Anderson, 'Kingship in Ford's *Perkin Warbeck*', *English Literary History*, 27 (1960), 177–93 and

'*Richard II* and *Perkin Warbeck*', *Shakespeare Quarterly*, 13 (1962), 260–3; Jonas A. Barish, '*Perkin Warbeck* as Anti-History', *Essays in Criticism*, 20 (1970), 151–71; Anne Barton, ' "He that plays the king": Ford's *Perkin Warbeck* and the Stuart History Play', in M. Axton and R. Williams (eds.), *English Drama: Forms and Development* (Cambridge, 1977), 69–93 and 'Oxymoron and the Structure of Ford's *The Broken Heart*', *Essays and Studies*, NS 33 (1980), 70–94; Joseph Candido, 'The "strange truth" of *Perkin Warbeck*', *Philological Quarterly* 59 (1980), 300–16; Terri Clerico, 'The Politics of Blood: John Ford's *'Tis Pity She's a Whore*', *English Literary Renaissance*, 22 (1992), 405–34; Philip Edwards, 'The Royal Pretenders in Massinger and Ford', *ES* 27 (1974), 18–36; Lisa Hopkins, 'Silence and the Language of the Body: Women in the Plays of John Ford', *Elizabethan Theatre XIV: Proceedings of the 14th Waterloo Conference on Elizabethan Theatre* (in press); R. J. Kaufmann, 'Ford's *Waste Land: The Broken Heart*', *Renaissance Drama*, NS 3 (1970), 167–87; Michael Neill, ' "Anticke Pageantrie": The Mannerist Art of *Perkin Warbeck*', *Renaissance Drama*, NS 7 (1976), 117–50 and 'Ford's Unbroken Art: The Moral Design of *The Broken Heart*' *Modern Language Review*, 75 (1980), 249–68; and Carol C. Rosen 'The Language of Cruelty in Ford's *'Tis Pity She's a Whore*', *Comparative Drama*, 8 (1974), 356–68.

A CHRONOLOGY OF JOHN FORD

1586 John Ford baptized at Ilsington, Devon, on 12 April.

1593 Death of Marlowe.

1599 Death of Spenser.

1601 'John Ford Devon gent.' matriculated as a member of Exeter College, Oxford, on 26 March.

1602 Ford enters Middle Temple for legal training, 16 November.

1603 Death of Elizabeth I. Accession of James I.

1605 Ford suspended from the Middle Temple for not paying his buttery bill.

1606 Publishes *Fame's Memorial*, an elegy on the death of Charles Blount, Earl of Devonshire, dedicated to his countess, Lady Penelope (née Devereux), and *Funeral Tears*, a shorter tribute to the earl.

Publishes *Honour Triumphant*, a prose pamphlet on love and beauty, dedicated to the Countesses of Pembroke and Montgomery.

1608 Ford reinstated at the Middle Temple.

1610 Ford's father dies and he receives a bequest of £10.

1612 Death of Henry, Prince of Wales.

1613 Publishes *The Golden Mean*, a prose work advocating stoic endurance, addressed to the imprisoned Earl of Northumberland.

A long poem, *Christ's Bloody Sweat*, dedicated to the Earl of Pembroke, was published by 'I.F.' Ford is considered by many to be the author.

An Ill Beginning Has a Good End, a comedy by Ford, acted at the Cockpit. This play was destroyed in the eighteenth century by John Warburton's cook.

1614 Commendatory verses to Sir Thomas Overbury's *The Wife*.

1615 *Sir Thomas Overbury's Ghost* entered in the Stationers' Register (now lost).

1616 Death of Shakespeare.

Ford granted an annual annuity of £20 by will of his elder brother, Henry.

A new edition of Overbury's *The Wife* published with elegiac verses on Overbury by 'Io. Fo.', often identified as Ford.

1617 Ford reprimanded for taking part in an organized protest at the Middle Temple against the wearing of lawyers' caps in hall.

1618 Execution of Raleigh.

1620 Publishes *A Line of Life*, a pamphlet urging stoicism in adversity.

1621 *The Witch of Edmonton*, a tragedy by Rowley, Dekker, and Ford, acted.

1623 *The Spanish Gipsy*, written with Middleton and Rowley, acted.

The Duchess of Malfi, by John Webster, published with commendatory verses by Ford.

1624 *The Bristol Merchant* and *The Fairy Knight*, written with Dekker, *The Late Murder of the Son upon the Mother*, and *Keep the Widow Waking*, written with Dekker, Rowley, and Webster (all lost plays) were probably acted now. (Elements of *The Bristol Merchant* may survive as the basis of Dekker's *Penny-Wise, Pound Foolish*, 1631.)

     The Sun's Darling, a masque written with Dekker, acted at the Cockpit.

1625 Death of James I. Accession of Charles I.

     Death of Fletcher.

1626 Death of Tourneur.

1628 *The Lover's Melancholy*, probably Ford's first sole-authorship play, licensed and acted at the Blackfriars and Globe theatres by the King's Men.

1629 *The Lover's Melancholy* published.

     Commendatory verses to Shirley's *The Wedding* and Massinger's *The Roman Actor*.

1632 Commendatory verses to Richard Brome's *The Northern Lass*.

1633 *'Tis Pity She's a Whore*, *The Broken Heart*, and *Love's Sacrifice*, published.

     Donne's *Poems* published.

1634 *Perkin Warbeck* published.

1636 Commendatory verses to Massinger's *The Great Duke of Florence* and (in Latin and English) Charles Saltonstall's *The Navigator*.

1637 Death of Ben Jonson.

1638 *The Fancies Chaste and Noble*, a comedy, published. *The Lady's Trial*, a tragicomedy, licensed and acted at the Cockpit.

     Verse tribute to Ben Jonson published in the collection *Jonsonus Virbius*.

1639 Death of Massinger.

     Publication of *The Lady's Trial*.

     Ford probably left London and returned to Devon about this time. Nothing more is known of him.

1642 Civil War begins. Theatres close.

1653 *The Queen*, now attributed to Ford, published anonymously but believed to have been written much earlier.

THE LOVER'S MELANCHOLY

To my worthily respected friends, Nathaniel Finch, John Ford, Esquires; Mr Henry Blunt, Mr Robert Ellice, and all the rest of the Noble Society of Gray's Inn

My Honoured Friends,
The account of some leisurable hours is here summed up and offered to examination. Importunity of others, or opinion of mine own, hath not urged on any confidence of running the hazard of a censure. As plurality hath reference to a multitude, so I care not to please many; but where there is a parity of condition, there the freedom of 5
construction makes the best music. This concord hath equally held between you the patrons, and me the presenter. I am cleared of all scruple of disrespect on your parts, as I am of too slack a merit in myself. My presumption of coming in print in this kind hath hitherto been unreprovable, this piece being the first that ever courted reader;° 10
and it is very possible that the like compliment with me may soon grow out of fashion. A practice of which that I may avoid now, I commend to the continuance of your loves the memory of his, who, without the protestation of a service, is readily your friend,

John Ford 15

To my Honoured Friend, Master John Ford, on his Lover's Melancholy

> If that thou think'st these lines thy worth can raise,
> Thou dost mistake; my liking is no praise:
> Nor can I think thy judgement is so ill,
> To seek for bays from such a barren quill.°
> Let your true critic, that can judge and mend, 5
> Allow thy scenes and style: I, as a friend
> That knows thy worth, do only stick my name,
> To show my love, not to advance thy fame.
>
> George Donne°

To his worthy Friend, the Author, Master John Ford

I write not to thy play: I'll not begin
To throw a censure upon what hath been
By th'best approved; it can nor fear, nor want
The rage, or liking of the ignorant.
Nor seek I fame for thee, when thine own pen   5
Hath forced a praise long since from knowing men.
I speak my thoughts, and wish unto the stage
A glory from thy studies; that the age
May be indebted to thee for reprieve
Of purer language, and that spite may grieve   10
To see itself outdone. When thou art read,
The theatre may hope arts are not dead,
Though long concealed; that poet-apes may fear°
To vent their weakness, mend, or quite forbear.
This I dare promise; and keep this in store,   15
As thou hast done enough, thou canst do more.

William Singleton°

To the Author, Master John Ford

Black choler, reason's overflowing spring,°
Where thirsty lovers drink, or any thing,
Passion, the restless current of dull plaints,
Affords their thoughts who deem lost beauties saints;
Here their best lectures read, collect, and see   5
Various conditions of humanity
Highly enlightened by thy muse's rage;
Yet all so couched that they adorned the stage.
Shun Phocion's blushes thou; for sure, to please°
It is no sin, then what is thy disease?   10
Judgement's applause? Effeminated smiles?
Study's delight? Thy wit mistrust beguiles;
Established fame will thy physician be,
Write but again to cure thy jealousy.°

Humfrey Howorth°   15

Of the Lover's Melancholy

'Tis not the language, nor the fore-placed rhymes
Of friends, that shall commend to after-times
The Lover's Melancholy; its own worth
Without a borrowed praise, shall set it forth.

ὁ Φιλος°   5

THE SCENE

Famagusta in Cyprus

THE PERSONS OF THE PLAY

PALADOR, Prince of Cyprus
MELEANDER, an old, former
  statesman to Palador's father
EROCLEA ⎫
  [PARTHENOPHILL] ⎬ daughters of Meleander
CLEOPHILA ⎭
RHETIAS, a courtier, protector of Eroclea
ARETUS, tutor to Palador
TROLLIO, servant to Meleander
CORAX, a physician
THAMASTA, cousin of Palador
AMETHUS, brother of Thamasta
MENAPHON, friend of Amethus
SOPHRONOS, father of Menaphon, brother of Meleander, and
  counsellor to Palador
KALA, maid to Thamasta
CUCULUS ⎱ foolish
PELIAS ⎰ courtiers
GRILLA, page to Cuculus (dressed as a female)
ATTENDANTS

THE NAMES OF SUCH AS ACTED°

John Lowin   Richard Sharpe
Joseph Taylor   Thomas Pollard
Robert Benfield   William Penn
John Schanck   Curteish Gr——
Eylyardt Swanston   George Vernon
Anthony Smith   Richard Baxter

              John Tomson
              John Honyman
              James Horne
              William Trigg
              Alexander Gough

6

THE PROLOGUE

To tell ye, gentlemen, in what true sense
The writer, actors, or the audience
Should mould their judgements for a play, might draw
Truth into rules, but we have no such law.
Our writer, for himself, would have ye know   5
That in his following scenes he doth not owe
To others' fancies, nor hath lain in wait
For any stol'n invention, from whose height
He might commend his own, more than the right
A scholar claims may warrant for delight.   10
It is art's scorn that some of late have made
The noble use of poetry a trade.
For your parts, gentlemen, to quit his pains,°
Yet you will please that, as you meet with strains
Of lighter mixtures, but to cast your eye   15
Rather upon the main than on the bye.°
His hopes stand firm, and we shall find it true,
The Lover's Melancholy cured by you.

The Lover's Melancholy

1.1

Enter Menaphon and Pelias

MENAPHON Dangers? How mean you dangers—that so courtly
  You gratulate my safe return from dangers?

PELIAS From travels, noble sir.

MENAPHON   These are delights,
  If my experience hath not truant-like
  Misspent the time, which I have strove to use   5
  For bettering my mind with observation.

PELIAS As I am modest, I protest 'tis strange;
  But is it possible?

MENAPHON   What?

PELIAS   To bestride
  The frothy foams of Neptune's surging waves
  When blust'ring Boreas tosseth up the deep   10
  And thumps a thunder bounce?

MENAPHON   Sweet sir, 'tis nothing.
  Straight comes a dolphin playing near your ship,
  Heaving his crookèd back up, and presents
  A feather-bed to waft'ee to the shore°
  As easily as if you slept i'th' court.   15

PELIAS Indeed, is't true, I pray?

MENAPHON   I will not stretch
  Your faith upon the tenters. Prithee, Pelias,
  Where didst thou learn this language?

PELIAS   I this language?
  Alas, sir, we that study words and forms
  Of compliment, must fashion all discourse   20
  According to the nature of the subject.
    Enter Amethus, Sophronos, and attendants
  But I am silent; now appears a sun
  Whose shadow I adore.

MENAPHON   My honoured father.

SOPHRONOS [*weeping with joy*] From mine eyes, son, son of my care,
  my love,

9

The joys that bid thee welcome do too much   25
Speak me a child.

MENAPHON [*to Amethus*] O princely sir, your hand.

AMETHUS Perform your duties where you owe them first;
I dare not be so sudden in the pleasures
Thy presence hath brought home.

SOPHRONOS   Here thou still find'st
A friend as noble, Menaphon, as when   30
Thou left'st at thy departure.

MENAPHON   Yes, I know it;
To him I owe more service.

AMETHUS [*to Sophronos*]   Pray give leave.
He shall attend your entertainments soon,
Next day, and next day; for an hour or two
I would engross him only.

SOPHRONOS   Noble lord.   35

AMETHUS Y'are both dismissed.

PELIAS   Your creature, and your servant.

Exeunt all but Amethus [and] Menaphon

AMETHUS Give me thy hand. I will not say, 'Th'art welcome';
That is the common road of common friends.
I am glad I have thee here—O, I want words
To let thee know my heart.

MENAPHON   'Tis pieced to mine.   40

AMETHUS Yes, 'tis; as firmly as that holy thing
Called friendship can unite it. Menaphon,
My Menaphon: now all the goodly blessings
That can create a heaven on earth, dwell with thee!
Twelve months we have been sundered; but henceforth   45
We never more will part till that sad hour
In which death leaves the one of us behind
To see the other's funerals performed.°
Let's now a while be free. How have thy travels
Disburdened thee abroad of discontents?   50

MENAPHON Such cure as sick men find in changing beds,
I found in change of airs; the fancy flattered
My hopes with ease, as theirs do, but the grief
Is still the same.

AMETHUS   Such is my case at home.
Cleophila, thy kinswoman, that maid   55
Of sweetness and humility, more pities

Her father's poor afflictions than the tide
Of my complaints.

MENAPHON   Thamasta, my great mistress,
Your princely sister, hath, I hope ere this,
Confirmed affection on some worthy choice.   60

AMETHUS Not any, Menaphon. Her bosom yet
Is intermured with ice, though by the truth
Of love, no day hath ever passed wherein
I have not mentioned thy deserts, thy constancy,
Thy—come, in troth I dare not tell thee what,   65
Lest thou mightst think I fawned upon a sin°
Friendship was never guilty of; for flattery
Is monstrous in a true friend.

MENAPHON   Does the court
Wear the old looks too?

AMETHUS   If thou mean'st the prince,
It does. He's the same melancholy man   70
He was at's father's death; sometimes speaks sense,
But seldom mirth; will smile, but seldom laugh;
Will lend an ear to business, deal in none;
Gaze upon revels, antic fopperies,
But is not moved; will sparingly discourse,   75
Hear music; but what most he takes delight in
Are handsome pictures. One so young and goodly,
So sweet in his own nature, any story
Hath seldom mentioned.

MENAPHON   Why should such as I am°
Groan under the light burdens of small sorrows,   80
Whereas a prince, so potent, cannot shun°
Motions of passion? To be man, my lord,
Is to be but the exercise of cares
In several shapes; as miseries do grow,
They alter as men's forms; but how, none know.   85

AMETHUS This little isle of Cyprus sure abounds
In greater wonders, both for change and fortune,
Than any you have seen abroad.

MENAPHON   Than any
I have observed abroad: all countries else°
To a free eye and mind yield something rare;   90
And I, for my part, have brought home one jewel
Of admirable value.

AMETHUS   Jewel, Menaphon?

MENAPHON   A jewel, my Amethus, a fair youth.
   A youth, whom if I were but superstitious,
   I should repute an excellence more high   95
   Than mere creations are; to add delight°
   I'll tell ye how I found him.

AMETHUS   Prithee do.

MENAPHON   Passing from Italy to Greece, the tales
   Which poets of an elder time have feigned
   To glorify their Tempe, bred in me°   100
   Desire of visiting that paradise.
   To Thessaly I came, and living private,
   Without acquaintance of more sweet companions
   Than the old inmates to my love, my thoughts,
   I day by day frequented silent groves   105
   And solitary walks. One morning early
   This accident encountered me: I heard
   The sweetest and most ravishing contention
   That art or nature ever were at strife in.°

AMETHUS   I cannot yet conceive what you infer   110
   By art and nature.

MENAPHON   I shall soon resolve ye.
   A sound of music touched mine ears, or rather,
   Indeed, entranced my soul. As I stole nearer,
   Invited by the melody, I saw
   This youth, this fair-faced youth, upon his lute,   115
   With strains of strange variety and harmony,
   Proclaiming (as it seemed) so bold a challenge
   To the clear choristers of the woods, the birds,
   That as they flocked about him, all stood silent,
   Wond'ring at what they heard. I wondered too.   120

AMETHUS   And so do I, good—on.

MENAPHON   A nightingale!
   Nature's best skilled musician undertakes
   The challenge, and for every several strain°
   The well-shaped youth could touch, she sung her down.°
   He could not run division with more art°   125
   Upon his quaking instrument than she,
   The nightingale, did with her various notes
   Reply to; for a voice and for a sound,
   Amethus, 'tis much easier to believe

That such they were than hope to hear again.   130
AMETHUS How did the rivals part?
MENAPHON   You term them rightly;
  For they were rivals, and their mistress, harmony.
  Some time thus spent, the young man grew at last
  Into a pretty anger that a bird
  Whom art had never taught clefs, moods, or notes,   135
  Should vie with him for mastery, whose study
  Had busied many hours to perfect practice.
  To end the controversy, in a rapture
  Upon his instrument he plays so swiftly,
  So many voluntaries, and so quick,°   140
  That there was curiosity and cunning,
  Concord in discord, lines of diff'ring method
  Meeting in one full centre of delight.°
AMETHUS Now for the bird.
MENAPHON   The bird, ordained to be
  Music's first martyr, strove to imitate   145
  These several sounds, which, when her warbling throat
  Failed in, for grief down dropped she on his lute,
  And brake her heart. It was the quaintest sadness
  To see the conqueror upon her hearse
  To weep a funeral elegy of tears,   150
  That trust me, my Amethus, I could chide
  Mine own unmanly weakness that made me
  A fellow-mourner with him.
AMETHUS   I believe thee.
MENAPHON He looked upon the trophies of his art,°
  Then sighed, then wiped his eyes, then sighed, and cried,   155
  'Alas, poor creature! I will soon revenge
  This cruelty upon the author of it.
  Henceforth this lute, guilty of innocent blood,
  Shall never more betray a harmless peace
  To an untimely end.' And in that sorrow,   160
  As he was pashing it against a tree,
  I suddenly stepped in.
AMETHUS   Thou hast discoursed
  A truth of mirth and pity.
MENAPHON   I reprieved°
  Th'intended execution with entreaties
  And interruption: but, my princely friend,   165

13

It was not strange the music of his hand
Did over-match birds, when his voice and beauty,
Youth, carriage, and discretion must, from men
Endued with reason, ravish admiration;
From me they did.

AMETHUS   But is this miracle   170
Not to be seen?

MENAPHON   I won him by degrees
To choose me his companion. Whence he is,
Or who, as I durst modestly enquire,
So gently he would woo not to make known;
Only—for reasons to himself reserved—   175
He told me that some remnant of his life
Was to be spent in travel; for his fortunes,
They were nor mean nor riotous; his friends°
Not published to the world, though not obscure;
His country, Athens, and his name, Parthenophill.   180

AMETHUS Came he with you to Cyprus?

MENAPHON   Willingly.
The fame of our young melancholy prince,
Meleander's rare distractions, the obedience°
Of young Cleophila, Thamasta's glory,
Your matchless friendship, and my desperate love,   185
Prevailed with him, and I have lodged him privately
In Famagusta.

AMETHUS   Now th'art doubly welcome:
I will not lose the sight of such a rarity
For one part of my hopes. When d'ee intend°
To visit my great-spirited sister?

MENAPHON   May I   190
Without offence?

AMETHUS   Without offence! Parthenophill
Shall find a worthy entertainment too.
Thou art not still a coward?

MENAPHON   She's too excellent,
And I too low in merit.

AMETHUS   I'll prepare
A noble welcome; and, friend, ere we part,   195
Unload to thee an over-chargèd heart.
        Exeunt

1.2

Enter Rhetias, carelessly attired

RHETIAS I will not court the madness of the times,
Nor fawn upon the riots that embalm
Our wanton gentry, to preserve the dust
Of their affected vanities in coffins
Of memorable shame. When commonwealths   5
Totter and reel from that nobility
And ancient virtue which renowns the great
Who steer the helm of government, while mushrooms
Grow up, and make new laws to license folly;
Why should not I, a May-game, scorn the weight   10
Of my sunk fortunes? Snarl at the vices
Which rot the land, and without fear or wit
Be mine own antic? 'Tis a sport to live
When life is irksome, if we will not hug
Prosperity in others and contemn   15
Affliction in ourselves. This rule is certain:
'He that pursues his safety from the school°
Of state, must learn to be madman, or fool.'
Ambition, wealth, ease; I renounce the devil
That damns ye here on earth, or I will be—   20
Mine own mirth, or mine own tormentor—So!
    Enter Pelias
Here comes intelligence, a buzz o' the court.

PELIAS Rhetias, I sought thee out to tell thee news,
New, excellent new news. Cuculus, sirrah,
That gull, that young old gull, is coming this way.   25

RHETIAS And thou art his forerunner?

PELIAS   Prithee, hear me:
Instead of a fine guarded page, we have got him°
A boy, tricked up in neat and handsome fashion;
Persuaded him that 'tis indeed a wench,
And he has entertained him. He does follow him,°   30
Carries his sword and buckler, waits on his trencher,°
Fills him his wine, tobacco, whets his knife,
Lackeys his letters, does what service else°
He would employ his man in. Being asked
Why he is so irregular in courtship,   35

His answer is, that since great ladies use
Gentlemen ushers to go bare before them,°
He knows no reason but he may reduce
The courtiers to have women wait on them,
And he begins the fashion. He is laughed at   40
Most complimentally. Thou'lt burst to see him.

RHETIAS Agelastus,° so surnamed for his gravity, was a very wise
fellow, kept his countenance all days of his life as demurely as a
judge that pronounceth sentence of death on a poor rogue for
stealing as much bacon as would serve at a meal with a calf's head.   45
Yet he smiled once, and never but once. Thou art no scholar?

PELIAS I have read pamphlets dedicated to me.
Dost call him Agelastus? Why did he laugh?

RHETIAS To see an ass eat thistles. Puppy, go study to be a singular
coxcomb. Cuculus is an ordinary ape, but thou art an ape of an ape.   50

PELIAS Thou hast a patent to abuse thy friends.

          Enter Cuculus and Grilla
. Look, look, he comes! Observe him seriously.

CUCULUS Reach me my sword and buckler.

GRILLA They are here, forsooth.

CUCULUS How now, minx, how now! Where is your duty, your   55
distance? Let me have service methodically tendered; you are now
one of us. Your curtsey. [*Grilla curtsies*] Good; remember that you
are to practise courtship. Was thy father a piper, say'st thou?

GRILLA A sounder of some such wind instrument,° forsooth.

CUCULUS Was he so? Hold up thy head. Be thou musical to me and   60
I will marry thee to a dancer;° one that shall ride on his footcloth,°
and maintain thee in thy muff and hood.°

GRILLA That will be fine indeed.

CUCULUS Thou art yet but simple.

GRILLA D'ee think so?   65

CUCULUS I have a brain, I have a head-piece.° O' my conscience, if
I take pains with thee, I should raise thy understanding,° girl, to
the height of a nurse, or a court-midwife at least; I will make thee
big° in time, wench.

GRILLA E'en do your pleasure with me, sir.   70

PELIAS [*coming forward*] Noble, accomplished Cuculus!

RHETIAS [*coming forward*] Give me thy fist, innocent.

CUCULUS Would 'twere in thy belly! There 'tis.

PELIAS That's well; he's an honest blade, though he be blunt.

CUCULUS Who cares? We can be as blunt as he, for's life.   75

RHETIAS Cuculus, there is within a mile or two a sow-pig hath sucked a brach,° and now hunts the deer, the hare, nay, most unnaturally, the wild boar, as well as any hound in Cyprus.

CUCULUS Monstrous sow-pig! Is't true?

PELIAS I'll be at charge of a banquet on thee° for a sight of her.   80

RHETIAS Everything takes after the dam that gave it suck: where hadst thou thy milk?

CUCULUS I? Why, my nurse's husband was a most excellent maker of shuttle-cocks.

PELIAS My nurse was a woman-surgeon.°   85

RHETIAS And who gave thee pap, mouse?

GRILLA I never sucked that I remember.

RHETIAS La, now, a shuttle-cock maker! All thy brains are stuck with cork and feather, Cuculus. This learned courtier takes after the nurse too, a she-surgeon, which is, in effect, a mere matcher of   90
colours. Go, learn to paint and daub compliments, 'tis the next step to run into a new suit. My Lady Periwinkle here never sucked; suck thy master, and bring forth moon-calves, fop, do. This is good philosophy, sirs, make use on't.

GRILLA Bless us, what a strange creature this is!   95

CUCULUS A gull, an arrant gull by proclamation.°

        Enter Corax, passing over°

PELIAS Corax, the prince's chief physician. What business speeds his haste?—Are all things well, sir?

CORAX Yes, yes, yes.

RHETIAS Phew! you may wheel about, man; we know y'are proud of   100
your slovenry and practice; 'tis your virtue. The prince's melancholy fit, I presume, holds still.

CORAX So do thy knavery and desperate beggary.

CUCULUS Aha! here's one will tickle the ban-dog.

RHETIAS You must not go yet.   105

CORAX I'll stay in spite of thy teeth.° There lies my gravity.° (*Casts off his gown*) Do what thou darest; I stand thee.

RHETIAS Mountebanks, empirics, quacksalvers, mineralists, wizards, alchemists, cast-apothecaries, old wives, and barbers, are all suppositors° to the right worshipful doctor, as I take it. Some of ye   110
are the head of your art—and the horns° too, but they come by nature. Thou livest single for no other end, but that thou fearest to be a cuckold.

CORAX Have at thee! Thou affect'st railing only for thy health; thy miseries are so thick and so lasting that thou hast not one poor   115

17

denier to bestow on opening a vein. Wherefore, to avoid a pleurisy, thou'lt be sure to prate thyself once a month into a whipping, and bleed in the breech instead of the arm.

RHETIAS Have at thee again!

CORAX Come!   120

CUCULUS There, there, there! O brave doctor!

PELIAS Let 'em alone.

RHETIAS Thou art in thy religion an atheist, in thy condition a cur, in thy diet an epicure, in thy lust a goat, in thy sleep a hog; thou tak'st upon thee the habit of a grave physician, but   125 art indeed an imposterous empiric. Physicians are the body's cobblers, rather the botchers of men's bodies; as the one patches our tattered clothes, so the other solders our diseased flesh. Come on.

CUCULUS To't, to't, hold him to't! Hold him to't! To't, to't, to't!   130

CORAX The best worth in thee is the corruption of thy mind, for that only entitles thee to the dignity of a louse, a thing bred out of the filth and superfluity of ill humours.° Thou bit'st anywhere, and any man who defends not himself with the clean linen of secure honesty; him thou darest not come near. Thou art fortune's idiot,   135 virtue's bankrupt, time's dunghill, manhood's scandal, and thine own scourge. Thou wouldst hang thyself, so wretchedly miserable thou art, but that no man will trust thee with as much money as will buy a halter; and all thy stock to be sold is not worth half as much as may procure it.   140

RHETIAS Ha, ha, ha! This is flattery, gross flattery.

CORAX I have employment for thee, and for ye all. Tut, these are but good-morrows between us.

RHETIAS Are thy bottles full?

CORAX Of rich wine; let's all suck together.   145

RHETIAS Like so many swine in a trough.

CORAX I'll shape ye all for a device before the prince; we'll try how that can move him.

RHETIAS He shall fret or laugh.

CUCULUS Must I make one?°   150

CORAX Yes, and your feminine page too.

GRILLA Thanks, most egregiously.

PELIAS I will not slack my part.

CUCULUS Wench, take my buckler.

CORAX Come all unto my chamber; the project is cast; the time only   155 we must attend.

RHETIAS The melody must agree well and yield sport,
When such as these are —knaves and fools—consort.°
        Exeunt

1.3

        Enter Amethus, Thamasta, and Kala
AMETHUS Does this show well?
THAMASTA   What would you have me do?
AMETHUS Not like a lady of the trim, new crept
Out of the shell of sluttish sweat and labour
Into the glittering pomp of ease and wantonness,
Embroideries, and all these antic fashions   5
That shape a woman monstrous; to transform
Your education and a noble birth
Into contempt and laughter. Sister, sister,
She who derives her blood from princes ought
To glorify her greatness by humility.   10
THAMASTA Then you conclude me proud.
AMETHUS   Young Menaphon,
My worthy friend, has loved you long and truly;
To witness his obedience to your scorn
Twelve months, wronged gentleman, he undertook
A voluntary exile. Wherefore, sister,   15
In this time of his absence, have you not
Disposed of your affections on some monarch?
Or sent ambassadors to some neighb'ring king
With fawning protestations of your graces,
Your rare perfections, admirable beauty?   20
This had been a new piece of modesty
Would have deserved a chronicle!
THAMASTA   You are bitter;
And, brother, by your leave, not kindly wise.°
My freedom is my birth's; I am not bound
To fancy your approvements, but my own.   25
Indeed, you are an humble youth! I hear of
Your visits and your loving commendation
To your heart's saint, Cleophila, a virgin
Of a rare excellence. What though she want

A portion to maintain a portly greatness?   30
Yet 'tis your gracious sweetness to descend
So low—the meekness of your pity leads ye!
She is your dear friend's sister, a good soul,°
An innocent.

AMETHUS   Thamasta!

THAMASTA   I have given°
Your Menaphon a welcome home as fits me;   35
For his sake entertained Parthenophill,
The handsome stranger, more familiarly
Than, I may fear, becomes me; yet, for his part,
I not repent my courtesies, but you—

AMETHUS No more, no more. Be affable to both;   40
Time may reclaim your cruelty.

THAMASTA   I pity
The youth; and trust me, brother, love his sadness.
He talks the prettiest stories; he delivers
His tales so gracefully that I could sit
And listen, nay, forget my meals and sleep,   45
To hear his neat discourses. Menaphon
Was well advised in choosing such a friend
For pleading his true love.

AMETHUS   Now I command thee;
Thou'lt change at last I hope.

> Enter Menaphon and Eroclea [as Parthenophill] in man's
> attire°

THAMASTA [aside]   I fear I shall.

AMETHUS Have ye surveyed the garden?

MENAPHON   'Tis a curious,   50
A pleasantly contrived delight.

THAMASTA   Your eye, sir,
Hath in your travels often met contents
Of more variety.

EROCLEA   Not any, lady.

MENAPHON [to Thamasta] It were impossible, since your fair
    presence
Makes every place where it vouchsafes to shine   55
More lovely than all other helps of art
Can equal.

THAMASTA What you mean by 'helps of art'
You know yourself best; be they as they are,

You need none, I am sure, to set me forth.

MENAPHON 'Twould argue want of manners more than skill   60
Not to praise praise itself.

THAMASTA   For your reward
Henceforth I'll call you servant.

AMETHUS   Excellent sister!°

MENAPHON 'Tis my first step to honour. May I fall
Lower than shame when I neglect all service
That may confirm this favour.

THAMASTA   Are you well, sir?   65

EROCLEA Great princess, I am well; to see a league
Between an humble love, such as my friend's is,
And a commanding virtue, such as yours is,
Are sure restoratives.

THAMASTA   You speak ingeniously.
Brother, be pleased to show the gallery   70
To this young stranger; use the time a while
And we will all together to the court.
I will present ye, sir, unto the prince.

EROCLEA Y'are all composed of fairness and true bounty.

AMETHUS Come, come. We'll wait thee, sister. This beginning   75
Doth relish happy process.

MENAPHON   You have blessed me.°

Exeunt all but Thamasta and Kala

THAMASTA Kala, O Kala!

KALA   Lady.

THAMASTA   We are private;
Thou art my closet.

KALA   Lock your secrets close then:
I am not to be forced.

THAMASTA   Never till now
Could I be sensible of being traitor   80
To honour and to shame.

KALA   You are in love.

THAMASTA I am grown base—Parthenophill—

KALA   He's handsome,
Richly endowed; he hath a lovely face,
A winning tongue.

THAMASTA   If ever I must fall,
In him my greatness sinks. Love is a tyrant,   85
Resisted. Whisper in his ear how gladly

I would steal time to talk with him one hour;
But do it honourably. Prithee, Kala,
Do not betray me.

KALA   Madam, I will make it
Mine own case; he shall think I am in love with him.   90

THAMASTA I hope thou art not, Kala.

KALA   'Tis for your sake:
I'll tell him so; but faith, I am not, lady.

THAMASTA Pray use me kindly; let me not too soon
Be lost in my new follies. 'Tis a fate
That overrules our wisdoms; whilst we strive   95
To live most free, we're caught in our own toils.
Diamonds cut diamonds; they who will prove°
To thrive in cunning, must cure love with love.

        Exeunt

2.1

Enter Sophronos and Aretus

SOPHRONOS Our commonwealth is sick: 'tis more than time
    That we should wake the head thereof, who sleeps
    In the dull lethargy of lost security.°
    The commons murmur and the nobles grieve,
    The court is now turned antic and grows wild,   5
    Whiles all the neighb'ring nations stand at gaze,
    And watch fit opportunity to wreak
    Their just-conceivèd fury on such injuries
    As the late prince, our living master's father,
    Committed against laws of truth or honour.   10
    Intelligence comes flying in on all sides,
    Whilst the unsteady multitude presume
    How that you, Aretus, and I, engross
    Out of particular ambition,
    Th'affairs of government—which I, for my part,   15
    Groan under and am weary of.
ARETUS   Sophronos,
    I am as zealous too of shaking off
    My gay state fetters, that I have bethought
    Of speedy remedy; and to that end,
    As I have told ye, have concluded with   20
    Corax, the prince's chief physician.
SOPHRONOS You should have done this sooner, Aretus;
    You were his tutor and could best discern
    His dispositions to inform them rightly.
ARETUS Passions of violent nature by degrees   25
    Are easiliest reclaimed. There's something hid
    Of his distemper, which we'll now find out.
    Enter Corax, Rhetias, Pelias, Cuculus, and Grilla
    You come on just appointment. Welcome, gentlemen!
    Have you won Rhetias, Corax?
CORAX   Most sincerely.
CUCULUS Save ye, nobilities! Do your lordships take notice of my   30
page? 'Tis a fashion of the newest edition, spick and span new,
without example. Do your honour, housewife.
GRILLA There's a curtsey for you, and a curtsey for you.

SOPHRONOS 'Tis excellent; we must all follow fashion
  And entertain she-waiters.

ARETUS   'Twill be courtly.   35

CUCULUS I think so; I hope the chronicles will rear me one day for
  a head-piece—°

RHETIAS Of woodcock without brains in't. Barbers shall wear thee
  on their citterns,° and hucksters set thee out in gingerbread.

CUCULUS Devil take thee! I say nothing to thee now; can'st let me   40
  be quiet?

GRILLA Y'are too perstreperous, sauce-box.

CUCULUS Good girl! If we begin to puff once—

PELIAS Prithee, hold thy tongue, the lords are in the presence.

RHETIAS Mum, butterfly!

PELIAS   O, the prince! Stand and keep silence.°   45

CUCULUS O, the prince! Wench, thou shalt see the prince now.

    Soft music. Enter Palador, the Prince, with a book in his hand

SOPHRONOS }
ARETUS   } Sir! Gracious sir!

PALADOR   Why all this company?

CORAX A book! Is this the early exercise
  I did prescribe? Instead of following health,
  Which all men covet, you pursue your disease.   50
  Where's your great horse, your hounds, your set at tennis,
  Your balloon ball, the practice of your dancing,°
  Your casting of the sledge, or learning how°
  To toss a pike?—All changed into a sonnet?
  Pray, sir, grant me free liberty to leave   55
  The court; it does infect me with the sloth
  Of sleep and surfeit. In the university
  I have employments, which to my profession
  Add profit and report; here I am lost
  And, in your wilful dulness, held a man   60
  Of neither art nor honesty. You may
  Command my head; pray take it, do; 'twere better
  For me to lose it than to lose my wits
  And live in bedlam. You will force me to't;
  I am almost mad already.

PALADOR   I believe it.   65

SOPHRONOS Letters are come from Crete which do require
  A speedy restitution of such ships,
  As by your father were long since detained;

    If not, defiance threatened.

ARETUS   These near parts
    Of Syria that adjoin, muster their friends;   70
    And by intelligence we learn for certain
    The Syrian will pretend an ancient interest
    Of tribute intermitted.

SOPHRONOS   Through your land°
    Your subjects mutter strangely, and imagine
    More than they dare speak publicly.

CORAX   And yet   75
    They talk but oddly of you.

CUCULUS   Hang 'em, mongrels.

PALADOR Of me? My subjects talk of me?

CORAX   Yes, scurvily,
    And think worse, prince.

PALADOR   I'll borrow patience
    A little time to listen to these wrongs,
    And from the few of you which are here present,   80
    Conceive the general voice.

CORAX [aside]   So, now he is nettled.°

PALADOR By all your loves I charge ye, without fear
    Or flattery, to let me know your thoughts,
    And how I am interpreted. Speak boldly.

SOPHRONOS For my part, sir, I will be plain and brief.   85
    I think you are of nature mild and easy,
    Not willingly provoked, but withal headstrong
    In any passion that misleads your judgement.
    I think you too indulgent to such motions
    As spring out of your own affections,°   90
    Too old to be reformed, and yet too young
    To take fit counsel from yourself of what
    Is most amiss.

PALADOR   So—Tutor, your conceit?

ARETUS I think you dote—with pardon let me speak it—
    Too much upon your pleasures, and these pleasures   95
    Are so wrapped up in self-love, that you covet
    No other change of fortune; would be still
    What your birth makes you, but are loath to toil
    In such affairs of state as break your sleeps.

CORAX I think you would be by the world reputed   100
    A man in every point complete, but are

In manners and effect indeed a child,
A boy, a very boy.
PELIAS   May it please your grace,
I think you do contain within yourself
The great elixir, soul, and quintessence   105
Of all divine perfections; are the glory
Of mankind, and the only strict example
For earthly monarchies to square out their lives by;
Time's miracle, fame's pride; in knowledge, wit,
Sweetness, discourse, arms, arts—
PALADOR   You are a courtier.   110
CUCULUS But not of the ancient fashion, an't like your highness.°
    'Tis I, I that am the credit of the court, noble prince; and if thou
    wouldst by proclamation or patent create me overseer of all the
    tailors in thy dominions, then, then the golden days° should appear
    again; bread should be cheaper, fools should have more wit; knaves   115
    more honesty, and beggars more money.
GRILLA I think now—
CUCULUS Peace, you squall.
PALADOR [to Rhetias] You have not spoken yet.
CUCULUS Hang him! He'll nothing but rail.   120
GRILLA Most abominable; out upon him!
CORAX Away, Cuculus; follow the lords.
CUCULUS Close, page, close.°
          They all fall back and steal out. Palador and Rhetias
          [remain]
PALADOR You are somewhat long a-thinking.
RHETIAS I do not think at all.   125
PALADOR Am I not worthy of your thought?
RHETIAS My pity you are—but not my reprehension.
PALADOR Pity?
RHETIAS Yes, for I pity such to whom I owe service, who exchange
    their happiness for a misery.   130
PALADOR Is it a misery to be a prince?
RHETIAS Princes who forget their sovereignty and yield to affected
    passion are weary of command. You had a father, sir.
PALADOR Your sovereign whiles he lived. But what of him?
RHETIAS Nothing. I only dared to name him; that's all.   135
PALADOR I charge thee by the duty that thou owest us,
    Be plain in what thou mean'st to speak; there's something
    That we must know; be free, our ears are open.

RHETIAS O, sir, I had rather hold a wolf by the ears than stroke a
 lion—the greatest danger is the last.   140
PALADOR This is mere trifling—Ha! are all stolen hence?
 We are alone. Thou hast an honest look;
 Thou hast a tongue, I hope, that is not oiled
 With flattery; be open. Though 'tis true
 That in my younger days I oft have heard   145
 Agenor's name, my father, more traduced
 Than I could then observe; yet, I protest,
 I never had a friend, a certain friend,
 That would inform me throughly of such errors
 As oftentimes are incident to princes.   150
RHETIAS All this may be. I have seen a man so curious in feeling of
 the edge of a keen knife that he has cut his fingers. My flesh is not
 of proof° against the metal I am to handle; the one is tenderer than
 the other.
PALADOR I see, then, I must court thee. Take the word   155
 Of a just prince; for anything thou speak'st
 I have more than a pardon—thanks and love.
RHETIAS I will remember you of an old tale that something con-
 cerns you. Meleander, the great but unfortunate statesman, was
 by your father treated with for a match between you and his 160
 eldest daughter, the Lady Eroclea. You were both near of an age.
 I presume you remember a contract, and cannot forget her.
PALADOR She was a lovely beauty. Prithee, forward.
RHETIAS To court was Eroclea brought; was courted by your father,
 not for Prince Palador, as it followed, but to be made a prey 165
 to some less noble design.—With your favour, I have forgot the
 rest.
PALADOR Good, call it back again into thy memory,
 Else, losing the remainder, I am lost too.
RHETIAS You charm me. In brief, a rape° by some bad agents 170
 was attempted; by the Lord Meleander, her father, rescued, she
 conveyed away, Meleander accused of treason, his land seized,
 he himself distracted, and confined to the castle where he yet
 lives. What had ensued was doubtful; but your father shortly after
 died.   175
PALADOR But what became of fair Eroclea?
RHETIAS She never since was heard of.
PALADOR   No hope lives then
 Of ever, ever seeing her again.

RHETIAS Sir, I feared I should anger ye. There was, as I said, an old
   tale: I have now a new one, which may perhaps season the first   180
   with a more delightful relish.

PALADOR I am prepared to hear; say what you please.

RHETIAS My Lord Meleander falling, on whose favour my fortunes
   relied, I furnished myself for travel and bent my course to Athens,
   where a pretty accident after a while came to my knowledge.   185

PALADOR My ear is open to thee.

RHETIAS A young lady contracted to a noble gentleman, as the lady
   we last mentioned and your highness were, being hindered by
   their jarring parents, stole from her home and was conveyed like
   a ship-boy in a merchant° from the country where she lived, into   190
   Corinth first, and afterwards to Athens; where in much solitari-
   ness she lived like a youth almost two years, courted by all for
   acquaintance, but friend to none by familiarity.

PALADOR In habit of a man?

RHETIAS A handsome young man; till within these three months or   195
   less—her sweetheart's father dying some year before or more—she
   had notice of it and with much joy returned home and, as report
   voiced it at Athens, enjoyed her happiness she was long an exile for.
   Now, noble sir, if you did love the Lady Eroclea, why may not such
   safety and fate direct her as directed the other? 'Tis not impossible.   200

PALADOR If I did love her, Rhetias. Yes, I did.
   Give me thy hand: as thou didst serve Meleander,
   And art still true to these, henceforth serve me.°

RHETIAS My duty and my obedience are my surety; but I have been
   too bold.   205

PALADOR Forget the sadder story of my father,
   And only, Rhetias, learn to read me well,°
   For I must ever thank thee. Th'ast unlocked
   A tongue was vowed to silence; for requital
   Open my bosom, Rhetias.

RHETIAS   What's your meaning?°   210

PALADOR To tie thee to an oath of secrecy—
   Unloose the buttons, man, thou dost it faintly.
   What find'st thou there?

RHETIAS   A picture in a tablet.

PALADOR Look well upon't.

RHETIAS   I do—yes—let me observe it—
   'Tis hers, the lady's.

PALADOR   Whose?

RHETIAS   Eroclea's.   215

PALADOR Hers that was once Eroclea. For her sake
  Have I advanced Sophronos to the helm
  Of government; for her sake will restore
  Mcleander's honours to him; will for her sake
  Beg friendship from thee, Rhetias. O, be faithful,   220
  And let no politic lord work from thy bosom
  My griefs. I know thou wert put on to sift me;
  But be not too secure.

RHETIAS   I am your creature.°

PALADOR Continue still thy discontented fashion,
  Humour the lords as they would humour me;   225
  I'll not live in thy debt.—We are discovered.

        Enter Amethus, Menaphon, Thamasta, Kala, [and] Eroclea
        [disguised as Parthenophill]

AMETHUS Honour and health still wait upon the prince!
  Sir, I am bold with favour to present°
  Unto your highness, Menaphon, my friend,
  Returned from travel.

MENAPHON   Humbly on my knees   230
  I kiss your gracious hand.

PALADOR   It is our duty
  To love the virtuous.

MENAPHON   If my prayers or service
  Hold any value, they are vowed yours ever.

RHETIAS I have a fist for thee too, stripling; th'art started up prettily
  since I saw thee. Hast learned any with abroad? Canst tell news,   235
  and swear lies with a grace like a true traveller? What new ouzel's
  this?

THAMASTA Your highness shall do right to your own judgement
  In taking more than common notice of
  This stranger, an Athenian named Parthenophill.   240
  One whom (if mine opinion do not soothe me
  Too grossly) for the fashion of his mind,
  Deserves a dear respect.

PALADOR   Your commendations,
  Sweet cousin, speak him nobly.

EROCLEA   All the powers°
  That sentinel just thrones, double their guards   245
  About your sacred excellence!

PALADOR   What fortune

29

Led him to Cyprus?

MENAPHON   My persuasions won him.

AMETHUS And if your highness please to hear the entrance°
Into their first acquaintance, you will say—

THAMASTA It was the newest, sweetest, prettiest accident   250
That e'er delighted your attention.
I can discourse it, sir.

PALADOR   Some other time.
How is 'a called?

THAMASTA   Parthenophill.

PALADOR   Parthenophill?
We shall sort time to take more notice of him.
        Exit [Palador]

MENAPHON His wonted melancholy still pursues him.   255

AMETHUS I told you so.

THAMASTA   You must not wonder at it.

EROCLEA I do not, lady.

AMETHUS   Shall we to the castle?

MENAPHON We will attend ye, both.

RHETIAS All three—I'll go too. [*To Amethus*] Hark in thine ear,
gallant: I'll keep the old madman in chat whilst thou gabblest to   260
the girl;° my thumb's upon my lips; not a word.

AMETHUS [*aside to Rhetias*] I need not fear thee, Rhetias.—Sister,
soon
Expect us; this day we will range the city.

THAMASTA Well, soon I shall expect ye.—[*Aside*] Kala!

KALA [*aside*]   Trust me.

RHETIAS Troop on—Love, love, what a wonder thou art!   265
        *Exeunt [Rhetias, Amethus, and Menaphon]. Kala and
        Eroclea [disguised as Parthenophill] stay*

KALA May I not be offensive, sir?

EROCLEA   Your pleasure?
Yet pray be brief.

KALA   Then briefly, good, resolve me:
Have you a mistress, or a wife?

EROCLEA   I have neither.

KALA Nor did you ever love in earnest any
Fair lady whom you wished to make your own?   270

EROCLEA Not any, truly.

KALA   What your friends or means are
I will not be inquisitive to know,

Nor do I care to hope for. But admit
A dowry were thrown down before your choice,
Of beauty, noble birth, and sincere affection,   275
How gladly would you entertain it? Young man,
I do not tempt you idly.
EROCLEA   I shall thank you
When my unsettled thoughts can make me sensible
Of what 'tis to be happy; for the present
I am your debtor; and, fair gentlewoman,   280
Pray give me leave as yet to study ignorance°
For my weak brains conceive not what concerns me.
—Another time—
        Enter Thamasta
THAMASTA   Do I break off your parley
That you are parting? Sure, my woman loves you.
Can she speak well, Parthenophill?
EROCLEA   Yes, madam,   285
Discreetly chaste she can; she hath much won
On my belief, and in few words, but pithy,°
Much moved my thankfulness. You are her lady;
Your goodness aims, I know, at her preferment;
Therefore I may be bold to make confession   290
Of truth: if ever I desire to thrive
In woman's favour, Kala is the first
Whom my ambition shall bend to.
THAMASTA   Indeed!
But say a nobler love should interpose?
EROCLEA Where real worth and constancy first settle   295
A hearty truth, there greatness cannot shake it,
Nor shall it mine. Yet I am but an infant
In that construction which must give clear light
To Kala's merit; riper hours hereafter
Must learn me how to grow rich in deserts.   300
Madam, my duty waits on you.
        Exit Eroclea
THAMASTA   Come hither.
'If ever henceforth I desire to thrive
In woman's favours, Kala is the first
Whom my ambition shall bend to.'—'Twas so.
KALA These very words he spake.
THAMASTA   These very words   305

Curse thee, unfaithful creature, to thy grave.
Thou wooed'st him for thyself?
KALA   You said I should.
THAMASTA My name was never mentioned!
KALA   Madam, no;
We were not come to that.
THAMASTA   Not come to that?
Art thou a rival fit to cross my fate?   310
Now poverty and a dishonest fame,°
The waiting-woman's wages, be thy payment.
False, faithless, wanton beast, I'll spoil your carriage;°
There's not a page, a groom, nay, not a citizen
That shall be cast upon ye. Kala,   315
I'll keep thee in my service all thy lifetime
Without hope of a husband or a suitor.
KALA I have not verily deserved this cruelty.
THAMASTA Parthenophill shall know, if he respect
My birth, the danger of a fond neglect.   320
      Exit Thamasta
KALA Are you so quick? Well, I may chance to cross
Your peevishness. Now, though I never meant
The young man for myself, yet if he love me,
I'll have him, or I'll run away with him,
And let her do her worst then. What! We are all   325
But flesh and blood; the same thing that will do
My lady good will please her woman too.
      Exit

2.2

Enter Cleophila and Trollio
CLEOPHILA Tread softly, Trollio, my father sleeps still.
TROLLIO Ay, forsooth; but he sleeps like a hare with his eyes
open,° and that's no good sign.
CLEOPHILA Sure, thou art weary of this sullen living
But I am not; for I take more content   5
In my obedience here than all delights
The time presents elsewhere.
MELEANDER (*within*)°   O!

CLEOPHILA   Dost hear that groan?

TROLLIO Hear it! I shudder. It was a strong blast, young mistress, able to root up heart, liver, lungs, and all.

CLEOPHILA My much-wronged father! Let me view his face.   10

      [Cleophila] draws the arras; Meleander [is] discovered in a
      chair, sleeping

TROLLIO Lady mistress, shall I fetch a barber to steal away his rough beard whiles he sleeps in's naps? He never looks in a glass, and 'tis high time, on conscience, for him to be trimmed; 'has not been under the shaver's hand almost these four years.°

CLEOPHILA Peace, fool.   15

TROLLIO *[aside]* I could clip the old ruffian; there's hair enough to stuff all the great codpieces in Switzerland. 'A begins to stir, 'a stirs. Bless us, how his eyes roll! *[To Meleander]* A good year keep your lordship in your right wits, I beseech ye.

MELEANDER Cleophila?

CLEOPHILA   Sir, I am here; how d'ee, sir?   20

TROLLIO Sir, is your stomach up yet?° Get some warm porridge in your belly, 'tis a very good settle-brain.

MELEANDER The raven croaked, and hollow shrieks of owls
Sung dirges at her funeral; I laughed
The whiles, for 'twas no boot to weep. The girl°   25
Was fresh and full of youth; but, O, the cunning
Of tyrants that look big—their very frowns
Doom poor souls guilty ere their cause be heard.
Good, what art thou? and thou?

CLEOPHILA   I am Cleophila,
Your woeful daughter.

TROLLIO   I am Trollia,°   30
Your honest implement.°

MELEANDER I know ye both. 'Las, why d'ee use me thus?
Thy sister, my Eroclea, was so gentle
That turtles in their down do feed more gall
Than her spleen mixed with; yet, when winds and storm°   35
Drive dirt and dust on banks of spotless snow,
The purest whiteness is no such defence
Against the sullying foulness of that fury.
So raved Agenor, that great man, mischief°
Against the girl—'twas a politic trick,   40
We were too old in honour.—I am lean°
And fallen away extremely; most assuredly

I have not dined these three days.

CLEOPHILA   Will you now, sir?

TROLLIO I beseech ye heartily, sir. I feel a horrible puking myself.

MELEANDER Am I stark mad?   45

TROLLIO No, no, you are but a little staring—there's difference
between staring and stark mad. You are but whimsied yet;
crotchetted, conundrumed,° or so.

MELEANDER Here's all my care; and I do often sigh
For thee, Cleophila; we are secluded   50
From all good people. But take heed; Amethus
Was son to Doryla, Agenor's sister.
There's some ill blood about him, if the surgeon
Have not been very skilful to let all out.

CLEOPHILA I am, alas, too grieved to think of love;   55
That must concern me least.

MELEANDER [to Trollio]   Sirrah, be wise, be wise.

TROLLIO Who I? I will be monstrous and wise—
        Enter Amethus, Menaphon, Eroclea [disguised as
        Parthenophill], and Rhetias°
immediately. Welcome, gentlemen, the more the merrier. I'll lay
the cloth and set the stools in a readiness, for I see here is some
hope of dinner now.   60
        Exit Trollio

AMETHUS My Lord Meleander, Menaphon, your kinsman,
Newly returned from travel, comes to tender
His duty t'ee; to you his love, fair mistress.

MENAPHON I would I could as easily remove
Sadness from your remembrance, sir, as study   65
To do you faithful service.—My dear cousin,
All best of comforts bless your sweet obedience!

CLEOPHILA One chief of 'em, worthy cousin, lives
In you and your well-doing.

MENAPHON   This young stranger
Will well deserve your knowledge.

AMETHUS   For my friend's sake,   70
Lady, pray give him welcome.

CLEOPHILA   He has met it,
If sorrows can look kindly.

EROCLEA   You much honour me.

RHETIAS [aside] How 'a eyes the company; sure my passion will
betray my weakness. [To Meleander] O my master, my noble

master, do not forget me; I am still the humblest and the most   75
faithful in heart of those that serve you.

MELEANDER Ha, ha, ha!

RHETIAS [*aside*] There's wormwood in that laughter; 'tis the usher to
a violent extremity.

MELEANDER I am a weak old man. All these are come   80
To jeer my ripe calamities.

MENAPHON   Good uncle!

MELEANDER But I'll outstare 'ee all; fools, desperate fools!
You are cheated, grossly cheated; range, range on
And roll about the world to gather moss,
The moss of honour, gay reports, gay clothes,   85
Gay wives, huge empty buildings, whose proud roofs
Shall, with their pinnacles, even reach the stars.
Ye work and work like moles, blind in the paths
That are bored through the crannies of the earth,
To charge your hungry souls with such full surfeits   90
As being gorged once, make 'ee lean with plenty.°
And when ye have skimmed the vomit of your riots,
Y'are fat in no felicity but folly;
Then your last sleeps seize on 'ee. Then the troops
Of worms crawl round and feast; good cheer, rich fare,   95
Dainty, delicious—here's Cleophila,
All the poor stock of my remaining thrift.
You, you, the prince's cousin, how d'ee like her?
Amethus, how d'ee like her?

AMETHUS   My intents
Are just and honourable.

MENAPHON   Sir, believe him.   100

MELEANDER Take her.—We two must part; go to him, do.

EROCLEA This sight is full of horror.

RHETIAS   There is sense yet
In this distraction.

MELEANDER In this jewel I have given away
All what I can call mine. When I am dead   105
Save charge; let me be buried in a nook.
No guns, no pompous whining; these are fooleries.
If, whiles we live, we stalk about the streets
Justled by carmen, footposts, and fine apes
In silken coats, unminded and scarce thought on,   110
It is not comely to be haled to the earth°

Like high-fed jades upon a tilting day,°
In antique trappings; scorn to useless tears!°
Eroclea was not coffined so; she perished
And no eye dropped save mine, and I am childish.°   115
I talk like one that dotes: laugh at me, Rhetias,
Or rail at me. They will not give me meat,
They have starved me; but I'll henceforth be mine own cook.
Good morrow! 'Tis too early for my cares
To revel. I will break my heart a little,   120
And tell ye more hereafter. Pray be merry.
       Exit Meleander
RHETIAS I'll follow him. [*Aside*] My Lord Amethus, use your time
Respectively. Few words to purpose soon'st prevail;
Study no long orations; be plain and short.
[*To them*] I'll follow him.   125
       Exit Rhetias
AMETHUS Cleophila, although these blacker clouds
Of sadness thicken and make dark the sky
Of thy fair eyes, yet give me leave to follow
The stream of my affections; they are pure,
Without all mixture of unnoble thoughts.   130
Can you be ever mine?
CLEOPHILA   I am so low
In mine own fortunes and my father's woes
That I want words to tell ye you deserve
A worthier choice.
AMETHUS   But give me leave to hope.
MENAPHON My friend is serious.
CLEOPHILA   Sir, this for answer: 135
If I ever thrive in an earthly happiness,
The next to my good father's wished recovery
Must be my thankfulness to your great merit,
Which I dare promise for the present time:
You cannot urge more from me.
MELEANDER [*within*]   Ho, Cleophila!   140
CLEOPHILA This gentleman is moved.
AMETHUS   Your eyes, Parthenophill,
Are guilty of some passion.
MENAPHON   Friend, what ails thee?
EROCLEA All is not well within me, sir.
MELEANDER [*within*]   Cleophila!

AMETHUS Sweet maid, forget me not; we now must part.
CLEOPHILA Still you shall have my prayer.
AMETHUS   Still you my truth.   145
        Exeunt

3.1

*Enter Cuculus and Grilla, Cuculus in a black velvet cap and
a white feather, with a paper in his hand*

CUCULUS Do not I look freshly, and like a youth of the trim?

GRILLA As rare an old youth as ever walked cross-gartered.°

CUCULUS Here are my mistresses mustered in white and black.
[*Reads*] 'Kala, the waiting-woman'. I will first begin at the foot:
stand thou for Kala.   5

GRILLA I stand for Kala; do your best and your worst.

CUCULUS I must look big, and care little or nothing for her, because
she is a creature that stands at livery.° Thus I talk wisely, and to
no purpose. Wench, as it is not fit that thou shouldst be either fair
or honest, so, considering thy service, thou art as thou art; and so   10
are thy betters, let them be what they can be. Thus, in despite and
defiance of all thy good parts, if I cannot endure thy baseness 'tis more
out of thy courtesy than my deserving; and so I expect thy answer.

GRILLA I must confess—

CUCULUS Well said.   15

GRILLA You are—

CUCULUS That's true too.

GRILLA To speak you right, a very scurvy fellow.

CUCULUS Away, Away! Dost think so?

GRILLA A very foul-mouthed and misshapen coxcomb.   20

CUCULUS I'll never believe it, by this hand.

GRILLA A maggot, most unworthy to creep in—to the least wrinkle
of a gentlewoman's, what d'ee call, good conceit, or so, or what
you will else—were you not refined by courtship and education,
which, in my blear eyes, makes you appear as sweet as any nosegay,   25
or savoury cod of musk new fallen from th'cat.°

CUCULUS This shall serve well enough for the waiting-woman. My
next mistress is Cleophila, the old madman's daughter. I must
come to her in whining tune; sigh, wipe mine eyes, fold my arms,
and blubber out my speech as thus: 'Even as a kennel of hounds,   30
sweet lady, cannot catch a hare when they are full paunched on
the carrion of a dead horse; so, even so, the gorge of my affections
being full crammed with the garboils of your condolements, doth
tickle me with the prick, as it were, about me, and fellow-feeling
of howling outright.'   35

38

GRILLA This will do't, if we will hear.°

CUCULUS Thou see'st I am crying ripe; I am such another tender-hearted fool.

GRILLA Even as the snuff of a candle that is burnt in the socket, goes out and leaves a strong perfume behind it; or as a piece of toasted cheese next the heart in a morning is a restorative for a sweet breath; so, even so, the odoriferous savour of your love doth perfume my heart (heigh-ho!) with the pure scent of an intolerable content, and not to be endured.

CUCULUS By this hand, 'tis excellent. Have at thee, last of all, for the Princess Thamasta, she that is my mistress indeed. She is abominably proud, a lady of a damnable, high, turbulent, and generous spirit; but I have a loud-mouthed cannon of mine own to batter her, and a penned speech of purpose. Observe it.

GRILLA Thus I walk by, hear and mind you not.°

CUCULUS [reads] 'Though haughty as the devil or his dam
Thou dost appear, great mistress, yet I am
Like to an ugly firework, and can mount
Above the region of thy sweet ac—count.°
Wert thou the moon herself, yet having seen thee,
Behold the man ordained to move within thee.'
—Look to yourself, housewife!° Answer me in strong lines, y'are best.

GRILLA Keep off, poor fool, my beams will strike thee blind;
Else, if thou touch me, touch me but behind.
In palaces, such as pass in before
Must be great princes; for at the back door
Tatterdemalions wait, who know not how
To get admittance; such a one—art thou.

CUCULUS 'Sfoot, this is downright roaring.

GRILLA I know how to present a big lady in her own cue.° But, pray, in earnest, are you in love with all these?

CUCULUS Pish, I have not a rag of love about me. 'Tis only a foolish humour I am possessed with, to be surnamed the Conquerer. I will court anything; be in love with nothing, nor no—thing.°

GRILLA A rare man you are, I protest.

CUCULUS Yes, I know I am a rare man, and I ever held myself so.

Enter Pelias and Corax

PELIAS In amorous contemplation, on my life;
Courting his page, by Helicon!

CUCULUS   'Tis false.

GRILLA A gross untruth; I'll justify it, sir,   75
  At any time, place, weapon.
CUCULUS   Marry, shall she.
CORAX No quarrels, Goody Whisk! Lay by your trumperies and
  fall to your practice. Instructions are ready for you all. Pelias is
  your leader; follow him. Get credit now or never. Vanish, doodles,
  vanish.   80
CUCULUS For the device?
CORAX The same; get'ee gone, and make no bawling.
      Exeunt [all but Corax]
  To waste my time thus drone-like in the court,
  And lose so many hours as my studies
  Have hoarded up, is to be like a man   85
  That creeps both on his hands and knees to climb
  A mountain's top; where, when he is ascended,
  One careless slip down, tumbles him again
  Into the bottom whence 'a first began.
  I need no prince's favour; princes need   90
  My art. Then, Corax, be no more a gull;
  The best of 'em cannot fool thee, nay, they shall not.
      Enter Sophronos and Aretus
SOPHRONOS We find him timely now; let's learn the cause.
ARETUS 'Tis fit we should.—Sir, we approve you learnèd,
  And since your skill can best discern the humours°   95
  That are predominant in bodies subject
  To alteration, tell us, pray, what devil
  This melancholy is which can transform
  Men into monsters.
CORAX   Y'are yourself a scholar,
  And quick of apprehension. Melancholy°   100
  Is not as you conceive, indisposition
  Of body, but the mind's disease. So ecstasy,
  Fantastic dotage, madness, frenzy, rapture
  Of mere imagination, differ partly
  From melancholy, which is briefly this: 105
  A mere commotion of the mind, o'ercharged
  With fear and sorrow; first begot i'th' brain,
  The seat of reason, and from thence derived
  As suddenly into the heart, the seat
  Of our affection.
ARETUS   There are sundry kinds   110

Of this disturbance?

CORAX   Infinite; it were
More easy to conjecture every hour
We have to live, than reckon up the kinds
Or causes of this anguish of the mind.

SOPHRONOS Thus you conclude: that as the cause is doubtful,   115
The cure must be impossible; and then
Our prince, poor gentleman, is lost for ever,
As well unto himself as to his subjects.

CORAX My lord, you are too quick. Thus much I dare
Promise and do; ere many minutes pass,   120
I will discover whence his sadness is,
Or undergo the censure of my ignorance.

ARETUS You are a noble scholar.

SOPHRONOS   For reward,
You shall make your own demand.

CORAX   May I be sure?

ARETUS We both will pledge our truth.

CORAX   'Tis soon performed: 125
That I may be discharged from my attendance
At court, and never more be sent for after;
Or, if I be, may rats gnaw all my books,
If I get home once and come here again.
Though my neck stretch a halter for't, I care not.   130

SOPHRONOS Come, come, you shall not fear it.

CORAX   I'll acquaint ye
With what is to be done, and you shall fashion it.

          Exeunt

3.2

          Enter Kala and Eroclea [disguised as Parthenophill]

KALA My lady does expect 'ee, thinks all time
Too slow till you come to her. Wherefore, young man,
If you intend to love me, and me only,
Before we part, without more circumstance
Let us betroth ourselves.

EROCLEA   I dare not wrong 'ee;   5
You are too violent.

KALA   Wrong me no more°
  Than I wrong you; be mine, and I am yours.
  I cannot stand on points.
EROCLEA   Then, to resolve°
  All further hopes, you never can be mine,
  Must not, and—pardon though I say—you shall not.   10
KALA [aside] The thing is sure a gelding—[to Eroclea] Shall not?
  Well,
  Y'are best to prate unto my lady now
  What proffer I have made.
EROCLEA   Never, I vow.
KALA Do, do; 'tis but a kind heart of mine own,
  And ill luck can undo me. [Aside] Be refused!   15
  O scurvy! [To Eroclea] Pray walk on, I'll overtake 'ee.
    Exit Eroclea
  What a green-sickness-livered boy is this!°
  My maidenhead will shortly grow so stale
  That 'twill be mouldy; but I'll mar her market.°
    Enter Menaphon
MENAPHON Parthenophill passed this way; prithee, Kala,   20
  Direct me to him.
KALA   Yes, I can direct 'ee;
  But you, sir, must forbear.
MENAPHON   Forbear!
KALA   I said so.
  Your bounty has engaged my truth; receive
  A secret that will, as you are a man,
  Startle your reason; 'tis but mere respect   25
  Of what I owe to thankfulness. Dear sir,
  The stranger whom your courtesy received
  For friend, is made your rival.
MENAPHON   Rival, Kala!
  Take heed, thou art too credulous.
KALA   My lady
  Dotes on him. I will place you in a room   30
  Where, though you cannot hear, yet you shall see
  Such passages as will confirm the truth
  Of my intelligence.
MENAPHON   'Twill make me mad.
KALA Yes, yes. It makes me mad, too, that a gentleman
  So excellently sweet, so liberal,   35

So kind, so proper, should be so betrayed
By a young smooth-chinned straggler; but, for love's sake,
Bear all with manly courage. Not a word;
I am undone then.
MENAPHON   That were too much pity;
Honest, most honest Kala, 'tis thy care,   40
Thy serviceable care.
KALA   You have even spoken
All can be said or thought.
MENAPHON   I will reward thee.
But as for him, ungentle boy, I'll whip
His falsehood with a vengeance.
KALA   O, speak little.
Walk up these stairs, and take this key; it opens°   45
A chamber door where, at that window yonder,
You may see all their courtship.
MENAPHON   I am silent.
KALA As little noise as may be, I beseech ye;
There is a back-stair to convey ye forth
Unseen or unsuspected.
        Exit Menaphon°
                        —He that cheats   50
A waiting-woman of a free good turn°
She longs for, must expect a shrewd revenge.
Sheep-spirited boy! Although he had not married me,
He might have proffered kindness in a corner
And ne'er have been the worse for't.
        Enter Thamasta and Eroclea [disguised as Parthenophill]
                        They are come;   55
On goes my set of faces most demurely.
THAMASTA Forbear the room.
KALA   Yes, Madam.
THAMASTA   Whosoever
Requires access to me, deny him entrance
Till I call thee; and wait without.
KALA   I shall.
[*Aside*] Sweet Venus, turn his courage to a snowball,   60
I heartily beseech it.
        Exit [Kala]
THAMASTA   I expose
The honour of my birth, my fame, my youth,

To hazard of much hard construction°
In seeking an adventure of a parley
So private with a stranger. If your thoughts   65
Censure me not with mercy, you may soon
Conceive I have laid by that modesty
Which should preserve a virtuous name unstained.

EROCLEA Lady—to shorten long excuses—time
And safe experience have so throughly armed   70
My apprehension with a real taste
Of your most noble nature, that to question
The least part of your bounties, or that freedom
Which heaven hath with a plenty made you rich in,
Would argue me uncivil; which is more,   75
Base-bred; and which is most of all, unthankful.

THAMASTA The constant lodestone and the steel are found
In several mines, yet is there such a league
Between these minerals, as if one vein
Of earth had nourished both. The gentle myrtle   80
Is not engraft upon an olive's stock,
Yet nature hath between them locked a secret
Of sympathy, that, being planted near,
They will both in their branches and their roots
Embrace each other. Twines of ivy round°   85
The well-grown oak; the vine doth court the elm;
Yet these are different plants. Parthenophill,
Consider this aright, then these slight creatures°
Will fortify the reasons I should frame
For that ungrounded—as thou think'st—affection   90
Which is submitted to a stranger's pity.
True love may blush when shame repents too late,
But in all actions, nature yields to fate.

EROCLEA Great lady, 'twere a dulness must exceed
The grossest and most sottish kind of ignorance   95
Not to be sensible of your intents;
I clearly understand them. Yet so much
The difference between that height and lowness
Which doth distinguish our unequal fortunes
Dissuades me from ambition, that I am   100
Humbler in my desires than love's own power
Can any way raise up.

THAMASTA   I am a princess

And know no law of slavery; to sue,
Yet be denied?

EROCLEA   I am so much a subject
To every law of noble honesty,   105
That to transgress the vows of perfect friendship°
I hold a sacrilege as foul and cursed
As if some holy temple had been robbed,
And I the thief.

THAMASTA   Thou art unwise, young man,
To enrage a lioness.

EROCLEA   It were unjust   110
To falsify a faith, and ever after,
Disrobed of that fair ornament, live naked,
A scorn to time and truth.

THAMASTA   Remember well
Who I am, and what thou art.

EROCLEA   That remembrance
Prompts me to worthy duty, O great lady.   115
If some few days have tempted your free heart
To cast away affection on a stranger;
If that affection have so overswayed
Your judgement, that it, in a manner, hath
Declined your sovereignty of birth and spirit;   120
How can ye turn your eyes off from that glass°
Wherein you may new trim and settle right
A memorable name?

THAMASTA   The youth is idle.°

EROCLEA Days, months, and years are passed since Menaphon
Hath loved and served you truly. Menaphon,   125
A man of no large distance in his blood
From yours; in qualities desertful, graced
With youth, experience, every happy gift
That can by nature, or by education
Improve a gentleman. For him, great lady,   130
Let me prevail, that you will yet at last
Unlock the bounty which your love and care
Have wisely treasured up, t'enrich his life.

THAMASTA Thou hast a moving eloquence; Parthenophill,
Parthenophill, in vain we strive to cross   135
The destiny that guides us. My great heart
Is stooped so much beneath that wonted pride

That first disguised it, that I now prefer
A miserable life with thee before
All other earthly comforts.

EROCLEA   Menaphon,   140
By me, repeats the self-same words to you;
You are too cruel if you can distrust
His truth or my report.

THAMASTA   Go where thou wilt,
I'll be an exile with thee; I will learn
To bear all change of fortunes.

EROCLEA   For my friend,   145
I plead with grounds of reason.

THAMASTA   For thy love,
Hard-hearted youth, I here renounce all thoughts
Of other hopes, of other entertainments—°

EROCLEA Stay, as you honour virtue!

THAMASTA   When the proffers
Of other greatness—

EROCLEA   Lady!

THAMASTA   When entreats   150
Of friends—

EROCLEA   I'll ease your grief.

THAMASTA   Respect of kindred—

EROCLEA Pray give me hearing.

THAMASTA   Loss of fame—

EROCLEA   I crave
But some few minutes.

THAMASTA   Shall infringe my vows,
Let heaven—

EROCLEA   My love speaks t'ee; hear, then go on.

THAMASTA Thy love! Why 'tis a charm to stop a vow   155
In its most violent course.

EROCLEA   Cupid has broke
His arrows here and, like a child unarmed,
Comes to make sport between us with no weapon
But feathers stolen from his mother's doves.°

THAMASTA This is mere trifling.

EROCLEA   Lady, take a secret.   160
I am as you are—in a lower rank,
Else of the self-same sex—a maid, a virgin.
And now, to use your own words, 'If your thoughts

Censure me not with mercy, you may soon
Conceive I have laid by that modesty   165
Which should preserve a virtuous name unstained.'

THAMASTA Are you not mankind then?

EROCLEA   When you shall read
The story of my sorrows, with the change
Of my misfortunes, in a letter printed
From my unforged relation, I believe°   170
You will not think the shedding of one tear
A prodigality that misbecomes
Your pity and my fortune.

THAMASTA   Pray conceal
The errors of my passions.

EROCLEA   Would I had
Much more of honour—as for life, I value't not—   175
To venture on your secrecy.

THAMASTA   It will be
A hard task for my reason to relinquish
The affection which was once devoted thine;
I shall awhile repute thee still the youth
I loved so dearly.

EROCLEA   You shall find me ever   180
Your ready faithful servant.

THAMASTA   O, the powers
Who do direct our hearts laugh at our follies!
We must not part yet.

EROCLEA   Let not my unworthiness
Alter your good opinion.

THAMASTA   I shall henceforth
Be jealous of thy company with any;   185
My fears are strong and many.

          Kala enters

KALA   Did your ladyship
Call me?

THAMASTA For what?

KALA   Your servant, Menaphon,°
Desires admittance.

          Enter Menaphon

MENAPHON   With your leave, great mistress, I come—
So private! Is this well, Parthenophill?

EROCLEA Sir, noble sir—

MENAPHON   You are unkind and treacherous;   190
  This 'tis to trust a straggler.
THAMASTA   Prithee, servant.
MENAPHON I dare not question you; you are my mistress,
  My prince's nearest kinswoman; but he—
THAMASTA Come, you are angry.
MENAPHON   Henceforth I will bury
  Unmanly passion in perpetual silence.   195
  I'll court mine own distraction, dote on folly,
  Creep to the mirth and madness of the age,°
  Rather than be so slaved again to woman,
  Which in her best of constancy is steadiest
  In change and scorn.
THAMASTA   How dare ye talk to me thus?   200
MENAPHON Dare! Were you not own sister to my friend,
  Sister to my Amethus, I would hurl ye
  As far off from mine eyes as from my heart;
  For I would never more look on ye. Take
  Your jewel t'ee. And, youth, keep under wing,°   205
  Or—boy—boy—
THAMASTA   If commands be of no force,
  Let me entreat thee, Menaphon.
MENAPHON   'Tis naught.
  Fie, fie, Parthenophill, have I deserved
  To be thus used?
EROCLEA   I do protest—
MENAPHON   You shall not;
  Henceforth I will be free, and hate my bondage.   210
      Enter Amethus
AMETHUS Away, away to court! The prince is pleased
  To see a masque tonight; we must attend him.
  'Tis near upon the time.—How thrives your suit?
MENAPHON The judge, your sister, will decide it shortly.
THAMASTA Parthenophill, I will not trust you from me.   215
      [*Exeunt*]

3.3

Enter Palador, [Sophronos,] Aretus, Corax with a paper
plot,° servants with torches

CORAX Lights and attendance! I will show your highness
A trifle of mine own brain. If you can,
Imagine you were now in the university,
You'll take it well enough; a scholar's fancy,
A quab; 'tis nothing else, a very quab.   5
PALADOR We will observe it.
SOPHRONOS   Yes, and grace it too, sir.
For Corax else is humorous and testy.°
ARETUS By any means; men singular in art
Have always some odd whimsy more than usual.
PALADOR The name of this conceit?
CORAX   Sir, it is called   10
'The Masque of Melancholy'.
ARETUS   We must look for
Nothing but sadness here then.
CORAX   Madness rather,
In several changes, melancholy is
The root as well of every apish frenzy,
Laughter and mirth, as dulness. Pray, my lord,   15
Hold and observe the plot; 'tis there expressed
In kind what shall be now expressed in action.
        Enter Amethus, Menaphon, Thamasta, Eroclea [disguised as
        Parthenophill]
No interruption, take your places quickly.
Nay, nay, leave ceremony: sound to the entrance.°
        Flourish. Enter Rhetias, his face whited, black shag hair, long
        nails, [and holding] a piece of raw meat
RHETIAS Bow, bow, wow, wow! the moon's eclipsed; I'll to the   20
churchyard and sup. Since I turned wolf,° I bark and howl, and
dig up graves; I will never have the sun shine again; 'tis midnight,
deep dark midnight. Get a prey and fall to—I have catched thee
now. Arre!
CORAX This kind is called Lycanthropia, sir,   25
When men conceive themselves wolves.
PALADOR   Here I find it.°
        Enter Pelias, a crown of feathers on, anticly rich

PELIAS I will hang 'em all, and burn my wife. Was I not an emperor?
My hand was kissed, and ladies lay down before me. In triumph
did I ride with my nobles about me till the mad dog bit me—I fell,
and I fell, and I fell. It shall be treason by statute for any man to   30
name water, or wash his hands, throughout all my dominions.
Break all the looking-glasses, I will not see my horns. My wife
cuckolds me; she is a whore, a whore, a whore, a whore!

PALADOR Hydrophobia° term you this?

CORAX And men possessed so shun all sight of water.   35
Sometimes, if mixed with jealousy, it renders them
Incurable, and oftentimes brings death.
    *Enter Philosopher in black rags, a copper chain on, an old
    gown half off, and [carrying a] book*

PHILOSOPHER Philosophers dwell in the moon. Speculation and
theory girdle the world about like a wall. Ignorance, like an atheist,
must be damned in the pit. I am very, very poor, and poverty is   40
the physic for the soul; my opinions are pure and perfect. Envy
is a monster, and I defy the beast.

CORAX Delirium this is called, which is mere dotage,
Sprung from ambition first and singularity,
Self-love, and blind opinion of true merit.   45

PALADOR I not dislike the course.°
    *Enter Grilla in a rich gown, great farthingale, great ruff,°
    muff, fan, and [with a] coxcomb on her head*

GRILLA Yes forsooth, and no forsooth; is not this fine? I pray your
blessing, gaffer—here, here, here! Did he give me a shough,
and cut off's tail! Buss, buss, nuncle; and there's a pum° for
daddy.   50

CORAX You find this noted there, Phrenitis.

PALADOR   True.°

CORAX Pride is the ground on't; it reigns most in women.
    Enter Cuculus like a bedlam, singing

CUCULUS   *They that will learn to drink a health in hell*
            Must learn on earth to take tobacco well,°
            To take tobacco well, to take tobacco well;   55
            For in hell they drink nor wine, nor ale, nor beer,
            But fire, and smoke, and stench, as we do here.

RHETIAS I'll sup° thee up.

PELIAS Thou'st straight to execution.

GRILLA Fool, fool, fool! Catch me an thou canst.   60

PHILOSOPHER Expel him the house, 'tis a dunce.

CUCULUS (*sings*)
> *Hark! did ye not hear a rumbling?*
> *The goblins are now a-tumbling;*
> *I'll tear 'em, I'll sear 'em,*
> *I'll roar 'em, I'll gore 'em;*   65
> *Now, now, now! My brains are a jumbling—*
Bounce! the gun's off.

PALADOR You name this here, Hypocondriacal.°

CORAX Which is a windy flatuous humour stuffing
The head, and thence derived to th' animal parts.   70
To be too over-curious, loss of goods
Or friends, excess of fear or sorrows, cause it.
> *Enter a Sea-Nymph big-bellied, singing and dancing*

NYMPH
> *Good your honours,*
> *Pray your worships,*
> *Dear your beauties,*   75

CUCULUS
> *Hang thee!*
> *To lash your sides,*
> *To tame your hides,*
> *To scourage your prides,*
> *And bang thee.*   80

NYMPH *We're pretty and dainty, and I will begin;*
> *See how they do jeer me, deride me, and grin.*
> *Come sport me, come court me, your topsail advance,*
> *And let us conclude our delights in a dance.°*

ALL A dance, a dance, a dance!   85

CORAX This is the Wanton Melancholy; women
With child, possessed with this strange fury, often
Have danced three days together without ceasing.°

PALADOR 'Tis very strange; but heaven is full of miracles.
> *The dance:—which ended, they all run out in couples*

PALADOR We are thy debtor, Corax, for the gift   90
Of this invention. But the plot deceives us;°
What means this empty space?

CORAX   One kind of melancholy
Is only left untouched; 'twas not in art
To personate the shadow of that fancy.
'Tis named Love-Melancholy. As, for instance,   95
Admit this stranger here—[*to Eroclea as Parthenophill*] young man,
    stand forth—
Entangled by the beauty of this lady,

The great Thamasta, cherished in his heart
The weight of hopes and fears, it were impossible
To limn his passions in such lively colours   100
As his own proper sufferance could express.

EROCLÆA You are not modest, sir.

THAMASTA   Am I your mirth?

CORAX Love is the tyrant of the heart; it darkens
Reason, confounds discretion; deaf to counsel,
It runs a headlong course to desperate madness.   105
O, were your highness but touched home, and throughly,
With this—what shall I call it—devil—

PALADOR   Hold!
Let no man henceforth name the word again.
Wait you my pleasure, youth. 'Tis late; to rest.
      [*Exit Palador*]

CORAX My lords—

SOPHRONOS   Enough; thou art a perfect arts-man.   110

CORAX Panthers may hide their heads, not change the skin;
And love pent ne'er so close yet will be seen.
      Exeunt

4.1

Enter Amethus and Menaphon

AMETHUS Dote on a stranger?

MENAPHON   Court him, plead, and sue to him.

AMETHUS Affectionately?

MENAPHON   Servilely; and pardon me
If I say basely.

AMETHUS   Women in their passions,
Like false fires, flash to fright our trembling senses,°
Yet in themselves contain nor light nor heat.   5
My sister do this? She, whose pride did scorn
All thoughts that were not busied on a crown!
To fall so far beneath her fortunes now?
You are my friend.

MENAPHON   What I confirm is truth.

AMETHUS Truth, Menaphon?

MENAPHON   If I conceived you were   10
Jealous of my sincerity and plainness,°
Then sir—

AMETHUS   What then, sir?

MENAPHON   I would then resolve
You were as changeable in vows of friendship
As is Thamasta in her choice of love.
That sin is double, running in a blood,   15
Which justifies another being worse.

AMETHUS My Menaphon, excuse me; I grow wild
And would not willingly believe the truth
Of my dishonour. She shall know how much
I am a debtor to thy noble goodness   20
By checking the contempt her poor desires
Have sunk her fame in. Prithee, tell me, friend,
How did the youth receive her?

MENAPHON   With a coldness
As modest and as hopeless as the trust
I did repose in him could wish or merit.   25

AMETHUS I will esteem him dearly.

Enter Thamasta and Kala

MENAPHON   Sir, your sister.

THAMASTA Servant, I have employment for ye.
AMETHUS   Hark ye;
  The mask of your ambition is fallen off;
  Your pride hath stooped to such an abject lowness
  That you have now discovered to report   30
  Your nakedness in virtue, honours, shame—
THAMASTA You are turned satire.
AMETHUS   All the flatteries
  Of greatness have exposed ye to contempt.
THAMASTA This is mere railing.
AMETHUS   You have sold your birth
  For lust.
THAMASTA Lust!
AMETHUS   Yes; and at a dear expense   35
  Purchased the only glories of a wanton.
THAMASTA A wanton!
AMETHUS   Let repentance stop your mouth;
  Learn to redeem your fault.
KALA [aside to Menaphon]   I hope your tongue
  Has not betrayed my honesty.
MENAPHON [aside to Kala]   Fear nothing.
THAMASTA If, Menaphon, I hitherto have strove   40
  To keep a wary guard about my fame;
  If I have used a woman's skill to sift
  The constancy of your protested love,
  You cannot, in the justice of your judgement,
  Impute that to a coyness or neglect,   45
  Which my discretion and your service aimed
  For noble purposes.
MENAPHON   Great mistress, no.
  I rather quarrel with mine own ambition,
  That durst to soar so high as to feed hope
  Of any least desert that might entitle   50
  My duty to a pension from your favours.°
AMETHUS And therefore, lady—pray, observe him well—
  He henceforth covets plain equality;
  Endeavouring to rank his fortunes low
  With some fit partner whom, without presumption,   55
  Without offence or danger, he may cherish,
  Yes and command too, as a wife—a wife,
  A wife, my most great lady!

KALA [*aside*]   All will out.
THAMASTA Now I perceive the league of amity,
    Which you have long between ye vowed and kept,   60
    Is sacred and inviolable; secrets
    Of every nature are in common t'ee.
    I have trespassed, and I have been faulty.
    Let not too rude a censure doom me guilty,
    Or judge my error wilful without pardon.   65
MENAPHON Gracious and virtuous mistress.
AMETHUS   'Tis a trick;
    There is no trust in female cunning, friend,
    Let her first purge her follies past, and clear
    The wrong done to her honour, by some sure
    Apparent testimony of her constancy,   70
    Or we will not believe these childish plots.°
    As you respect my friendship, lend no ear
    To a reply. Think on't.
MENAPHON   Pray, love your fame.
    Exeunt Menaphon [and] Amethus
THAMASTA Gone! I am sure awaked. Kala, I find
    You have not been so trusty as the duty   75
    You owed required.
KALA   Not I? I do protest
    I have been, madam.
THAMASTA   Be no matter what,
    I'm paid in mine own coin. Something I must,°
    And speedily—So!—Seek out Cuculus;
    Bid him attend me instantly.
KALA   That antic!   80
    The trim old youth shall wait ye.°
THAMASTA Wounds may be mortal which are wounds indeed;
    But no wounds deadly till our honours bleed.
    Exeunt

4.2

Enter Rhetias and Corax

RHETIAS Thou'rt an excellent fellow. Diabolo! O these lousy close-
stool empirics that will undertake all cures yet know not the
causes of any disease. Dog-leeches!° By the four elements, I
honour thee; could find in my heart to turn knave and be thy
flatterer.   5

CORAX Sirrah, 'tis pity thou'st not been a scholar;
Thou'rt honest, blunt, and rude enough, o'conscience.
But for thy lord, now, I have put him to't.

RHETIAS He chafes hugely, fumes like a stew-pot. Is he not mon-
strously overgone in frenzy?   10

CORAX Rhetias, 'tis not a madness, but his sorrow's
Close-griping grief and anguish of the soul
That torture him; he carries hell on earth
Within his bosom. 'Twas a prince's tyranny
Caused his distraction, and a prince's sweetness°   15
Must qualify that tempest of his mind.

RHETIAS Corax, to praise thy art were to assure
The misbelieving world that the sun shines
When 'tis in th'full meridian of his beauty;
No cloud of black detraction can eclipse   20
The light of thy rare knowledge. Henceforth, casting
All poor disguises off, that play in rudeness,°
Call me your servant only; for the present,
I wish a happy blessing to your labours.
Heaven crown your undertakings! And, believe me,   25
Ere many hours can pass, at our next meeting,
The bonds my duty owes shall be full cancelled.
    Exit [Rhetias]

CORAX Farewell—a shrewd-brain whoreson; there's pith°
In his untoward plainness.
    Enter Trollio with a morion on
                        Now, the news?

TROLLIO Worshipful Master Doctor, I have a great deal of I cannot   30
tell what, to say t'ee. My lord thunders; every word that comes out
of his mouth roars like a cannon. The house shook once; my young
lady dares not be seen.

CORAX We will roar with him, Trollio, if he roar.

TROLLIO He has got a great pole-axe in his hand, and fences it up   35
  and down the house, as if he were to make room for the pageants.°
  I have provided me a morion, for fear of a clap on the coxcomb.
CORAX No matter for the morion, here's my cap;
  Thus I will pull it down, and thus outstare him.°
    [*Corax pulls down his physician's cap*]
TROLLIO [*aside*] The physician is got as mad as my lord.—   40
  [*to him*] O brave! a man of worship.°
CORAX Let him come, Trollio; I will firk his trangdido,°
  And bounce and bounce in mettle, honest Trollio.°
TROLLIO [*aside*] He vapours like a tinker, and struts like a juggler.
MELEANDER *within* So-ho, so-ho!   45
TROLLIO There, there, there! Look to your right worshipful, look to
  yourself.
    Enter Meleander with a pole-axe
MELEANDER Show me the dog whose triple-throated noise
  Hath roused a lion from his uncouth den
  To tear the cur in pieces.
CORAX   Stay thy paws,°   50
  Courageous beast; else, lo! the Gorgon's skull°
  That shall transform thee to that restless stone
  Which Sisyphus rolls up against the hill,°
  Whence, tumbling down again, it, with his weight,
  Shall crush thy bones and puff thee into air.   55
MELEANDER Hold, hold thy conqu'ring breath; 'tis stronger far
  Than gunpowder and garlic. If the fates
  Have spun my thread, and my spent clew of life°
  Be now untwisted, let us part like friends.
  Lay up my weapon, Trollio, and be gone.   60
TROLLIO Yes, sir, with all my heart.
    Exit Trollio [with the pole-axe]
MELEANDER   This friend and I
  Will walk, and gabble wisely.
CORAX   I allow
  The motion; on! [*Corax pushes up his cap*]
MELEANDER   So politicians thrive,
  That with their crabbèd faces and sly tricks,
  Legerdemain, ducks, cringes, formal beards,   65
  Crisped hairs, and punctual cheats, do wriggle in
  Their heads first, like a fox, to rooms of state,
  Then the whole body follows.

CORAX   Then they fill
  Lordships, steal women's hearts; with them and theirs
  The world runs round; yet these are square men still.   70
MELEANDER There are none poor but such as engross offices.
CORAX None wise but unthrifts, bankrupts, beggars, rascals.
MELEANDER The hangman is a rare physician.
CORAX [aside] That's not so good. [To him] It shall be granted.
MELEANDER All the buzz of drugs and minerals and simples,   75
  Blood-lettings, vomits, purges, or what else
  Is conjured up by men of art to gull
  Liege-people and rear golden piles, are trash
  To a strong well-wrought halter; there the gout,°
  The stone, yes, and the melancholy devil,   80
  Are cured in less time than a pair of minutes.
  Build me a gallows in this very plot
  And I'll dispatch your business.
CORAX   Fix the knot
  Right under the left ear.
MELEANDER   Sirrah, make ready.
CORAX Yet do not be too sudden; grant me leave   85
  To give a farewell to a creature long
  Absented from me. 'Tis a daughter, sir,
  Snatched from me in her youth, a handsome girl;
  She comes to ask a blessing.
MELEANDER   Pray, where is she?
  I cannot see her yet.
CORAX   She makes more haste   90
  In her quick prayers than her trembling steps,
  Which many griefs have weakened.
MELEANDER   Cruel man!
  How canst thou rip a heart that's cleft already
  With injuries of time? Whilst I am frantic,
  Whilst throngs of rude divisions huddle on,   95
  And do disrank my brains from peace and sleep,
  So long I am insensible of cares.
  As balls of wild-fire may be safely touched,°
  Not violently sundered and thrown up,
  So my distempered thoughts rest in their rage,   100
  Not hurried in the air of repetition,
  Or memory of my misfortunes past.
  Then are my griefs struck home when they are reclaimed

To their own pity of themselves.—Proceed;
What of your daughter now?
CORAX   I cannot tell ye,   105
'Tis now out of my head again; my brains
Are crazy; I have scarce slept one sound sleep
These twelve months.
MELEANDER   'Las, poor man! canst thou imagine
To prosper in the task thou tak'st in hand
By practising a cure upon my weakness,   110
And yet be no physician for thyself?
Go, go, turn over all thy books once more,
And learn to thrive in modesty; for impudence
Does least become a scholar. Thou art a fool,
A kind of learnèd fool.
CORAX   I do confess it.   115
MELEANDER If thou canst wake with me, forget to eat,
Renounce the thought of greatness, tread on fate,
Sigh out a lamentable tale of things
Done long ago, and ill done; and, when sighs
Are wearied, piece up what remains behind   120
With weeping eyes, and hearts that bleed to death,
Thou shalt be a companion fit for me,
And we will sit together like true friends
And never be divided. With what greediness
Do I hug my afflictions! There's no mirth   125
Which is not truly seasoned with some madness:
As, for example—
        Exit Meleander
CORAX   What new crotchet next?
There is so much sense in this wild distraction
That I am almost out of my wits too,
To see and hear him; some few hours more   130
Spent here would turn me apish, if not frantic.
        Enter Meleander and Cleophila
MELEANDER In all the volumes thou has turned, thou man
Of knowledge, hast thou met with any rarity
Worthy thy contemplation like to this?
The model of the heavens, the earth, the waters,   135
The harmony and sweet consent of times,
Are not of such an excellence, in form
Of their creation, as the infinite wonder

That dwells within the compass of this face.
And yet I tell thee, scholar, under this   140
Well-ordered sign is lodged such an obedience°
As will hereafter, in another age
Strike all comparison into a silence.
She had a sister too; but as for her,
If I were given to talk, I could describe   145
A pretty piece of goodness; let that pass—
We must be wise sometimes. What would you with her?

CORAX I with her! Nothing, by your leave, sir, I;
     It is not my profession.

MELEANDER   You are saucy,°
     And, as I take it, scurvy in your sauciness,   150
     To use no more respect. [*To Cleophila*] Good soul, be patient;
     We are a pair of things the world doth laugh at.
     Yet be content, Cleophila; those clouds
     Which bar the sun from shining on our miseries
     Will never be chased off till I am dead,   155
     And then some charitable soul will take thee
     Into protection. I am hasting on;
     The time cannot be long.

CLEOPHILA   I do beseech ye,
     Sir, as you love your health, as you respect
     My safety, let not passion overrule you.   160

MELEANDER It shall not; I am friends with all the world.
     Get me some wine; to witness that I will be
     An absolute good fellow I will drink with thee.

CORAX [*aside to Cleophila*] Have you prepared his cup?

CLEOPHILA [*aside to Corax*]   'Tis in readiness.
          Enter Cuculus and Grilla

CUCULUS By your leave, gallants, I come to speak with a young lady,   165
     as they say, the old Trojan's daughter of the house.

MELEANDER Your business with my lady daughter, toss-pot?

GRILLA Toss-pot! O base! Toss-pot!

CUCULUS [*aside to Grilla*] Peace! Dost not see in what case he is?
     [*To Meleander*] I would do my own commendations to her, that's   170
     all.

MELEANDER Do. [*To Corax*] Come, my genius, we will quaff in wine
     Till we grow wise.

CORAX   True nectar is divine.
          Exeunt Meleander and Corax

CUCULUS So; I am glad he is gone. Page, walk aside. Sweet beauty,
I am sent ambassador from the mistress of my thoughts, to you,   175
the mistress of my desires.

CLEOPHILA So, sir, I pray be brief.

CUCULUS That you may know I am not, as they say, an animal,
which is, as they say, a kind of cokes, which is, as the learned term,
an ass, a puppy, a widgeon, a dolt, a noddy, a—   180

CLEOPHILA As you please.

CUCULUS Pardon me for that, it shall be as you please indeed.
Forsooth, I love to be courtly and in fashion.

CLEOPHILA Well, to your embassy; what, or from whom?

CUCULUS Marry, *what* is more than I know; for to know *what's what*,   185
is to know *what's what* and for *what's what*—but these are foolish
figures and to little purpose.

CLEOPHILA From whom, then, are you sent?

CUCULUS There you come to me again. O, to be in favour of great
ladies is as much to say as to be great in ladies' favours.   190

CLEOPHILA Good time a day t'ee; I can stay no longer.

CUCULUS By this light, but you must, for now I come to't. The most
excellent, most wise, most dainty, precious, loving, kind, sweet,
intolerably fair lady Thamasta commends to your little hands this
letter of importance. By your leave, let me first kiss, and then   195
deliver it in fashion to your own proper beauty.

CLEOPHILA To me from her? 'Tis strange; I dare peruse it.

CUCULUS Good. [*Aside*] O that I had not resolved to live a single life!
Here's temptation able to conjure up a spirit with a witness.° So,
so; she has read it.   200

CLEOPHILA Is't possible? Heaven, thou art great and bountiful.
Sir, I much thank your pains; and to the princess
Let my love, duty, service, be remembered.

CUCULUS They shall, mad-dame.

CLEOPHILA When we of hopes or helps are quite bereaven,   205
Our humble prayers have entrance into heaven.

CUCULUS That's my opinion clearly and without doubt.
  Exeunt

4.3

Enter Aretus and Sophronos

ARETUS The prince is throughly moved.

SOPHRONOS   I never saw him
So much distempered.

ARETUS   What should this young man be,
Or whither can he be conveyed?

SOPHRONOS   'Tis to me
A mystery; I understand it not.

ARETUS   Nor I.
Enter Palador, Amethus, and Pelias

PALADOR Ye have consented all to work upon   5
The softness of my nature; but take heed:
Though I can sleep in silence, and look on
The mockery ye make of my dull patience,
Yet 'ee shall know, the best of ye, that in me
There is a masculine, a stirring spirit,   10
Which provoked, shall like a bearded comet°
Set ye at gaze, and threaten horror.

PELIAS   Good sir—

PALADOR Good sir! 'Tis not your active wit or language,
Nor your grave politic wisdoms, lords, shall dare
To checkmate and control my just commands.   15
Enter Menaphon
Where is the youth, your friend? Is he found yet?

MENAPHON Not to be heard of.

PALADOR   Fly then to the desert
Where thou didst first encounter this fantastic,
This airy apparition. Come no more
In sight; get ye all from me; he that stays   20
Is not my friend.

AMETHUS [*aside*] 'Tis strange.

ARETUS   ⎱
                                We must obey.
SOPHRONOS ⎰
Exeunt all but Palador

PALADOR Some angry power cheats with rare delusions
My credulous sense; the very soul of reason
Is troubled in me—the physician
Presented a strange masque, the view of it   25

62

Puzzled my understanding; but the boy—
    Enter Rhetias
Rhetias, thou art acquainted with my griefs;
Parthenophill is lost, and I would see him,
For he is like to something I remember
A great while since, a long, long time ago.   30

RHETIAS I have been diligent, sir, to pry into every corner for
discovery, but cannot meet with him. There is some trick, I am
confident.

PALADOR There is; there is some practice, sleight or plot.

RHETIAS I have apprehended a fair wench in an odd private lodging   35
in the city, as like the youth in face as can by possibility be
discerned.

PALADOR How, Rhetias!

RHETIAS If it be not Parthenophill in long coats, 'tis a spirit in his
likeness; answer I can get none from her; you shall see her.   40

PALADOR The young man in disguise, upon my life,
    To steal out of the land.

RHETIAS   I'll send him t'ee.
    Exit Rhetias

PALADOR Do, do, my Rhetias.
    Enter Eroclea in woman's attire, and listens
                    As there is by nature
In everything created, contrariety,
So likewise is there unity and league   45
Between them in their kind; but man, the abstract
Of all perfection, which the workmanship
Of heaven hath modelled, in himself contains
Passions of several quality; the music
Of man's fair composition best accords   50
When 'tis in consort, not in single strains.°
My heart has been untuned these many months
Wanting her presence, in whose equal love
True harmony consisted. Living here
We are heaven's bounty all, but fortune's exercise.°   55

EROCLEA Minutes are numbered by the fall of sands,
As by an hour-glass; the span of time
Doth waste us to our graves, and we look on it.°
An age of pleasures, revelled out, comes home
At last and ends in sorrow; but the life   60
Weary of riot, numbers every sand,

Wailing in sighs, until the last drop down,
So to conclude calamity in rest.

PALADOR   What echo yields a voice to my complaints?
Can I be nowhere private?

EROCLEA [*coming forward*]   Let the substance   65
As suddenly be hurried from your eyes
As the vain sound can pass your ear,
If no impression of a troth vowed yours [*she kneels*]
Retain a constant memory.

PALADOR   Stand up;
'Tis not the figure stamped upon thy cheeks,°   70
The cozenage of thy beauty, grace, or tongue,
Can draw from me a secret that hath been
The only jewel of my speechless thoughts.

EROCLEA   I am so worn away with fears and sorrows,
So wintered with the tempests of affliction,   75
That the bright sun of your life-quick'ning presence
Hath scarce one beam of force to warm again
That spring of cheerful comfort which youth once
Apparelled in fresh looks.

PALADOR   Cunning imposter!
Untruth hath made thee subtle in thy trade.   80
If any neighbouring greatness hath seduced°
A free-born resolution to attempt
Some bolder act of treachery by cutting
My weary days off, wherefore, cruel mercy,
Hast thou assumed a shape that would make treason   85
A piety, guilt pardonable, bloodshed
As holy as the sacrifice of peace?

EROCLEA   The incense of my love-desires are flamed°
Upon an altar of more constant proof.°
Sir, O sir, turn me back into the world,   90
Command me to forget my name, my birth,
My father's sadness, and my death alive,
If all remembrance of my faith hath found
A burial without pity in your scorn.

PALADOR   My scorn, disdainful boy, shall soon unweave°   95
The web thy art hath twisted. Cast thy shape off,°
Disrobe the mantle of a feignèd sex,
And so I may be gentle; as thou art
There's witchcraft in thy language, in thy face,

In thy demeanours. Turn, turn from me, prithee, 100
For my belief is armèd else. Yet, fair subtlety,°
Before we part—for part we must—be true;
Tell me thy country.

EROCLEA   Cyprus.

PALADOR   Ha! Thy father?

EROCLEA Meleander.

PALADOR   Hast a name?

EROCLEA   A name of misery;
The unfortunate Eroclea.

PALADOR   There is danger 105
In this seducing counterfeit. Great goodness!
Hath honesty and virtue left the time?
Are we become so impious, that to tread
The path of impudence is law and justice?
Thou vizard of a beauty ever sacred, 110
Give me thy name.

EROCLEA   Whilst I was lost to memory
Parthenophill did shroud my shame in change
Of sundry rare misfortunes; but since now
I am, before I die, returned to claim
A convoy to my grave, I must not blush 115
To let Prince Palador, if I offend,
Know when he dooms me, that he dooms Eroclea.
I am that woeful maid.

PALADOR   Join not too fast
Thy penance with the story of my suff'rings.
So dwelt simplicity with virgin truth, 120
So martyrdom and holiness are twins,
As innocence and sweetness on thy tongue.
But let me by degrees collect my senses;
I may abuse my trust. Tell me, what air
Hast thou perfumed since tyranny first ravished° 125
The contract of our hearts?

EROCLEA   Dear sir, in Athens
Have I been buried.

PALADOR   Buried! Right, as I
In Cyprus. Come to trial; if thou beest
Eroclea, in my bosom I can find thee.°

EROCLEA As I, Prince Palador, in mine; this gift 130
        She shows him a tablet°

His bounty blest me with, the only physic
My solitary cares have hourly took
To keep me from despair.

PALADOR   We are but fools
To trifle in disputes, or vainly struggle
With that eternal mercy which protects us.   135
Come home, home to my heart, thou banished peace!
My ecstasy of joys would speak in passion
But that I would not lose that part of man
Which is reserved to entertain content.
Eroclea, I am thine; O, let me seize thee   140
As my inheritance. Hymen shall now
Set all his torches burning to give light
Throughout this land, new-settled in thy welcome.

EROCLEA You are still gracious. Sir, how I have lived,
By what means been conveyed, by what preserved,   145
By what returned, Rhetias, my trusty servant,
Directed by the wisdom of my uncle,
The good Sophronos, can inform at large.

PALADOR Enough. Instead of music, every night,
To make our sleeps delightful, thou shalt close   150
Our weary eyes with some part of thy story.

EROCLEA O, but my father!

PALADOR   Fear not; to behold
Eroclea safe will make him young again;
It shall be our first task. Blush, sensual follies,
Which are not guarded with thoughts chastely pure.   155
There is no faith in lust, but baits of arts;
'Tis virtuous love keeps clear contracted hearts.

        [*Exeunt*]

5.1

Enter Corax and Cleophila

CORAX 'Tis well, 'tis well; the hour is at hand
  Which must conclude the business that no art
  Could all this while make ripe for wished content.
  O, lady, in the turmoils of our lives,
  Men are like politic states, or troubled seas, 5
  Tossed up and down with several storms and tempests,
  Change and variety of wrecks and fortunes,°
  Till, labouring to the havens of our homes,
  We struggle for the calm that crowns our ends.
CLEOPHILA A happy end heaven bless us with!
CORAX   'Tis well said. 10
  The old man sleeps still soundly?
CLEOPHILA   May soft dreams
  Play in his fancy that, when he awakes,
  With comfort he may, by degrees, digest
  The present blessings in a moderate joy.
CORAX I drenched his cup to purpose; he ne'er stirred 15
  At barber or at tailor; 'a will laugh
  At his own metamorphosis, and wonder.
  We must be watchful. Does the coach stand ready?
CLEOPHILA All as you commanded.
       Enter Trollio
                     What's your haste for?
TROLLIO A brace of big women,° ushered by the young old ape° 20
  with his she-clog° at his bum, are entered the castle. Shall they
  come on?
CORAX By any means; the time is precious now.
  Lady, be quick and careful. Follow, Trollio.
TROLLIO I owe all sir-reverence to your right worshipfulness. 25
      [*Exeunt Corax and Trollio*]
CLEOPHILA So many fears, so many joys encounter
  My doubtful expectations, that I waver
  Between the resolution of my hopes
  And my obedience. 'Tis not—O my fate!—
  The apprehension of a timely blessing 30
  In pleasures shakes my weakness; but the danger

Of a mistaken duty that confines
The limits of my reason. Let me live,
Virtue, to thee as chaste as truth to time.
       Enter Thamasta
THAMASTA [*to attendants within*]° Attend me till I call.—My sweet
       Cleophila!   35
CLEOPHILA Great princess—
THAMASTA   I bring peace, to sue a pardon
For my neglect of all those noble virtues
Thy mind and duty are apparelled with.
I have deserved ill from thee, and must say
Thou art too gentle if thou canst forget it.   40
CLEOPHILA Alas, you have not wronged me; for, indeed,
Acquaintance with my sorrows and my fortune
Were grown to such familiarity,
That 'twas an impudence more than presumption
To wish so great a lady as you are   45
Should lose affection on my uncle's son;
But that your brother, equal in your blood,
Should stoop to such a lowness as to love
A castaway, a poor despisèd maid,
Only for me to hope was almost sin;   50
Yet, troth, I never tempted him.
THAMASTA   Chide not
The grossness of my trespass, lovely sweetness,
In such an humble language; I have smarted
Already in the wounds my pride hath made
Upon thy sufferings. Henceforth 'tis in you   55
To work my happiness.
CLEOPHILA   Call any service
Of mine a debt, for such it is; the letter
You lately sent me, in the blest contents
It made me privy to, hath largely quitted
Every suspicion of your grace or goodness.   60
THAMASTA Let me embrace thee with a sister's love,
A sister's love, Cleophila; for should
My brother henceforth study to forget
The vows that he hath made thee, I would ever
Solicit thy deserts.
AMETHUS ⎫
MENAPHON⎭ [*within*] We must have entrance.   65

THAMASTA Must? Who are they, say 'must'? You are unmannerly.
 Enter Amethus and Menaphon
 Brother, is't you? and you too, sir?
AMETHUS   Your ladyship
 Has had a time of scolding to your humour:
 Does the storm hold still?
CLEOPHILA   Never fell a shower
 More seasonably gentle on the barren   70
 Parched thirsty earth, than showers of courtesy
 Have from this princess been distilled on me,
 To make my growth in quiet of my mind
 Secure and lasting.
THAMASTA   You may both believe
 That I was not uncivil.
AMETHUS   Pish! I know   75
 Her spirit and her envy.
CLEOPHILA   Now, in troth, sir—
 Pray credit me, I do not use to swear—
 The virtuous princess hath in words and carriage
 Been kind, so over-kind, that I do blush:
 I am not rich enough in thanks sufficient   80
 For her unequalled bounty.—My good cousin,
 I have a suit to you.
MENAPHON   It shall be granted.
CLEOPHILA That no time, no persuasion, no respects
 Of jealousies past, present, or hereafter
 By possibility to be conceived,   85
 Draw you from that sincerity and pureness
 Of love which you have oftentimes protested
 To this great worthy lady; she deserves
 A duty more than what the ties of marriage
 Can claim or warrant. Be for ever hers,   90
 As she is yours, and heaven increase your comforts!
AMETHUS Cleophila hath played the churchman's part;
 I'll not forbid the banns.
MENAPHON [*to Thamasta*] Are you consented?
THAMASTA I have one task in charge first which concerns me:
 Brother, be not more cruel than this lady;   95
 She hath forgiven my follies, so may you.
 Her youth, her beauty, innocence, discretion,
 Without additions of estate or birth,

Are dower for a prince indeed. You loved her,
For sure you swore you did; else, if you did not,   100
Here fix your heart and thus resolve; if now
You miss this heaven on earth you cannot find
In any other choice ought but a hell.

AMETHUS The ladies are turned lawyers, and plead handsomely
Their clients' cases. I am an easy judge,   105
And so shalt thou be, Menaphon. I give thee
My sister for a wife; a good one, friend.

MENAPHON Lady, will you confirm the gift?

THAMASTA   The errors
Of my mistaken judgement being lost
To your remembrance, I shall ever strive   110
In my obedience to deserve your pity.

MENAPHON My love, my care, my all!

AMETHUS   What rests for me?
I'm still a bachelor. Sweet maid, resolve me:
. May I yet call you mine?

CLEOPHILA   My Lord Amethus,
Blame not my plainness; I am young and simple,   115
And have not any power to dispose
Mine own will without warrant from my father;
That purchased, I am yours.

AMETHUS   It shall suffice me.

    Enter Cuculus, Pelias, Trollio, and Grilla plucked in by 'em

CUCULUS Revenge! I must have revenge; I will have revenge, bitter
and abominable revenge; I will have revenge. This unfashion-   120
able mongrel, this linsey-woolsey° of mortality—by this hand,
mistress—this she-rogue is drunk, and clapper-clawed me without
any reverence to my person or good garments. Why d'ee not speak,
gentlemen?

PELIAS Some certain blows have passed, an't like your highness.   125

TROLLIO Some few knocks of friendship, some love-toys, some cuffs
in kindness, or so.

GRILLA I'll turn him away; he shall be my master no longer.

MENAPHON Is this your she-page, Cuculus? 'Tis a boy, sure.

CUCULUS A boy, an arrant boy in long coats.   130

TROLLIO He has mumbled his nose, that 'tis as big as a great
codpiece.

CUCULUS O, thou cock-vermin of iniquity!

THAMASTA Pelias, take hence the wag and school him for't.

For your part, servant, I'll entreat the prince   135
To grant you some fit place about his wardrobe.

CUCULUS Ever after a bloody nose do I dream of good luck. I
horribly thank your ladyship.
Whilst I'm in office, the old garb shall again°
Grow in request, and tailors shall be men.°   140
Come, Trollio, help to wash my face, prithee.

TROLLIO Yes, and to scour it too.
        Exeunt Cuculus, Trollio, Pelias, [and] Grill[a].
        Enter Rhetias [and] Corax

RHETIAS The prince and princess are at hand; give over
Your amorous dialogues.—Most honoured lady,
Henceforth forbear your sadness; are you ready   145
To practise your instructions?

CLEOPHILA   I have studied
My part with care, and will perform it, Rhetias,
With all the skill I can.

CORAX   I'll pass my word for her.
        Flourish. Enter Palador, Sophronos, Aretus, and Eroclea

PALADOR Thus princes should be circled, with a guard
Of truly noble friends and watchful subjects.   150
O, Rhetias, thou art just; the youth thou told'st me
That lived at Athens, is returned at last
To her own fortunes and contracted love.

RHETIAS My knowledge made me sure of my report, sir.

PALADOR Eroclea, clear thy fears; when the sun shines   155
Clouds must not dare to muster in the sky,
Nor shall they here
        [Cleophila and Amethus kneel]
                        —Why do they kneel? Stand up;
The day and place is privileged.

SOPHRONOS   Your presence,
Great sir, makes every room a sanctuary.°
        [Amethus stands]

PALADOR Wherefore does this young virgin use such circumstance   160
In duty to us? Rise.

EROCLEA   'Tis I must raise her.
        [Eroclea helps Cleophila to her feet]
Forgive me, sister; I have been too private
In hiding from your knowledge any secret
That should have been in common 'twixt our souls;

But I was ruled by counsel.

CLEOPHILA   That I show   165
Myself a girl, sister, and bewray
Joy in too soft a passion 'fore all these,
I hope you cannot blame me.
          [*They weep and embrace*]

PALADOR   We must part
The sudden meeting of these two fair rivulets
With th'island of our arms. Cleophila,   170
The custom of thy piety hath built,
Even to thy younger years, a monument
Of memorable fame; some great reward
Must wait on thy desert.

SOPHRONOS   The prince speaks t'ee, niece.

CORAX Chat low, I pray; let's about our business.   175
The good old man wakes. My lord, withdraw.
Rhetias, let's settle here the coach.

PALADOR   Away then!°
          Exeunt

5.2

*Soft music. Enter Meleander in a coach [drawn or carried by
attendants], his hair and beard trimmed, habit and gown
changed; Rhetias and Corax and Boy that sings*

THE SONG
*Fly hence, shadows, that do keep
Watchful sorrows charmed in sleep!
Though the eyes be overtaken,
Yet the heart doth ever waken
Thoughts chained up in busy snares   5
Of continual woes and cares:
Love and griefs are so expressed
As they rather sigh than rest.
Fly hence, shadows, that do keep
Watchful sorrows charmed in sleep!*   10

MELEANDER [*awakening*] Where am I? Ha! What sounds are these?
     'Tis day, sure.

O, I have slept belike; 'tis but the foolery
Of some beguiling dream. So, so! I will not
Trouble the play of my delighted fancy,
But dream my dream out.

CORAX   Morrow to your lordship!   15
You took a jolly nap, and slept it soundly.

MELEANDER Away beast! Let me alone.

Cease music

CORAX   O by your leave, sir,
I must be bold to raise ye, else your physic
Will turn to further sickness.

MELEANDER   Physic, bear-leech?

CORAX Yes, physic; you are mad.   20

MELEANDER Trollio! Cleophila!

RHETIAS   Sir, I am here.

MELEANDER I know thee, Rhetias; prithee rid the room
Of this tormenting noise. He tells me, sirrah,°
I have took physic, Rhetias; physic, physic!

RHETIAS Sir, true, you have; and this most learnèd scholar   25
Applied't 'ee. O, you were in dangerous plight
Before he took ye in hand.

MELEANDER   These things are drunk,
Directly drunk. Where did you get your liquor?

CORAX I never saw a body in the wane
Of age so overspread with several sorts   30
Of such diseases as the strength of youth
Would groan under and sink.

RHETIAS   The more your glory
In the miraculous cure.

CORAX   Bring me the cordial
Prepared for him to take after his sleep;
'Twill do him good at heart.

RHETIAS   I hope it will, sir.   35

Exit [Rhetias]

MELEANDER What dost think I am, that thou shouldst fiddle
So much upon my patience? Fool, the weight
Of my disease sits on my heart so heavy,
That all the hands of art cannot remove
One grain to ease my grief. If thou couldst poison   40
My memory, or wrap my senses up
Into a dulness, hard and cold as flints;

If thou couldst make me walk, speak, eat, and laugh,
Without a sense or knowledge of my faculties,
Why, then, perhaps, at marts thou mightst make benefit   45
Of such an antic motion, and get credit
From credulous gazers, but not profit me.
Study to gull the wise; I am too simple
To be wrought on.

CORAX   I'll burn my books, old man,
But I will do thee good, and quickly too.   50

          Enter Aretus with a patent

ARETUS Most honoured Lord Meleander, our great master,
Prince Palador of Cyprus, hath by me
Sent you this patent, in which is contained
Not only confirmation of the honours
You formerly enjoyed, but the addition   55
Of the marshalship of Cyprus; and ere long
He means to visit you. Excuse my haste,
I must attend the prince.

          Exit [Aretus]

CORAX   There's one pill works.

MELEANDER Dost know that spirit? 'Tis a grave familiar,°
And talked I know not what.

CORAX   He's like, methinks,   60
The prince his tutor, Aretus.

MELEANDER   Yes, yes;
It may be I have seen such a formality;
No matter where or when.

          Enter Amethus with a staff

AMETHUS   The prince hath sent ye,
My lord, this staff of office, and withal
Salutes you Grand Commander of the Ports   65
Throughout his principalities. He shortly
Will visit you himself: I must attend him.

          Exit [Amethus]

CORAX D'ee feel your physic stirring yet?

MELEANDER   A devil
Is a rare juggler, and can cheat the eye
But not corrupt the reason, in the throne   70
Of a pure soul.

          Enter Sophronos with a tablet°

                    —Another? I will stand thee,

Be what thou canst, I care not.
SOPHRONOS   From the prince,
    Dear brother, I present you this rich relic,
    A jewel he hath long worn in his bosom.
    Henceforth, he bade me say, he does beseech you   75
    To call him son, for he will call you father.
    It is an honour, brother, that a subject
    Cannot but entertain with thankful prayers.
    Be moderate in your joys; he will in person
    Confirm my errand, but commands my service.   80
        Exit [Sophronos]
CORAX What hope now of your cure?
MELEANDER   Stay, stay!—what earthquakes
    Roll in my flesh? Here's prince, and prince, and prince;
    Prince upon prince! The dotage of my sorrows
    Revels in magic of ambitious scorn:
    Be they enchantments deadly as the grave,   85
    I'll look upon 'em; patent, staff, and relic.
    To the last first. [*Taking up the miniature*] Round me, ye guarding
        ministers,°
    And ever keep me waking till the cliffs°
    That overhang my sight fall off, and leave
    These hollow spaces to be crammed with dust.   90
CORAX 'Tis time, I see, to fetch the cordial. Prithee,
    Sit down; I'll instantly be here again.
        Exit [Corax]
MELEANDER Good, give me leave, I will sit down indeed;
    Here's company enough for me to prate to.
    [*Looking at the miniature*] Eroclea! 'Tis the same; the cunning
        artsman   95
    Faltered not in a line. Could he have fashioned
    A little hollow space here, and blown breath
    To have made it move and whisper, 't had been excellent.
    But, faith, 'tis well, 'tis very well as 'tis;
    Passing, most passing well.
        Enter Cleophila, Eroclea, [and] Rhetias
CLEOPHILA   The sovereign greatness,   100
    Who, by commission from the powers of heaven,
    Sways both this land and us, our gracious prince,
    By me presents you, sir, with this large bounty,
    A gift more precious to him than his birthright.

Here let your cares take end; now set at liberty   105
Your long-imprisoned heart, and welcome home
The solace of your soul, too long kept from you.
EROCLEA [*kneeling*] Dear sir, you know me.
MELEANDER   Yes, thou art my daughter,
My eldest blessing. Know thee? Why, Eroclea,
I never did forget thee in thy absence.   110
Poor soul, how dost?
EROCLEA   The best of my well-being
Consists in yours.
MELEANDER   Stand up: the gods who hitherto
Have kept us both alive, preserve thee ever!
Cleophila, I thank thee and the prince.
I thank thee too, Eroclea, that thou wouldst,   115
In pity of my age, take so much pains
To live till I might once more look upon thee
Before I broke my heart. O, 'twas a piece
Of piety and duty unexampled!
RHETIAS [*aside*] The good man relisheth his comforts strangely; 120
The sight doth turn me child.
EROCLEA   I have not words
That can express my joys.
CLEOPHILA   Nor I.
MELEANDER   Nor I:
Yet let us gaze on one another freely,
And surfeit with our eyes. Let me be plain:°
If I should speak as much as I should speak,   125
I should talk of a thousand things at once,
And all of thee, of thee, my child, of thee!
My tears, like ruffling winds locked up in caves,
Do bustle for a vent—on t'other side,
To fly out into mirth were not so comely.   130
[*To Eroclea*] Come hither, let me kiss thee—with a pride,
Strength, courage, and fresh blood, which now thy presence
Hath stored me with, I kneel before their altars
Whose sovereignty kept guard about thy safety.
Ask, ask thy sister, prithee; she'll tell thee   135
How I have been much mad.
CLEOPHILA   Much discontented,
Shunning all means that might procure him comfort.
EROCLEA Heaven has at last been gracious.

76

MELEANDER   So say I;
But wherefore drop thy words in such a sloth,
As if thou wert afraid to mingle truth   140
With thy misfortunes? Understand me throughly:
I would not have thee to report at large,
From point to point, a journal of thy absence;
'Twill take up too much time. I would securely
Engross the little remnant of my life   145
That thou mightst every day be telling somewhat
Which might convey me to my rest with comfort.
Let me bethink me; how we parted first
Puzzles my faint remembrance—but soft,
Cleophila, thou toldst me that the prince   150
Sent me this present.
CLEOPHILA   From his own fair hands
I did receive my sister.
MELEANDER   To requite him,
We will not dig his father's grave anew,
Although the mention of him much concerns
The business we inquire of.—As I said,   155
We parted in a hurry at the court;
I to this castle, after made my jail.
But whither thou, dear heart?
RHETIAS   Now they fall to't;
I looked for this.
EROCLEA   I, by my uncle's care—
Sophronos, my good uncle—suddenly   160
Was, like a sailor's boy, conveyed o'shipboard
That very night.
MELEANDER   A policy quick and strange.
EROCLEA The ship was bound for Corinth; whither first,
Attended only with your servant, Rhetias,
And all fit necessaries, we arrived: 165
From thence, in habit of a youth, we journeyed
To Athens, where till our return of late,
Have we lived safe.
MELEANDER   O, what a thing is man,
To bandy factions of distempered passions
Against the sacred providence above him!   170
Here, in the legend of thy two years' exile,°
Rare pity and delight are sweetly mixed.

And still thou wert a boy?
EROCLEA   So I obeyed
My uncle's wise command.
MELEANDER   'Twas safely carried,
I humbly thank thy fate.
EROCLEA   If earthly treasures   175
Are poured in plenty down from heaven on mortals,
They reign amongst those oracles that flow
In schools of sacred knowledge; such is Athens.
Yet Athens was to me but a fair prison:
The thoughts of you, my sister, country, fortunes,   180
And something of the prince, barred all contents
Which else might ravish sense. For had not Rhetias
Been always comfortable to me, certainly°
Things had gone worse.
MELEANDER   Speak low, Eroclea;
That 'something of the prince' bears danger in it.   185
Yet thou hast travelled, wench, for such endowments°
As might create a prince a wife fit for him
Had he the world to guide; but touch not there.
How cam'st thou home?
RHETIAS   Sir, with your noble favour,
Kissing your hand first, that point I can answer.   190
MELEANDER Honest, right honest Rhetias.
RHETIAS   Your grave brother
Perceived with what a hopeless love his son,
Lord Menaphon, too eagerly pursued
Thamasta, cousin to our present prince;
And to remove the violence of affection,   195
Sent him to Athens, where for twelve months space,
Your daughter, my young lady, and her cousin
Enjoyed each other's griefs; till by his father,
The Lord Sophronos, we were all called home.
MELEANDER Enough, enough; the world shall henceforth witness   200
My thankfulness to heaven and those people
Who have been pitiful to me and mine.
Lend me a looking-glass—How now! How came I
So courtly in fresh raiments?
RHETIAS   Here's the glass, sir.
MELEANDER [looking in the mirror] I'm in the trim too.—O Cleophila,° 205
This was the goodness of thy care and cunning.

Loud music
Whence comes this noise?
RHETIAS   The prince, my lord, in person.°
      Enter Palador, Sophronos, Aretus, Menaphon, Thamasta,
      Corax, Kala. [The others kneel]
PALADOR Ye shall not kneel to us; rise all, I charge ye. [*They rise*]
      Father, you wrong your age; henceforth my arms
      And heart shall be your guard. We have o'erheard   210
      All passages of your united loves.
      Be young again, Meleander; live to number
      A happy generation, and die old
      In comforts as in years! The offices
      And honours which I late on thee conferred   215
      Are not fantastic bounties, but thy merit;
      Enjoy them liberally.
MELEANDER   My tears must thank ye,
      For my tongue cannot.
CORAX   I have kept my promise
      And given you a sure cordial.
MELEANDER   O, a rare one!
PALADOR Good man, we both have shared enough of sadness,   220
      Though thine has tasted deeper of th'extreme;
      Let us forget it henceforth. Where's the picture
      I sent ye? Keep it, 'tis a counterfeit;
      And in exchange of that I seize on this,
      The real substance. [*Palador takes Eroclea by the hand*] With this
         other hand   225
      I give away, before her father's face,
      His younger joy, Cleophila, to thee,
      Cousin Amethus: take her, and be to her
      More than a father, a deserving husband.—
      Thus robbed of both thy children in a minute,   230
      Thy cares are taken off.
MELEANDER   My brains are dulled;
      I am entranced and know not what you mean.
      Great, gracious sir, alas, why do you mock me?
      I am a weak old man, so poor and feeble
      That my untoward joints can scarcely creep   235
      Unto the grave where I must seek my rest.
PALADOR Eroclea was, you know, contracted mine;
      Cleophila, my cousin's, by consent

79

Of both their hearts; we both now claim our own.
It only rests in you to give a blessing   240
For confirmation.
RHETIAS   Sir, 'tis truth and justice.
MELEANDER   The gods that lent ye to me, bless your vows!
O children, children, pay your prayers to heaven,
For they have showed much mercy. But, Sophronos,°
Thou art my brother—I can say no more—   245
A good, good brother.
PALADOR   Leave the rest to time.
Cousin Thamasta, I must give you too.
She's thy wife, Menaphon. Rhetias, for thee
And Corax, I have more than common thanks.
On to the temple! There all solemn rites   250
Performed, a general feast shall be proclaimed.
The Lover's Melancholy hath found cure;
Sorrows are changed to bride-songs. So they thrive
Whom fate, in spite of storms, hath kept alive.
        Exeunt

EPILOGUE

To be too confident is as unjust
In any work, as too much to distrust;
Who from the laws of study have not swerved,
Know begged applauses never were deserved.
We must submit to censure: so doth he,   5
Whose hours begot this issue; yet, being free,°
For his part, if he have not pleased you, then
In this kind he'll not trouble you again.

THE BROKEN HEART

To the most worthy deserver of the noblest titles in honour,
William, Lord Craven,° Baron of Hamstead Marshall

My Lord,
The glory of a great name, acquired by a greater glory of action, hath in all ages lived the truest chronicle to his own memory. In the practice of which argument, your growth to perfection, even in youth,° hath appeared so sincere, so unflattering a pen-man, that posterity cannot with more delight read the merit of noble endeavours 5 than noble endeavours merit thanks from posterity to be read with delight. Many nations, many eyes, have been witnesses of your deserts and loved them. Be pleased then, with the freedom of your own nature, to admit one, amongst all, particularly into the list of such as honour a fair example of nobility. There is a kind of humble ambition, 10 not uncommendable, when the silence of study breaks forth into discourse, coveting rather encouragement than applause. Yet herein censure commonly is too severe an auditor without the moderation of an able patronage. I have ever been slow in courtship of greatness, not ignorant of such defects as are frequent to opinion; but the justice of 15 your inclination to industry emboldens my weakness of confidence to relish an experience of your mercy, as many brave dangers have tasted of your courage. Your lordship strove to be known to the world (when the world knew you least) by voluntary but excellent attempts. Like allowance I plead of being known to your lordship (in this low 20 presumption) by tendering to a favourable entertainment, a devotion offered from a heart that can be as truly sensible of any least respect,° as ever profess the owner in my best, my readiest services, a lover of your natural love to virtue.

John Ford   25

Sparta

THE PERSONS OF THE PLAY,
NAMES FITTED TO THEIR QUALITIES

AMYCLAS, King of Sparta	*common to the kings of Laconia°*
CALANTHA, the king's daughter	*flower of beauty*
ITHOCLES, a favourite	*honour of loveliness*
PROPHILUS, friend of Ithocles	*dear*
ARMOSTES, a counsellor of state	*an appeaser*
CROTOLON, another counsellor	*noise*
NEARCHUS, Prince of Argos	*young prince*
AMELUS, friend of Nearchus	*trusty*
EUPHRANIA, a maid of honour, daughter of Crotolon	*joy*
CHRYSTALLA ⎱ maids of honour	*crystal*
PHILEMA ⎰	*a kiss*
LEMOPHIL ⎱ two courtiers	*glutton*
GRONEAS ⎰	*tavernhaunter*
PENTHEA, twin-sister of Ithocles	*complaint*
BASSANES, a jealous nobleman, husband of Penthea	*vexation*
ORGILUS [APLOTES], son of Crotolon	*angry [simplicity]*
TECNICUS, a philosopher	*artist*
GRAUSIS, overseer of Penthea	*old beldam*
PHULAS, servant to Bassanes	*watchful*
LORDS, COURTIERS, OFFICERS, SERVANTS, MUSICIANS	

Other persons mentioned

THRASUS, father of Ithocles and Penthea	*fierceness*

THE PROLOGUE

Our scene is Sparta. He whose best of art
Hath drawn this piece calls it *The Broken Heart*.
The title lends no expectation here
Of apish laughter, or of some lame jeer
At place or persons; no pretended clause   5
Of jests fit for a brothel courts applause
From vulgar admiration. Such low songs,
Tuned to unchaste ears, suit not modest tongues.
The virgin sisters then deserved fresh bays°
When innocence and sweetness crowned their lays.   10
Then vices gasped for breath, whose whole commerce
Was whipped to exile by unblushing verse.
This law we keep in our presentment now,
Not to take freedom more than we allow.°
What may be here thought a fiction, when time's youth   15
Wanted some riper years, was known *A Truth*;°
In which, if words have clothed the subject right,
You may partake a pity with delight.

The Broken Heart

1.1

Enter Crotolon and Orgilus

CROTOLON Dally not further. I will know the reason
    That speeds thee to this journey.

ORGILUS   Reason? Good sir,
    I can yield many.

CROTOLON   Give me one, a good one.
    Such I expect, and ere we part must have.
    Athens? Pray why to Athens? You intend not   5
    To kick against the world, turn Cynic, Stoic,°
    Or read the logic lecture, or become°
    An Areopagite, and judge in causes°
    Touching the commonwealth? For as I take it,
    The budding of your chin cannot prognosticate   10
    So grave an honour.

ORGILUS   All this I acknowledge.

CROTOLON You do! Then, son, if books and love of knowledge
    Inflame you to this travel, here in Sparta
    You may as freely study.

ORGILUS   'Tis not that, sir.

CROTOLON Not that, sir? As a father I command thee   15
    To acquaint me with the truth.

ORGILUS   Thus I obey 'ee.
    After so many quarrels as dissension,
    Fury, and rage had broached in blood, and sometimes
    With death to such confederates as sided
    With now dead Thrasus and yourself, my lord,   20
    Our present king, Amyclas, reconciled
    Your eager swords and sealed a gentle peace.
    Friends you professed yourselves; which to confirm,
    A resolution for a lasting league
    Betwixt your families was entertained,   25
    By joining in a Hymenean bond°
    Me, and the fair Penthea, only daughter
    To Thrasus.

CROTON   What of this?
ORGILUS   Much, much, dear sir.
  A freedom of converse, an interchange
  Of holy and chaste love, so fixed our souls   30
  In a firm growth of union, that no time
  Can eat into the pledge. We had enjoyed°
  The sweets our vows expected, had not cruelty
  Prevented all those triumphs we prepared for,
  By Thrasus his untimely death.
CROTOLON   Most certain.   35
ORGILUS From this time sprouted up that poisonous stalk
  Of aconite, whose ripened fruit hath ravished°
  All health, all comfort of a happy life.
  For Ithocles her brother, proud of youth,
  And prouder in his power, nourished closely   40
  The memory of former discontents.
  To glory in revenge, by cunning partly,
  Partly by threats, 'a woos at once, and forces
  His virtuous sister to admit a marriage
  With Bassanes, a nobleman, in honour   45
  And riches, I confess, beyond my fortunes.
CROTOLON All this is no sound reason to importune
  My leave for thy departure.
ORGILUS   Now it follows.
  Beauteous Penthea, wedded to this torture
  By an insulting brother, being secretly   50
  Compelled to yield her virgin freedom up
  To him, who never can usurp her heart,
  Before contracted mine, is now so yoked
  To a most barbarous thraldom, misery,
  Affliction, that he savours not humanity°   55
  Whose sorrow melts not into more than pity
  In hearing but her name.
CROTOLON   As how, pray?
ORGILUS   Bassanes,
  The man that calls her wife, considers truly
  What heaven of perfections he is lord of,
  By thinking fair Penthea his. This thought   60
  Begets a kind of monster-love, which love
  Is nurse unto a fear so strong and servile
  As brands all dotage with a jealousy.

All eyes who gaze upon that shrine of beauty,
He doth resolve, do homage to the miracle.   65
Someone, he is assured, may now or then
(If opportunity but sort) prevail.
So much out of a self-unworthiness
His fears transport him; not that he finds cause
In her obedience, but his own distrust.   70
CROTOLON You spin out your discourse.
ORGILUS   My griefs are violent.
    For knowing how the maid was heretofore
    Courted by me, his jealousies grow wild
    That I should steal again into her favours,
    And undermine her virtues; which the gods   75
    Know I nor dare nor dream of. Hence, from hence,
    I undertake a voluntary exile.
    First, by my absence to take off the cares
    Of jealous Bassanes; but chiefly, sir,
    To free Penthea from a hell on earth.   80
    Lastly, to lose the memory of something
    Her presence makes to live in me afresh.
CROTOLON Enough, my Orgilus, enough. To Athens.
    I give a full consent.—Alas, good lady!—
    We shall hear from thee often?
ORGILUS   Often.
        Enter Euphrania
CROTOLON   See,   85
    Thy sister comes to give a farewell.
EUPHRANIA   Brother.
ORGILUS Euphrania, thus upon thy cheeks I print
    A brother's kiss, more careful of thine honour,
    Thy health, and thy well-doing, than my life.
    Before we part, in presence of our father,   90
    I must prefer a suit to 'ee.
EUPHRANIA   You may style it,°
    My brother, a command.
ORGILUS   That you will promise
    To pass never to any man, however
    Worthy, your faith, till with our father's leave,
    I give a free consent.
CROTOLON   An easy motion.   95
    I'll promise for her, Orgilus.

ORGILUS   Your pardon;
  Euphrania's oath must yield me satisfaction.
EUPHRANIA By Vesta's sacred fires I swear.
CROTOLON   And I,°
  By great Apollo's beams, join in the vow,°
  Not, without thy allowance, to bestow her   100
  On any living.
ORGILUS   Dear Euphrania,
  Mistake me not. Far, far 'tis from my thought,
  As far from any wish of mine, to hinder
  Preferment to an honourable bed°
  Or fitting fortune. Thou art young and handsome;   105
  And 'twere injustice—more, a tyranny—
  Not to advance thy merit. Trust me, sister,
  It shall be my first care to see thee matched
  As may become thy choice and our contents.
  I have your oath.
EUPHRANIA   You have. But mean you, brother,   110
  To leave us as you say?
CROTOLON   Ay, ay, Euphrania;
  He has just grounds direct him. I will prove°
  A father and a brother to thee.
EUPHRANIA   Heaven
  Does look into the secrets of all hearts.
  Gods, you have mercy with 'ee, else—
CROTOLON   Doubt nothing;   115
  Thy brother will return in safety to us.
ORGILUS Souls sunk in sorrows never are without 'em;
  They change fresh airs, but bear their griefs about 'em.°
     Exeunt

1.2

Flourish. Enter Amyclas the king, Armostes, Prophilus, and
attendants

AMYCLAS The Spartan gods are gracious. Our humility
  Shall bend before their altars, and perfume
  Their temples with abundant sacrifice.
  See lords, Amyclas, your old king, is ent'ring

Into his youth again. I shall shake off   5
This silver badge of age, and change this snow
For hairs as gay as are Apollo's locks.°
Our heart leaps in new vigour.

ARMOSTES   May old time
Run back to double your long life, great sir.

AMYCLAS It will, it must, Armostes. Thy bold nephew,   10
Death-braving Ithocles, brings to our gates
Triumphs and peace upon his conquering sword.
Laconia is a monarchy at length,°
Hath in this latter war trod underfoot
Messene's pride; Messene bows her neck°   15
To Lacedaemon's royalty. O, 'twas
A glorious victory, and doth deserve
More than a chronicle; a temple, lords,
A temple, to the name of Ithocles.—
Where didst thou leave him, Prophilus?

PROPHILUS   At Pephnon,°   20
Most gracious sovereign. Twenty of the noblest
Of the Messenians there attend your pleasure
For such conditions as you shall propose,
In settling peace, and liberty of life.

AMYCLAS When comes your friend the general?

PROPHILUS   He promised   25
To follow with all speed convenient.

> *Enter Crotolon, Calantha, Chrystalla, Philema, and*
> *Euphrania. [Chrystalla and Philema carry a laurel wreath]*

AMYCLAS Our daughter.—Dear Calantha, the happy news
The conquest of Messene, hath already
Enriched thy knowledge.

CALANTHA   With the circumstance
And manner of the fight, related faithfully   30
By Prophilus himself. But pray, sir, tell me,
How doth the youthful general demean
His actions in these fortunes?

PROPHILUS   Excellent princess,
Your own fair eyes may soon report a truth
Unto your judgement, with what moderation,   35
Calmness of nature, measure, bounds and limits
Of thankfulness and joy, 'a doth digest
Such amplitude of his success as would

In others, moulded of a spirit less clear,
Advance 'em to comparison with heaven.   40
But Ithocles—
CALANTHA   Your friend—
PROPHILUS   He is so, madam,
In which the period of my fate consists.°
He in this firmament of honour stands
Like a star fixed, not moved with any thunder
Of popular applause, or sudden lightning   45
Of self-opinion. He hath served his country,
And thinks 'twas but his duty.
CROTOLON   You describe
A miracle of man.
AMYCLAS   Such, Crotolon,
On forfeit of a king's word, thou wilt find him.
         Flourish
Hark, warning of his coming! All attend him.   50
         Enter Ithocles [with] Lemophil and Groneas; the rest of the
         lords ushering him in
AMYCLAS Return into these arms, thy home, thy sanctuary,
Delight of Sparta, treasure of my bosom,
Mine own, own Ithocles.
ITHOCLES   Your humblest subject.
ARMOSTES Proud of the blood I claim an interest in,
As brother to thy mother, I embrace thee,   55
Right noble nephew.
ITHOCLES   Sir, your love's too partial.
CROTOLON Our country speaks by me, who by thy valour,
Wisdom, and service, shares in this great action;
Returning thee, in part of thy due merits,°
A general welcome.
ITHOCLES   You exceed in bounty.   60
CALANTHA Chrystalla, Philema, the chaplet! [*They give her the laurel*
         wreath]—Ithocles,
Upon the wings of fame the singular
And chosen fortune of an high attempt
Is borne so past the view of common sight
That I myself, with mine own hands, have wrought   65
To crown thy temples, this provincial garland.°
Accept, wear, and enjoy it, as our gift
Deserved, not purchased. [*She places it on Ithocles' head*]

ITHOCLES   Y'are a royal maid.

AMYCLAS She is in all our daughter.

ITHOCLES   Let me blush,
  Acknowledging how poorly I have served,   70
  What nothings I have done, compared with th'honours
  Heaped on the issue of a willing mind.°
  In that lay mine ability, that only.
  For who is he so sluggish from his birth,
  So little worthy of a name, or country,   75
  That owes not, out of gratitude for life,
  A debt of service, in what kind soever
  Safety or counsel of the commonwealth
  Requires for payment?

CALANTHA   'A speaks truth.

ITHOCLES   Whom heaven
  Is pleased to style victorious, there, to such,   80
  Applause runs madding, like the drunken priests
  In Bacchus' sacrifices, without reason°
  Voicing the leader-on a demigod;°
  Whereas, indeed, each common soldier's blood
  Drops down as current coin in that hard purchase   85
  As his whose much more delicate condition
  Hath sucked the milk of ease. Judgement commands,
  But resolution executes. I use not,
  Before this royal presence, these fit slights°
  As in contempt of such as can direct.   90
  My speech hath other end: not to attribute
  All praise to one man's fortune, which is strengthed
  By many hands. For instance, here is Prophilus,
  A gentleman (I cannot flatter truth)
  Of much desert; and, though in other rank,   95
  Both Lemophil and Groneas were not missing
  To wish their country's peace. For, in a word,
  All there did strive their best, and 'twas our duty.

AMYCLAS Courtiers turn soldiers?—[*To Lemophil and Groneas*] We
  vouchsafe our hand.°
  Observe your great example.

LEMOPHIL   With all diligence.°   100

GRONEAS Obsequiously and hourly.

AMYCLAS   Some repose
  After these toils are needful. We must think on°

Conditions for the conquered; they expect 'em.
On!—Come, my Ithocles.
    [Prophilus offers to escort Euphrania out]
EUPHRANIA *[to Prophilus]*   Sir, with your favour,
I need not a supporter.
PROPHILUS   Fate instructs me.°   105
    Exeunt [all but Lemophil, Groneas, Chrystalla, and
    Philema]. Lemophil stays Chrystalla [and] Groneas, Philema
CHRYSTALLA With me?
PHILEMA   Indeed I dare not stay.
LEMOPHIL   Sweet lady,
Soldiers are blunt.—Your lip. *[Kisses Chrystalla]*
CHRYSTALLA   Fie, this is rudeness!
You went not hence such creatures.
GRONEAS   Spirit of valour
Is of a mounting nature.
PHILEMA   It appears so.°
Pray, in earnest, how many men apiece   110
Have you two been the death of?
GRONEAS   Faith, not many;°
We were composed of mercy.
LEMOPHIL   For our daring,
You heard the general's approbation
Before the king.
CHRYSTALLA   You wished your country's peace;°
That showed your charity. Where are your spoils,   115
Such as the soldier fights for?
PHILEMA   They are coming.°
CHRYSTALLA By the next carrier, are they not?
GRONEAS   Sweet Philema,
When I was in the thickest of mine enemies,
Slashing off one man's head, another's nose,
Another's arms and legs—
PHILEMA   And all together—   120
GRONEAS Then would I with a sigh remember thee,
And cry, 'Dear Philema, 'tis for thy sake
I do these deeds of wonder!' Dost not love me
With all thy heart now?
PHILEMA   Now as heretofore.
I have not put my love to use; the principal°   125
Will hardly yield an interest.

GRONEAS   By Mars,°
I'll marry thee!
PHILEMA   By Vulcan, y'are forsworn,°
Except my mind do alter strangely.
GRONEAS [*taking Philema aside to talk to her*] One word.
CHRYSTALLA [*to Lemophil*] You lie beyond all modesty.—Forbear me.
LEMOPHIL I'll make thee mistress of a city; 'tis   130
Mine own by conquest.
CHRYSTALLA   By petition; sue for't
In forma pauperis. City? Kennel! Gallants,°
Off with your feathers; put on aprons, gallants.°
Learn to reel, thrum, or trim a lady's dog,
And be good quiet souls of peace, hobgoblins.   135
LEMOPHIL Chrystalla!
CHRYSTALLA   Practise to drill hogs, in hope
To share in the acorns. Soldiers? Corn-cutters,°
But not so valiant; they oft-times draw blood,
Which you durst never do. When you have practised
More wit, or more civility, we'll rank 'ee   140
I'th' list of men. Till then, brave things at-arms,
Dare not to speak to us.—Most potent Groneas—
PHILEMA And Lemophil the hardy—at your services.
          Exeunt Chrystalla and Philema
GRONEAS They scorn us as they did before we went.
LEMOPHIL Hang 'em; let us scorn them and be revenged.   145
GRONEAS Shall we?
LEMOPHIL   We will; and when we slight them thus,
Instead of following them, they'll follow us.
It is a woman's nature.
GRONEAS   'Tis a scurvy one.
          Exeunt

1.3

*Enter Tecnicus, a philosopher, and Orgilus disguised like a
scholar of his*

TECNICUS Tempt not the stars, young man; thou canst not play
With the severity of fate. This change
Of habit, and disguise in outward view,

Hides not the secrets of thy soul within thee
From their quick-piercing eyes, which dive at all times°   5
Down to thy thoughts. In thy aspect I note°
A consequence of danger.

ORGILUS   Give me leave,
Grave Tecnicus, without fore-dooming destiny,
Under thy roof to ease my silent griefs,
By applying to my hidden wounds the balm   10
Of thy oraculous lectures. If my fortune
Run such a crooked by-way as to wrest
My steps to ruin, yet thy learnèd precepts
Shall call me back, and set my footings straight.
I will not court the world.

TECNICUS   Ah, Orgilus,   15
Neglects in young men of delights, and life,
Run often to extremities. They care not
For harms to others who contemn their own.

ORGILUS But I, most learned artist, am not so much
At odds with nature that I grudge the thrift°   20
Of any true deserver. Nor doth malice
Of present hopes so check them with despair
As that I yield to thought of more affliction
Than what is incident to frailty. Wherefore,°
Impute not this retired course of living   25
Some little time to any other cause°
Than what I justly render: the information°
Of an unsettled mind, as the effect
Must clearly witness.

TECNICUS   Spirit of truth inspire thee!
On these conditions I conceal thy change,   30
And willingly admit thee for an auditor.
I'll to my study.

ORGILUS   I to contemplations
In these delightful walks.

    [*Exit Tecnicus*]

                              Thus metamorphosed,
I may without suspicion hearken after°
Penthea's usage and Euphrania's faith.   35
Love, thou art full of mystery! The deities
Themselves are not secure in searching out
The secrets of those flames which, hidden, waste

A breast made tributary to the laws
Of beauty; physic yet hath never found   40
A remedy to cure a lover's wound.

> *Prophilus passeth over,° supporting° Euphrania, and*
> *whispering*

Ha! Who are those that cross yon private walk
Into the shadowing grove, in amorous foldings?°
My sister; O, my sister! 'Tis Euphrania
With Prophilus; supported too. I would   45
It were an apparition. Prophilus
Is Ithocles his friend. It strangely puzzles me.

> *Enter again Prophilus and Euphrania°*

Again? Help me, my book; this scholar's habit
Must stand my privilege. My mind is busy,°
Mine eyes and ears are open. *Walks by, reading*

PROPHILUS   Do not waste   50
The span of this stol'n time (lent by the gods
For precious use) in niceness! Bright Euphrania,
Should I repeat old vows, or study new,
For purchase of belief to my desires—
ORGILUS [*aside*] Desires?
PROPHILUS   My service, my integrity—   55
ORGILUS [*aside*] That's better.
PROPHILUS   I should but repeat a lesson
Oft conned without a prompter—but thine eyes.°
My love is honourable—
ORGILUS [*aside*]   So was mine
To my Penthea; chastely honourable.
PROPHILUS Nor wants there more addition to my wish   60
Of happiness than having thee a wife;
Already sure of Ithocles, a friend
Firm and unalterable.
ORGILUS [*aside*]   But a brother
More cruel than the grave.
EUPHRANIA   What can you look for,
In answer to your noble protestations,   65
From an unskilful maid, but language suited
To a divided mind?
ORGILUS [*aside*]   Hold out, Euphrania.
EUPHRANIA Know, Prophilus, I never undervalued
(From the first time you mentioned worthy love)

Your merit, means, or person. It had been   70
A fault of judgement in me, and a dullness
In my affections, not to weigh and thank
My better stars, that offered me the grace
Of so much blissfulness. For, to speak truth,
The law of my desires kept equal pace°   75
With yours, nor have I left that resolution;
But only, in a word, whatever choice
Lives nearest in my heart must first procure
Consent both from my father, and my brother,
Ere he can own me his.
ORGILUS [*aside*]   She is forsworn else.   80
PROPHILUS Leave me that task.
EUPHRANIA   My brother, ere he parted
To Athens, had my oath.
ORGILUS [*aside*]   Yes, yes, 'a had sure.
PROPHILUS I doubt not, with the means the court supplies,
· But to prevail at pleasure.
ORGILUS [*aside*]   Very likely.
PROPHILUS Meantime, best, dearest, I may build my hopes   85
On the foundation of thy constant suff'rance
In any opposition.
EUPHRANIA   Death shall sooner°
Divorce life and the joys I have in living,
Than my chaste vows from truth.
PROPHILUS   On thy fair hand
I seal the like. [*He kisses her hand*]
ORGILUS [*aside*] There is no faith in woman—°   90
Passion, O, be contained! My very heartstrings
Are on the tenters.
EUPHRANIA   Sir, we are overheard.
Cupid protect us! 'Twas a stirring, sir,
Of someone near.
PROPHILUS   Your fears are needless, lady.
None have access into these private pleasures,°   95
Except some near in court, or bosom student
From Tecnicus his oratory, granted
By special favour lately from the king
Unto the grave philosopher.
EUPHRANIA   Methinks
I hear one talking to himself. I see him.   100

PROPHILUS 'Tis a poor scholar, as I told you, lady.

ORGILUS [*aside*] I am discovered. [*Aloud*] Say it. Is it possible°
With a smooth tongue, a leering countenance,
Flattery, or force of reason—I come t'ee, sir—°
To turn or to appease the raging sea?   105
Answer to that. Your art? What art to catch
And hold fast in a net the sun's small atoms?
No, no; they'll out, they'll out. Ye may as easily
Outrun a cloud driven by a northern blast
As fiddle-faddle so. Peace, or speak sense.   110

EUPHRANIA Call you this thing a scholar? 'Las, he's lunatic.

PROPHILUS Observe him, sweet; 'tis but his recreation.

ORGILUS But will you hear a little! You are so tetchy,
You keep no rule in argument. Philosophy
Works not upon impossibilities,   115
But natural conclusions.—Mew!—Absurd!
The metaphysics are but speculations°
Of the celestial bodies, or such accidents
As, not mixed perfectly, in the air engendered,
Appear to us unnatural; that's all.   120
Prove it. Yet, with a reverence to your gravity,
I'll balk illiterate sauciness, submitting
My sole opinion to the touch of writers.°

PROPHILUS Now let us fall in with him.

ORGILUS   Ha, ha, ha!
These apish boys, when they but taste the grammates°   125
And principles of theory, imagine
They can oppose their teachers. Confidence
Leads many into errors.

PROPHILUS   By your leave, sir.

EUPHRANIA Are you a scholar, friend?

ORGILUS   I am, gay creature,
With pardon of your deities, a mushroom   130
On whom the dew of heaven drops now and then.
The sun shines on me too, I thank his beams.
Sometime I feel their warmth, and eat, and sleep.

PROPHILUS Does Tecnicus read to thee?

ORGILUS   Yes, forsooth,°
He is my master surely. Yonder door   135
Opens upon his study.

PROPHILUS   Happy creatures!

Such people toil not, sweet, in heats of state,
Nor sink in thaws of greatness. Their affections
Keep order with the limits of their modesty.°
Their love is love of virtue.—What's thy name?   140
ORGILUS Aplotes, sumptuous master; a poor wretch.
EUPHRANIA Dost thou want anything?
ORGILUS   Books, Venus, books.
PROPHILUS Lady, a new conceit comes in my thought,
And most available for both our comforts.
EUPHRANIA My lord—
PROPHILUS   Whiles I endeavour to deserve   145
Your father's blessing to our loves, this scholar
May daily at some certain hours attend
What notice I can write of my success,
Here in this grove, and give it to your hands.
The like from you to me. So can we never,   150
Barred of our mutual speech, want sure intelligence;
And thus our hearts may talk when our tongues cannot.
EUPHRANIA Occasion is most favourable; use it.
PROPHILUS Aplotes, wilt thou wait us twice a day,
At nine i'th' morning, and at four at night,   155
Here in this bower, to convey such letters
As each shall send to other? Do it willingly,
Safely, and secretly, and I will furnish
Thy study, or what else thou canst desire.
ORGILUS Jove, make me thankful, thankful, I beseech thee,   160
Propitious Jove! I will prove sure and trusty.
You will not fail me books?
PROPHILUS   Nor aught besides
Thy heart can wish. This lady's name's Euphrania;
Mine Prophilus.
ORGILUS   I have a pretty memory;
It must prove my best friend. I will not miss   165
One minute of the hours appointed.
PROPHILUS   Write
The books thou wouldst have bought thee in a note,
Or take thyself some money.
ORGILUS   No, no money.
Money to scholars is a spirit invisible;
We dare not finger it. Or books, or nothing.   170

PROPHILUS Books of what sort thou wilt. Do not forget
  Our names.
ORGILUS   I warrant 'ee, I warrant 'ee.
PROPHILUS Smile, Hymen, on the growth of our desires;
  We'll feed thy torches with eternal fires.
     Exeunt [Euphrania and Prophilus]
ORGILUS Put out thy torches, Hymen, or their light   175
  Shall meet a darkness of eternal night.
  Inspire me, Mercury, with swift deceits;°
  Ingenious fate has leapt into mine arms,
  Beyond the compass of my brain. Mortality
  Creeps on the dung of earth, and cannot reach   180
  The riddles which are purposed by the gods.
  Great acts best write themselves in their own stories.
  They die too basely who outlive their glories.
     Exit

2.1

Enter Bassanes and Phulas

BASSANES I'll have that window next the street dammed up;
It gives too full a prospect to temptation,°
And courts a gazer's glances. There's a lust
Committed by the eye, that sweats and travails,
Plots, wakes, contrives, till the deformed bear-whelp,   5
Adultery, be licked into the act,°
The very act. That light shall be dammed up.
D'ee hear, sir?
PHULAS   I do hear, my lord; a mason
Shall be provided suddenly.
BASSANES   Some rogue,
Some rogue of your confederacy—factor   10
For slaves and strumpets—to convey close packets°
From this spruce springal and the tother youngster,
That gaudy earwig, or my lord, your patron,°
Whose pensioner you are.—I'll tear thy throat out,
Son of a cat, ill-looking hound's head; rip up   15
Thy ulcerous maw, if I but scent a paper,°
A scroll, but half as big as what can cover
A wart upon thy nose, a spot, a pimple,
Directed to my lady. It may prove
A mystical preparative to lewdness.   20
PHULAS Care shall be had. I will turn every thread
About me to an eye. [*Aside*] Here's a sweet life!°
BASSANES The city housewives, cunning in the traffic°
Of chamber-merchandise, set all at price°
By wholesale, yet they wipe their mouths and simper,°   25
Cull, kiss, and cry 'sweetheart', and stroke the head
Which they have branched, and all is well again.°
Dull clods of dirt, who dare not feel the rubs°
Stuck on their foreheads!
PHULAS   'Tis a villainous world;
One cannot hold his own in't.
BASSANES   Dames at court,   30
Who flaunt in riots, run another bias.°
Their pleasure heaves the patient ass that suffers

Up on the stilts of office, titles, incomes.°
Promotion justifies the shame, and sues for't.
Poor honour! Thou art stabbed, and bleed'st to death   35
By such unlawful hire. The country mistress
Is yet more wary, and in blushes hides
Whatever trespass draws her troth to guilt;
But all are false. On this truth I am bold:
No woman but can fall, and doth, or would.—   40
Now for the newest news about the city;
What blab the voices, sirrah?

PHULAS   O my lord,
The rarest, quaintest, strangest, tickling news
That ever—

BASSANES   Heyday, up and ride me, rascal!°
What is't?

PHULAS   Forsooth, they say, the king has mewed   45
All his grey beard, instead of which is budded
Another of a pure carnation colour,
Speckled with green and russet.

BASSANES   Ignorant block!

PHULAS Yes, truly, and 'tis talked about the streets
That, since Lord Ithocles came home, the lions   50
Never left roaring, at which noise the bears
Have danced their very hearts out.

BASSANES   Dance out thine too.

PHULAS Besides, Lord Orgilus is fled to Athens
Upon a fiery dragon, and 'tis thought°
'A never can return.

BASSANES   Grant it, Apollo!   55

PHULAS Moreover, please your lordship, 'tis reported
For certain that whoever is found jealous
Without apparent proof that's wife is wanton°
Shall be divorced. But this is but she-news;°
I had it from a midwife. I have more yet.   60

BASSANES Antic, no more! Idiots and stupid fools
Grate my calamities. Why, to be fair
Should yield presumption of a faulty soul!
Look to the doors.

PHULAS [aside]   The horn of plenty crest him.°
          Exit Phulas

BASSANES Swarms of confusion huddle in my thoughts   65

In rare distemper. Beauty! O, it is
An unmatched blessing or a horrid curse.
    Enter Penthea and Grausis, an old lady
She comes, she comes! So shoots the morning forth,
Spangled with pearls of transparent dew.
The way to poverty is to be rich;   70
As I in her am wealthy, but for her
In all contents a bankrupt.—Loved Penthea,
How fares my heart's best joy?
GRAUSIS   In sooth not well,
She is so oversad.
BASSANES [*to Grausis*] Leave chattering, magpie.
[*To Penthea*] Thy brother is returned, sweet, safe, and honoured   75
With a triumphant victory. Thou shalt visit him.
We will to court, where, if it be thy pleasure,
Thou shalt appear in such a ravishing lustre
Of jewels above value, that the dames
Who brave it there, in rage to be out-shined,°   80
Shall hide them in their closets and, unseen,°
Fret in their tears; whiles every wond'ring eye
Shall crave none other brightness but thy presence.
Choose thine own recreations. Be a queen
Of what delights thou fanciest best; what company,   85
What place, what times. Do anything, do all things
Youth can command; so thou wilt chase these clouds
From the pure firmament of thy fair looks.
GRAUSIS Now 'tis well said, my lord.—What, lady? Laugh,
Be merry. Time is precious.
BASSANES [*to Grausis*]   Furies whip thee!°   90
PENTHEA Alas, my lord, this language to your handmaid°
Sounds as would music to the deaf. I need
No braveries nor cost of art to draw
The whiteness of my name into offence.
Let such, if any such there are, who covet   95
A curiosity of admiration,
By laying out their plenty to full view,
Appear in gaudy outsides. My attires
Shall suit the inward fashion of my mind;
From which, if your opinion, nobly placed,   100
Change not the livery your words bestow,
My fortunes with my hopes are at the highest.

BASSANES This house, methinks, stands somewhat too much inward.
    It is too melancholy. We'll remove
    Nearer the court. Or what thinks my Penthea   105
    Of the delightful island we command?
    Rule me as thou canst wish.
PENTHEA   I am no mistress.
    Whither you please, I must attend; all ways
    Are alike pleasant to me.
GRAUSIS   Island? Prison!
    A prison is as gaysome. We'll no islands.   110
    Marry, out upon 'em! Whom shall we see there?
    Seagulls, and porpoises, and water rats,
    And crabs, and mews, and dogfish? Goodly gear
    For a young lady's dealing, or an old one's.
    On no terms islands; I'll be stewed first.
BASSANES [aside]   Grausis,°   115
    You are a juggling bawd. [To Penthea] This sadness, sweetest,
    Becomes not youthful blood. [To Grausis] I'll have you pounded.
    [To Penthea] For my sake put on a more cheerful mirth.
    Thou'lt mar thy cheeks, and make me old in griefs.
    [To Grausis] Damnable bitch-fox!
GRAUSIS   I am thick of hearing   120
    Still when the wind blows southerly. What think 'ee
    If your fresh lady breed young bones, my lord?
    Would not a chopping boy d'ee good at heart?
    But as you said—
BASSANES   I'll spit thee on a stake,
    Or chop thee into collops.
GRAUSIS   Pray speak louder.   125
    Sure, sure, the wind blows south still.
PENTHEA   Thou prat'st madly.
BASSANES 'Tis very hot; I sweat extremely.
    Enter Phulas

                     —Now?
PHULAS A herd of lords, sir.
BASSANES   Ha?
PHULAS   A flock of ladies.
BASSANES Where?
PHULAS   Shoals of horses.
BASSANES   Peasant, how?
PHULAS   Caroches

In drifts—th'one enter, th'other stand without, sir.   130
And now I vanish.
> *Exit Phulas. Enter Prophilus, Lemophil, Groneas, Chrystalla,*
> *and Philema*

PROPHILUS   Noble Bassanes.
BASSANES Most welcome Prophilus, ladies, gentlemen;
To all, my heart is open. You all honour me—
[*Aside*] A tympany swells in my head already—°
Honour me bountifully. [*Aside*] How they flutter,   135
Wagtails and jays together!
PROPHILUS   From your brother,°
By virtue of your love to him, I require
Your instant presence, fairest.
PENTHEA   He is well, sir?
PROPHILUS The gods preserve him ever. Yet, dear beauty,
I find some alteration in him lately,   140
Since his return to Sparta. [*To Bassanes*] My good lord,
I pray use no delay.
BASSANES   We had not needed
An invitation if his sister's health
Had not fallen into question.—Haste, Penthea,
Slack not a minute. Lead the way, good Prophilus;   145
I'll follow step by step.
PROPHILUS   Your arm, fair madam.
> *Exeunt all but Bassanes and Grausis*

BASSANES One word with your old bawdship: th'hadst been better
Railed at the sins thou worshipp'st than have thwarted°
My will. I'll use thee cursedly.
GRAUSIS   You dote,
You are beside yourself. A politician   150
In jealousy? No, y'are too gross, too vulgar.
Pish, teach not me my trade; I know my cue.
My crossing you sinks me into her trust,
By which I shall know all. My trade's a sure one.
BASSANES Forgive me, Grausis; 'twas consideration   155
I relished not. But have a care now.
GRAUSIS   Fear not;°
I am no new-come-to't.
BASSANES   Thy life's upon it,
And so is mine. My agonies are infinite.
> *Exeunt*

2.2

Enter Ithocles, alone

ITHOCLES Ambition? 'Tis of viper's breed, it gnaws
A passage through the womb that gave it motion.°
Ambition, like a seelèd dove, mounts upward,°
Higher and higher still, to perch on clouds,
But tumbles headlong down with heavier ruin.   5
So squibs and crackers fly into the air;
Then, only breaking with a noise, they vanish
In stench and smoke. Morality applied
To timely practice keeps the soul in tune,
At whose sweet music all our actions dance.   10
But this is form of books and school tradition;°
It physics not the sickness of a mind
Broken with griefs. Strong fevers are not eased
With counsel, but with best receipts and means.
Means, speedy means and certain; that's the cure.   15

Enter Armostes and Crotolon

ARMOSTES You stick, Lord Crotolon, upon a point
Too nice, and too unnecessary. Prophilus
Is every way desertful. I am confident
Your wisdom is too ripe to need instruction
From your son's tutelage.

CROTOLON   Yet not so ripe,   20
My Lord Armostes, that it dares to dote
Upon the painted meat of smooth persuasion
Which tempts me to a breach of faith.

ITHOCLES   Not yet
Resolved, my lord? Why, if your son's consent
Be so available, we'll write to Athens   25
For his repair to Sparta. The king's hand
Will join with our desires; he has been moved to't.

ARMOSTES Yes, and the king himself importuned Crotolon
For a dispatch.

CROTOLON   Kings may command; their wills
Are laws not to be questioned.

ITHOCLES   By this marriage   30
You knit an union so devout, so hearty,
Between your loves to me, and mine to yours,

As if mine own blood had an interest in it;
For Prophilus is mine, and I am his.
CROTOLON My lord, my lord!
ITHOCLES   What, good sir? Speak your thought.   35
CROTOLON Had this sincerity been real once,
My Orgilus had not been now unwived,
Nor your lost sister buried in a bride-bed.
Your uncle here, Armostes, knows this truth,
For had your father Thrasus lived—but peace   40
Dwell in his grave. I have done.
ARMOSTES   Y'are bold and bitter.
ITHOCLES [aside] 'A presses home the injury; it smarts.
[To Armostes] No reprehensions, uncle; I deserve 'em.
Yet, gentle sir, consider what the heat
Of an unsteady youth, a giddy brain,   45
Green indiscretion, flattery of greatness,
Rawness of judgement, wilfulness in folly,
Thoughts vagrant as the wind, and as uncertain,
Might lead a boy-in-years to. 'Twas a fault,
A capital fault, for then I could not dive   50
Into the secrets of commanding love;
Since when, experience by the extremities (in others)
Hath forced me to collect. And trust me, Crotolon,
I will redeem those wrongs with any service
Your satisfaction can require for current.   55
ARMOSTES Thy acknowledgement is satisfaction.
[To Crotolon] What would you more?
CROTOLON   I'm conquered. If Euphrania
Herself admit the motion, let it be so.
I doubt not my son's liking.
ITHOCLES   Use my fortunes,
Life, power, sword, and heart; all are your own.   60
    Enter Bassanes, Prophilus, Calantha, Penthea, Euphrania,
    Chrystalla, Philema, and Grausis
ARMOSTES The princess, with your sister.
CALANTHA   I present 'ee
A stranger here in court, my lord, for did not
Desire of seeing you draw her abroad,
We had not been made happy in her company.°
ITHOCLES You are a gracious princess.—Sister, wedlock   65
Holds too severe a passion in your nature,

Which can engross all duty to your husband
Without attendance on so dear a mistress.—°
'Tis not my brother's pleasure, I presume,°
T'immure her in a chamber.

BASSANES   'Tis her will;   70
She governs her own hours. Noble Ithocles,
We thank the gods for your success and welfare.
Our lady has of late been indisposed,
Else we had waited on you with the first.

ITHOCLES How does Penthea now?

PENTHEA   You best know, brother,   75
From whom my health and comforts are derived.

BASSANES [aside] I like the answer well; 'tis sad and modest.
There may be tricks yet, tricks.—Have an eye, Grausis.

CALANTHA Now, Crotolon, the suit we joined in must not
Fall by too long demur.

CROTOLON   'Tis granted, princess,   80
For my part.

ARMOSTES   With condition, that his son
Favour the contract.

CALANTHA   Such delay is easy.
The joys of marriage make thee, Prophilus,
A proud deserver of Euphrania's love,
And her of thy desert.

PROPHILUS   Most sweetly gracious!   85

BASSANES The joys of marriage are the heaven on earth,
Life's paradise, great princess, the soul's quiet,
Sinews of concord, earthly immortality,
Eternity of pleasures; no restoratives
Like to a constant woman.—[Aside] But where is she?   90
'Twould puzzle all the gods but to create
Such a new monster.—I can speak by proof,
For I rest in Elysium; 'tis my happiness.

CROTOLON Euphrania, how are you resolved—speak freely—
In your affections to this gentleman?   95

EUPHRANIA Nor more nor less than as his love assures me,
Which (if your liking, with my brother's, warrants)
I cannot but approve in all points worthy.

CROTOLON So, so; [to Prophilus] I know your answer.

ITHOCLES   'T had been pity
To sunder hearts so equally consented.   100

Enter Lemophil

LEMOPHIL The king, Lord Ithocles, commands your presence;
  And, fairest princess, yours.
CALANTHA   We will attend him.
  Enter Groneas
GRONEAS Where are the lords? All must unto the king
  Without delay. The Prince of Argos—
CALANTHA   Well, sir?°
GRONEAS Is coming to the court, sweet lady.
CALANTHA   How!   105
  The Prince of Argos?
GRONEAS   'Twas my fortune, madam,
  T'enjoy the honour of these happy tidings.
ITHOCLES Penthea.
PENTHEA   Brother.
ITHOCLES   Let me an hour hence
  Meet you alone, within the palace grove.
  I have some secret with you. [*To Prophilus*] Prithee, friend,   110
  Conduct her thither, and have special care
  The walks be cleared of any to disturb us.
PROPHILUS I shall.
BASSANES [*aside*]   How's that?
ITHOCLES   Alone, pray be alone.—
  I am your creature, princess.—On, my lords.
  Exeunt [all but Bassanes]°
BASSANES Alone, alone? What means that word 'alone'?   115
  Why might not I be there?—Hum!—He's her brother;
  Brothers and sisters are but flesh and blood,
  And this same whoreson court-ease is temptation
  To a rebellion in the veins. Besides,
  His fine friend Prophilus must be her guardian.   120
  Why may not he dispatch a business nimbly°
  Before the other come?—Or, pand'ring; pand'ring
  For one another? Be't to sister, mother,
  Wife, cousin, anything—'mongst youths of mettle,
  Is in request. It is so—stubborn fate.°   125
  But if I be a cuckold, and can know it,
  I will be fell, and fell.
  Enter Groneas
GRONEAS   My lord, y'are called for.
BASSANES Most heartily I thank ye. Where's my wife, pray?

GRONEAS Retired amongst the ladies.

BASSANES   Still I thank 'ee.

There's an old waiter with her; saw you her too?   130

GRONEAS She sits i'th' presence lobby fast asleep, sir.°

BASSANES Asleep? Sleep, sir!

GRONEAS   Is your lordship troubled?

You will not to the king?

BASSANES   Your humblest vassal.

GRONEAS Your servant, my good lord.

BASSANES   I wait your footsteps.

Exeunt

2.3

[Enter] Prophilus [and] Penthea

PROPHILUS In this walk, lady, will your brother find you.

And with your favour, give me leave a little

To work a preparation. In his fashion

I have observed of late some kind of slackness

To such alacrity as nature   5

And custom took delight in. Sadness grows

Upon his recreations, which he hoards

In such a willing silence that to question

The grounds will argue little skill in friendship,°

And less good manners.

PENTHEA   Sir, I'm not inquisitive   10

Of secrecies without an invitation.

PROPHILUS With pardon, lady, not a syllable

Of mine implies so rude a sense. The drift—

Enter Orgilus [disguised as before]

[To Orgilus] Do thy best

To make this lady merry for an hour.   15

ORGILUS Your will shall be a law, sir.

Exit [Prophilus]

PENTHEA   Prithee leave me;

I have some private thoughts I would account with.°

Use thou thine own.

ORGILUS   Speak on, fair nymph. Our souls

Can dance as well to music of the spheres°

As any's who have feasted with the gods.   20
PENTHEA Your school terms are too troublesome.
ORGILUS   What heaven°
Refines mortality from dross of earth
But such as uncompounded beauty hallows
With glorified perfection?
PENTHEA   Set thy wits
In a less wild proportion.
ORGILUS   Time can never   25
On the white table of unguilty faith
Write counterfeit dishonour. Turn those eyes,
The arrows of pure love, upon that fire
Which once rose to a flame, perfumed with vows
As sweetly scented as the incense smoking   30
The holiest altars; virgin tears (like°
On Vesta's odours) sprinkled dews to feed 'em°
And to increase their fervour.
PENTHEA   Be not frantic.
ORGILUS All pleasures are but mere imagination,
Feeding the hungry appetite with steam   35
And sight of banquet, whilst the body pines,
Not relishing the real taste of food.
Such is the leanness of a heart divided
From intercourse of troth-contracted loves;
No horror should deface that precious figure   40
Sealed with the lively stamp of equal souls.
PENTHEA Away! Some fury hath bewitched thy tongue.
The breath of ignorance that flies from thence
Ripens a knowledge in me of afflictions
Above all suff'rance.—Thing of talk, be gone;   45
Be gone without reply.
ORGILUS   Be just, Penthea,
In thy commands. When thou send'st forth a doom
Of banishment, know first on whom it lights.
Thus I take off the shroud in which my cares
Are folded up from view of common eyes.   50
        [*Orgilus throws off his disguise*]
What is thy sentence next?
PENTHEA   Rash man, thou layest
A blemish on mine honour with the hazard
Of thy too desperate life. Yet I profess,
By all the laws of ceremonious wedlock,

I have not given admittance to one thought 55
Of female change, since cruelty enforced°
Divorce betwixt my body and my heart.
Why would you fall from goodness thus?

ORGILUS   O, rather
Examine me how I could live to say
I have been much, much wronged. 'Tis for thy sake 60
I put on this imposture. Dear Penthea,
If thy soft bosom be not turned to marble,
Thou'lt pity our calamities. My interest°
Confirms me thou art mine still.

PENTHEA   Lend your hand.
With both of mine I clasp it thus, thus kiss it, 65
Thus kneel before ye. [Kneels]

ORGILUS   You instruct my duty. [Kneels]

PENTHEA We may stand up. Have you aught else to urge
Of new demand? As for the old, forget it;
'Tis buried in an everlasting silence,
And shall be, shall be ever. What more would ye? 70

ORGILUS I would possess my wife; the equity
Of very reason bids me.

PENTHEA   Is that all?

ORGILUS Why 'tis the all of me myself.

PENTHEA   Remove
Your steps some distance from me. At this space
A few words I dare change; but first put on° 75
Your borrowed shape.
          [Orgilus resumes his disguise]

ORGILUS   You are obeyed, 'tis done.

PENTHEA How, Orgilus, by promise I was thine,
The heavens do witness; they can witness, too,
A rape done on my truth. How I do love thee°
Yet, Orgilus, and yet, must best appear 80
In tendering thy freedom; for I find°
The constant preservation of thy merit
By thy not daring to attempt my fame
With injury of any loose conceit,
Which might give deeper wounds to discontents. 85
Continue this fair race; then, though I cannot
Add to thy comfort, yet I shall more often
Remember from what fortune I am fallen,
And pity mine own ruin.—Live, live happy,

Happy in thy next choice, that thou mayst people   90
This barren age with virtues in thy issue.
And O, when thou art married, think on me
With mercy, not contempt. I hope thy wife,
Hearing my story, will not scorn my fall.
Now let us part.
ORGILUS   Part! Yet advise thee better.°   95
Penthea is the wife to Orgilus,
And ever shall be.
PENTHEA   Never shall nor will.
ORGILUS How!
PENTHEA   Hear me; in a word I'll tell thee why.
The virgin dowry, which my birth bestowed,
Is ravished by another. My true love   100
Abhors to think that Orgilus deserved
No better favours than a second bed.
ORGILUS I must not take this reason.
PENTHEA   To confirm it,
Should I outlive my bondage let me meet
Another worse than this, and less desired,   105
If of all the men alive thou shouldst but touch
My lip or hand again.
ORGILUS   Penthea, now
I tell 'ee you grow wanton in my sufferance.°
Come sweet, th'art mine. [*Orgilus makes an advance*]
PENTHEA   Uncivil sir, forbear,
Or I can turn affection into vengeance.   110
Your reputation, if you value any,
Lies bleeding at my feet. Unworthy man,
If ever henceforth thou appear in language,
Message, or letter to betray my frailty,
I'll call thy former protestations lust,   115
And curse my stars for forfeit of my judgement.
Go thou, fit only for disguise and walks°
To hide thy shame. This once I spare thy life.
I laugh at mine own confidence; my sorrows
By thee are made inferior to my fortunes.   120
If ever thou didst harbour worthy love,
Dare not to answer. My good genius guide me,
That I may never see thee more.—Go from me.
ORGILUS I'll tear my veil of politic French off,°
And stand up like a man resolved to do.   125

Action, not words, shall show me. O, Penthea!
    Exit Orgilus
PENTHEA 'A sighed my name, sure, as he parted from me;
    I fear I was too rough. Alas, poor gentleman,
    'A looked not like the ruins of his youth,
    But like the ruins of those ruins. Honour,   130
    How much we fight with weakness to preserve thee.
    Enter Bassanes and Grausis
BASSANES Fie on thee! Damn thee, rotten maggot, damn thee!
    Sleep? Sleep at court? And now? Aches, convulsions,
    Impostumes, rheums, gouts, palsies clog thy bones
    A dozen years more yet.
GRAUSIS   Now y'are in humours.°   135
BASSANES She's by herself; there's hope of that. She's sad, too;
    She's in strong contemplation. Yes, and fixed.
    The signs are wholesome.
GRAUSIS   Very wholesome, truly.
BASSANES Hold your chops, nightmare.—Lady, come. Your brother
    Is carried to his closet; you must thither.   140
PENTHEA Not well, my lord?
BASSANES   A sudden fit, 'twill off;
    Some surfeit or disorder.—How dost, dearest?
PENTHEA Your news is none o'th' best.
    Enter Prophilus
PROPHILUS   The chief of men,
    The excellentest Ithocles, desires
    Your presence, madam.
BASSANES   We are hasting to him.   145
PENTHEA In vain we labour in this course of life
    To piece our journey out at length, or crave
    Respite of breath. Our home is in the grave.
BASSANES Perfect philosophy. Then let us care
    To live so that our reckonings may fall even   150
    When w'are to make account.
PROPHILUS   He cannot fear
    Who builds on noble grounds. Sickness or pain
    Is the deserver's exercise, and such
    Your virtuous brother to the world is known.
    Speak comfort to him, lady; be all gentle.   155
    Stars fall but in the grossness of our sight;
    A good man dying, th'earth doth lose a light.
    Exeunt

3.1

Enter Tecnicus, and Orgilus in his own shape°

TECNICUS Be well advised; let not a resolution
  Of giddy rashness choke the breath of reason.

ORGILUS It shall not, most sage master.

TECNICUS   I am jealous.
  For if the borrowed shape so late put on
  Inferred a consequence, we must conclude   5
  Some violent design of sudden nature
  Hath shook that shadow off, to fly upon
  A new-hatched execution. Orgilus,°
  Take heed thou hast not, under our integrity,
  Shrouded unlawful plots. Our mortal eyes   10
  Pierce not the secrets of your heart; the gods
  Are only privy to them.

ORGILUS   Learnèd Tecnicus,
  Such doubts are causeless; and to clear the truth
  From misconceit, the present state commands me.°
  The Prince of Argos comes himself in person   15
  In quest of great Calantha for his bride,
  Our kingdom's heir; besides, mine only sister,
  Euphrania, is disposed to Prophilus.°
  Lastly, the king is sending letters for me
  To Athens, for my quick repair to court.   20
  Please to accept these reasons.

TECNICUS   Just ones, Orgilus,
  Not to be contradicted. Yet beware
  Of an unsure foundation; no fair colours
  Can fortify a building faintly jointed.
  I have observed a growth in thy aspect°   25
  Of dangerous extent, sudden, and (look to't)
  I might add, certain—

ORGILUS   My aspect? Could art
  Run through mine inmost thoughts, it should not sift
  An inclination there, more than what suited
  With justice of mine honour.

TECNICUS   I believe it.   30
  But know then, Orgilus, what honour is.

114

Honour consists not in a bare opinion
By doing any act that feeds content,°
Brave in appearance 'cause we think it brave.
Such honour comes by accident, not nature;   35
Proceeding from the vices of our passion,
Which makes our reason drunk. But real honour
Is the reward of virtue, and acquired
By justice, or by valour which, for basis,
Hath justice to uphold it. He then fails   40
In honour who for lucre of revenge
Commits thefts, murders, treasons and adulteries,
With such like, by entrenching on just laws,
Whose sov'reignty is best preserved by justice.
Thus, as you see how honour must be grounded   45
On knowledge, not opinion—for opinion
Relies on probability and accident,
But knowledge on necessity and truth—
I leave thee to the fit consideration
Of what becomes the grace of real honour,   50
Wishing success to all thy virtuous meanings.

ORGILUS The gods increase thy wisdom, reverend oracle,
And in thy precepts make me ever thrifty.°

TECNICUS I thank thy wish.

      Exit Orgilus°

               —Much mystery of fate
Lies hid in that man's fortunes. Curiosity°   55
May lead his actions into rare attempts.°
But let the gods be moderators still;
No human power can prevent their will.

      Enter Armostes

From whence come 'ee?

ARMOSTES   From King Amyclas. (Pardon
My interruption of your studies.)—Here   60
In this sealed box he sends a treasure dear
To him as his crown. 'A prays your gravity
You would examine, ponder, sift, and bolt
The pith and circumstance of every tittle
The scroll within contains.

TECNICUS   What is't, Armostes?   65

ARMOSTES It is the health of Sparta, the king's life,
Sinews and safety of the commonwealth,

The sum of what the oracle delivered,
When last he visited the prophetic temple
At Delphos. What his reasons are, for which°   70
After so long a silence he requires
Your counsel now, grave man, his majesty
Will soon himself acquaint you with.
TECNICUS   Apollo
Inspire my intellect!—The Prince of Argos
Is entertained?
ARMOSTES   He is, and has demanded   75
Our princess for his wife; which I conceive
One special cause the king importunes you
For resolution of the oracle.
TECNICUS My duty to the king, good peace to Sparta,
And fair day to Armostes.
ARMOSTES   Like to Tecnicus.°   80
    Exeunt

3.2

Soft music. A song [within]
        Can you paint a thought? or number
        Every fancy in a slumber?
        Can you count soft minutes roving
        From a dial's point by moving?
        Can you grasp a sigh? or lastly,   5
        Rob a virgin's honour chastely?
    No, O no; Yet you may
        Sooner do both that and this,
        This and that, and never miss,
    Than by any praise display   10
        Beauty's beauty, such a glory
        As beyond all fate, all story,
            All arms, all arts,
            All loves, all hearts,
        Greater than those, or they,   15
        Do, shall, and must obey.
During which time, enter Prophilus, Bassanes, Penthea,
[and] Grausis, passing over the stage;° Bassanes and

*Grausis enter again softly, stealing to several stands, and
     listen*

BASSANES All silent, calm, secure.—Grausis, no creaking?
     No noise? Dost hear nothing?
GRAUSIS   Not a mouse,
     Or whisper of the wind.
BASSANES   The floor is matted,
     The bedposts, sure, are steel or marble.—Soldiers   20
     Should not affect, methinks, strains so effeminate;
     Sounds of such delicacy are but fawnings
     Upon the sloth of luxury. They heighten
     Cinders of covert lust up to a flame.
GRAUSIS What do you mean, my lord? Speak low; that gabbling   25
     Of yours will but undo us.
BASSANES   Chamber-combats°
     Are felt, not heard.
PROPHILUS [*within*] 'A wakes.
BASSANES   What's that?
ITHOCLES [*within*]   Who's there?°
     Sister?—All quit the room else.
BASSANES   'Tis consented.
     Enter Prophilus
PROPHILUS Lord Bassanes, your brother would be private;°
     We must forbear; his sleep hath newly left him.   30
     Please 'ee withdraw?
BASSANES   By any means; 'tis fit.
PROPHILUS Pray, gentlewoman, walk too.
GRAUSIS   Yes, I will, sir.
     Exeunt [Bassanes, Prophilus, and Grausis].
     Ithocles discovered° in a chair, and Penthea
ITHOCLES Sit nearer, sister, to me; nearer yet.
     We had one father, in one womb took life,
     Were brought up twins together, yet have lived   35
     At distance like two strangers. I could wish
     That the first pillow whereon I was cradled
     Had proved to me a grave.
PENTHEA   You had been happy:
     Then had you never known that sin of life
     Which blots all following glories with a vengeance   40
     For forfeiting the last will of the dead,
     From whom you had your being.

ITHOCLES   Sad Penthea,°
  Thou canst not be too cruel. My rash spleen
  Hath with a violent hand plucked from thy bosom
  A lover-blessed heart, to grind it into dust,   45
  For which mine's now a-breaking.
PENTHEA   Not yet, heaven,
  I do beseech thee. First let some wild fires
  Scorch, not consume it; may the heat be cherished
  With desires infinite, but hopes impossible.
ITHOCLES Wronged soul, thy prayers are heard.
PENTHEA   Here, lo, I breathe,   50
  A miserable creature led to ruin
  By an unnatural brother.
ITHOCLES   I consume
  In languishing affections for that trespass,
  Yet cannot die.
PENTHEA   The handmaid to the wages
  Of country toil drinks the untroubled streams   55
  With leaping kids and with the bleating lambs,
  And so allays her thirst secure, whiles I
  Quench my hot sighs with fleetings of my tears.
ITHOCLES The labourer doth eat his coarsest bread,
  Earned with his sweat, and lies him down to sleep,   60
  While every bit I touch turns in digestion
  To gall, as bitter as Penthea's curse.
  Put me to any penance for my tyranny,
  And I will call thee merciful.
PENTHEA   Pray kill me;
  Rid me from living with a jealous husband.   65
  Then we will join in friendship, be again
  Brother and sister.—Kill me, pray. Nay, will 'ee?
ITHOCLES How does thy lord esteem thee?
PENTHEA   Such an one
  As only you have made me: a faith-breaker,
  A spotted whore. Forgive me. I am one°   70
  In act, not in desires, the gods must witness.
ITHOCLES Thou dost belie thy friend.
PENTHEA   I do not, Ithocles;°
  For she that's wife to Orgilus, and lives
  In known adultery with Bassanes
  Is at the best a whore. Wilt kill me now?   75

The ashes of our parents will assume
Some dreadful figure, and appear to charge
Thy bloody guilt, that hast betrayed their name
To infamy in this reproachful match.

ITHOCLES After my victories abroad, at home   80
I meet despair; ingratitude of nature
Hath made my actions monstrous. Thou shalt stand
A deity, my sister, and be worshipped
For thy resolvèd martyrdom. Wronged maids
And married wives shall to thy hallowed shrine   85
Offer their orisons, and sacrifice
Pure turtles crowned with myrtle, if thy pity°
Unto a yielding brother's pressure lend
One finger but to ease it.

PENTHEA   O, no more!

ITHOCLES Death waits to waft me to the Stygian banks,°   90
And free me from this chaos of my bondage;
And till thou wilt forgive, I must endure.

PENTHEA Who is the saint you serve?

ITHOCLES   Friendship, or nearness°
Of birth to any but my sister, durst not
Have moved that question as a secret, sister,°   95
I dare not murmur to myself.

PENTHEA   Let me,
By your new protestations I conjure 'ee,
Partake her name.

ITHOCLES   Her name—'tis,—'tis,—I dare not.

PENTHEA All you respects are forged.

ITHOCLES   They are not.—Peace!
Calantha is the princess; the king's daughter,   100
Sole heir of Sparta—me most miserable!
Do I now love thee? For my injuries°
Revenge thyself with bravery, and gossip
My treasons to the king's ears. Do. Calantha
Knows it not yet, nor Prophilus my nearest.   105

PENTHEA Suppose you were contracted to her, would it not
Split even your very soul to see her father
Snatch her out of your arms against her will,
And force her on the Prince of Argos?

ITHOCLES   Trouble not
The fountains of mine eyes with thine own story;   110

I sweat in blood for't.
PENTHEA   We are reconciled.
Alas, sir, being children, but two branches
Of one stock, 'tis not fit we should divide.
Have comfort; you may find it.
ITHOCLES   Yes, in thee:
Only in thee, Penthea mine.
PENTHEA   If sorrows   115
Have not too much dulled my infected brain,
I'll cheer invention for an active strain.°
ITHOCLES Mad man! Why have I wronged a maid so excellent?
        Enter Bassanes with a poniard; Prophilus, Groneas,
        Lemophil, and Grausis
BASSANES I can forbear no longer. More, I will not.
Keep off your hands, or fall upon my point.°   120
Patience is tired, for like a slow-paced ass
Ye ride my easy nature, and proclaim
My sloth to vengeance a reproach and property.°
ITHOCLES The meaning of this rudeness?
PROPHILUS   He's distracted.
PENTHEA O my grieved lord.
GRAUSIS   Sweet lady, come not near him;   125
He holds his perilous weapon in his hand
To prick 'a cares not whom nor where.—See, see, see!
BASSANES My birth is noble, though the popular blast
Of vanity, as giddy as thy youth,°
Hath reared thy name up to bestride a cloud   130
Or progress in the chariot of the sun.°
I am no clod of trade, to lackey pride,
Nor, like your slave of expectation, wait
The bawdy hinges of your doors, or whistle°
For mystical conveyance to your bed-sports.   135
GRONEAS Fine humours! They become him.
LEMOPHIL   How 'a stares,
Struts, puffs, and sweats. Most admirable lunacy!
ITHOCLES But that I may conceive the spirit of wine
Has took possession of your soberer custom,
I'd say you were unmannerly.
PENTHEA   Dear brother—   140
BASSANES Unmannerly!—Mew, kitling!—Smooth formality
Is usher to the rankness of the blood,

But impudence bears up the train. Indeed, sir,
Your fiery mettle, or your springal blaze
Of huge renown, is no sufficient royalty   145
To print upon my forehead the scorn 'cuckold'.
ITHOCLES His jealousy has robbed him of his wits;
  'A talks 'a knows not what.
BASSANES   Yes, and 'a knows
To whom 'a talks; to one that franks his lust°
In swine-security of bestial incest.   150
ITHOCLES Ha, devil!
BASSANES   I will halloo't, though I blush more
To name the filthiness than thou to act it.
ITHOCLES Monster!
PROPHILUS   Sir, by our friendship—
PENTHEA   By our bloods,
Will you quite both undo us, brother?
GRAUSIS   Out on him,
These are his megrims, firks, and melancholies.   155
LEMOPHIL Well said, old touch-hole.
GRONEAS   Kick him out at doors.°
PENTHEA With favour, let me speak.—My lord, what slackness
In my obedience hath deserved this rage?
Except humility and silent duty
Have drawn on your unquiet, my simplicity   160
Ne'er studied your vexation.
BASSANES   Light of beauty,°
Deal not ungently with a desperate wound!
No breach of reason dares make war with her
Whose looks are sovereignty, whose breath is balm.
O that I could preserve thee in fruition°   165
As in devotion!
PENTHEA   Sir, may every evil
Locked in Pandora's box show'r, in your presence,°
On my unhappy head, if since you made me
A partner in your bed, I have been faulty
In one unseemly thought against your honour.   170
ITHOCLES Purge not his griefs, Penthea.
BASSANES   Yes, say on,
Excellent creature.—Good, be not a hindrance
To peace and praise of virtue.—O, my senses
Are charmed with sounds celestial.—On, dear, on.

I never gave you one ill word; say, did I?   175
Indeed I did not.
PENTHEA   Nor, by Juno's forehead,°
Was I e'er guilty of a wanton error.
BASSANES A goddess! Let me kneel.
GRAUSIS   Alas, kind animal.
ITHOCLES No; but for penance—
BASSANES   Noble sir, what is it?
With gladness I embrace it; yet pray let not   180
My rashness teach you to be too unmerciful.
ITHOCLES When you shall show good proof that manly wisdom,
Not overswayed by passion or opinion,
Knows how to lead your judgement, then this lady,°
Your wife, my sister, shall return in safety   185
Home, to be guided by you. But till first
I can out of clear evidence approve it,°
She shall be my care.
BASSANES   Rip my bosom up,
I'll stand the execution with a constancy.
This torture is unsufferable.
ITHOCLES   Well, sir,   190
I dare not trust her to your fury.
BASSANES   But
Penthea says not so.
PENTHEA   She needs no tongue
To plead excuse, who never purposed wrong.
       [*They begin to leave*]
LEMOPHIL [*to Grausis*] Virgin of reverence and antiquity,
Stay you behind.
GRONEAS [*to Grausis*] The court wants not your diligence.   195
       Exeunt all but Bassanes and Grausis
GRAUSIS What will you do, my lord? My lady's gone;
I am denied to follow.
BASSANES   I may see her,
Or speak to her once more.
GRAUSIS   And feel her too, man.
Be of good cheer; she's your own flesh and bone.
BASSANES Diseases desperate must find cures alike.°   200
She swore she has been true.
GRAUSIS   True, on my modesty.
BASSANES Let him want truth who credits not her vows.

Much wrong I did her, but her brother infinite.
Rumour will voice me the contempt of manhood
Should I run on thus. Some way I must try   205
To outdo art and cry a jealousy.°
    Exeunt

3.3

Flourish. Enter Amyclas, Nearchus leading Calantha, Armostes,
Crotolon, Euphrania, Chrystalla, Philema, and Amelus

AMYCLAS Cousin of Argos, what the heavens have pleased
    In their unchanging counsels to conclude
    For both our kingdoms' weal, we must submit to.
    Nor can we be unthankful to their bounties,
    Who, when we were even creeping to our grave,   5
    Sent us a daughter, in whose birth our hope
    Continues of succession. As you are
    In title next, being grandchild to our aunt,
    So we in heart desire you may sit nearest
    Calantha's love, since we have ever vowed   10
    Not to enforce affection by our will,
    But by her own choice to confirm it gladly.
NEARCHUS You speak the nature of a right just father.
    I come not hither roughly to demand
    My cousin's thraldom, but to free mine own.   15
    Report of great Calantha's beauty, virtue,
    Sweetness, and singular perfections, courted
    All ears to credit what I find was published
    By constant truth; from which, if any service
    Of my desert can purchase fair construction,   20
    This lady must command it.
CALANTHA   Princely sir,
    So well you know how to profess observance
    That you instruct your hearers to become
    Practitioners in duty; of which number
    I'll study to be chief.
NEARCHUS   Chief, glorious virgin,   25
    In my devotions, as in all men's wonder.
AMYCLAS Excellent cousin, we deny no liberty;

123

Use thine own opportunities.—Armostes,°
We must consult with the philosophers;
The business is of weight.

ARMOSTES   Sir, at your pleasure.   30

AMYCLAS You told me, Crotolon, your son's returned
From Athens. Wherefore comes 'a not to court
As we commanded?

CROTOLON   He shall soon attend
Your royal will, great sir.

AMYCLAS   The marriage
Between young Prophilus and Euphrania   35
Tastes of too much delay.

CROTOLON   My lord.

AMYCLAS   Some pleasures
At celebration of it would give life
To th'entertainment of the prince our kinsman.
Our court wears gravity more than we relish.

ARMOSTES Yet the heavens smile on all your high attempts,°   40
Without a cloud.

CROTOLON   So may the gods protect us.

CALANTHA [to Nearchus] A prince a subject?

NEARCHUS   Yes, to beauty's sceptre.
As all hearts kneel, so mine.

CALANTHA   You are too courtly.
    [Enter] to them, Ithocles, Orgilus, Prophilus

ITHOCLES [to Orgilus] Your safe return to Sparta is most welcome.
I joy to meet you here, and as occasion   45
Shall grant us privacy, will yield you reasons
Why I should covet to deserve the title
Of your respected friend. For, without compliment,
Believe it, Orgilus, 'tis my ambition.

ORGILUS Your lordship may command me your poor servant.   50

ITHOCLES [aside, seeing Nearchus with Calantha] So amorously
    close?—So soon?—My heart!

PROPHILUS What sudden change is next?

ITHOCLES   Life to the king,
To whom I here present this noble gentleman,
New come from Athens. Royal sir, vouchsafe
Your gracious hand in favour of his merit.   55

CROTOLON [aside] My son preferred by Ithocles!

AMYCLAS   Our bounties

Shall open to thee, Orgilus. For instance—
Hark in thine ear—if out of those inventions
Which flow in Athens thou hast there engrossed
Some rarity of wit to grace the nuptials   60
Of thy fair sister, and renown our court
In th'eyes of this young prince, we shall be debtor
To thy conceit. Think on't.
ORGILUS   Your highness honours me.
NEARCHUS [to Calantha] My tongue and heart are twins.
CALANTHA   A noble birth,
Becoming such a father.—Worthy Orgilus,   65
You are a guest most wished for.
ORGILUS   May my duty
Still rise in your opinion, sacred princess.
ITHOCLES [to Nearchus] Euphrania's brother, sir; a gentleman
Well worthy of your knowledge.
NEARCHUS   We embrace him,
Proud of so dear acquaintance.
AMYCLAS   All prepare   70
For revels and disport. The joys of Hymen,
Like Phoebus in his lustre, puts to flight°
All mists of dullness. Crown the hours with gladness.
No sounds but music; no discourse but mirth.
CALANTHA Thine arm, I prithee, Ithocles. [To Nearchus] Nay, good 75
My lord, keep on your way; I am provided.
NEARCHUS I dare not disobey.
ITHOCLES   Most heavenly lady.
        Exeunt

3.4

Enter Crotolon [and] Orgilus
CROTOLON The king hath spoke his mind.
ORGILUS   His will he hath;
But were it lawful to hold plea against°
The power of greatness, not the reason, haply
Such undershrubs as subjects sometimes might
Borrow of nature justice, to inform   5
That licence sovereignty holds without check

Over a meek obedience.

CROTOLON   How resolve you
Touching your sister's marriage? Prophilus
Is a deserving and a hopeful youth.

ORGILUS I envy not his merit, but applaud it;°   10
Could wish him thrift in all his best desires,
And with a willingness enleague our blood
With his, for purchase of full growth in friendship.
He never touched on any wrong that maliced°
The honour of our house, nor stirred our peace;   15
Yet, with your favour, let me not forget
Under whose wing he gathers warmth and comfort,
Whose creature he is bound, made, and must live so.

CROTOLON Son, son, I find in thee a harsh condition.°
No courtesy can win it; 'tis too rancorous.   20

ORGILUS Good sir, be not severe in your construction.
I am no stranger to such easy calms
As sit in tender bosoms. Lordly Ithocles
Hath graced my entertainment in abundance;
Too humbly hath descended from that height   25
Of arrogance and spleen which wrought the rape
On grieved Penthea's purity. His scorn
Of my untoward fortunes is reclaimed°
Unto a courtship, almost to a fawning.
I'll kiss his foot, since you will have it so.   30

CROTOLON Since I will have it so? Friend, I will have it so,
Without our ruin by your politic plots,
Or wolf of hatred snarling in your breast.
You have a spirit, sir, have ye? A familiar°
That posts i'th' air for your intelligence?   35
Some such hobgoblin hurried you from Athens,
For yet you come unsent for.

ORGILUS   If unwelcome,
I might have found a grave there.

CROTOLON   Sure your business
Was soon dispatched, or your mind altered quickly.

ORGILUS 'Twas care, sir, of my health cut short my journey;   40
For there a general infection°
Threatens a desolation.

CROTOLON   And I fear
Thou hast brought back a worse infection with thee,

Infection of thy mind; which, as thou say'st,
Threatens the desolation of our family.   45
ORGILUS Forbid it, our dear genius! I will rather
Be made a sacrifice on Thrasus' monument,
Or kneel to Ithocles his son in dust,
Than woo a father's curse. My sister's marriage
With Prophilus is from my heart confirmed.   50
May I live hated, may I die despised,
If I omit to further it in all
That can concern me.
CROTOLON   I have been too rough.
My duty to my king made me so earnest;
Excuse it, Orgilus.
ORGILUS   Dear sir.
    Enter to them, Prophilus, Euphrania, Ithocles, Groneas,
        [and] Lemophil
CROTOLON   Here comes   55
Euphrania, with Prophilus and Ithocles.
ORGILUS Most honoured, ever famous.
ITHOCLES   Your true friend;
On earth not any truer.—With smooth eyes°
Look on this worthy couple. Your consent
Can only make them one.
ORGILUS   They have it.—Sister,   60
Thou pawn'dst to me an oath, of which engagement
I never will release thee, if thou aim'st
At any other choice than this.
EUPHRANIA   Dear brother,
At him or none.
CROTOLON   To which my blessing's added.
ORGILUS Which till a greater ceremony perfect,°   65
Euphrania, lend thy hand.—Here, take her, Prophilus.
Live long a happy man and wife; and further,
That these in presence may conclude an omen,
Thus for a bridal song I close my wishes:
            Comforts lasting, loves increasing,   70
            Like soft hours never ceasing;
            Plenty's pleasure, peace complying
            Without jars or tongues envying;
            Hearts by holy union wedded,
            More than theirs by custom bedded;   75

> *Fruitful issues; life so graced,*
> *Not by age to be defaced,*
> *Budding, as the year ensu'th,*
> *Every spring another youth:*
> *All what thought can add beside,*   80
> *Crown this bridegroom and this bride.*

PROPHILUS You have sealed joy close to my soul.—Euphrania,
Now I may call thee mine.

ITHOCLES   I but exchange
One good friend for another.

ORGILUS   If these gallants
Will please to grace a poor invention,   85
By joining with me in some slight device,
I'll venture on a strain my younger days
Have studied for delight.

LEMOPHIL   With thankful willingness
I offer my attendance.

GRONEAS   No endeavour
Of mine shall fail to show itself.

ITHOCLES   We will   90
All join to wait on thy directions, Orgilus.

ORGILUS O my good lord, your favours flow towards
A too unworthy worm. But as you please;
I am what you will shape me.

ITHOCLES   A fast friend.

CROTOLON I thank thee, son, for this acknowledgement;   95
It is a sight of gladness.

ORGILUS   But my duty.°

>   *Exeunt*

3.5

>   *Enter Calantha, Penthea, Chrystalla, [and] Philema*

CALANTHA Whoe'er would speak with us, deny his entrance.
Be careful of our charge.

CHRYSTALLA   We shall, madam.

CALANTHA Except the king himself, give none admittance;
Not any.

PHILEMA   Madam, it shall be our care.

>   [*Exeunt Chrystalla and Philema*]

CALANTHA Being alone, Penthea, you have granted   5
  The opportunity you sought, and might
  At all times have commanded.
PENTHEA   'Tis a benefit
  Which I shall owe your goodness even in death for.
  My glass of life, sweet princess, hath few minutes°
  Remaining to run down; the sands are spent;   10
  For by an inward messenger I feel
  The summons of departure short and certain.°
CALANTHA You feed too much your melancholy.
PENTHEA   Glories
  Of human greatness are but pleasing dreams
  And shadows soon decaying. On the stage   15
  Of my mortality, my youth hath acted
  Some scenes of vanity, drawn out at length
  By varied pleasures, sweetened in the mixture,
  But tragical in issue. Beauty, pomp—
  With every sensuality our giddiness   20
  Doth frame an idol—are inconstant friends°
  When any troubled passion makes assault
  On the unguarded castle of the mind.
CALANTHA Contemn not your condition for the proof
  Of bare opinion only. To what end°   25
  Reach all these moral texts?
PENTHEA   To place before 'ee
  A perfect mirror, wherein you may see
  How weary I am of a ling'ring life,
  Who count the best a misery.
CALANTHA   Indeed
  You have no little cause; yet none so great   30
  As to distrust a remedy.
PENTHEA   That remedy
  Must be a winding-sheet, a fold of lead,°
  And some untrod-on corner in the earth.
  Not to detain your expectation, princess,
  I have an humble suit.
CALANTHA   Speak; I enjoin it.°   35
PENTHEA Vouchsafe, then, to be my executrix,
  And take that trouble on 'ee, to dispose
  Such legacies as I bequeath impartially.
  I have not much to give; the pains are easy.
  Heaven will reward your piety, and thank it   40

When I am dead; for sure I must not live,
I hope I cannot.

CALANTHA   Now beshrew thy sadness;
Thou turn'st me too much woman. [*Calantha weeps*]

PENTHEA [*aside*]   Her fair eyes
Melt into passion. Then I have assurance
Encouraging my boldness. [*To her*]—In this paper   45
My will was charactered; which you, with pardon,
Shall now know from mine own mouth.

CALANTHA   Talk on, prithee;
It is a pretty earnest.

PENTHEA   I have left me
But three poor jewels to bequeath. The first is
My youth; for though I am much old in griefs,   50
In years I am a child.

CALANTHA   To whom that?

PENTHEA To virgin wives, such as abuse not wedlock°
By freedom of desires, but covet chiefly
The pledges of chaste beds for ties of love,
Rather than ranging of their blood. And next   55
To married maids, such as prefer the number°
Of honourable issue in their virtues
Before the flattery of delights by marriage.
May those be ever young.

CALANTHA   A second jewel
You mean to part with.

PENTHEA   'Tis my fame, I trust   60
By scandal yet untouched. This I bequeath
To memory, and Time's old daughter, Truth.°
If ever my unhappy name find mention
When I am fall'n to dust, may it deserve
Beseeming charity without dishonour.   65

CALANTHA How handsomely thou play'st with harmless sport
Of mere imagination. Speak the last:
I strangely like thy will.

PENTHEA   This jewel, madam,
Is dearly precious to me; you must use
The best of your discretion to employ   70
This gift as I intend it.

CALANTHA   Do not doubt me.

PENTHEA 'Tis long agone since first I lost my heart.

Long I have lived without it, else for certain
I should have given that too. But instead
Of it, to great Calantha, Sparta's heir,   75
By service bound, and by affection vowed,
I do bequeath in holiest rites of love,
Mine only brother, Ithocles.

CALANTHA   What saidst thou?

PENTHEA Impute not, heaven-blest lady, to ambition
A faith as humbly perfect as the prayers   80
Of a devoted suppliant can endow it.
Look on him, princess, with an eye of pity;
How like the ghost of what he late appeared,
'A moves before you.

CALANTHA   Shall I answer here,
Or lend my ear too grossly?

PENTHEA   First his heart   85
Shall fall in cinders, scorched by your disdain,
Ere he will dare, poor man, to ope an eye
On these divine looks, but with low-bent thoughts
Accusing such presumption. As for words,
'A dares not utter any but of service.   90
Yet this lost creature loves 'ee.—Be a princess
In sweetness as in blood; give him his doom,
Or raise him up to comfort.

CALANTHA   What new change
Appears in my behaviour, that thou dar'st
Tempt my displeasure?

PENTHEA   I must leave the world   95
To revel Elysium, and 'tis just
To wish my brother some advantage here.
Yet, by my best hopes, Ithocles is ignorant
Of this pursuit. But if you please to kill him,°
Lend him one angry look, or one harsh word,   100
And you shall soon conclude how strong a power
Your absolute authority holds over
His life and end.

CALANTHA   You have forgot, Penthea,
How still I have a father.

PENTHEA   But remember
I am a sister, though to me this brother   105
Hath been, you know, unkind. O, most unkind!

CALANTHA Chrystalla, Philema, where are 'ee?—Lady,
     Your check lies in my silence.
          Enter Chrystalla and Philema
BOTH   Madam, here.
CALANTHA I think 'ee sleep, 'ee drones; wait on Penthea
     Unto her lodging.—[*Aside*] Ithocles? Wronged lady!   110
PENTHEA My reckonings are made even. Death or fate°
     Can now nor strike too soon, nor force too late.
          Exeunt

4.1

Enter Ithocles and Armostes

ITHOCLES Forbear your inquisition. Curiosity
  Is of too subtle and too searching nature:
  In fears of love too quick; too slow of credit.
  I am not what you doubt me.
ARMOSTES   Nephew, be then
  As I would wish.—All is not right.—Good heaven   5
  Confirm your resolutions for dependence
  On worthy ends which may advance your quiet.
ITHOCLES I did the noble Orgilus much injury,
  But grieved Penthea more. I now repent it;
  Now, uncle, now. This 'now' is now too late.   10
  So provident is folly in sad issue
  That after-wit, like bankrupts' debts, stand tallied°
  Without all possibilities of payment.
  Sure he's an honest, very honest gentleman;
  A man of single meaning.
ARMOSTES   I believe it.   15
  Yet nephew, 'tis the tongue informs our ears;
  Our eyes can never pierce into the thoughts,
  For they are lodged too inward. But I question
  No truth in Orgilus.
      Enter Nearchus, leading Calantha [accompanied by] Amelus,
      Chrystalla, [and] Philema
           —The princess, sir.
ITHOCLES The princess? Ha!
ARMOSTES   With her, the Prince of Argos.   20
NEARCHUS Great fair one, grace my hopes with any instance
  Of livery, from the allowance of your favour.
  This little spark—[*indicating Calantha's ring*]
CALANTHA   A toy.
NEARCHUS   Love feasts on toys,
  For Cupid is a child.—Vouchsafe this bounty.
  It cannot be denied.
CALANTHA   You shall not value,   25
  Sweet cousin, at a price, what I count cheap;
  So cheap, that let him take it who dares stoop for't,

And give it at next meeting to a mistress:
She'll thank him for't, perhaps.
     [She] casts it [close] to Ithocles. [He picks it up]
AMELUS   The ring, sir, is
The princess's. I could have took it up.   30
ITHOCLES Learn manners, prithee.—To the blessed owner,
Upon my knees. *[He offers the ring to Calantha]*
NEARCHUS   Y'are saucy.
CALANTHA   This is pretty.
I am, belike, a mistress!—Wondrous pretty.
Let the man keep his fortune, since he found it;
He's worthy on't.—On, cousin.
ITHOCLES *[to Amelus]*   Follow, spaniel;   35
I'll force 'ee to a fawning else.
AMELUS   You dare not.
    Exeunt [all but] Ithocles and Armostes
ARMOSTES My lord, you were too forward.
ITHOCLES   Look 'ee, uncle:
Some such there are whose liberal contents
Swarm without care in every sort of plenty;
Who, after full repasts, can lay them down   40
To sleep; and they sleep, uncle: in which silence
Their very dreams present 'em choice of pleasures;
Pleasures (observe me, uncle) of rare object:
Here heaps of gold, there increments of honours;
Now change of garments, then the votes of people;   45
Anon varieties of beauties, courting°
In flatteries of the night, exchange of dalliance.
Yet these are still but dreams. Give me felicity
Of which my senses waking are partakers;
A real, visible, material happiness—   50
And then, too, when I stagger in expectance
Of the least comfort that can cherish life.
I saw it, sir, I saw it; for it came
From her own hand.
ARMOSTES   The princess threw it t'ee.
ITHOCLES True, and she said—well I remember what.   55
Her cousin prince would beg it.
ARMOSTES   Yes, and parted
In anger at your taking on't.
ITHOCLES   Penthea!

O, thou hast pleaded with a powerful language!
I want a fee to gratify thy merit.
But I will do—
ARMOSTES   What is't you say?
ITHOCLES   In anger,   60
In anger let him part; for could his breath,
Like whirlwinds, toss such servile slaves as lick
The dust his footsteps print into a vapour,
It durst not stir a hair of mine. It should not;
I'd rend it up by th'roots first. To be anything°   65
Calantha smiles on is to be a blessing
More sacred than a petty-prince of Argos
Can wish to equal, or in worth or title.
ARMOSTES Contain yourself, my lord. Ixion, aiming°
To embrace Juno, bosomed but a cloud,°   70
And begat centaurs. 'Tis an useful moral:
Ambition, hatched in clouds of mere opinion,
Proves but in birth a prodigy.
ITHOCLES   I thank 'ee;
Yet, with your licence, I should seem uncharitable
To gentler fate, if, relishing the dainties   75
Of a soul's settled peace, I were so feeble
Not to digest it.
ARMOSTES   He deserves small trust
Who is not privy counsellor to himself.
        Enter Nearchus, Orgilus, and Amelus
NEARCHUS Brave me?
ORGILUS   Your excellence mistakes his temper,
For Ithocles, in fashion of his mind,   80
Is beautiful, soft, gentle, the clear mirror
Of absolute perfection.
AMELUS   Was't your modesty
Termed any of the prince his servants 'spaniel'?°
Your nurse, sure, taught you other language.
ITHOCLES   Language!
NEARCHUS A gallant man at arms is here, a doctor°   85
In feats of chivalry; blunt and rough-spoken,
Vouchsafing not the fustian of civility,
Which less rash spirits style good manners.
ITHOCLES   Manners!°
ORGILUS No more, illustrious sir; 'tis matchless Ithocles.

NEARCHUS You might have understood who I am.
ITHOCLES   Yes,   90
  I did—else—but the presence calmed th'affront.°
  Y'are cousin to the princess.
NEARCHUS   To the king too;
  A certain instrument that lent supportance
  To your colossic greatness—to that king too,
  You might have added.
ITHOCLES   There is more divinity   95
  In beauty than in majesty.
ARMOSTES   O fie, fie!
NEARCHUS This odd youth's pride turns heretic in loyalty.
  Sirrah! Low mushrooms never rival cedars.°
      Exeunt Nearchus and Amelus
ITHOCLES Come back! What pitiful dull thing am I
  So to be tamely scolded at? Come back!   100
  Let him come back and echo once again
  That scornful sound of 'mushroom'! Painted colts,°
  Like heralds' coats gilt o'er with crowns and sceptres,
  May bait a muzzled lion.
ARMOSTES   Cousin, cousin,
  Thy tongue is not thy friend.
ORGILUS   In point of honour   105
  Discretion knows no bounds. Amelus told me
  'Twas all about a little ring.
ITHOCLES   A ring
  The princess threw away, and I took up.
  Admit she threw't to me, what arm of brass
  Can snatch it hence? No, could 'a grind the hoop   110
  To powder, 'a might sooner reach my heart
  Than steal and wear one dust on't.—Orgilus,°
  I am extremely wronged.
ORGILUS   A lady's favour
  Is not to be so slighted.
ITHOCLES   Slighted!
ARMOSTES   Quiet
  These vain unruly passions, which will render ye   115
  Into a madness.
ORGILUS   Griefs will have their vent.
      Enter Tecnicus
ARMOSTES Welcome; thou com'st in season, reverend man,
  To pour the balsam of a supplying patience

Into the festering wound of ill-spent fury.
ORGILUS [*aside*] What makes he here?
TECNICUS   The hurts are yet but mortal,°   120
Which shortly will prove deadly. To the king,
Armostes, see in safety thou deliver
This sealed up counsel; bid him with a constancy°
Peruse the secrets of the gods.—O Sparta,
O Lacedaemon! Double-named, but one   125
In fate. When kingdoms reel (mark well my saw)
Their heads must needs be giddy.—Tell the king
That henceforth he no more must enquire after
My agèd head; Apollo wills it so.
I am for Delphos.
ARMOSTES   Not without some conference   130
With our great master.
TECNICUS   Never more to see him;
A greater prince commands me.—Ithocles,°
When youth is ripe, and age from time doth part,
The lifeless trunk shall wed the broken heart.
ITHOCLES What's this, if understood?
TECNICUS   List, Orgilus.   135
Remember what I told thee long before;°
These tears shall be my witness.
ARMOSTES   'Las, good man.
TECNICUS Let craft with courtesy a while confer,
Revenge proves its own executioner.
ORGILUS Dark sentences are for Apollo's priests: 140
I am not Oedipus.
TECNICUS   My hour is come;°
Cheer up the king. Farewell to all.—O Sparta,
O Lacedaemon!
          Exit Tecnicus
ARMOSTES   If prophetic fire
Have warmed this old man's bosom, we might construe
His words to fatal sense.
ITHOCLES   Leave to the powers   145
Above us, the effects of their decrees;
My burden lies within me. Servile fears
Prevent no great effects.—Divine Calantha!
ARMOSTES The gods be still propitious.
          Exeunt [Ithocles and Armostes]
ORGILUS   Something oddly

The book-man prated; yet 'a talked it weeping: 150
'Let craft with courtesy a while confer,
Revenge proves its own executioner.'
Con it again. For what? It shall not puzzle me;
'Tis dotage of a withered brain. Penthea
Forbade me not her presence; I may see her,   155
And gaze my fill. Why see her then I may;
When if I faint to speak, I must be silent.
    Exit Orgilus

4.2

    Enter Bassanes, Grausis, and Phulas

BASSANES Pray use your recreations; all the service
  I will expect is quietness amongst 'ee.
  Take liberty at home, abroad, at all times,
  And in your charities appease the gods
  Whom I, with my distractions, have offended.   5
GRAUSIS Fair blessings on thy heart!
PHULAS [*aside*]   Here's a rare change.
  My lord, to cure the itch, is surely gelded;
  The cuckold in conceit, hath cast his horns.
BASSANES Betake 'ee to your several occasions,
  And wherein I have heretofore been faulty,   10
  Let your constructions mildly pass it over.
  Henceforth I'll study reformation—more
  I have not for employment.
GRAUSIS   O sweet man!
  Thou art the very honeycomb of honesty.
PHULAS The garland of good will.—Old lady, hold up°   15
  Thy reverend snout, and trot behind me softly,
  As it becomes a mule of ancient carriage.°
    Exeunt [Grausis and Phulas]
BASSANES Beasts only capable of sense, enjoy°
  The benefit of food and ease with thankfulness.
  Such silly creatures, with a grudging, kick not   20
  Against the portion nature hath bestowed.
  But men, endowed with reason and the use

Of reason to distinguish from the chaff
Of abject scarcity the quintessence,
Soul, and elixir of the earth's abundance,   25
The treasures of the sea, the air, nay, heaven,
Repining at these glories of creation,
Are verier beasts than beasts. And of those beasts
The worse am I. I, who was made a monarch
Of what a heart could wish for, a chaste wife,   30
Endeavoured what in me lay to pull down
That temple built for adoration only,
And level't in the dust of causeless scandal.
But, to redeem a sacrilege so impious,
Humility shall pour before the deities   35
I have incensed a largeness of more patience
Than their displeasèd altars can require.
No tempests of commotion shall disquiet
The calms of my composure.
             Enter Orgilus
ORGILUS   I have found thee,
     Thou patron of more horrors than the bulk   40
     Of manhood, hooped about with ribs of iron,
     Can cram within thy breast. Penthea, Bassanes,
     Cursed by thy jealousies—more, by thy dotage—
     Is left a prey to words.
BASSANES   Exercise°
     Your trials for addition to my penance;   45
     I am resolved.
ORGILUS   Play not with misery
     Past cure: some angry minister of fate hath
     Deposed the empress of her soul, her reason,
     From its most proper throne; but, what's the miracle
     More new, I, I have seen it, and yet live.   50
BASSANES You may delude my senses, not my judgement:
     'Tis anchored into a firm resolution.
     Dalliance of mirth or wit can ne'er unfix it.
     Practise yet further.
ORGILUS   May thy death of love to her
     Damn all thy comforts to a lasting fast   55
     From every joy of life: thou barren rock,
     By thee we have been split in ken of harbour.°

Enter Ithocles, Penthea, her hair about her ears,° Philema,
Chrystalla, [and Armostes]

ITHOCLES Sister, look up; your Ithocles, your brother,
Speaks t'ee. Why do you weep? Dear, turn not from me.—
Here is a killing sight: lo, Bassanes,   60
A lamentable object.
ORGILUS   Man, dost see't?
Sports are more gamesome; am I yet in merriment?
Why dost not laugh?
BASSANES   Divine, and best of ladies,
Please to forget my outrage. Mercy ever
Cannot but lodge under a roof so excellent.   65
I have cast off that cruelty of frenzy
Which once appeared impostorous, and then juggled
To cheat my sleeps of rest.
ORGILUS   Was I in earnest?
PENTHEA Sure if we were all sirens, we should sing pitifully;°
And 'twere a comely music when in parts°   70
One sung another's knell. The turtle sighs
When he hath lost his mate, and yet some say
'A must be dead first. 'Tis a fine deceit
To pass away in a dream. Indeed, I've slept
With mine eyes open a great while. No falsehood   75
Equals a broken faith. There's not a hair
Sticks on my head but like a leaden plummet
It sinks me to the grave. I must creep thither;
The journey is not long.
ITHOCLES   But thou, Penthea,
Hast many years, I hope, to number yet   80
Ere thou canst travel that way.
BASSANES   Let the sun first
Be wrapped up in an everlasting darkness,
Before the light of nature, chiefly formed
For the whole world's delight, feel an eclipse
So universal.
ORGILUS   Wisdom, look 'ee, begins   85
To rave.—Art thou mad too, antiquity?°
PENTHEA Since I was first a wife, I might have been
Mother to many pretty prattling babes.
They would have smiled when I smiled; and, for certain,
I should have cried when they cried.—Truly, brother,   90

My father would have picked me out a husband,
And then my little ones had been no bastards.
But 'tis too late for me to marry now,
I am past child-bearing; 'tis not my fault.°
BASSANES Fall on me, if there be a burning Etna,°   95
And bury me in flames! Sweats hot as sulphur
Boil through my pores! Affliction hath in store
No torture like to this.
ORGILUS   Behold a patience!
Lay by thy whining, grey dissimulation;
Do something worth a chronicle. Show justice   100
Upon the author of this mischief; dig out
The jealousies that hatched this thraldom first
With thine own poniard. Every antic rapture
Can roar as thine does.
ITHOCLES   Orgilus, forbear.
BASSANES Disturb him not, it is a talking motion   105
Provided for my torment. What a fool am I
To bandy passion. Ere I'll speak a word
I will look on and burst.
PENTHEA [to Orgilus]   I loved you once.
ORGILUS Thou didst, wronged creature, in despite of malice.
For it I love thee ever.
PENTHEA   Spare your hand;   110
Believe me, I'll not hurt it.
ORGILUS [giving Penthea his hand] Pain my heart too.
PENTHEA Complain not though I wring it hard. I'll kiss it;
O, 'tis a fine soft palm. Hark in thine ear—
Like whom do I look, prithee? Nay, no whispering.
Goodness! We had been happy. Too much happiness   115
Will make folk proud, they say—but that is he—
        (Points at Ithocles)
And yet he paid for't home. Alas, his heart°
Is crept into the cabinet of the princess;°
We shall have points and bride-laces. Remember°
When we last gathered roses in the garden   120
I found my wits, but truly you lost yours.
That's he, and still 'tis he.
        [Points again at Ithocles]
ITHOCLES   Poor soul, how idly
Her fancies guide her tongue.

BASSANES [*aside*]   Keep in, vexation,
And break not into clamour.
ORGILUS [*aside*]   She has tutored me:
Some powerful inspiration checks my laziness.—   125
Now let me kiss your hand, grieved beauty.
PENTHEA   Kiss it.
Alack, alack, his lips be wondrous cold;
Dear soul, h'as lost his colour. Have 'ee seen
A straying heart? All crannies, every drop
Of blood is turnèd to an amethyst,   130
Which married bachelors hang in their ears.
ORGILUS Peace usher her into Elysium.
If this be madness, madness is an oracle.°
        Exit Orgilus
ITHOCLES Chrystalla, Philema, when slept my sister,
Her ravings are so wild?
CHRYSTALLA   Sir, not these ten days.   135
PHILEMA We watch by her continually; besides,
We cannot any way pray her to eat.
BASSANES O, misery of miseries!
PENTHEA [*to Bassanes*]   Take comfort;
You may live well and die a good old man.
By yea and nay, an oath not to be broken,   140
[*to Crotolon*] If you had joined our hands once in the temple—
'Twas since my father died, for had he lived
He would have done't—I must have called you father.
O, my wracked honour, ruined by those tyrants,
A cruel brother, and a desperate dotage!   145
There is no peace left for a ravished wife
Widowed by lawless marriage; to all memory
Penthea's, poor Penthea's name is strumpeted.
But since her blood was seasoned by the forfeit
Of noble shame, with mixtures of pollution,   150
Her blood—'tis just—be henceforth never heightened
With taste of sustenance. Starve; let that fullness
Whose pleurisy hath fevered faith and modesty—°
Forgive me. O, I faint!
ARMOSTES   Be not so wilful,
Sweet niece, to work thine own destruction.
ITHOCLES   Nature   155
Will call her daughter, monster.—What? Not eat?

Refuse the only ordinary means
Which are ordained for life? Be not, my sister,
A murd'ress to thyself.—Hear'st thou this, Bassanes?
BASSANES Foh! I am busy; for I have not thoughts   160
Enough to think all shall be well anon;°
'Tis tumbling in my head. There is a mastery
In art to fatten and keep smooth the outside;
Yes, and to comfort up the vital spirits
Without the help of food, fumes or perfumes,°   165
Perfumes or fumes. Let her alone; I'll search out
The trick on't.
PENTHEA   Lead me gently; heavens reward ye.
Griefs are sure friends; they leave, without control,
Nor cure nor comforts for a leprous soul.°
        Exeunt [Chrystalla and Philema], supporting Penthea
BASSANES I grant t'ee and will put in practice instantly   170
What you shall still admire. 'Tis wonderful,
'Tis super-singular, not to be matched.
Yet when I've done't, I've done't; ye shall all thank me.
        Exit Bassanes
ARMOSTES The sight is full of terror.
ITHOCLES   On my soul
Lies such an infinite clog of massy dullness   175
As that I have not sense enough to feel it.
        Enter Nearchus and Amelus
See, uncle, th'augury thing returns again;°
Shall's welcome him with thunder? We are haunted,
And must use exorcism to conjure down
This spirit of malevolence.
ARMOSTES   Mildly, nephew.   180
NEARCHUS I come not, sir, to chide your late disorder,
Admitting that th'inurement to a roughness
In soldiers of your years and fortunes, chiefly
So lately prosperous, hath not yet shook off
The custom of the war in hours of leisure.   185
Nor shall you need excuse, since y'are to render
Account to that fair excellence, the princess,
Who in her private gallery expects it
From your own mouth alone: I am a messenger
But to her pleasure.
ITHOCLES   Excellent Nearchus,   190

Be prince still of my services, and conquer
Without the combat of dispute. I honour 'ee.°
NEARCHUS The king is on a sudden indisposed;
Physicians are called for. 'Twere fit, Armostes,
You should be near him.
ARMOSTES   Sir, I kiss your hands.   195
    Exeunt [all but Nearchus and Amelus]
NEARCHUS Amelus, I perceive Calantha's bosom
Is warmed with other fires than such as can
Take strength from any fuel of the love
I might address to her. Young Ithocles,
Or ever I mistake, is lord ascendant°   200
Of her devotions; one, to speak him truly,
In every disposition nobly fashioned.
AMELUS But can your Highness brook to be so rivalled,
Considering th'inequality of the persons?
NEARCHUS I can, Amelus; for affections injured   205
By tyranny, or rigour of compulsion,
Like tempest-threatened trees unfirmly rooted,
Ne'er spring to timely growth. Observe, for instance,
Life-spent Penthea and unhappy Orgilus.
AMELUS How does your grace determine?
NEARCHUS   To be jealous°   210
In public of what privately I'll further;
And though they shall not know, yet they shall find it.
    Exeunt

4.3

*Enter Lemophil and Groneas, leading Amyclas and placing
him in a chair, followed by Armostes [carrying a box],
Crotolon, and Prophilus*

AMYCLAS Our daughter is not near?
ARMOSTES   She is retired, sir,
Into her gallery.
AMYCLAS   Where's the prince our cousin?
PROPHILUS New walked into the grove, my lord.
AMYCLAS   All leave us
Except Armostes, and you, Crotolon;

We would be private.
PROPHILUS   Health unto your majesty.   5
        Exeunt Prophilus, Lemophil, and Groneas
AMYCLAS What, Tecnicus is gone?
ARMOSTES   He is to Delphos;
And to your royal hands presents this box.
AMYCLAS Unseal it, good Armostes; therein lies
    The secrets of the oracle. Out with it.
        [*Armostes lifts out the scroll and breaks the seal*]
    Apollo live our patron! Read, Armostes.   10
ARMOSTES   *The plot in which the vine takes root*
                Begins to dry, from head to foot;
                The stock soon withering, want of sap
                Doth cause to quail the budding grape.
                But from the neighbouring elm, a dew   15
                Shall drop and feed the plot anew.
AMYCLAS That is the oracle. What exposition
    Makes the philosopher?
ARMOSTES   This brief one only:
        The plot is Sparta, the dried vine the king.
        The quailing grape his daughter; but the thing   20
        Of most importance, not to be revealed,
        Is a near prince, the elm; the rest concealed.
                                        Tecnicus.
AMYCLAS Enough. Although the opening of this riddle°
    Be but itself a riddle, yet we construe   25
    How near our labouring age draws to a rest.
    But must Calantha quail too, that young grape
    Untimely budded? I could mourn for her.
    Her tenderness hath yet deserv'd no rigour
    So to be cross'd by fate.
ARMOSTES   You misapply, sir—   30
    With favour let me speak it—what Apollo
    Hath clouded in hid sense. I here conjecture
    Her marriage with some neighb'ring prince, the dew
    Of which befriending elm shall ever strengthen
    Your subjects with a sovereignty of power.   35
CROTOLON Besides, most gracious lord, the pith of oracles
    Is to be then digested when th'events
    Expound their truth, not brought as soon to light
    As uttered. Truth is child of Time, and herein

I find no scruple; rather cause of comfort,   40
With unity of kingdoms.
AMYCLAS   May it prove so
For weal of this dear nation.—Where is Ithocles?
Armostes, Crotolon, when this withered vine
Of my frail carcass, on the funeral pile
Is fired into its ashes, let that young man   45
Be hedged about still with your cares and loves.
Much owe I to his worth, much to his service.
Let such as wait come in now.
ARMOSTES   All attend here!
    Enter Ithocles, Calantha, Prophilus, Orgilus, Euphrania,
    Lemophil, and Groneas
CALANTHA Dear sir, king, father!
ITHOCLES   O my royal master!
AMYCLAS Cleave not my heart, sweet twins of my life's solace,   50
With your forejudging fears. There is no physic
So cunningly restorative to cherish
The fall of age, or call back youth and vigour,
As your consents in duty. I will shake off
This languishing disease of time, to quicken   55
Fresh pleasures in these drooping hours of sadness.
Is fair Euphrania married yet to Prophilus?
CROTOLON This morning, gracious lord.
ORGILUS   This very morning;
Which, with your highness' leave, you may observe too.
Our sister looks, methinks, mirthful and sprightly;   60
As if her chaster fancy could already
Expound the riddle of her gain in losing
A trifle; maids know only that they know not.°
Pish! prithee blush not; 'tis but honest change
Of fashion in the garment, loose for strait,°   65
And so the modest maid is made a wife.
Shrewd business, is't not, sister?
EUPHRANIA   You are pleasant.°
AMYCLAS We thank thee, Orgilus; this mirth becomes thee.
But wherefore sits the court in such a silence?
A wedding without revels is not seemly.   70
CALANTHA Your late indisposition, sir, forbade it.
AMYCLAS Be it thy charge, Calantha, to set forward
The bridal sports, to which I will be present;

If not, at least consenting.—Mine own Ithocles,
I have done little for thee yet.

ITHOCLES   Y'have built me   75
To the full height I stand in.

CALANTHA [*aside*]   Now or never!—
May I propose a suit?

AMYCLAS   Demand and have it.

CALANTHA Pray, sir, give me this young man, and no further
Account him yours than he deserves in all things
To be thought worthy mine. I will esteem him   80
According to his merit.

AMYCLAS   Still th'art my daughter,
Still grow'st upon my heart.—[*To Ithocles*] Give me thine hand.—
Calantha, take thine own. In noble actions
Thou'lt find him firm and absolute.—I would not
Have parted with thee, Ithocles, to any   85
But to a mistress who is all what I am.

ITHOCLES A change, great king, most wished for, 'cause the same.

CALANTHA Th'art mine.—Have I now kept my word?

ITHOCLES   Divinely.

ORGILUS Rich fortunes guard the favour of a princess;°
Rock thee, brave man, in ever-crownèd plenty.   90
Y'are minion of the time; be thankful for it.—
[*Aside*] Ho, here's a swinge in destiny!—Apparent,
The youth is up on tiptoe, yet may stumble.°

AMYCLAS On to your recreations. Now convey me
Unto my bedchamber. None on his forehead   95
Wear a distempered look.

ALL   The gods preserve 'ee.

CALANTHA [*aside to Ithocles*] Sweet, be not from my sight.

ITHOCLES [*aside to Calantha*]   My whole felicity!

        Exeunt, carrying out the king; Orgilus stays Ithocles

ORGILUS Shall I be bold, my lord?

ITHOCLES   Thou canst not, Orgilus.
Call me thine own, for Prophilus must henceforth
Be all thy sister's; friendship, though it cease not   100
In marriage, yet is oft at less command
Than when a single freedom can dispose it.

ORGILUS Most right, my most good lord, my most great lord,
My gracious princely lord—I might add, royal.

ITHOCLES Royal? A subject royal?

ORGILUS   Why not, pray, sir?   105
  The sovereignty of kingdoms in their nonage
  Stooped to desert, not birth. There's as much merit
  In clearness of affection as in puddle
  Of generation. You have conquered love
  Even in the loveliest; if I greatly err not,   110
  The son of Venus hath bequeathed his quiver
  To Ithocles his manage, by whose arrows°
  Calantha's breast is opened.
ITHOCLES   Can't be possible?
ORGILUS I was myself a piece of suitor once,
  And forward in preferment too; so forward,   115
  That, speaking truth, I may without offence, sir,
  Presume to whisper that my hopes and, hark 'ee,
  My certainty of marriage, stood assured
  With as firm footing (by your leave) as any's
  Now at this very instant—but—
ITHOCLES   'Tis granted.   120
  And for a league of privacy between us,
  Read o'er my bosom and partake a secret.
  The princess is contracted mine.
ORGILUS   Still: why not?
  I now applaud her wisdom. When your kingdom
  Stands seated in your will, secure and settled,   125
  I dare pronounce you will be a just monarch.
  Greece must admire, and tremble.
ITHOCLES   Then the sweetness
  Of so imparadised a comfort, Orgilus!
  It is to banquet with the gods.
ORGILUS   The glory
  Of numerous children, potency of nobles,   130
  Bent knees, hearts paved to tread on.
ITHOCLES   With a friendship
  So dear, so fast as thine.
ORGILUS   I am unfitting
  For office, but for service.
ITHOCLES   We'll distinguish
  Our fortunes merely in the title; partners
  In all respects else but the bed.
ORGILUS   The bed?   135
  Forfend it, Jove's own jealousy, till lastly

We slip down in the common earth together;
And there our beds are equal, save some monument
To show this was the king, and this the subject.
  Soft sad music
List, what sad sounds are these? Extremely sad ones. 140
ITHOCLES Sure from Penthea's lodgings.
ORGILUS   Hark, a voice too.

     A Song [within]°
PHILEMA *O no more, no more; too late*
   Sighs are spent. The burning tapers
   Of a life as chaste as fate,
   Pure as are unwritten papers, 145
    Are burnt out. No heat, no light
    Now remains; 'tis ever night.
   Love is dead; let lovers' eyes,
    Locked in endless dreams,
    Th'extremes of all extremes, 150
   Ope no more, for now love dies,
    Now love dies, implying
   Love's martyrs must be ever, ever dying.

ITHOCLES O my misgiving heart!
ORGILUS   A horrid stillness
Succeeds this deathful air; let's know the reason. 155
Tread softly; there is mystery in mourning.
  Exeunt

4.4

  Enter Chrystalla and Philema, bringing in Penthea in a
  chair, veiled; two other servants placing two chairs, one on
  the one side, and the other with an engine° on the other. The
  maids sit down at her feet, mourning. The servants go out;
  meet them Ithocles and Orgilus
SERVANT [*aside to Orgilus*] 'Tis done; that on her right hand.
ORGILUS   Good, begone.
  [*Exeunt servants*]
ITHOCLES Soft peace enrich this room.
ORGILUS   How fares the lady?

PHILEMA Dead.
CHRYSTALLA   Dead!
PHILEMA   Starved.
CHRYSTALLA   Starved!
ITHOCLES   Me miserable!
ORGILUS   Tell us
  How parted she from life?
PHILEMA   She called for music,
  And begged some gentle voice to tune a farewell   5
  To life and griefs. Chrystalla touched the lute;
  I wept the funeral song.
CHRYSTALLA   Which scarce was ended,
  But her last breath sealed up these hollow sounds,
  'O cruel Ithocles, and injured Orgilus!'
  So down she drew her veil; so died.
ITHOCLES   So died!   10
ORGILUS [*To Chrystalla and Philema*] Up! You are messengers of
  death, go from us.
  Here's woe enough to court without a prompter.
  Away; and hark ye, till you see us next,
  No syllable that she is dead.—Away;
  Keep a smooth brow.
      Exeunt Philema and Chystalla
        —My lord.
ITHOCLES   Mine only sister;   15
  Another is not left me.
ORGILUS   Take that chair;
  I'll seat me here in this. Between us sits
  The object of our sorrows. Some few tears
  We'll part among us; I perhaps can mix
  One lamentable story to prepare 'em.   20
  There, there, sit there, my lord.
ITHOCLES   Yes, as you please.
    (*Ithocles sits down, and is catched in the engine*)
  What means this treachery?
ORGILUS   Caught, you are caught,
  Young master; 'tis thy throne of coronation,
  Thou fool of greatness. See, I take this veil off;
  Survey a beauty withered by the flames   25
  Of an insulting Phaethon, her brother.°
ITHOCLES Thou mean'st to kill me basely.

ORGILUS   I foreknew
  The last act of her life, and trained thee hither
  To sacrifice a tyrant to a turtle.
  You dreamt of kingdoms, did 'ee? How to bosom   30
  The delicacies of a youngling princess,
  How with this nod to grace that subtle courtier,
  How with that frown to make this noble tremble,
  And so forth; whiles Penthea's groans, and tortures,
  Her agonies, her miseries, afflictions,   35
  Ne'er touched upon your thought. As for my injuries,
  Alas, they were beneath your royal pity,
  But yet they lived, thou proud man, to confound thee.
  Behold thy fate, this steel. [*Draws a dagger*]
ITHOCLES   Strike home; a courage
  As keen as thy revenge shall give it welcome.   40
  But prithee faint not; if the wound close up,
  Tent it with double force, and search it deeply.
  Thou look'st that I should whine, and beg compassion,
  As loth to leave the vainness of my glories.
  A statelier resolution arms my confidence,   45
  To cozen thee of honour. Neither could I,
  With equal trial of unequal fortune,
  By hazard of a duel; 'twere a bravery
  Too mighty for a slave intending murder.
  On to the execution, and inherit   50
  A conflict with thy horrors.
ORGILUS   By Apollo,
  Thou talk'st a goodly language; for requital,
  I will report thee to thy mistress richly.
  And take this peace along: some few short minutes
  Determined, my resolves shall quickly follow°   55
  Thy wrathful ghost. Then, if we tug for mastery,
  Penthea's sacred eyes shall lend new courage.
  Give me thy hand; be healthful in thy parting
  From lost mortality. Thus, thus, I free it.
    [*Stabs him*]
ITHOCLES Yet, yet, I scorn to shrink.
ORGILUS   Keep up thy spirit.   60
  I will be gentle even in blood; to linger
  Pain, which I strive to cure, were to be cruel.
    [*Stabs him again*]

ITHOCLES Nimble in vengeance, I forgive thee. Follow
     Safety, with best success. O, may it prosper!
     Penthea, by thy side thy brother bleeds: 65
     The earnest of his wrongs to thy forced faith.
     Thoughts of ambition, or delicious banquet,
     With beauty, youth, and love, together perish
     In my last breath, which on the sacred altar
     Of a long-looked-for peace—now—moves—to heaven.   70
          Dies
ORGILUS Farewell, fair spring of manhood; henceforth welcome
     Best expectation of a noble suff'rance.
     I'll lock the bodies safe, till what must follow
     Shall be approved.—Sweet twins, shine stars forever.
     In vain they build their hopes, whose life is shame;   75
     No monument lasts but a happy name.
          Exit Orgilus°

5.1

Enter Bassanes, alone

BASSANES Athens, to Athens I have sent, the nursery
Of Greece for learning, and the fount of knowledge.
For here in Sparta there's not left amongst us
One wise man to direct; we're all turned madcaps.
'Tis said Apollo is the god of herbs;   5
Then certainly he knows the virtue of 'em.
To Delphos I have sent too; if there can be
A help for nature, we are sure yet.
    Enter Orgilus

ORGILUS   Honour°
Attend thy counsels ever.

BASSANES   I beseech thee
With all my heart, let me go from thee quietly;   10
I will not aught to do with thee of all men.
The doublers of a hare, or, in a morning,°
Salutes from a splay-footed witch, to drop
Three drops of blood at th'nose, just and no more,
Croaking of ravens, or the screech of owls,   15
Are not so boding mischief as thy crossing
My private meditations. Shun me, prithee;
And if I cannot love thee heartily,
I'll love thee as well as I can.

ORGILUS   Noble Bassanes,
Mistake me not.

BASSANES   Phew, then we shall be troubled.   20
Thou wert ordained my plague; heaven make me thankful,
And give me patience too, heaven, I beseech thee.

ORGILUS Accept a league of amity; for henceforth,
I vow by my best genius, in a syllable
Never to speak vexation. I will study   25
Service and friendship with a zealous sorrow
For my past incivility towards 'ee.

BASSANES Heyday! Good words, good words. I must believe 'em,
And be a coxcomb for my labour.

ORGILUS   Use not
So hard a language; your misdoubt is causeless.   30

153

For instance, if you promise to put on
A constancy of patience—such a patience
As chronicle or history ne'er mentioned,
As follows not example, but shall stand
A wonder and a theme for imitation,   35
The first, the index pointing to a second—
I will acquaint 'ee with an unmatched secret,
Whose knowledge to your griefs shall set a period.

BASSANES Thou canst not, Orgilus; 'tis in the power
Of the gods only. Yet, for satisfaction,   40
Because I note an earnest in thine utterance,
Unforced and naturally free, be resolute
The virgin bays shall not withstand the lightning
With a more careless danger, than my constancy°
The full of thy relation. Could it move   45
Distraction in a senseless marble statue,
It should find me a rock. I do expect now
Some truth of unheard moment.

ORGILUS   To your patience°
You must add privacy, as strong in silence
As mysteries locked up in Jove's own bosom.   50

BASSANES A skull hid in the earth a treble age
Shall sooner prate.

ORGILUS   Lastly, to such direction
As the severity of a glorious action
Deserves to lead your wisdom and your judgement,
You ought to yield obedience.

BASSANES   With assurance   55
Of will and thankfulness.

ORGILUS   With manly courage
Please then to follow me.

BASSANES   Where'er, I fear not.
     Exeunt

5.2

Loud music. Enter Groneas and Lemophil leading Euphrania;
Chrystalla and Philema leading Prophilus; Nearchus
supporting Calantha;° Crotolon and Amelus. Loud music
ceases;° all make a stand

CALANTHA We miss our servant Ithocles and Orgilus;
On whom attend they?

CROTOLON   My son, gracious princess,
Whispered some new device, to which these revels
Should be but usher, wherein I conceive
Lord Ithocles and he himself are actors.   5

CALANTHA A fair excuse for absence. As for Bassanes,
Delights to him are troublesome. Armostes
Is with the king?

CROTOLON   He is.

CALANTHA   On to the dance.—
Dear cousin, hand you the bride; the bridegroom must be
Intrusted to my courtship.—Be not jealous,   10
Euphrania; I shall scarcely prove a temptress.—
Fall to our dance.

Music. Nearchus dance[s] with Euphrania, Prophilus with
Calantha, Chrystalla with Lemophil, Philema with
Groneas. [They] dance the first change,° during which, enter
Armostes

ARMOSTES (*in Calantha's ear*) The king your father's dead.

CALANTHA To the other change.

ARMOSTES   Is't possible?

Dance again. Enter Bassanes

BASSANES [*in Calantha's ear*]   O, madam!
Penthea, poor Penthea's starved.

CALANTHA   Beshrew thee.—
Lead to the next.

BASSANES   Amazement dulls my senses.   15

Dance again. Enter Orgilus

ORGILUS [*in Calantha's ear*] Brave Ithocles is murdered, murdered
cruelly.

CALANTHA How dull this music sounds! Strike up more sprightly;
Our footings are not active like our heart
Which treads the nimbler measure.

ORGILUS   I am thunderstruck.
      Last change. Cease music
CALANTHA So, let us breathe awhile. Hath not this motion   20
      Raised fresh colour on your cheeks?
NEARCHUS   Sweet princess,
      A perfect purity of blood enamels
      The beauty of your white.
CALANTHA   We all look cheerfully.
      And cousin, 'tis, methinks, a rare presumption
      In any who prefers our lawful pleasures   25
      Before their own sour censure, to interrupt
      The custom of this ceremony bluntly.
NEARCHUS None dares, lady.
CALANTHA Yes, yes; some hollow voice delivered to me
      How that the king was dead.
ARMOSTES   The king is dead.   30
      That fatal news was mine; for in mine arms
      He breathed his last, and with his crown bequeathed 'ee
      Your mother's wedding ring, which here I tender.
CROTOLON Most strange!
CALANTHA   Peace crown his ashes. We are queen, then.
NEARCHUS Long live Calantha, Sparta's sovereign queen!   35
ALL Long live the queen!
CALANTHA   What whispered Bassanes?
BASSANES That my Penthea, miserable soul,
      Was starved to death.
CALANTHA   She's happy; she hath finished
      A long and painful progress.—A third murmur
      Pierced mine unwilling ears.
ORGILUS   That Ithocles   40
      Was murdered; rather butchered, had not bravery
      Of an undaunted spirit, conquering terror,
      Proclaimed his last act triumph over ruin.
ARMOSTES How? Murdered!
CALANTHA   By whose hand?
ORGILUS [*draws his dagger*]   By mine; this weapon
      Was instrument to my revenge. The reasons   45
      Are just and known; quit him of these, and then
      Never lived gentleman of greater merit,
      Hope, or habiliment to steer a kingdom.°
CROTOLON Fie, Orgilus!

EUPHRANIA   Fie, brother!
CALANTHA   You have done it.
BASSANES How it was done let him report, the forfeit   50
      Of whose allegiance to our laws doth covet
      Rigour of justice; but that done it is,
      Mine eyes have been an evidence of credit
      Too sure to be convinced. Armostes, rend not°
      Thine arteries with hearing the bare circumstances   55
      Of these calamities. Thou'st lost a nephew,
      A niece, and I a wife. Continue man still;
      Make me the pattern of digesting evils,
      Who can outlive my mighty ones, not shrinking
      At such a pressure as would sink a soul   60
      Into what's most of death, the worst of horrors.
      But I have sealed a covenant with sadness,
      And entered into bonds without condition
      To stand these tempests calmly.—Mark me, nobles,
      I do not shed a tear, not for Penthea.   65
      Excellent misery!
CALANTHA   We begin our reign
      With a first act of justice.—Thy confession,
      Unhappy Orgilus, dooms thee a sentence.
      But yet thy father's or thy sister's presence
      Shall be excused.—Give, Crotolon, a blessing   70
      To thy lost son.—Euphrania, take a farewell,
      And both be gone.
CROTOLON   Confirm thee, noble sorrow,
      In worthy resolution.
EUPHRANIA   Could my tears speak,
      My griefs were slight.
ORGILUS   All goodness dwell amongst ye.
      Enjoy my sister, Prophilus; my vengeance   75
      Aimed never at thy prejudice.
CALANTHA   Now withdraw.
      Exeunt Crotolon, Prophilus, and Euphrania
      Bloody relater of thy stains in blood;
      For that thou hast reported him whose fortunes
      And life by thee are both at once snatched from him
      With honourable mention, make thy choice   80
      Of what death likes thee best; there's all our bounty.
      But to excuse delays, let me, dear cousin,

Entreat you and these lords see execution
Instant, before 'ee part.

NEARCHUS   Your will commands us.

ORGILUS One suit, just queen; my last. Vouchsafe your clemency   85
That by no common hand I be divided
From this my humble frailty.

CALANTHA   To their wisdoms°
Who are to be spectators of thine end,
I make the reference. Those that are dead°
Are dead. Had they not now died, of necessity   90
They must have paid the debt they owed to nature,
One time or other. Use dispatch, my lords;
We'll suddenly prepare our coronation.
    Exeunt Calantha, Philema, [and] Chrystalla

ARMOSTES 'Tis strange these tragedies should never touch on
Her female pity.

BASSANES   She has a masculine spirit.   95
And wherefore should I pule, and like a girl
Put finger in the eye? Let's be all toughness,
Without distinction betwixt sex and sex.

NEARCHUS Now Orgilus, thy choice.

ORGILUS   To bleed to death.°

ARMOSTES The executioner?

ORGILUS   Myself; no surgeon.   100
I am well skilled in letting blood. Bind fast
This arm, that so the pipes may from their conduits°
Convey a full stream. Here's a skilful instrument.
    [*Shows his dagger*]
Only I am a beggar to some charity
To speed me in this execution,   105
By lending th'other prick to th'tother arm,
When this is bubbling life out.

BASSANES   I am for 'ee.
It most concerns my art, my care, my credit.
Quick, fillet both these arms.

ORGILUS   Gramercy, friendship.°
Such courtesies are real which flow cheerfully   110
Without an expectation of requital.
Reach me a staff in this hand. If a proneness
Or custom in my nature, from my cradle,
Had been inclined to fierce and eager bloodshed,

A coward guilt, hid in a coward quaking,   115
Would have betrayed fame to ignoble flight
And vagabond pursuit of dreadful safety.
But look upon my steadiness, and scorn not
The sickness of my fortune, which since Bassanes
Was husband to Penthea, had lain bed-rid.   120
We trifle time in words. Thus I show cunning
In opening of a vein too full, too lively.
     [*Opens a vein*]
ARMOSTES Desperate courage!
ORGILUS   Honourable infamy.°
LEMOPHIL I tremble at the sight.
GRONEAS   Would I were loose.°
BASSANES It sparkles like a lusty wine new broached;   125
The vessel must be sound from which it issues.
Grasp hard this other stick. I'll be as nimble.
But prithee look not pale. Have at 'ee; stretch out
Thine arm with vigour and unshook virtue.
     [*Opens another vein*]
Good. O, I envy not a rival fitted   130
To conquer in extremities. This pastime
Appears majestical. Some high-tuned poem
Hereafter shall deliver to posterity
The writer's glory and his subject's triumph.
How is't, man? Droop not yet.
ORGILUS   I feel no palsies.   135
On a pair-royal do I wait in death:°
My sovereign, as his liegeman; on my mistress,
As a devoted servant; and on Ithocles,
As if no brave, yet no unworthy enemy.
Nor did I use an engine to entrap   140
His life out of a slavish fear to combat
Youth, strength, or cunning, but for that I durst not
Engage the goodness of a cause on fortune,°
By which his name might have outfaced my vengeance.
Ah Tecnicus, inspired with Phoebus' fire,   145
I call to mind thy augury; 'twas perfect:
'Revenge proves its own executioner.'
When feeble man is bending to his mother,°
The dust 'a was first framed on, thus he totters.
BASSANES Life's fountain is dried up.

ORGILUS   So falls the standards°   150
　　Of my prerogative in being a creature.
　　A mist hangs o'er mine eyes; the sun's bright splendour
　　Is clouded in an everlasting shadow.
　　Welcome, thou ice that sitt'st about my heart;
　　No heat can ever thaw thee.
　　　　Dies
NEARCHUS   Speech hath left him.   155
BASSANES 'A has shook hands with time. His funeral urn
　　Shall be my charge. Remove the bloodless body.
　　The coronation must require attendance;
　　That past, my few days can be but one mourning.
　　　　Exeunt [with the body]

5.3

An altar covered with white. Two lights of virgin wax. Music
of recorders, during which enter four bearing Ithocles on a
hearse, or in a chair, in a rich robe, and a crown on his head.
[They] place him on one side of the altar. After him enter
Calantha in a white robe and crowned; Euphrania, Philema,
Chrystalla in white; Nearchus, Armostes, Crotolon, Prophilus,
Amelus, Bassanes, Lemophil, and Groneas. Calantha goes and
kneels before the altar. The rest stand off, the women kneeling
behind. Cease recorders during her devotions. Soft music.
Calantha and the rest rise, doing obeisance to the altar.

CALANTHA Our orisons are heard; the gods are merciful.
　　Now tell me, you whose loyalties pays tribute
　　To us your lawful sovereign, how unskilful
　　Your duties or obedience is to render
　　Subjection to the sceptre of a virgin,   5
　　Who have been ever fortunate in princes
　　Of masculine and stirring composition.
　　A woman has enough to govern wisely
　　Her own demeanours, passions, and divisions.
　　A nation, warlike and inured to practice   10
　　Of policy and labour, cannot brook
　　A feminate authority. We therefore
　　Command your counsel, how you may advise us

In choosing of a husband whose abilities
Can better guide this kingdom.

NEARCHUS   Royal lady,   15
Your law is in your will.

ARMOSTES   We have seen tokens
Of constancy too lately to mistrust it.

CROTOLON Yet if your highness settle on a choice
By your own judgement both allowed and liked of,
Sparta may grow in power, and proceed   20
To an increasing height.

CALANTHA [*to Bassanes*] Hold you the same mind?

BASSANES Alas, great mistress, reason is so clouded
With the thick darkness of my infinite woes
That I forecast nor dangers, hopes, or safety.
Give me some corner of the world to wear out   25
The remnant of the minutes I must number,
Where I may hear no sounds but sad complaints
Of virgins who have lost contracted partners,
Of husbands howling that their wives were ravished
By some untimely fate, of friends, divided   30
By churlish opposition, or of fathers
Weeping upon their children's slaughtered carcasses,
Or daughters groaning o'er their fathers' hearses,
And I can dwell there, and with these keep consort°
As musical as theirs. What can you look for   35
From an old, foolish, peevish, doting man,
But craziness of age?

CALANTHA Cousin of Argos.

NEARCHUS   Madam.

CALANTHA   Were I presently
To choose you for my lord, I'll open freely
What articles I would propose to treat on°   40
Before our marriage.

NEARCHUS   Name them, virtuous lady.

CALANTHA I would presume you would retain the royalty°
Of Sparta in her own bounds. Then in Argos
Armostes might be viceroy; in Messene
Might Crotolon bear sway; and Bassanes—   45

BASSANES I, queen? Alas! What I?

CALANTHA   Be Sparta's marshal.
The multitudes of high employments could not

But set a peace to private griefs. These gentlemen,
Groneas and Lemophil, with worthy pensions,
Should wait upon your person in your chamber.   50
I would bestow Chrystalla on Amelus;
She'll prove a constant wife. And Philema
Should into Vesta's temple.
BASSANES   This is a testament;°
    It sounds not like conditions on a marriage.
NEARCHUS All this should be performed.
CALANTHA   Lastly, for Prophilus,   55
    He should be, cousin, solemnly invested
    In all those honours, titles, and preferments
    Which his dear friend, and my neglected husband,
    Too short a time enjoyed.
PROPHILUS   I am unworthy
    To live in your remembrance.
EUPHRANIA   Excellent lady!   60
NEARCHUS Madam, what means that word 'neglected husband'?
CALANTHA Forgive me. [*To Ithocles' corpse*] Now I turn to thee, thou
        shadow
    Of my contracted lord.—Bear witness all,
    I put my mother's wedding ring upon
    His finger; 'twas my father's last bequest.   65
    Thus I new marry him whose wife I am;
    Death shall not separate us. O my lords,
    I but deceived your eyes with antic gesture,
    When one news straight came huddling on another,
    Of death, and death, and death. Still I danced forward;   70
    But it struck home, and here, and in an instant.
    Be such mere women, who with shrieks and outcries
    Can vow a present end to all their sorrows,
    Yet live to vow new pleasures, and outlive them.°
    They are the silent griefs which cut the heartstrings.   75
    Let me die smiling.
NEARCHUS   'Tis a truth too ominous.
CALANTHA One kiss on these cold lips; my last. [*Kisses Ithocles'
        corpse*] Crack, crack!
    Argos now's Sparta's king. Command the voices°
    Which wait at th'altar now to sing the song
    I fitted for my end.
NEARCHUS   Sirs, the song.   80

A Song°

ALL   *Glories, pleasures, pomps, delights, and ease*
      Can but please
     The outward senses, when the mind
    Is not untroubled, or by peace refined.

1 [VOICE] *Crowns may flourish and decay;*   85
     Beauties shine, but fade away.

2 [VOICE] *Youth may revel, yet it must*
     Lie down in a bed of dust.

3 [VOICE] *Earthly honours flow and waste;*
     Time alone doth change and last. 90

ALL   *Sorrows mingled with contents prepare*
      Rest for care.
     Love only reigns in death; though art
    Can find no comfort for a broken heart.
  [*Calantha dies*]

ARMOSTES Look to the queen!

BASSANES   Her heart is broke indeed. 95
O royal maid, would thou hadst missed this part;°
Yet 'twas a brave one. I must weep to see
Her smile in death.

ARMOSTES   Wise Tecnicus, thus said he:
'When youth is ripe, and age from time doth part
The lifeless trunk shall wed the broken heart.' 100
'Tis here fulfilled.

NEARCHUS   I am your king.

ALL   Long live
Nearchus, King of Sparta!

NEARCHUS   Her last will
Shall never be digressed from. Wait in order
Upon these faithful lovers as becomes us.
The counsels of the gods are never known° 105
Till men can call th'effects of them their own.
  [*Exeunt*]

THE EPILOGUE

Where noble judgements and clear eyes are fixed
To grace endeavour, there sits truth not mixed
With ignorance. Those censures may command
Belief which talk not till they understand.
Let some say, 'This was flat'; some, 'Here the scene   5
Fell from its height'; another, that the mean°
Was 'ill observed' in such a growing passion
As it transcended either state or fashion.
Some few may cry, ' 'Twas pretty', 'Well', or 'So,°
But—', and there shrug in silence. Yet we know   10
Our writer's aim was in the whole addressed
Well to deserve of all, but please the best.
Which granted, by th'allowance of this strain,°
The Broken Heart may be pieced up again.

'TIS PITY SHE'S A WHORE

To my Friend the Author

With admiration I beheld this Whore
Adorned with beauty, such as might restore
(If ever being as thy Muse hath famed)
Her Giovanni, in his love unblamed.
The ready Graces lent their willing aid,°   5
Pallas herself now played the chambermaid°
And helped to put her dressings on. Secure
Rest thou, that thy name herein shall endure
To th'end of age; and Annabella be
Gloriously fair, even in her infamy.   10

                       Thomas Ellice°

To the truly noble John, Earl of Peterborough, Lord Mordaunt,° Baron of Turvey

My Lord,

Where a truth of merit hath a general warrant, there love is but a debt, acknowledgement a justice. Greatness cannot often claim virtue by inheritance; yet, in this, yours appears most eminent, for that you are not more rightly heir to your fortunes than glory shall be to your memory. Sweetness of disposition ennobles a freedom° of birth; in   5 both, your lawful interest adds honour to your own name, and mercy to my presumption. Your noble allowance of these first fruits of my leisure in the action, emboldens my confidence of your as noble construction in this presentment; especially since my service must ever owe particular duty to your favours, by a particular engagement.   10 The gravity of the subject may easily excuse the lightness of the title; otherwise, I had been a severe judge against mine own guilt. Princes have vouchsafed grace to trifles offered from a purity of devotion; your Lordship may likewise please to admit into your good opinion, with these weak endeavours, the constancy of affection from the   15 sincere lover of your deserts in honour,

                          John Ford

THE SCENE

Parma

THE PERSONS OF THE PLAY°

FLORIO, a citizen of Parma
GIOVANNI, son of Florio
ANNABELLA, daughter of Florio
BONAVENTURA, a friar, tutor to Giovanni
PUTANA, tutoress to Annabella

SORANZO, a nobleman
VASQUES, servant to Soranzo
RICHARDETTO, a supposed physician
HIPPOLITA, wife of Richardetto
PHILOTIS, niece of Richardetto
DONADO, a citizen of Parma
BERGETTO, nephew of Donado
POGGIO, servant to Bergetto

A CARDINAL, nuncio of the Pope
GRIMALDI, a Roman gentleman
BANDITTI
OFFICERS
ATTENDANTS

'Tis Pity She's a Whore

1.1

Enter Friar and Giovanni

FRIAR Dispute no more in this, for know, young man,
  These are no school-points; nice philosophy
  May tolerate unlikely arguments,
  But Heaven admits no jest; wits that presumed
  On wit too much, by striving how to prove   5
  There was no God, with foolish grounds of art,
  Discovered first the nearest way to Hell;
  And filled the world with devilish atheism.
  Such questions, youth, are fond; for better 'tis,
  To bless the sun, than reason why it shines;   10
  Yet he thou talk'st of is above the sun—
  No more! I may not hear it.
GIOVANNI   Gentle Father,
  To you I have unclasped my burdened soul,
  Emptied the storehouse of my thoughts and heart,
  Made myself poor of secrets; have not left   15
  Another word untold, which hath not spoke
  All what I ever durst, or think, or know;
  And yet is here the comfort I shall have?
  Must I not do what all men else may—love?
FRIAR Yes, you may love, fair son.
GIOVANNI   Must I not praise   20
  That beauty, which if framed anew, the gods
  Would make a god of, if they had it there,
  And kneel to it, as I do kneel to them?
FRIAR Why, foolish madman!
GIOVANNI   Shall a peevish sound,
  A customary form, from man to man,°   25
  Of brother and of sister, be a bar
  'Twixt my perpetual happiness and me?
  Say that we had one father, say one womb
  (Curse to my joys) gave both us life and birth;
  Are we not therefore each to other bound   30

So much the more by nature; by the links
Of blood, of reason? nay, if you will have't,
Even of religion, to be ever one:
One soul, one flesh, one love, one heart, one all?

FRIAR Have done, unhappy youth, for thou art lost.   35

GIOVANNI Shall then, for that I am her brother born,
My joys be ever banished from her bed?
No, Father; in your eyes I see the change
Of pity and compassion: from your age,
As from a sacred oracle, distils   40
The life of counsel. Tell me, holy man,
What cure shall give me ease in these extremes?

FRIAR Repentance, son, and sorrow for this sin
—For thou hast moved a Majesty above
With thy unrangèd almost blasphemy.   45

GIOVANNI O do not speak of that, dear confessor.

FRIAR Art thou, my son, that miracle of wit
Who once, within these three months, wert esteemed
A wonder of thine age, throughout Bologna?°
How did the university applaud   50
Thy government, behaviour, learning, speech,
Sweetness, and all that could make up a man!
I was proud of my tutelage, and chose
Rather to leave my books than part with thee.
I did so: but the fruits of all my hopes   55
Are lost in thee, as thou art in thyself.
O Giovanni! Hast thou left the schools
Of knowledge, to converse with lust and death?°
For death waits on thy lust. Look through the world,
And thou shalt see a thousand faces shine   60
More glorious than this idol thou ador'st:
Leave her, and take thy choice; 'tis much less sin,°
Though in such games as those, they lose that win.

GIOVANNI It were more ease to stop the ocean
From floats and ebbs, than to dissuade my vows.   65

FRIAR Then I have done, and in thy wilful flames°
Already see thy ruin; Heaven is just,
Yet hear my counsel.

GIOVANNI   As a voice of life.

FRIAR Hie to thy father's house, there lock thee fast
Alone within thy chamber, then fall down   70

On both thy knees, and grovel on the ground.
Cry to thy heart, wash every word thou utter'st
In tears (and if 't be possible) of blood:°
Beg Heaven to cleanse the leprosy of lust
That rots thy soul. Acknowledge what thou art,   75
A wretch, a worm, a nothing: weep, sigh, pray
Three times a day, and three times every night.
For seven days' space do this, then if thou find'st
No change in thy desires, return to me:
I'll think on remedy. Pray for thyself   80
At home, whilst I pray for thee here—away,
My blessing with thee; we have need to pray.
GIOVANNI All this I'll do, to free me from the rod
Of vengeance; else I'll swear, my fate's my god.
    Exeunt

1.2

Enter Grimaldi and Vasques ready to fight

VASQUES Come sir, stand to your tackling;° if you prove craven, I'll
    make you run quickly.
GRIMALDI Thou art no equal match for me.°
VASQUES Indeed I never went to the wars to bring home news, nor
    cannot play the mountebank for a meal's meat, and swear I got my   5
    wounds in the field. See you these grey hairs? They'll not flinch
    for a bloody nose. Wilt thou to this gear?°
GRIMALDI Why slave, think'st thou I'll balance my reputation with
    a cast-suit? Call thy master, he shall know that I dare—
VASQUES Scold like a cot-quean—that's your profession. Thou poor   10
    shadow of a soldier, I will make thee know my master keeps
    servants, thy betters in quality and performance. Com'st thou to
    fight or prate?
GRIMALDI Neither with thee. I am a Roman and a gentleman; one
    that have got mine honour with expense of blood.   15
VASQUES You are a lying coward, and a fool. Fight, or by these hilts
    I'll kill thee—brave my lord!—You'll fight.°
GRIMALDI Provoke me not, for if thou dost—
VASQUES Have at you! (*They fight, Grimaldi hath the worst*)
    Enter Florio, Donado, [and] Soranzo

FLORIO What mean these sudden broils so near my doors?   20
   Have you not other places but my house
   To vent the spleen of your disordered bloods?°
   Must I be haunted still with such unrest
   As not to eat, or sleep in peace at home?
   Is this your love, Grimaldi? Fie, 'tis naught.   25
DONADO And Vasques, I may tell thee, 'tis not well
   To broach these quarrels; you are ever forward
   In seconding contentions.
          Enter above° Annabella and Putana
FLORIO   What's the ground?
SORANZO That, with your patience, Signiors, I'll resolve:
   This gentleman, whom fame reports a soldier,   30
   (For else I know not) rivals me in love
   To Signior Florio's daughter, to whose ears
   He still prefers his suit, to my disgrace—
   Thinking the way to recommend himself
   Is to disparage me in his report.   35
   But know Grimaldi, though, may be, thou art
   My equal in thy blood, yet this bewrays
   A lowness in thy mind; which wert thou noble
   Thou wouldst as much disdain, as I do thee
   For this unworthiness; [*to Donado and Florio*] and on this ground   40
   I willed my servant to correct this tongue,°
   Holding a man so base no match for me.
VASQUES And had not your sudden coming prevented us, I had let
   my gentleman blood under the gills;° [*to Grimaldi*] I should have
   wormed° you, sir, for running mad.°   45
GRIMALDI I'll be revenged Soranzo.
VASQUES On a dish of warm broth to stay your stomach°—do,
   honest innocence, do; spoon-meat is a wholesomer diet than a
   Spanish blade.
GRIMALDI Remember this.
SORANZO   I fear thee not, Grimaldi.   50
        Exit Grimaldi
FLORIO My Lord Soranzo, this is strange to me,
   Why you should storm, having my word engaged:
   Owing her heart, what need you doubt her ear?
   Losers may talk by law of any game.°
VASQUES Yet the villainy of words, Signior Florio, may be such as would   55
   make any unspleened dove° choleric. Blame not my lord in this.

FLORIO Be you more silent.
I would not for my wealth my daughter's love
Should cause the spilling of one drop of blood.
Vasques, put up, let's end this fray in wine.°   60
    Exeunt [Florio, Donado, Soranzo, and Vasques]

PUTANA How like you this, child? Here's threatening, challenging,
quarrelling, and fighting, on every side, and all is for your sake;
you had need look to yourself, charge, you'll be stol'n away
sleeping else shortly.

ANNABELLA But, tutoress, such a life gives no content   65
To me, my thoughts are fixed on other ends;
Would you would leave me.

PUTANA Leave you? No marvel else; leave me no leaving, charge;
this is love outright. Indeed I blame you not; you have choice fit
for the best lady in Italy.   70

ANNABELLA Pray do not talk so much.

PUTANA Take the worst with the best—there's Grimaldi the soldier,
a very well-timbered fellow: they say he is a Roman, nephew to
the Duke Monferrato;° they say he did good service in the wars
against the Milanese, but faith, charge, I do not like him, an't be   75
for nothing but for being a soldier; not one amongst twenty of your
skirmishing captains but have some privy maim° or other, that
mars their standing upright. I like him the worse, he crinkles so
much in the hams;° though he might serve° if there were no more
men, yet he's not the man I would choose.   80

ANNABELLA Fie, how thou prate'st.

PUTANA As I am a very woman, I like Signior Soranzo well; he is
wise, and what is more, rich; and what is more than that, kind;
and what is more than all this, a nobleman; such a one, were I
the fair Annabella myself, I would wish and pray for. Then he   85
is bountiful; besides he is handsome, and, by my troth, I think
wholesome° (and that's news in a gallant of three-and-twenty);
liberal,° that I know; loving, that you know; and a man sure, else
he could never ha' purchased such a good name° with Hippolita,
the lusty widow, in her husband's lifetime: and 'twere but for that 90
report, sweetheart, would 'a were thine. Commend a man for his
qualities, but take a husband as he is a plain-sufficient, naked man:
such a one is for your bed, and such a one is Signior Soranzo, my
life for't.

ANNABELLA Sure the woman took her morning's draught too soon.   95
    Enter Bergetto and Poggio

PUTANA But look, sweetheart, look what thing comes now: here's another of your ciphers to fill up the number. O, brave old ape in a silken coat!° Observe.

BERGETTO Didst thou think, Poggio, that I would spoil my new clothes, and leave my dinner, to fight? 100

POGGIO No sir, I did not take you for so arrant a baby.

BERGETTO I am wiser than so: for I hope, Poggio, thou never heard'st of an elder brother that was a coxcomb, didst, Poggio?

POGGIO Never indeed sir, as long as they had either land or money left them to inherit. 105

BERGETTO Is it possible, Poggio? O monstrous! Why, I'll undertake, with a handful of silver, to buy a headful of wit at any time; but sirrah, I have another purchase in hand, I shall have the wench, mine° uncle says. I will but wash my face, and shift socks, and then have at her i'faith!—Mark my pace, Poggio. 110
    [Walks affectedly]

POGGIO Sir, I have seen an ass and a mule trot the Spanish pavan with a better grace, I know not how often.
    Exeunt [Bergetto and Poggio]

ANNABELLA This idiot haunts me too.

PUTANA Ay, ay, he needs no description. The rich magnifico that is below with your father, charge, Signior Donado his uncle—for that 115 he means to make this, his cousin, a golden calf°—thinks that you will be a right Israelite, and fall down to him presently: but I hope I have tutored you better. They say a fool's bauble° is a lady's playfellow: yet you having wealth enough, you need not cast upon the dearth of flesh at any rate.° Hang him, innocent! 120
    Enter Giovanni [below]

ANNABELLA But see, Putana, see: what blessèd shape
    Of some celestial creature now appears?
    What man is he, that with such sad aspect°
    Walks careless of himself?

PUTANA   Where?

ANNABELLA   Look below.

PUTANA O, 'tis your brother, sweet—

ANNABELLA   Ha!

PUTANA   'Tis your brother. 125

ANNABELLA Sure 'tis not he; this is some woeful thing
    Wrapped up in grief, some shadow of a man.
    Alas, he beats his breast, and wipes his eyes
    Drowned all in tears: methinks I hear him sigh.

Let's down, Putana, and partake the cause;   130
I know my brother, in the love he bears me,
Will not deny me partage in his sadness.
My soul is full of heaviness and fear.
            Exeunt [Annabella and Putana]°
GIOVANNI Lost, I am lost: my fates have doomed my death.
The more I strive, I love; the more I love,   135
The less I hope: I see my ruin, certain.
What judgement or endeavours could apply
To my incurable and restless wounds
I throughly have examined, but in vain.
O that it were not in religion sin   140
To make our love a god, and worship it.
I have even wearied Heaven with prayers, dried up
The spring of my continual tears, even starved
My veins with daily fasts. What wit or art
Could counsel, I have practised; but alas   145
I find all these but dreams, and old men's tales
To fright unsteady youth; I'm still the same.
Or I must speak, or burst; 'tis not I know,
My lust, but 'tis my fate that leads me on.
Keep fear and low faint-hearted shame with slaves!   150
I'll tell her that I love her, though my heart
Were rated at the price of that attempt.
Oh me! She comes.
            Enter Annabella and Putana
ANNABELLA   Brother.
GIOVANNI [*aside*]   If such a thing
As courage dwell in men, ye heavenly powers,
Now double all that virtue in my tongue.   155
ANNABELLA Why brother, will you not speak to me?
GIOVANNI Yes; how d'ee sister?
ANNABELLA Howsoever I am, methinks you are not well.
PUTANA Bless us, why are you so sad, sir?
GIOVANNI Let me entreat you leave us awhile, Putana.   160
Sister, I would be private with you.
ANNABELLA Withdraw Putana.
PUTANA I will. [*Aside*] If this were any other company for her, I
should think my absence an office of some credit;° but I will leave
them together.   165
            Exit Putana

GIOVANNI Come sister, lend your hand, let's walk together.
  I hope you need not blush to walk with me;
  Here's none but you and I.
ANNABELLA How's this?
GIOVANNI Faith, I mean no harm.   170
ANNABELLA Harm?
GIOVANNI No good faith; how is't with 'ee?
ANNABELLA [*aside*] I trust he be not frantic—[*to him*] I am very well,
  brother.
GIOVANNI Trust me but I am sick; I fear so sick,   175
  'Twill cost my life.
ANNABELLA Mercy forbid it! 'Tis not so, I hope.
GIOVANNI I think you love me, sister.
ANNABELLA Yes, you know I do.
GIOVANNI I know't indeed—y'are very fair.   180
ANNABELLA Nay, then I see you have a merry sickness.
GIOVANNI That's as it proves. The poets feign, I read,
  That Juno for her forehead did exceed
  All other goddesses: but I durst swear
  Your forehead exceeds hers, as hers did theirs.   185
ANNABELLA Troth, this is pretty.
GIOVANNI   Such a pair of stars
  As are thine eyes, would (like Promethean fire,°
  If gently glanced) give life to senseless stones.
ANNABELLA Fie upon 'ee!
GIOVANNI The lily and the rose, most sweetly strange,   190
  Upon your dimpled cheeks do strive for change.°
  Such lips would tempt a saint; such hands as those
  Would make an anchorite lascivious.
ANNABELLA D'ee mock me, or flatter me?
GIOVANNI If you would see a beauty more exact   195
  Than art can counterfeit, or nature frame,
  Look in your glass, and there behold your own.
ANNABELLA O you are a trim youth.
GIOVANNI Here.
          Offers his dagger to her
ANNABELLA   What to do?
GIOVANNI   And here's my breast, strike home.
  Rip up my bosom; there thou shalt behold   200
  A heart, in which is writ the truth I speak.
  Why stand 'ee?

ANNABELLA   Are you earnest?
GIOVANNI   Yes, most earnest.
  You cannot love?
ANNABELLA   Whom?
GIOVANNI   Me. My tortured soul
  Hath felt affliction in the heat of death.°
  O Annabella, I am quite undone.   205
  The love of thee, my sister, and the view
  Of thy immortal beauty hath untuned
  All harmony both of my rest and life.°
  Why d'ee not strike?
ANNABELLA   Forbid it my just fears;
  If this be true, 'twere fitter I were dead.   210
GIOVANNI True, Annabella; 'tis no time to jest.
  I have too long suppressed the hidden flames
  That almost have consumed me; I have spent
  Many a silent night in sighs and groans,
  Ran over all my thoughts, despised my fate,   215
  Reasoned against the reasons of my love,
  Done all that smoothed-cheek Virtue could advise,°
  But found all bootless; 'tis my destiny
  That you must either love, or I must die.
ANNABELLA Comes this in sadness from you?
GIOVANNI   Let some mischief°   220
  Befall me soon, if I dissemble aught.
ANNABELLA You are my brother Giovanni.
GIOVANNI   You,
  My sister Annabella; I know this:°
  And could afford you instance why to love
  So much the more for this; to which intent   225
  Wise Nature first in your creation meant
  To make you mine: else't had been sin and foul
  To share one beauty to a double soul.°
  Nearness in birth or blood doth but persuade
  A nearer nearness in affection.   230
  I have asked counsel of the holy Church,
  Who tells me I may love you, and 'tis just°
  That since I may, I should; and will, yes will:
  Must I now live, or die?
ANNABELLA   Live; thou hast won
  The field, and never fought; what thou hast urged,   235

My captive heart had long ago resolved.
I blush to tell thee—but I'll tell thee now—
For every sigh that thou hast spent for me,
I have sighed ten; for every tear, shed twenty:°
And not so much for that I loved, as that   240
I durst not say I loved; nor scarcely think it.

GIOVANNI Let not this music be a dream, ye gods,
    For pity's sake I beg 'ee.

ANNABELLA   On my knees, (*she kneels*)
    Brother, even by our mother's dust, I charge you,
    Do not betray me to your mirth or hate;   245
    Love me, or kill me, brother.

GIOVANNI   On my knees, (*he kneels*)
    Sister, even by my mother's dust I charge you,
    Do not betray me to your mirth or hate;
    Love me, or kill me, sister.

ANNABELLA You mean good sooth then?

GIOVANNI   In good troth I do,   250
    And so do you I hope: say, I'm in earnest.

ANNABELLA I'll swear't; and I.

GIOVANNI   And I, and by this kiss—
        (*Kisses her*)
    Once more, yet once more; now let's rise, by this,
    I would not change this minute for Elysium.
    What must we now do?

ANNABELLA   What you will.

GIOVANNI   Come then,   255
    After so many tears as we have wept,
    Let's learn to court in smiles, to kiss and sleep.
        Exeunt

1.3

Enter Florio and Donado

FLORIO Signior Donado, you have said enough;
    I understand you, but would have you know
    I will not force my daughter 'gainst her will.
    You see I have but two, a son and her;
    And he is so devoted to his book,   5

As I must tell you true, I doubt his health:
Should he miscarry, all my hopes rely
Upon my girl. As for worldly fortune,
I am, I thank my stars, blessed with enough.
My care is how to match her to her liking;   10
I would not have her marry wealth, but love,
And if she like your nephew, let him have her.
Here's all that I can say.
DONADO   Sir, you say well,
Like a true father, and for my part, I,
If the young folks can like ('twixt you and me),   15
Will promise to assure my nephew presently,
Three thousand florins yearly during life,
And after I am dead, my whole estate.
FLORIO 'Tis a fair proffer, sir; meantime your nephew
Shall have free passage to commence his suit: 20
If he can thrive, he shall have my consent.
So for this time I'll leave you, signior.
        Exit
DONADO   Well,
Here's hope yet, if my nephew would have wit;
But he is such another dunce, I fear
He'll never win the wench. When I was young   25
I could have done't i'faith, and so shall he
If he will learn of me;
        Enter Bergetto and Poggio
                    and in good time°
He comes himself.
How now Bergetto, whither away so fast?°
BERGETTO Oh uncle, I have heard the strangest news that ever came   30
    out of the mint,° have I not, Poggio?
POGGIO Yes indeed, sir.
DONADO What news, Bergetto?
BERGETTO Why look ye uncle?° My barber° told me just now that
    there is a fellow come to town, who undertakes to make a mill go   35
    without the mortal help of any water or wind, only with sandbags:°
    and this fellow hath a strange horse, a most excellent beast, I'll
    assure you uncle, (my barber says), whose head, to the wonder of
    all Christian people, stands just behind where his tail is;° is't not
    true, Poggio?   40
POGGIO So the barber swore forsooth.

DONADO And you are running thither?

BERGETTO Ay forsooth uncle.

DONADO Wilt thou be a fool still? Come, sir, you shall not go; you
have more mind of° a puppet-play, than on the business I told ye.   45
Why, thou great baby, wilt never have wit; wilt make thyself a
May-game to all the world?

POGGIO Answer for yourself, master.

BERGETTO Why uncle, should I sit at home still, and not go abroad
to see fashions like other gallants?   50

DONADO To see hobby-horses! What wise talk, I pray, had you with
Annabella, when you were at Signior Florio's house?

BERGETTO Oh, the wench! Uds sa' me, uncle, I tickled her with
a rare speech, that I made her almost burst her belly with
laughing.   55

DONADO Nay I think so, and what speech was't?

BERGETTO What did I say, Poggio?

POGGIO Forsooth, my master said that he loved her almost as well
as he loved parmesan,° and swore (I'll be sworn for him) that she
wanted but such a nose as his was, to be as pretty a young woman   60
as any was in Parma.

DONADO Oh gross!

BERGETTO Nay uncle, then she asked me whether my father had any
more children than myself: and I said, 'No, 'twere better he should
have had his brains knocked out first.'   65

DONADO This is intolerable.

BERGETTO Then said she, 'Will Signior Donado, your uncle, leave
you all his wealth?'

DONADO Ha! that was good, did she harp upon that string?

BERGETTO Did she harp upon that string? Ay that she did. I   70
answered, 'Leave me all his wealth? Why, woman, he hath no other
wit; if he had he should hear on't to his everlasting glory° and
confusion: I know', quoth I, 'I am his white boy, and will not be
gulled'; and with that she fell into a great smile, and went away.
Nay, I did fit her.°   75

DONADO Ah sirrah, then I see there is no changing of nature. Well,
Bergetto, I fear thou wilt be a very ass still.

BERGETTO I should be sorry for that, uncle.

DONADO Come, come you home with me; since you are no better a
speaker, I'll have you write to her after some courtly manner, and   80
enclose some rich jewel in the letter.

BERGETTO Ay, marry, that will be excellent.

DONADO Peace, innocent.
Once in my time I'll set my wits to school;
If all fail, 'tis but the fortune of a fool.   85
BERGETTO Poggio, 'twill do, Poggio!
      Exeunt

2.1

Enter Giovanni and Annabella, as from their chamber°

GIOVANNI Come Annabella, no more sister now,
But love, a name more gracious; do not blush,
Beauty's sweet wonder, but be proud to know
That yielding thou hast conquered, and inflamed
A heart whose tribute is thy brother's life.   5

ANNABELLA And mine is his. O, how these stol'n contents
Would print a modest crimson on my cheeks,
Had any but my heart's delight prevailed.

GIOVANNI I marvel why the chaster of your sex
Should think this pretty toy called maidenhead   10
So strange a loss, when being lost, 'tis nothing,
And you are still the same.

ANNABELLA   'Tis well for you;
Now you can talk.

GIOVANNI   Music as well consists
In th'ear, as in the playing.

ANNABELLA   O, y'are wanton!°
Tell on't, y'are best, do.

GIOVANNI   Thou wilt chide me then.°   15
Kiss me, so: thus hung Jove on Leda's neck,°
And sucked divine ambrosia from her lips.
I envy not the mightiest man alive,
But hold myself in being king of thee,
More great, than were I king of all the world: 20
But I shall lose you, sweetheart.

ANNABELLA   But you shall not.

GIOVANNI You must be married, mistress.

ANNABELLA   Yes, to whom?

GIOVANNI Someone must have you.

ANNABELLA   You must.

GIOVANNI   Nay, some other.°

ANNABELLA Now prithee do not speak so without jesting;°
You'll make me weep in earnest.

GIOVANNI   What, you will not!°   25
But tell me sweet, canst thou be dared to swear
That thou wilt live to me, and to no other?°

ANNABELLA By both our loves I dare, for didst thou know
   My Giovanni, how all suitors seem
   To my eyes hateful, thou wouldst trust me then.   30
GIOVANNI Enough, I take thy word. Sweet, we must part:
   Remember what thou vow'st; keep well my heart.
ANNABELLA Will you begone?
GIOVANNI   I must.
ANNABELLA   When to return?
GIOVANNI Soon.
ANNABELLA   Look you do.
GIOVANNI   Farewell.
     Exit [Giovanni]
ANNABELLA Go where thou wilt, in mind I'll keep thee here,   35
   And where thou art, I know I shall be there.
   Guardian!
     Enter Putana
PUTANA Child, how is't child? Well, thank Heaven, ha?
ANNABELLA O Guardian, what a paradise of joy
   Have I passed over!°   40
PUTANA Nay, what a paradise of joy have you passed under! Why,
   now I commend thee, charge; fear nothing, sweetheart. What
   though he be your brother? Your brother's a man I hope, and I
   say still, if a young wench feel the fit upon her, let her take
   anybody, father or brother, all is one.   45
ANNABELLA I would not have it known for all the world.
PUTANA Nor I indeed, for the speech of the people;° else 'twere
   nothing.
FLORIO (*within*) Daughter Annabella!
ANNABELLA O me, my father!—Here, sir! [*To Putana*]—Reach my
   work.°   50
FLORIO (*within*) What are you doing?
ANNABELLA   So, let him come now.
     Enter Florio, Richardetto like a Doctor of Physic, and
     Philotis with a lute in her hand
FLORIO So hard at work, that's well; you lose no time.
   Look, I have brought you company: here's one,
   A learnèd doctor, lately come from Padua,°
   Much skilled in physic; and for that I see   55
   You have of late been sickly, I entreated
   This reverend man to visit you some time.
ANNABELLA Y'are very welcome, sir.

RICHARDETTO   I thank you mistress.
   Loud fame in large report hath spoke your praise,
   As well for virtue as perfection: 60
   For which I have been bold to bring with me
   A kinswoman of mine, a maid, for song
   And music, one perhaps will give content.
   Please you to know her.
ANNABELLA   They are parts I love,
   And she for them most welcome.
PHILOTIS   Thank you, lady.   65
FLORIO Sir, now you know my house, pray make not strange,°
   And if you find my daughter need your art,
   I'll be your paymaster.
RICHARDETTO   Sir, what I am
   She shall command.
FLORIO   You shall bind me to you.°
   Daughter, I must have conference with you   70
   About some matters that concerns us both.
   Good master doctor, please you but walk in,
   We'll crave a little of your cousin's cunning:
   I think my girl hath not quite forgot
   To touch an instrument; she could have done't°—   75
   We'll hear them both.
RICHARDETTO   I'll wait upon you, sir.
    Exeunt

2.2

Enter Soranzo in his study, reading a book
SORANZO 'Love's measure is extreme, the comfort, pain,
   The life unrest, and the reward disdain.'
   What's here? Look't o'er again: 'tis so, so writes
   This smooth licentious poet in his rhymes.°
   But Sannazar thou liest, for had thy bosom   5
   Felt such oppression as is laid on mine,
   Thou wouldst have kissed the rod that made the smart.
   To work then, happy Muse, and contradict
   What Sannazar hath in his envy writ.°
   'Love's measure is the mean, sweet his annoys,°   10

His pleasure's life, and his reward all joys.'
Had Annabella lived when Sannazar
Did in his brief encomium celebrate
Venice, that queen of cities, he had left
That verse which gained him such a sum of gold,   15
And for one only look from Annabell
Had writ of her, and her diviner cheeks.
O how my thoughts are—
VASQUES (*within*) Pray forbear; in rules of civility, let me give notice
   on't: I shall be taxed of° my neglect of duty and service.   20
SORANZO What rude intrusion interrupts my peace?
   Can I be nowhere private?
VASQUES (*within*) Troth you wrong your modesty.
SORANZO What's the matter Vasques, who is't?
     Enter Hippolita [in mourning clothes] and Vasques
HIPPOLITA 'Tis I: 25
   Do you know me now? Look, perjured man, on her°
   Whom thou and thy distracted lust have wronged.
   Thy sensual rage of blood hath made my youth
   A scorn to men and angels, and shall I
   Be now a foil to thy unsated change?°   30
   Thou know'st, false wanton, when my modest fame°
   Stood free from stain or scandal, all the charms
   Of Hell or sorcery could not prevail
   Against the honour of my chaster bosom.
   Thine eyes did plead in tears, thy tongue in oaths   35
   Such and so many, that a heart of steel
   Would have been wrought to pity, as was mine:
   And shall the conquest of my lawful bed,
   My husband's death urged on by his disgrace,
   My loss of womanhood, be ill rewarded°   40
   With hatred and contempt? No, know Soranzo,
   I have a spirit doth as much distaste
   The slavery of fearing thee, as thou
   Dost loathe the memory of what hath passed.
SORANZO Nay, dear Hippolita—
HIPPOLITA   Call me not dear,   45
   Nor think with supple words to smooth the grossness
   Of my abuses; 'tis not your new mistress,
   Your goodly Madam Merchant, shall triumph°
   On my dejection; tell her thus from me,

My birth was nobler, and by much, more free.   50
SORANZO You are too violent.
HIPPOLITA   You are too double
   In your dissimulation. Seest thou this,
   This habit, these black mourning weeds of care?°
   'Tis thou art cause of this, and hast divorced
   My husband from his life and me from him,   55
   And made me widow in my widowhood.°
SORANZO Will you yet hear?
HIPPOLITA   More of thy perjuries?
   Thy soul is drowned too deeply in those sins;
   Thou need'st not add to th'number.
SORANZO   Then I'll leave you;
   You are past all rules of sense.
HIPPOLITA   And thou of grace.   60
VASQUES Fie, mistress, you are not near the limits of reason: if my
   lord had a resolution as noble as virtue itself, you take the course
   to unedge it all. Sir, I beseech you do not perplex her; griefs, alas,
   will have a vent. I dare undertake Madam Hippolita will now freely
   hear you.   65
SORANZO Talk to a woman frantic! Are these the fruits of your love?
HIPPOLITA They are the fruits of thy untruth, false man.
   Didst thou not swear, whilst yet my husband lived,
   That thou wouldst wish no happiness on earth
   More than to call me wife? Didst thou not vow   70
   When he should die to marry me? For which
   The devil in my blood, and thy protests,
   Caused me to counsel him to undertake
   A voyage to Leghorn, for that we heard°
   His brother there was dead, and left a daughter   75
   Young and unfriended, who with much ado
   I wished him to bring hither: he did so,
   And went; and as thou know'st, died on the way.
   Unhappy man, to buy his death so dear
   With my advice! Yet thou for whom I did it   80
   Forget'st thy vows, and leav'st me to my shame.
SORANZO Who could help this?
HIPPOLITA   Who? Perjured man, thou couldst,
   If thou hadst faith or love.
SORANZO   You are deceived.
   The vows I made, if you remember well,

Were wicked and unlawful; 'twere more sin   85
To keep them than to break them. As for me,
I cannot mask my penitence. Think thou
How much thou hast digressed from honest shame
In bringing of a gentleman to death
Who was thy husband; such a one as he,   90
So noble in his quality, condition,
Learning, behaviour, entertainment, love,
As Parma could not show a braver man.

VASQUES You do not well; this was not your promise.

SORANZO I care not; let her know her monstrous life.   95
Ere I'll be servile to so black a sin,
I'll be a corse.—Woman, come here no more,°
Learn to repent and die; for by my honour
I hate thee and thy lust; you have been too foul.
    [Exit Soranzo]

VASQUES This part has been scurvily played.   100

HIPPOLITA How foolishly this beast contemns his fate,°
And shuns the use of that which I more scorn
Than I once loved, his love. But let him go;
My vengeance shall give comfort to his woe.°
    She offers to go away

VASQUES Mistress, mistress, Madam Hippolita, pray, a word or two. 105

HIPPOLITA With me, sir?

VASQUES With you, if you please.

HIPPOLITA What is't?

VASQUES I know you are infinitely moved now, and you think you
have cause: some I confess you have, but sure not so much as   110
you imagine.

HIPPOLITA Indeed.

VASQUES O, you were miserably bitter, which you followed even to
the last syllable. Faith, you were somewhat too shrewd. By my life,
you could not have took my lord in a worse time since I first knew 115
him: tomorrow you shall find him a new man.

HIPPOLITA Well, I shall wait his leisure.

VASQUES Fie, this is not a hearty patience, it comes sourly from you;
troth, let me persuade you for once.

HIPPOLITA *[aside]* I have it, and it shall be so; thanks, opportunity! 120
[To him] Persuade me to what?

VASQUES Visit him in some milder temper. O, if you could but
master a little your female spleen, how might you win him!

HIPPOLITA He will never love me. Vasques, thou hast been a too
    trusty servant to such a master, and I believe thy reward in the end   125
    will fall out like mine.

VASQUES So, perhaps too.°

HIPPOLITA Resolve thyself it will. Had I one so true, so truly honest,
    so secret to my counsels, as thou hast been to him and his, I should
    think it a slight acquittance, not only to make him master of all I   130
    have, but even of myself.

VASQUES O, you are a noble gentlewoman!

HIPPOLITA Wilt thou feed always upon hopes? Well, I know thou
    art wise, and seest the reward of an old servant daily what it is.

VASQUES Beggary and neglect.   135

HIPPOLITA True; but Vasques, wert thou mine, and wouldst be
    private to° me and my designs, I here protest, myself and all what
    I can else call mine, should be at thy dispose.

VASQUES [aside] Work you that way, old mole? Then I have the wind
    of you. [To her] I were not worthy of it by any desert that could   140
    lie within my compass; if I could—

HIPPOLITA What then?

VASQUES I should then hope to live in these my old years with rest
    and security.

HIPPOLITA Give me thy hand: now promise but thy silence,   145
    And help to bring to pass a plot I have,
    And here in sight of Heaven, that being done,
    I make thee lord of me and mine estate.

VASQUES Come, you are merry; this is such a happiness that I can
    neither think or believe.   150

HIPPOLITA Promise thy secrecy, and 'tis confirmed.

VASQUES Then here I call our good genii for witnesses, whatsoever
    your designs are, or against whomsoever, I will not only be a
    special actor therein, but never disclose it till it be effected.

HIPPOLITA I take thy word, and with that, thee for mine.   155
    Come then, let's more confer of this anon.
    On this delicious bane my thoughts shall banquet:
    Revenge shall sweeten what my griefs have tasted.
       Exeunt

2.3

Enter Richardetto and Philotis

RICHARDETTO Thou seest, my lovely niece, these strange mishaps,
How all my fortunes turn to my disgrace,
Wherein I am but as a looker-on,
Whiles others act my shame and I am silent.°

PHILOTIS But uncle, wherein can this borrowed shape°   5
Give you content?

RICHARDETTO   I'll tell thee, gentle niece.
Thy wanton aunt in her lascivious riots
Lives now secure, thinks I am surely dead
In my late journey to Leghorn for you°
(As I have caused it to be rumoured out).   10
Now would I see with what an impudence
She gives scope to her loose adultery,
And how the common voice allows hereof;°
Thus far I have prevailed.

PHILOTIS   Alas, I fear
You mean some strange revenge.

RICHARDETTO   O, be not troubled;   15
Your ignorance shall plead for you in all.
But to our business: what, you learnt for certain
How Signior Florio means to give his daughter
In marriage to Soranzo?

PHILOTIS   Yes, for certain.

RICHARDETTO But how find you young Annabella's love   20
Inclined to him?

PHILOTIS   For aught I could perceive,
She neither fancies him or any else.

RICHARDETTO There's mystery in that which time must show.
She used you kindly?

PHILOTIS   Yes.

RICHARDETTO   And craved your company?°

PHILOTIS Often.

RICHARDETTO   'Tis well; it goes as I could wish.   25
I am the doctor now, and as for you,
None knows you; if all fail not, we shall thrive.
        Enter Grimaldi°
But who comes here? I know him: 'tis Grimaldi,

A Roman and a soldier, near allied
Unto the Duke of Monferrato, one°   30
Attending on the nuncio of the Pope
That now resides in Parma, by which means
He hopes to get the love of Annabella.

GRIMALDI Save you, sir.

RICHARDETTO   And you, sir.

GRIMALDI   I have heard
Of your approved skill, which through the city   35
Is freely talked of, and would crave your aid.

RICHARDETTO For what, sir?

GRIMALDI   Marry, sir, for this—
But I would speak in private.

RICHARDETTO   Leave us, cousin.
          [*Exit Philotis*]

GRIMALDI I love fair Annabella, and would know
Whether in arts there may not be receipts   40
To move affection.

RICHARDETTO   Sir, perhaps there may,°
But these will nothing profit you.

GRIMALDI   Not me?

RICHARDETTO Unless I be mistook, you are a man
Greatly in favour with the Cardinal.

GRIMALDI What of that?

RICHARDETTO   In duty to his grace,   45
I will be bold to tell you, if you seek
To marry Florio's daughter, you must first
Remove a bar 'twixt you and her.

GRIMALDI   Who's that?

RICHARDETTO Soranzo is the man that hath her heart,
And while he lives, be sure you cannot speed.   50

GRIMALDI Soranzo! What, mine enemy! Is't he?

RICHARDETTO Is he your enemy?

GRIMALDI   The man I hate
Worse than confusion—
I'll kill him straight.

RICHARDETTO   Nay, then take mine advice,
Even for his grace's sake, the Cardinal.   55
I'll find a time when he and she do meet,
Of which I'll give you notice, and to be sure
He shall not 'scape you, I'll provide a poison

To dip your rapier's point in; if he had
As many heads as Hydra had, he dies.   60
GRIMALDI But shall I trust thee, doctor?
RICHARDETTO   As yourself;
  Doubt not in aught. [*Aside*] Thus shall the fates decree:
  By me Soranzo falls, that ruined me.
      Exeunt

2.4

Enter Donado, Bergetto, and Poggio

DONADO Well, sir, I must be content to be both your secretary and
  your messenger myself. I cannot tell what this letter may work, but
  as sure as I am alive, if thou come once to talk with her, I fear thou
  wilt mar whatsoever I make.
BERGETTO You make, uncle? Why, am not I big enough to carry   5
  mine own letter, I pray?
DONADO Ay, ay, carry a fool's head° o' thy own. Why, thou dunce,
  wouldst thou write a letter and carry it thyself?
BERGETTO Yes, that I would, and read it to her with my own mouth;
  for you must think, if she will not believe me myself when she   10
  hears me speak, she will not believe another's handwriting. O, you
  think I am a blockhead, uncle. No, sir; Poggio knows I have indited
  a letter myself, so I have.
POGGIO Yes truly, sir, I have it in my pocket.
DONADO A sweet one no doubt, pray let's see't.   15
BERGETTO I cannot read my own hand very well, Poggio; read it,
  Poggio.
DONADO Begin.
POGGIO (*reads*) 'Most dainty and honey-sweet mistress, I could call
  you fair, and lie as fast as any that loves you, but my uncle being   20
  the elder man, I leave it to him as more fit for his age and the
  colour of his beard. I am wise enough to tell you I can board°
  where I see occasion, or if you like my uncle's wit better than mine,
  you shall marry me; if you like mine better than his, I will marry
  you in spite of your teeth.° So, commending my best parts to   25
  you, I rest. Yours upwards and downwards, or you may choose,
  Bergetto.'
BERGETTO Aha! here's stuff, uncle!

DONADO Here's stuff indeed to shame us all. Pray, whose advice did
you take in this learnèd letter?   30

POGGIO None, upon my word, but mine own.

BERGETTO And mine, uncle, believe it, nobody's else; 'twas mine
own brain, I thank a good wit for't.

DONADO Get you home sir, and look you keep within doors till I
return.   35

BERGETTO How! That were a jest indeed; I scorn it i'faith.

DONADO What! You do not?

BERGETTO Judge me, but I do now.

POGGIO Indeed, sir, 'tis very unhealthy.

DONADO Well, sir, if I hear any of your apish running to motions   40
and fopperies till I come back, you were as good no;° look to't.
          Exit [*Donado*]

BERGETTO Poggio, shall's steal to see this horse with the head in's
tail?

POGGIO Ay, but you must take heed of whipping.

BERGETTO Dost take me for a child, Poggio? Come, honest Poggio.   45
          Exeunt

2.5

          Enter Friar and Giovanni

FRIAR Peace! Thou hast told a tale whose every word
Threatens eternal slaughter to the soul.
I'm sorry I have heard it; would mine ears
Had been one minute deaf, before the hour
That thou cam'st to me. O young man, cast away°   5
By the religious number of mine order,°
I day and night have waked my agèd eyes
Above my strength, to weep on thy behalf.
But Heaven is angry, and be thou resolved,
Thou art a man remarked to taste a mischief.   10
Look for't; though it come late, it will come sure.

GIOVANNI Father, in this you are uncharitable;
What I have done, I'll prove both fit and good.
It is a principle (which you have taught
When I was yet your scholar) that the frame   15
And composition of the mind doth follow

The frame and composition of the body.
So where the body's furniture is beauty,
The mind's must needs be virtue, which allowed,
Virtue itself is reason but refined,   20
And love the quintessence of that. This proves
My sister's beauty, being rarely fair,
Is rarely virtuous; chiefly in her love,
And chiefly in that love, her love to me.
If hers to me, then so is mine to her;   25
Since in like causes are effects alike.

FRIAR O ignorance in knowledge! Long ago,
How often have I warned thee this before!
Indeed, if we were sure there were no Deity,
Nor Heaven nor Hell, then to be led alone   30
By Nature's light (as were philosophers
Of elder times), might instance some defence.°
But 'tis not so. Then, madman, thou wilt find
That Nature is in Heaven's positions blind.°

GIOVANNI Your age o'errules you; had you youth like mine,   35
You'd make her love your heaven, and her divine.

FRIAR Nay, then I see th'art too far sold to Hell,
It lies not in the compass of my prayers
To call thee back; yet let me counsel thee:
Persuade thy sister to some marriage.   40

GIOVANNI Marriage? Why, that's to damn her! That's to prove
Her greedy of variety of lust.

FRIAR O fearful! If thou wilt not, give me leave
To shrive her, lest she should die unabsolved.°

GIOVANNI At your best leisure, father; then she'll tell you   45
How dearly she doth prize my matchless love;
Then you will know what pity 'twere we two
Should have been sundered from each other's arms.
View well her face, and in that little round
You may observe a world of variety: 50
For colour, lips; for sweet perfumes, her breath;
For jewels, eyes; for threads of purest gold,
Hair; for delicious choice of flowers, cheeks;
Wonder in every portion of that throne.°
Hear her but speak, and you will swear the spheres   55
Make music to the citizens in Heaven;°
But father, what is else for pleasure framed,

Lest I offend your ears, shall go unnamed.
FRIAR The more I hear, I pity thee the more,
  That one so excellent should give those parts   60
  All to a second death. What I can do°
  Is but to pray; and yet I could advise thee,
  Wouldst thou be ruled.
GIOVANNI   In what?
FRIAR   Why, leave her yet,
  The throne of mercy is above your trespass;°
  Yet time is left you both—
GIOVANNI   To embrace each other,   65
  Else let all time be struck quite out of number.
  She is, like me, and I like her, resolved.
FRIAR No more! I'll visit her. This grieves me most,
  Things being thus, a pair of souls are lost.
     Exeunt

2.6

     Enter Florio, Donado, Annabella, [and] Putana
FLORIO Where's Giovanni?
ANNABELLA   Newly walked abroad,
  And, as I heard him say, gone to the friar,
  His reverend tutor.
FLORIO   That's a blessed man,
  A man made up of holiness; I hope
  He'll teach him how to gain another world.   5
DONADO Fair gentlewoman, here's a letter sent
    [*He offers a letter to Annabella*]
  To you from my young cousin. I dare swear
  He loves you in his soul: would you could hear
  Sometimes, what I see daily, sighs and tears,
  As if his breast were prison to his heart.   10
FLORIO Receive it, Annabella.
ANNABELLA   Alas, good man!
    [*She takes the letter*]
DONADO What's that she said?
PUTANA And° please you, sir, she said 'Alas, good man!' [*Aside to*
  Donado] Truly, I do commend him to her every night before her

first sleep, because I would have her dream of him, and she   15
hearkens to that most religiously.

DONADO [*aside to Putana*] Say'st so? Godamercy, Putana, there's
something for thee [*gives her money*] and prithee do what thou
canst on his behalf; sha'not be lost labour, take my word for't.

PUTANA [*aside to Donado*] Thank you most heartily, sir, now I have   20
a feeling of your mind,° let me alone to work.

ANNABELLA Guardian!

PUTANA Did you call?

ANNABELLA Keep this letter.

DONADO Signior Florio, in any case bid her read it instantly.   25

FLORIO Keep it for what? Pray read it me here right.

ANNABELLA I shall, sir.

    She reads

DONADO How d'ee find her inclined, Signior?

FLORIO Troth, sir, I know not how; not all so well
  As I could wish.   30

ANNABELLA Sir, I am bound to rest your cousin's debtor.
  The jewel I'll return, for if he love,
  I'll count that love a jewel.

DONADO   Mark you that?
  Nay, keep them both, sweet maid.

ANNABELLA   You must excuse me;
  Indeed I will not keep it.

FLORIO   Where's the ring,   35
  That which your mother in her will bequeathed,
  And charged you on her blessing not to give't
  To any but your husband? Send back that.

ANNABELLA I have it not.

FLORIO   Ha, have it not! Where is't?

ANNABELLA My brother in the morning took it from me,   40
  Said he would wear't today.

FLORIO   Well, what do you say
  To young Bergetto's love? Are you content
  To match with him? Speak.

DONADO   There's the point indeed.

ANNABELLA [*aside*] What shall I do? I must say something now.

FLORIO What say? Why d'ee not speak?

ANNABELLA   Sir, with your leave,°   45
  Please you to give me freedom.

FLORIO   Yes, you have't.°

ANNABELLA Signior Donado, if your nephew mean
　　To raise his better fortunes in his match,°
　　The hope of me will hinder such a hope.
　　Sir, if you love him, as I know you do,　　　　　　　　　50
　　Find one more worthy of his choice than me.
　　In short, I'm sure I sha'not be his wife.
DONADO Why, here's plain dealing, I commend thee for't,
　　And all the worst I wish thee, is Heaven bless thee!
　　Your father yet and I will still be friends,　　　　　　55
　　Shall we not, Signior Florio?
FLORIO　　　　　　　　　　　　Yes, why not?
　　Look, here your cousin comes.
　　　　　Enter Bergetto and Poggio
DONADO [*aside*] O coxcomb, what doth he make° here?
BERGETTO Where's my uncle, sirs?
DONADO What's the news now?　　　　　　　　　　　　　60
BERGETTO Save you, uncle, save you! You must not think I come
　. for nothing, masters. And how, and how is't? What, you have read
　　my letter? Ah, there I—tickled you i'faith!
POGGIO [*aside*]° But 'twere better you had tickled her in another
　　place.　　　　　　　　　　　　　　　　　　　　　　65
BERGETTO Sirrah sweetheart, I'll tell thee a good jest, and riddle
　　what 'tis.
ANNABELLA You say you'd tell me.
BERGETTO As I was walking just now in the street, I met a
　　swaggering fellow would needs take the wall° of me; and because　70
　　he did thrust me, I very valiantly called him rogue. He hereupon
　　bade me draw. I told him I had more wit than so; but when he
　　saw that I would not, he did so maul me with the hilts° of his
　　rapier that my head sung whilst my feet capered in the kennel.
DONADO [*aside*] Was ever the like ass seen?　　　　　　　75
ANNABELLA And what did you all this while?
BERGETTO Laugh at him for a gull, till I see the blood run about
　　mine ears, and then I could not choose but find in my heart to cry;
　　till a fellow with a broad beard—they say he is a new-come
　　doctor—called me into this house and gave me a plaster—look you,　80
　　here 'tis; and sir, there was a young wench washed my face and
　　hands most excellently, i'faith I shall love her as long as I live
　　for't—did she not, Poggio?
POGGIO Yes, and kissed him too.
BERGETTO Why la now, you think I tell a lie, uncle, I warrant.　85

DONADO Would he that beat thy blood out of thy head, had beaten
 some wit into it; for I fear thou never wilt have any.

BERGETTO O uncle, but there was a wench would have done a man's
 heart good to have looked on her; by this light, she had a face
 methinks worth twenty of you, Mistress Annabella.   90

DONADO [aside] Was ever such a fool born?

ANNABELLA I am glad she liked you, sir.

BERGETTO Are you so? By my troth, I thank you forsooth.

FLORIO Sure 'twas the doctor's niece, that was last day with us here.

BERGETTO 'Twas she, 'twas she!   95

DONADO How do you know that, simplicity?

BERGETTO Why, does not he say so? If I should have said no, I
 should have given him the lie,° uncle, and so have deserved a dry
 beating again; I'll none of that.

FLORIO A very modest, well-behaved young maid as I have seen.   100

DONADO Is she indeed?

FLORIO Indeed she is, if I have any judgement.

DONADO Well, sir, now you are free, you need not care for sending
 letters: now you are dismissed; your mistress here will none of you.

BERGETTO No? Why, what care I for that; I can have wenches enough   105
 in Parma for half-a-crown° apiece, cannot I, Poggio?

POGGIO I'll warrant you, sir.

DONADO Signior Florio, I thank you for your free recourse you gave
 for my admittance; and to you, fair maid, that jewel I will give you
 'gainst your marriage. Come, will you go, sir?   110

BERGETTO Ay, marry will I. Mistress, farewell mistress; I'll come
 again tomorrow. Farewell mistress.

    Exeunt Donado, Bergetto, and Poggio. Enter Giovanni

FLORIO Son, where have you been? What, alone, alone still, still?°
 I would not have it so; you must forsake
 This over-bookish humour. Well, your sister   115
 Hath shook the fool off.

GIOVANNI   'Twas no match for her.

FLORIO 'Twas not indeed, I meant it nothing less;
 Soranzo is the man I only like—
 Look on him, Annabella. Come, 'tis supper-time,
 And it grows late.

    Exit [Florio]

GIOVANNI   Whose jewel's that?

ANNABELLA   Some sweetheart's.   120

GIOVANNI So I think.

ANNABELLA   A lusty youth—°
  Signior Donado gave it me to wear
  Against my marriage.
GIOVANNI   But you shall not wear it:
  Send it him back again.
ANNABELLA   What, you are jealous?
GIOVANNI That you shall know anon, at better leisure.   125
  Welcome, sweet night! The evening crowns the day.
    Exeunt

3.1

Enter Bergetto and Poggio

BERGETTO Does my uncle think to make me a baby still? No, Poggio, he shall know I have a sconce now.

POGGIO Ay, let him not bob you off° like an ape with an apple.

BERGETTO 'Sfoot, I will have the wench, if he were ten uncles, in despite of his nose,° Poggio.   5

POGGIO Hold him to the grindstone, and give not a jot of ground. She hath, in a manner, promised you already.

BERGETTO True, Poggio, and her uncle the doctor swore I should marry her.

POGGIO He swore, I remember.   10

BERGETTO And I will have her, that's more; didst see the codpiece-point° she gave me, and the box° of marmalade?

POGGIO Very well; and kissed you that my chops watered at the sight on't. There's no way but to clap up a marriage in hugger-mugger.°

BERGETTO I will do't, for I tell thee, Poggio, I begin to grow valiant   15
methinks, and my courage begins to rise.°

POGGIO Should you be afraid of your uncle?

BERGETTO Hang him, old doting rascal! No, I say I will have her.

POGGIO Lose no time then.

BERGETTO I will beget a race of wise men and constables, that shall   20
cart whores° at their own charges,° and break the Duke's peace ere
I have done myself.° Come away!

Exeunt

3.2

Enter Florio, Giovanni, Soranzo, Annabella, Putana, and
Vasques

FLORIO My lord Soranzo, though I must confess
The proffers that are made me have been great
In marriage of my daughter, yet the hope
Of your still rising honours have prevailed
Above all other jointures. Here she is,°   5

She knows my mind, speak for yourself to her;
And hear you, daughter, see you use him nobly.
For any private speech I'll give you time.
Come son, and you [*to Putana*];° the rest, let them alone;
Agree as they may.
SORANZO   I thank you, sir.   10
GIOVANNI [*aside*] Sister, be not all woman: think on me.°
SORANZO Vasques?
VASQUES   My lord.
SORANZO   Attend me without.
        Exeunt all but Soranzo and Annabella
ANNABELLA Sir, what's your will with me?
SORANZO   Do you not know
    What I should tell you?
ANNABELLA   Yes, you'll say you love me.°
SORANZO And I'll swear it too; will you believe it?   15
ANNABELLA 'Tis not point of faith.
        Enter Giovanni above
SORANZO   Have you not will to love?°
ANNABELLA Not you.
SORANZO   Whom then?
ANNABELLA   That's as the fates infer.
GIOVANNI [*aside*] Of those I'm regent now.
SORANZO   What mean you, sweet?
ANNABELLA To live and die a maid.
SORANZO   O, that's unfit.
GIOVANNI [*aside*] Here's one can say that's but a woman's note.°   20
SORANZO Did you but see my heart, then would you swear—
ANNABELLA That you were dead.
GIOVANNI [*aside*]   That's true, or somewhat near it.
SORANZO See you these true love's tears?
ANNABELLA   No.
GIOVANNI [*aside*]   Now she winks.
SORANZO They plead to you for grace.
ANNABELLA   Yet nothing speak.
SORANZO O, grant my suit!
ANNABELLA   What is't?
SORANZO   To let me live—   25
ANNABELLA Take it.
SORANZO   —still yours.
ANNABELLA   That is not mine to give.

GIOVANNI [*aside*] One such another word would kill his hopes.
SORANZO Mistress, to leave those fruitless strifes of wit,
  I know I have loved you long, and loved you truly;
  Not hope of what you have, but what you are   30
  Have drawn me on: then let me not in vain°
  Still feel the rigour of your chaste disdain.
  I'm sick, and sick to th'heart.
ANNABELLA   Help! Aqua-vitae!°
SORANZO What mean you?
ANNABELLA   Why, I thought you had been sick.
SORANZO Do you mock my love?
GIOVANNI [*aside*]   There, sir, she was too nimble.   35
SORANZO [*aside*] 'Tis plain, she laughs at me! [*To her*] These scornful
    taunts
  Neither become your modesty or years.
ANNABELLA You are no looking-glass; or if you were,
  I'd dress my language by you.
GIOVANNI [*aside*]   I'm confirmed.
ANNABELLA To put you out of doubt, my lord, methinks   40
  Your common sense should make you understand
  That if I loved you, or desired your love,
  Some way I should have given you better taste;°
  But since you are a nobleman, and one
  I would not wish should spend his youth in hopes,   45
  Let me advise you here to forbear your suit,
  And think I wish you well; I tell you this.
SORANZO Is't you speak this?
ANNABELLA   Yes, I myself; yet know—
  Thus far I give you comfort—if mine eyes
  Could have picked out a man (amongst all those   50
  That sued to me) to make a husband of,
  You should have been that man. Let this suffice;
  Be noble in your secrecy, and wise.
GIOVANNI [*aside*] Why now I see she loves me.
ANNABELLA   One word more.
  As ever virtue lived within your mind,   55
  As ever noble courses were your guide,
  As ever you would have me know you loved me,
  Let not my father know hereof by you:
  If I hereafter find that I must marry,
  It shall be you or none.

SORANZO   I take that promise.   60
ANNABELLA O, O my head!
SORANZO   What's the matter? Not well?
ANNABELLA O, I begin to sicken.
GIOVANNI [aside]   Heaven forbid!
        Exit [Giovanni] from above
SORANZO Help, help, within there, ho!
    Look to your daughter, Signior Florio!°
        Enter Florio, Giovanni, [and] Putana
FLORIO Hold her up; she swoons.   65
GIOVANNI Sister, how d'ee?
ANNABELLA   Sick, brother, are you there?
FLORIO Convey her to bed instantly, whilst I send for a physician;
    quickly, I say.
PUTANA Alas, poor child!
        Exeunt. Soranzo [remains]. Enter Vasques
VASQUES My lord.   70
SORANZO O Vasques, now I doubly am undone,
    Both in my present and my future hopes:
    She plainly told me that she could not love,
    And thereupon soon sickened, and I fear
    Her life's in danger.   75
VASQUES [aside] By'r Lady, sir, and so is yours, if you knew all. [To
    him] 'Las sir, I am sorry for that; may be 'tis but the maid's
    sickness,° an overflux of youth—and then, sir, there is no such
    present remedy as present marriage. But hath she given you an
    absolute denial?   80
SORANZO She hath and she hath not; I'm full of grief,
    But what she said I'll tell thee as we go.
        Exeunt

3.3

Enter Giovanni and Putana

PUTANA Oh sir, we are all undone, quite undone, utterly undone,
    and shamed forever; your sister, O your sister!
GIOVANNI What of her? For Heaven's sake speak; how does she?
PUTANA Oh that ever I was born to see this day!
GIOVANNI She is not dead, ha, is she?   5

PUTANA Dead? No, she is quick;° 'tis worse, she is with child. You
  know what you have done, Heaven forgive 'ee. 'Tis too late to
  repent, now Heaven help us!

GIOVANNI With child? How dost thou know't?

PUTANA How do I know't? Am I at these years ignorant what the   10
  meanings of qualms and water-pangs° be? Of changing of colours,
  queasiness of stomachs, pukings, and another thing° that I could
  name? Do not (for her and your credit's° sake) spend the time in
  asking how, and which way; 'tis so. She is quick, upon my word;
  if you let a physician see her water y'are undone.   15

GIOVANNI But in what case is she?

PUTANA Prettily amended; 'twas but a fit which I soon espied, and
  she must look for often henceforward.

GIOVANNI Commend me to her; bid her take no care.°
  Let not the doctor visit her, I charge you,   20
  Make some excuse till I return—O me,
  I have a world of business in my head.°
  Do not discomfort her.—
  How does this news perplex me! If my father
  Come to her, tell him she's recovered well.   25
  Say 'twas but some ill diet; d'ee hear woman?
  Look you to't.

PUTANA I will, sir.
          Exeunt

3.4

Enter Florio and Richardetto

FLORIO And how d'ee find her, sir?

RICHARDETTO   Indifferent well:
  I see no danger, scarce perceive she's sick,
  But that she told me she had lately eaten
  Melons, and as she thought, those disagreed
  With her young stomach.

FLORIO   Did you give her aught?   5

RICHARDETTO An easy surfeit-water, nothing else.°
  You need not doubt her health; I rather think
  Her sickness is a fullness of her blood—
  You understand me?

FLORIO   I do; you counsel well,
    And once within these few days, will so order't   10
    She shall be married, ere she know the time.
RICHARDETTO Yet let not haste, sir, make unworthy choice;
    That were dishonour.
FLORIO   Master doctor, no,
    I will not do so neither; in plain words,
    My lord Soranzo is the man I mean.   15
RICHARDETTO A noble and a virtuous gentleman.
FLORIO As any is in Parma. Not far hence
    Dwells Father Bonaventure, a grave friar,
    Once tutor to my son; now at his cell
    I'll have 'em married.
RICHARDETTO   You have plotted wisely.   20
FLORIO I'll send one straight to speak with him tonight.
RICHARDETTO Soranzo's wise, he will delay no time.
FLORIO It shall be so.
            Enter Friar and Giovanni
FRIAR   Good peace be here and love.
FLORIO Welcome, religious friar, you are one
    That still bring blessing to the place you come to.   25
GIOVANNI Sir, with what speed I could, I did my best
    To draw this holy man from forth his cell
    To visit my sick sister, that with words
    Of ghostly comfort in this time of need,
    He might absolve her, whether she live or die.   30
FLORIO 'Twas well done Giovanni; thou herein
    Hast showed a Christian's care, a brother's love.
    Come, father, I'll conduct you to her chamber,
    And one thing would entreat you.
FRIAR   Say on, sir.
FLORIO I have a father's dear impression,°   35
    And wish, before I fall into my grave,
    That I might see her married, as 'tis fit;
    A word from you, grave man, will win her more
    Than all our best persuasions.
FRIAR   Gentle sir,
    All this I'll say, that Heaven may prosper her.   40
            Exeunt

3.5

Enter Grimaldi

GRIMALDI Now if the doctor keep his word, Soranzo,
 Twenty to one you miss your bride. I know
 'Tis an unnoble act, and not becomes
 A soldier's valour; but in terms of love,
 Where merit cannot sway, policy must.°   5
 I am resolved; if this physician
 Play not on both hands, then Soranzo falls.°
   Enter Richardetto

RICHARDETTO You are come as I could wish; this very night
 Soranzo, 'tis ordained, must be affied
 To Annabella; and for aught I know,   10
 Married.

GRIMALDI How!

RICHARDETTO   Yet your patience.
 The place, 'tis Friar Bonaventure's cell.
 Now I would wish you to bestow this night
 In watching thereabouts. 'Tis but a night;
 If you miss now, tomorrow I'll know all.°   15

GRIMALDI Have you the poison?

RICHARDETTO   Here 'tis in this box.
 Doubt nothing, this will do't; in any case,
 As you respect your life, be quick and sure.

GRIMALDI I'll speed him.

RICHARDETTO   Do. Away, for 'tis not safe°
 You should be seen much here.—Ever my love!   20

GRIMALDI And mine to you.
   Exit Grimaldi

RICHARDETTO So, if this hit, I'll laugh and hug revenge;
 And they that now dream of a wedding-feast
 May chance to mourn the lusty bridegroom's ruin.
 But to my other business.—Niece Philotis!   25
   Enter Philotis

PHILOTIS Uncle.

RICHARDETTO   My lovely niece, you have bethought 'ee?

PHILOTIS Yes, and as you counselled,
 Fashioned my heart to love him; but he swears
 He will tonight be married, for he fears

His uncle else, if he should know the drift,   30
Will hinder all, and call his coz to shrift.°
RICHARDETTO Tonight? Why, best of all! But let me see,
   Ay—ha—yes,—so it shall be; in disguise
   We'll early to the friar's, I have thought on't.
      Enter Bergetto and Poggio
PHILOTIS Uncle, he comes!
RICHARDETTO   Welcome, my worthy coz.   35
BERGETTO Lass, pretty lass, come buss, lass! [*Kisses her*] Aha, Poggio!
PHILOTIS There's hope of this yet.°
RICHARDETTO You shall have time enough; withdraw a little,
   We must confer at large.
BERGETTO Have you not sweetmeats or dainty devices for me?   40
PHILOTIS You shall have enough, sweetheart.
BERGETTO Sweetheart! Mark that, Poggio; by my troth I cannot
   choose but kiss thee once more for that word 'sweetheart'. [*Kisses
   her*] Poggio, I have a monstrous swelling about my stomach,
   whatsoever the matter be.   45
POGGIO You shall have physic for't, sir.
RICHARDETTO Time runs apace.
BERGETTO Time's a blockhead.
RICHARDETTO Be ruled; when we have done what's fit to do,
   Then you may kiss your fill, and bed her too.   50
      Exeunt

3.6

*Enter the Friar in his study,° sitting in a chair, Annabella
kneeling and whispering to him, a table before them and
wax-lights; she weeps, and wrings her hands*
FRIAR I am glad to see this penance; for believe me,
   You have unripped a soul so foul and guilty,°
   As I must tell you true, I marvel how
   The earth hath borne you up. But weep, weep on,
   These tears may do you good; weep faster yet,   5
   Whiles I do read a lecture.
ANNABELLA   Wretched creature!°
FRIAR Ay, you are wretched, miserably wretched,
   Almost condemned alive. There is a place—

List, daughter—in a black and hollow vault,
Where day is never seen; there shines no sun,   10
But flaming horror of consuming fires;
A lightless sulphur, choked with smoky fogs
Of an infected darkness. In this place
Dwell many thousand thousand sundry sorts
Of never-dying deaths: there, damnèd souls   15
Roar without pity; there, are gluttons fed
With toads and adders; there, is burning oil
Poured down the drunkard's throat; the usurer
Is forced to sup whole draughts of molten gold;
There is the murderer forever stabbed,   20
Yet can he never die; there lies the wanton
On racks of burning steel, whiles in his soul
He feels the torment of his raging lust.

ANNABELLA Mercy, oh mercy!

FRIAR   There stands these wretched things
Who have dreamt out whole years in lawless sheets   25
And secret incests, cursing one another.
Then you will wish each kiss your brother gave
Had been a dagger's point; then you shall hear
How he will cry, 'O, would my wicked sister
Had first been damned, when she did yield to lust!'   30
But soft, methinks I see repentance work
New motions in your heart; say, how is't with you?

ANNABELLA Is there no way left to redeem my miseries?

FRIAR There is, despair not: Heaven is merciful,
And offers grace even now. 'Tis thus agreed,   35
First, for your honour's safety, that you marry
The Lord Soranzo; next, to save your soul,°
Leave off this life, and henceforth live to him.

ANNABELLA Ay me!

FRIAR   Sigh not; I know the baits of sin
Are hard to leave—O, 'tis a death to do't.   40
Remember what must come! Are you content?

ANNABELLA I am.

FRIAR   I like it well; we'll take the time.°
Who's near us there?
       Enter Florio [and] Giovanni

FLORIO   Did you call, father?

FRIAR Is Lord Soranzo come?

FLORIO   He stays below.
FRIAR Have you acquainted him at full?
FLORIO   I have,   45
  And he is overjoyed.
FRIAR   And so are we;
  Bid him come near.
GIOVANNI [*aside*]   My sister weeping, ha?
  I fear this friar's falsehood. [*To them*] I will call him.
          Exit [*Giovanni*]
FLORIO Daughter, are you resolved?
ANNABELLA   Father, I am.
          Enter Giovanni, Soranzo, and Vasques
FLORIO My lord Soranzo, here   50
  Give me your hand; for that I give you this.°
          [*He joins their hands*]
SORANZO Lady, say you so too?
ANNABELLA   I do, and vow
  To live with you and yours.
FRIAR   Timely resolved:
  My blessing rest on both. More to be done,
  You may perform it on the morning sun.°   55
          Exeunt

3.7

          Enter Grimaldi with his rapier drawn, and a dark lantern°
GRIMALDI 'Tis early night as yet, and yet too soon
  To finish such a work. Here I will lie
  To listen who comes next.°
          He lies down
          Enter Bergetto and Philotis disguised, and after,° *Richardetto*
          and Poggio
BERGETTO We are almost at the place, I hope, sweetheart.
GRIMALDI [*aside*] I hear them near, and heard one say 'sweetheart'.   5
  'Tis he; now guide my hand, some angry Justice,
  Home to his bosom. [*Aloud*] Now have at you, sir!
          Strikes Bergetto and exit[*s*]
BERGETTO O help, help! Here's a stitch fallen° in my guts. O for a
  flesh-tailor° quickly!—Poggio!

PHILOTIS What ails my love?   10

BERGETTO I am sure I cannot piss forward and backward, and yet I
am wet before and behind. Lights, lights, ho, lights!

PHILOTIS Alas, some villain here has slain my love!

RICHARDETTO O, Heaven forbid it!—Raise up the next neighbours
Instantly, Poggio, and bring lights.   15
          Exit Poggio
How is't, Bergetto? Slain? It cannot be!
Are you sure y'are hurt?

BERGETTO O, my belly seethes like a porridge-pot: some cold water,
I shall boil over else. My whole body is in a sweat, that you may
wring my shirt; feel here—why, Poggio!   20
          Enter Poggio with officers, and lights and halberts

POGGIO Here! Alas, how do you?

RICHARDETTO Give me a light—what's here? All blood! O sirs,
Signior Donado's nephew now is slain!
Follow the murderer with all thy haste
Up to the city; he cannot be far hence.   25
Follow, I beseech you!

OFFICERS   Follow, follow, follow!
          Exeunt officers

RICHARDETTO Tear off thy linen, coz, to stop his wounds;
Be of good comfort, man.

BERGETTO Is all this mine own blood? Nay, then good-night with
me. Poggio, commend me to my uncle, dost hear? Bid him, for my   30
sake, make much of this wench. O—I am going the wrong way°
sure, my belly aches so.—O, farewell, Poggio!—O!—O!—
          Dies

PHILOTIS O, he is dead!

POGGIO   How! Dead!

RICHARDETTO   He's dead indeed.
'Tis now too late to weep; let's have him home,
And with what speed we may, find out the murderer.   35

POGGIO O my master, my master, my master!
          Exeunt

3.8

Enter Vasques and Hippolita

HIPPOLITA Betrothed?

VASQUES I saw it.

HIPPOLITA And when's the marriage-day?

VASQUES Some two days hence.

HIPPOLITA Two days? Why, man, I would but wish two hours   5
　　To send him to his last and lasting sleep.
　　And Vasques, thou shalt see, I'll do it bravely.

VASQUES I do not doubt your wisdom, nor (I trust) you my secrecy;
　　I am infinitely yours.

HIPPOLITA I will be thine in spite of my disgrace.   10
　　So soon? O wicked man, I durst be sworn
　　He'd laugh to see me weep.

VASQUES And that's a villainous fault in him.

HIPPOLITA No, let him laugh; I'm armed in my resolves,
　　Be thou still true.   15

VASQUES I should get little by treachery against so hopeful° a
　　preferment as I am like to climb to.

HIPPOLITA Even to my bosom, Vasques. Let my youth°
　　Revel in these new pleasures. If we thrive,
　　He now hath but a pair of days to live.   20
　　　Exeunt

3.9

Enter Florio, Donado [weeping], Richardetto, Poggio, and officers

FLORIO 'Tis bootless now to show yourself a child,
　　Signior Donado; what is done, is done.
　　Spend not the time in tears, but seek for justice.

RICHARDETTO I must confess, somewhat I was in fault,
　　That had not first acquainted you what love   5
　　Passed 'twixt him and my niece; but as I live,
　　His fortune grieves me as it were mine own.

DONADO Alas, poor creature, he meant no man harm,
　　That I am sure of.

FLORIO　　　　　　　I believe that too.

But stay, my masters, are you sure you saw   10
  The murderer pass here?

OFFICER And it please you sir, we are sure we saw a ruffian with a
naked weapon in his hand, all bloody, get into my lord Cardinal's
grace's gate—that,° we are sure of; but for fear of his grace (bless
us!) we durst go no further.   15

DONADO Know you what manner of man he was?

OFFICER Yes, sure I know the man; they say 'a is a soldier—he that
loved your daughter, sir, an't please ye, 'twas he for certain.

FLORIO Grimaldi, on my life!

OFFICER   Ay, ay, the same.

RICHARDETTO The Cardinal is noble; he no doubt   20
  Will give true justice.

DONADO Knock someone at the gate.

POGGIO I'll knock, sir.
    Poggio knocks

SERVANT (*within*) What would 'ee?

FLORIO We require speech with the lord Cardinal   25
  About some present business; pray inform
  His grace that we are here.
    Enter Cardinal and Grimaldi

CARDINAL Why, how now, friends! What saucy mates are you°
  That know nor duty nor civility?
  Are we a person fit to be your host?   30
  Or is our house become your common inn,
  To beat our doors at pleasure? What such haste
  Is yours, as that it cannot wait fit times?
  Are you the masters of this commonwealth,
  And know no more discretion? O, your news   35
  Is here before you; you have lost a nephew,
  Donado, last night by Grimaldi slain:
  Is that your business? Well, sir, we have knowledge on't.
  Let that suffice.

GRIMALDI   In presence of your grace,
  In thought I never meant Bergetto harm;   40
  But Florio, you can tell with how much scorn
  Soranzo, backed with his confederates,
  Hath often wronged me. I, to be revenged,
  (For that I could not win him else to fight)
  Had thought by way of ambush to have killed him,   45
  But was unluckily therein mistook;

Else he had felt what late Bergetto did.
And though my fault to him were merely chance,
Yet humbly I submit me to your grace, [*kneels*]
To do with me as you please.
CARDINAL   Rise up, Grimaldi.   50
     [*He rises*]
You citizens of Parma, if you seek
For justice, know, as nuncio from the Pope,
For this offence I here receive Grimaldi
Into his Holiness' protection.
He is no common man, but nobly born;   55
Of princes' blood, though you, Sir Florio,°
Thought him too mean a husband for your daughter.
If more you seek for, you must go to Rome,
For he shall thither; learn more wit, for shame.
Bury your dead.—Away, Grimaldi—leave 'em!   60
     Exeunt Cardinal and Grimaldi
DONADO Is this a churchman's voice? Dwells Justice here?
FLORIO Justice is fled to Heaven and comes no nearer.°
Soranzo! Was't for him? O impudence!
Had he the face to speak it, and not blush?
Come, come Donado, there's no help in this,   65
When cardinals think murder's not amiss.
Great men may do their wills; we must obey,
But Heaven will judge them for't another day.
     Exeunt

4.1

A banquet.° Hautboys.
Enter the Friar, Giovanni, Annabella, Philotis, Soranzo,
Donado, Florio, Richardetto, Putana, and Vasques

FRIAR These holy rites performed, now take your times,
To spend the remnant of the day in feast;
Such fit repasts are pleasing to the saints
Who are your guests, though not with mortal eyes
To be beheld. Long prosper in this day,   5
You happy couple, to each other's joy!

SORANZO Father, your prayer is heard. The hand of goodness
Hath been a shield for me against my death;
And, more to bless me, hath enriched my life
With this most precious jewel; such a prize   10
As earth hath not another like to this.
Cheer up, my love; and gentlemen, my friends,
Rejoice with me in mirth: this day we'll crown
With lusty cups to Annabella's health.

GIOVANNI (*aside*) O, torture! Were the marriage yet undone,   15
Ere I'd endure this sight, to see my love
Clipped by another, I would dare confusion,
And stand the horror of ten thousand deaths.

VASQUES Are you not well, sir?

GIOVANNI   Prithee, fellow, wait;°
I need not thy officious diligence.   20

FLORIO Signior Donado, come, you must forget
Your late mishaps, and drown your cares in wine.

SORANZO Vasques!

VASQUES   My lord.

SORANZO   Reach me that weighty bowl.
Here, brother Giovanni, here's to you;
Your turn comes next, though now a bachelor: 25
Here's to your sister's happiness and mine!
    [*Drinks, and offers him the bowl*]

GIOVANNI I cannot drink.

SORANZO   What?

GIOVANNI   'Twill indeed offend me.°

ANNABELLA Pray, do not urge him if he be not willing.

Hautboys

FLORIO How now, what noise is this?°

VASQUES O sir, I had forgot to tell you; certain young maidens of   30
Parma, in honour to Madam Annabella's marriage, have sent
their loves to her in a masque,° for which they humbly crave your
patience and silence.

SORANZO We are much bound to them, so much the more
As it comes unexpected; guide them in.   35

*Enter Hippolita and ladies [masked,] in white robes with
garlands of willows.° Music and a dance*

SORANZO Thanks, lovely virgins; now might we but know
To whom we have been beholding for this love,°
We shall acknowledge it.

HIPPOLITA   Yes, you shall know.
    [*Unmasks*]
What think you now?

ALL   Hippolita!

HIPPOLITA   'Tis she.
Be not amazed; nor blush, young lovely bride.   40
I come not to defraud you of your man.
[*To Soranzo*] 'Tis now no time to reckon up the talk
What Parma long hath rumoured of us both.
Let rash report run on; the breath that vents it
Will, like a bubble, break itself at last.   45
[*To Annabella*] But now to you, sweet creature; lend's your hand.
Perhaps it hath been said that I would claim
Some interest in Soranzo, now your lord.
What I have right to do, his soul knows best:
But in my duty to your noble worth,   50
Sweet Annabella, and my care of you,
Here take Soranzo; take this hand from me.°
    [*She joins their hands*]
I'll once more join what by the holy Church
Is finished and allowed: have I done well?

SORANZO You have too much engaged us.

HIPPOLITA   One thing more.°   55
That you may know my single charity,°
Freely I here remit all interest
I e'er could claim, and give you back your vows;
And to confirm't—reach me a cup of wine—
My Lord Soranzo, in this draught I drink   60

Long rest t'ee! [*Aside*] Look to it, Vasques.

VASQUES [*aside*] Fear nothing.

    He gives her a poisoned cup; she drinks

SORANZO Hippolita, I thank you, and will pledge

This happy union as another life.—

Wine there!   65

VASQUES You shall have none, neither shall you pledge her.

HIPPOLITA How!

VASQUES Know now, mistress she-devil, your own mischievous
treachery hath killed you. I must not marry you.

HIPPOLITA Villain!   70

ALL What's the matter?

VASQUES Foolish woman, thou art now like a firebrand, that hath
kindled others and burnt thyself. *Troppo sperare inganna;*° thy vain
hope hath deceived thee. Thou art but° dead; if thou hast any
grace, pray.   75

HIPPOLITA Monster!

VASQUES Die in charity,° for shame!—This thing of malice, this
woman, had privately corrupted me with promise of marriage,
under this politic reconciliation to poison my lord, whiles she
might laugh at his confusion on his marriage-day. I promised her   80
fair, but I knew what my reward should have been; and would
willingly have spared her life, but that I was acquainted with the
danger of her disposition—and now have fitted her a just payment
in her own coin. There she is, she hath yet—and° end thy days in
peace, vile woman; as for life there's no hope, think not on't.   85

ALL Wonderful justice!

RICHARDETTO   Heaven, thou art righteous.

HIPPOLITA O, 'tis true,

I feel my minute coming. Had that slave°

Kept promise—O, my torment!—thou this hour

Hadst died, Soranzo.—Heat above hell-fire!—   90

Yet ere I pass away—cruel, cruel flames!—

Take here my curse amongst you: may thy bed

Of marriage be a rack unto thy heart;

Burn, blood, and boil in vengeance.—O my heart,

My flame's intolerable!—Mayst thou live°   95

To father bastards, may her womb bring forth

Monsters, and die together in your sins,

Hated, scorned, and unpitied!—O!—O!—

    Dies

FLORIO Was e'er so vile a creature?

RICHARDETTO   Here's the end
  Of lust and pride.

ANNABELLA   It is a fearful sight.   100

SORANZO Vasques, I know thee now a trusty servant,
  And never will forget thee.—Come, my love,
  We'll home, and thank the heavens for this escape.
  Father and friends, we must break up this mirth;
  It is too sad a feast.

DONADO   Bear hence the body.   105

FRIAR [*aside to Giovanni*] Here's an ominous change;
  Mark this, my Giovanni, and take heed.
  I fear the event; that marriage seldom's good,°
  Where the bride-banquet so begins in blood.
          Exeunt [*with Hippolita's body*]

4.2

          Enter Richardetto and Philotis

RICHARDETTO My wretched wife, more wretched in her shame
  Than in her wrongs to me, hath paid too soon
  The forfeit of her modesty and life.
  And I am sure, my niece, though vengeance hover,
  Keeping aloof yet from Soranzo's fall,   5
  Yet he will fall, and sink with his own weight.
  I need not—now my heart persuades me so—
  To further his confusion. There is One
  Above begins to work, for, as I hear,
  Debates already 'twixt his wife and him°   10
  Thicken and run to head; she (as 'tis said)
  Slightens his love, and he abandons hers.
  Much talk I hear. Since things go thus, my niece,
  In tender love and pity of your youth,
  My counsel is that you should free your years   15
  From hazard of these woes, by flying hence
  To fair Cremona, there to vow your soul
  In holiness a holy votaress.
  Leave me to see the end of these extremes.
  All human worldly courses are uneven;°   20

216

No life is blessed but the way to Heaven.

PHILOTIS Uncle, shall I resolve to be a nun?

RICHARDETTO Ay, gentle niece, and in your hourly prayers
Remember me, your poor unhappy uncle.
Hie to Cremona now, as fortune leads,   25
Your home your cloister, your best friends your beads.°
Your chaste and single life shall crown your birth;
Who dies a virgin lives a saint on earth.

PHILOTIS Then farewell, world, and worldly thoughts adieu!
Welcome, chaste vows; myself I yield to you.   30

> *Exeunt*

4.3

Enter Soranzo unbraced,° and Annabella dragged in

SORANZO Come, strumpet, famous whore! Were every drop
Of blood that runs in thy adulterous veins
A life, this sword—dost see't?—should in one blow
Confound them all. Harlot, rare, notable harlot,
That with thy brazen face maintain'st thy sin,°   5
Was there no man in Parma to be bawd
To your loose cunning whoredom else but I?
Must your hot itch and pleurisy of lust,°
The heyday of your luxury, be fed
Up to a surfeit, and could none but I   10
Be picked out to be cloak to your close tricks,°
Your belly-sports? Now I must be the dad
To all that gallimaufry that's stuffed
In thy corrupted bastard-bearing womb!
Why must I?

ANNABELLA   Beastly man, why, 'tis thy fate.   15
I sued not to thee, for, but that I thought
Your over-loving lordship would have run
Mad on denial, had ye lent me time,
I would have told 'ee in what case I was.
But you would needs be doing.

SORANZO   Whore of whores!°   20
Dar'st thou tell me this?

ANNABELLA   O yes, why not?

You were deceived in me: 'twas not for love
I chose you, but for honour. Yet know this,
Would you be patient yet, and hide your shame,
I'd see whether I could love you.

SORANZO   Excellent quean!   25
Why, art thou not with child?

ANNABELLA   What needs all this,
When 'tis superfluous? I confess I am.

SORANZO Tell me by whom.

ANNABELLA   .   Soft, sir, 'twas not in my bargain.
Yet somewhat, sir, to stay your longing stomach,°
I'm content t'acquaint you with. The man,   30
The more than man that got this sprightly boy—
For 'tis a boy; that for your glory, sir;
Your heir shall be a son.

SORANZO   Damnable monster!

ANNABELLA Nay, and you will not hear, I'll speak no more.°

SORANZO Yes, speak, and speak thy last.

ANNABELLA   A match, a match!°   35
This noble creature was in every part
So angel-like, so glorious, that a woman
Who had not been but human, as was I,
Would have kneeled to him, and have begged for love.
You, why you are not worthy once to name   40
His name without true worship, or indeed,
Unless you kneeled, to hear another name him.

SORANZO What was he called?

ANNABELLA   We are not come to that;
Let it suffice that you shall have the glory
To father what so brave a father got.   45
In brief, had not this chance fall'n out as't doth,
I never had been troubled with a thought
That you had been a creature. But for marriage,°
I scarce dream yet of that.°

SORANZO Tell me his name.

ANNABELLA   Alas, alas, there's all.   50
Will you believe?

SORANZO   What?

ANNABELLA   You shall never know.

SORANZO How!

ANNABELLA   Never; if you do, let me be cursed.

SORANZO Not know it, strumpet! I'll rip up thy heart,
And find it there.
ANNABELLA   Do, do!
SORANZO   And with my teeth
Tear the prodigious lecher joint by joint.   55
ANNABELLA Ha, ha, ha, the man's merry!
SORANZO   Dost thou laugh?
Come, whore, tell me your lover, or by truth
I'll hew thy flesh to shreds! Who is't?
ANNABELLA (*sings*) *Che morte più dolce che morire per amore?*°
SORANZO Thus will I pull thy hair, and thus I'll drag   60
Thy lust-belepered body through the dust.
Yet tell his name.
ANNABELLA (*sings*) *Morendo in grazia a lui, morirei senza dolore.*°
SORANZO Dost thou triumph? The treasure of the earth
Shall not redeem thee; were there kneeling kings   65
Did beg thy life, or angels did come down
To plead in tears, yet should not all prevail
Against my rage. Dost thou not tremble yet?
ANNABELLA At what? To die? No, be a gallant hangman.
I dare thee to the worst; strike, and strike home.   70
I leave revenge behind, and thou shalt feel't.
SORANZO Yet tell me ere thou diest, and tell me truly,
Knows thy old father this?
ANNABELLA   No, by my life.
SORANZO Wilt thou confess, and I will spare thy life?
ANNABELLA My life! I will not buy my life so dear.   75
SORANZO I will not slack my vengeance. [*Draws his sword*]
        Enter Vasques
VASQUES   What d'ee mean, sir?
SORANZO Forbear, Vasques; such a damnèd whore
Deserves no pity.
VASQUES   Now the gods forfend!
And would you be her executioner, and kill her in your rage
too? O, 'twere most unmanlike! She is your wife; what faults   80
hath been done by her before she married you, were not against
you; alas, poor lady, what hath she committed which any lady
in Italy in the like case would not? Sir, you must be ruled by
your reason, and not by your fury; that were unhuman and
beastly.   85
SORANZO She shall not live.

VASQUES Come, she must. You would have her confess the author
of her present misfortunes, I warrant 'ee; 'tis an unconscionable
demand, and she should lose the estimation that I, for my part,
hold of her worth, if she had done it. Why sir, you ought not of   90
all men living to know it. Good sir, be reconciled; alas, good
gentlewoman!

ANNABELLA Pish, do not beg for me; I prize my life
As nothing. If the man will needs be mad,
Why let him take it.

SORANZO   Vasques, hear'st thou this?   95

VASQUES Yes, and commend her for it. In this she shows the
nobleness of a gallant spirit, and beshrew my heart but it becomes
her rarely. [*Aside to Soranzo*] Sir, in any case° smother your revenge;
leave the scenting-out your wrongs to me. Be ruled, as you respect
your honour, or you mar all. [*Aloud*] Sir, if ever my service were   100
of any credit with you, be not so violent in your distractions. You
are married now; what a triumph might the report of this give to
other neglected suitors! 'Tis as manlike to bear extremities, as
godlike to forgive.

SORANZO O Vasques, Vasques, in this piece of flesh,   105
This faithless face of hers, had I laid up
The treasure of my heart!—Hadst thou been virtuous,
Fair, wicked woman, not the matchless joys
Of life itself had made me wish to live
With any saint but thee. Deceitful creature,   110
How hast thou mocked my hopes, and in the shame
Of thy lewd womb, even buried me alive!
I did too dearly love thee.

VASQUES [*aside*] (*to Soranzo*) This is well. Follow this temper with
some passion.° Be brief and moving; 'tis for the purpose.   115

SORANZO Be witness to my words thy soul and thoughts,
And tell me, didst not think that in my heart
I did too superstitiously adore thee?

ANNABELLA I must confess, I know you loved me well.

SORANZO And wouldst thou use me thus? O Annabella,   120
Be thou assured, whatsoe'er the villain was
That thus hath tempted thee to this disgrace,
Well he might lust, but never loved like me.
He doted on the picture that hung out
Upon thy cheeks, to please his humorous eye;°   125
Not on the part I loved, which was thy heart,

And, as I thought, thy virtues.

ANNABELLA   O my lord!
These words wound deeper than your sword could do.

VASQUES Let me not ever take comfort, but I begin to weep myself,
so much I pity him; why, madam, I knew when his rage was   130
overpassed what it would come to.

SORANZO Forgive me, Annabella. Though thy youth
Hath tempted thee above thy strength to folly,
Yet will not I forget what I should be,
And what I am, a husband; in that name   135
Is hid divinity. If I do find
That thou wilt yet be true, here I remit
All former faults, and take thee to my bosom.

VASQUES By my troth, and that's a point° of noble charity.

ANNABELLA Sir, on my knees—

SORANZO   Rise up; you shall not kneel.   140
Get you to your chamber, see you make no show
Of alteration; I'll be with you straight.°
My reason tells me now that 'tis as common
To err in frailty as to be a woman.
Go to your chamber.   145

        Exit Annabella

VASQUES So, this was somewhat to the matter;° what do you think
of your heaven of happiness now, sir?

SORANZO I carry Hell about me; all my blood
Is fired in swift revenge.

VASQUES That may be, but know you how, or on whom? Alas, to   150
marry a great woman,° being made great in the stock° to your
hand, is a usual sport in these days; but to know what ferret it was
that haunted your cony-berry,° there's the cunning.

SORANZO I'll make her tell herself, or—

VASQUES Or what? You must not do so. Let me yet persuade your   155
sufferance a little while. Go to her, use her mildly, win her if it be
possible to a voluntary,° to a weeping tune; for the rest, if all hit,
I will not miss my mark. Pray, sir, go in; the next news I tell you
shall be wonders.

SORANZO Delay in vengeance gives a heavier blow.   160

        Exit [Soranzo]

VASQUES Ah, sirrah, here's work for the nonce! I had a suspicion of
a bad matter in my head a pretty whiles ago; but after my madam's
scurvy looks here at home, her waspish perverseness and loud

fault-finding, then I remembered the proverb, that where hens crow and cocks hold their peace there are sorry houses.° 'Sfoot, if the 165 lower parts of a she-tailor's cunning can cover such a swelling in the stomach, I'll never blame a false stitch in a shoe whiles I live again. Up, and up so quick?° And so quickly too? 'Twere a fine policy to learn by whom. This° must be known; and I have thought on't.

[*Enter Putana in tears*]

Here's the way, or none.—What, crying, old mistress? Alas, alas, 170 I cannot blame 'ee; we have a lord, Heaven help us, is so mad as the devil himself, the more shame for him.

PUTANA O Vasques, that ever I was born to see this day! Doth he use thee so too, sometimes, Vasques?

VASQUES Me? Why, he makes a dog of me; but if some were of my 175 mind, I know what we would do. As sure as I am an honest man, he will go near to kill my lady with unkindness. Say she be with child, is that such a matter for a young woman of her years to be blamed for?

PUTANA Alas, good heart, it is against her will full sore. 180

VASQUES I durst be sworn, all his madness is for that she will not confess whose 'tis; which he will know, and when he doth know it, I am so well acquainted with his humour, that he will forget all straight. Well I could wish she would in plain terms tell all, for that's the way indeed. 185

PUTANA Do you think so?

VASQUES Foh, I know't; provided that he did not win her to't by force. He was once in a mind that you could tell, and meant to have wrung it out of you, but I somewhat pacified him for that; yet sure you know a great deal. 190

PUTANA Heaven forgive us all, I know a little, Vasques.

VASQUES Why should you not? Who else should? Upon my conscience, she loves you dearly, and you would not betray her to any affliction for the world.

PUTANA Not for all the world, by my faith and troth, Vasques. 195

VASQUES 'Twere pity of your life if you should; but in this you should both relieve her present discomforts, pacify my lord, and gain yourself everlasting love and preferment.

PUTANA Dost think so, Vasques?

VASQUES Nay, I know't. Sure 'twas some near and entire friend.° 200

PUTANA 'Twas a dear° friend indeed; but—

VASQUES But what? Fear not to name him; my life between you and danger. Faith, I think 'twas no base fellow.

PUTANA Thou wilt stand between me and harm?

VASQUES Ud's pity, what else? You shall be rewarded too; trust me.   205

PUTANA 'Twas even no worse than her own brother.

VASQUES Her brother Giovanni, I warrant 'ee?

PUTANA Even he, Vasques; as brave a gentleman as ever kissed fair
lady. O, they love most perpetually.

VASQUES A brave gentleman indeed; why, therein I commend her   210
choice. [*Aside*] Better and better! [*To her*]—You are sure 'twas
he?

PUTANA Sure; and you shall see he will not be long from her too.

VASQUES He were to blame if he would; but may I believe thee?

PUTANA Believe me! Why, dost think I am a Turk or a Jew? No,   215
Vasques, I have known their dealings too long to belie them now.

VASQUES Where are you? There within, sirs!

Enter Banditti

PUTANA How now, what are these?

VASQUES You shall know presently. Come sirs, take me this old
damnable hag, gag her instantly, and put out her eyes. Quickly,   220
quickly!

PUTANA Vasques, Vasques!

VASQUES Gag her I say. 'Sfoot, d'ee suffer her to prate? What d'ee
fumble about? Let me come to her.—I'll help your old gums, you
toad-bellied bitch! [*He gags Putana*]—Sirs, carry her closely into   225
the coal-house and put out her eyes instantly. If she roars, slit her
nose; d'ee hear, be speedy and sure.

Exeunt [Banditti] with Putana

Why, this is excellent and above expectation. Her own brother?
O horrible! To what a height of liberty in damnation hath the devil
trained our age. Her brother, well! There's yet but a beginning; I   230
must to my lord, and tutor him better in his points of vengeance.
Now I see how a smooth tale goes beyond a smooth tail. But
soft—What thing comes next?

Enter Giovanni

Giovanni! As I would wish. My belief is strengthened; 'tis as firm
as winter and summer.   235

GIOVANNI Where's my sister?

VASQUES Troubled with a new sickness, my lord; she's somewhat ill.

GIOVANNI Took too much of the flesh,° I believe.

VASQUES Troth, sir, and you I think have e'en hit it;° but my
virtuous lady—   240

GIOVANNI Where's she?

223

VASQUES In her chamber. Please you visit her; she is alone. [*Giovanni gives him money*] Your liberality° hath doubly made me your servant, and ever shall, ever—

Exit Giovanni. Enter Soranzo

Sir, I am made a man,° I have plied my cue° with cunning and   245
success; I beseech you, let's be private.

SORANZO My lady's brother's come; now he'll know all.

VASQUES Let him know't; I have made some of them fast enough.
How have you dealt with my lady?

SORANZO Gently, as thou hast counselled. O, my soul   250
Runs circular in sorrow for revenge!
But Vasques, thou shalt know—

VASQUES Nay, I will know no more, for now comes your turn to
know. I would not talk so openly with you. Let my young master
take time enough, and go at pleasure; he is sold to death, and the   255
devil shall not ransom him. Sir, I beseech you, your privacy.

SORANZO No conquest can gain glory of my fear.°

[*Exeunt*]

5.1

Enter Annabella above [with a letter written in blood]

ANNABELLA Pleasures farewell, and all ye thriftless minutes
Wherein false joys have spun a weary life;
To these my fortunes now I take my leave.
Thou precious Time, that swiftly rid'st in post
Over the world, to finish up the race   5
Of my last fate; here stay thy restless course,
And bear to ages that are yet unborn
A wretched woeful woman's tragedy.
My conscience now stands up against my lust
With depositions charactered in guilt,°   10
          Enter Friar [below]
And tells me I am lost. Now I confess
Beauty that clothes the outside of the face
Is cursèd if it be not clothed with grace.
Here like a turtle, mewed up in a cage
Unmated, I converse with air and walls,°   15
And descant on my vile unhappiness.
O Giovanni, that hast had the spoil°
Of thine own virtues and my modest fame,
Would thou hadst been less subject to those stars
That luckless reigned at my nativity!   20
O, would the scourge due to my black offence
Might pass from thee, that I alone might feel
The torment of an uncontrollèd flame!
FRIAR [*aside*] What's this I hear?
ANNABELLA   That man, that blessed friar,
Who joined in ceremonial knot my hand   25
To him whose wife I now am, told me oft
I trod the path to death, and showed me how.
But they who sleep in lethargies of lust
Hug their confusion, making Heaven unjust,
And so did I.
FRIAR [*aside*]   Here's music to the soul!   30
ANNABELLA Forgive me, my good genius, and this once
Be helpful to my ends. Let some good man
Pass this way, to whose trust I may commit

This paper double-lined with tears and blood;
Which being granted, here I sadly vow   35
Repentance, and a leaving of that life
I long have died in.
FRIAR   Lady, Heaven hath heard you,
And hath by providence ordained that I
Should be his minister for your behoof.
ANNABELLA Ha, what are you?
FRIAR   Your brother's friend, the friar;   40
Glad in my soul that I have lived to hear
This free confession 'twixt your peace and you.
What would you, or to whom? Fear not to speak.
ANNABELLA Is Heaven so bountiful? Then I have found
More favour than I hoped. Here, holy man—   45
        (*Throws a letter*)
Commend me to my brother, give him that,
That letter; bid him read it and repent.
Tell him that I—imprisoned in my chamber,
Barred of all company, even of my guardian,
Who gives me cause of much suspect—have time   50
To blush at what hath passed; bid him be wise,
And not believe the friendship of my lord.
I fear much more than I can speak. Good father,
The place is dangerous, and spies are busy;
I must break off—you'll do't?
FRIAR   Be sure I will,   55
And fly with speed. My blessing ever rest
With thee, my daughter; live to die more blessed!
        Exit [Friar]
ANNABELLA Thanks to the Heavens, who have prolonged my breath
To this good use. Now I can welcome death.
        Exit

5.2

Enter Soranzo and Vasques

VASQUES Am I to be believed now? First marry a strumpet that cast
herself away upon you but to laugh at your horns?° To feast on
your disgrace, riot in your vexations, cuckold you in your bride-
bed, waste your estate upon panders and bawds?

SORANZO No more, I say, no more!   5

VASQUES A cuckold is a goodly tame beast, my lord.

SORANZO I am resolved; urge not another word.
My thoughts are great, and all as resolute°
As thunder. In mean time I'll cause our lady
To deck herself in all her bridal robes,   10
Kiss her, and fold her gently in my arms.
Begone—yet hear you, are the banditti ready
To wait in ambush?

VASQUES Good sir, trouble not yourself about other business than
your own resolution; remember that time lost cannot be recalled.   15

SORANZO With all the cunning words thou canst, invite
The states of Parma to my birthday's feast;°
Haste to my brother rival and his father,
Entreat them gently, bid them not to fail.
Be speedy and return.   20

VASQUES Let not your pity betray you. Till my coming back, think
upon incest and cuckoldry.

SORANZO Revenge is all the ambition I aspire;
To that I'll climb or fall: my blood's on fire.
Exeunt

5.3

Enter Giovanni

GIOVANNI Busy opinion is an idle fool,°
That, as a school-rod keeps a child in awe,
Frights the unexperienced temper of the mind.
So did it me; who, ere my precious sister
Was married, thought all taste of love would die   5
In such a contract. But I find no change

Of pleasure in this formal law of sports.°
She is still one to me, and every kiss°
As sweet and as delicious as the first
I reaped, when yet the privilege of youth   10
Entitled her a virgin. O, the glory
Of two united hearts like hers and mine!
Let poring book-men dream of other worlds,
My world, and all of happiness, is here,
And I'd not change it for the best to come: 15
A life of pleasure is Elysium.
        Enter Friar
Father, you enter on the jubilee°
Of my retired delights. Now I can tell you,
The Hell you oft have prompted is nought else
But slavish and fond superstitious fear;   20
And I could prove it, too—

FRIAR   Thy blindness slays thee.
Look there, 'tis writ to thee.
        (*Gives the letter*)
GIOVANNI From whom?
FRIAR Unrip the seals and see.
The blood's yet seething hot, that will anon   25
Be frozen harder than congealed coral.°
Why d'ee change colour, son?
GIOVANNI   'Fore Heaven, you make
Some petty devil factor 'twixt my love
And your religion-maskèd sorceries.
Where had you this?
FRIAR   Thy conscience, youth, is seared,°   30
Else thou wouldst stoop to warning.
GIOVANNI   'Tis her hand,°
I know't; and 'tis all written in her blood.
She writes I know not what. Death? I'll not fear
An armèd thunderbolt aimed at my heart.
She writes we are discovered—pox on dreams   35
Of low faint-hearted cowardice! Discovered?
The devil we are! Which way is't possible?
Are we grown traitors to our own delights?
Confusion take such dotage; 'tis but forged!
This is your peevish chattering, weak old man.   40
        Enter Vasques

Now, sir, what news bring you?

VASQUES My lord, according to his yearly custom keeping this day a
feast in honour of his birthday, by me invites you thither. Your
worthy father, with the Pope's reverend nuncio, and other
magnificoes of Parma, have promised their presence; will't please   45
you to be of the number?

GIOVANNI Yes, tell them I dare come.

VASQUES Dare come?

GIOVANNI So I said; and tell him more, I will come.

VASQUES These words are strange to me.   50

GIOVANNI Say I will come.

VASQUES You will not miss?°

GIOVANNI Yet more? I'll come! Sir, are you answered?

VASQUES So I'll say.—My service to you.

    Exit Vasques

FRIAR You will not go, I trust.

GIOVANNI   Not go! For what?   55

FRIAR O do not go! This feast, I'll gage my life,
Is but a plot to train you to your ruin;
Be ruled, you sha'not go.

GIOVANNI   Not go? Stood Death
Threat'ning his armies of confounding plagues,
With hosts of dangers hot as blazing stars,°   60
I would be there. Not go! Yes; and resolve
To strike as deep in slaughter as they all.
For I will go.

FRIAR   Go where thou wilt; I see
The wildness of thy fate draws to an end,
To a bad, fearful end. I must not stay   65
To know thy fall; back to Bologna I
With speed will haste, and shun this coming blow.
Parma farewell; would I had never known thee,
Or aught of thine! Well, youngman, since no prayer°
Can make thee safe, I leave thee to despair.   70

    Exit Friar

GIOVANNI° Despair, or tortures of a thousand hells,
All's one to me; I have set up my rest.°
Now, now, work serious thoughts on baneful plots.
Be all a man, my soul; let not the curse
Of old prescription rend from me the gall°   75
Of courage, which enrols a glorious death.

If I must totter like a well-grown oak,
Some under-shrubs shall in my weighty fall
Be crushed to splits: with me they all shall perish.
          Exit

5.4

Enter Soranzo, Vasques, and Banditti

SORANZO You will not fail, or shrink in the attempt?

VASQUES I will undertake° for their parts. [*To Banditti*]—Be sure,
my masters, to be bloody enough, and as unmerciful as if you were
preying upon a rich booty on the very mountains of Liguria.° For
your pardons, trust to my lord; but for reward you shall trust none   5
but your own pockets.

BANDITTI We'll make a murder.

SORANZO Here's gold, here's more; want nothing. What you do
Is noble, and an act of brave revenge.
I'll make ye rich banditti, and all free.°   10

BANDITTI Liberty, liberty!

VASQUES Hold, take every man a vizard. When ye are withdrawn,
keep as much silence as you can possibly. You know the watchword, till which be spoken, move not, but when you hear that, rush
in like a stormy flood; I need not instruct ye in your own   15
profession.

BANDITTI No, no, no.

VASQUES In, then; your ends are profit and preferment—away!
          [*Exeunt*] *Banditti*

SORANZO The guests will all come, Vasques?

VASQUES Yes, sir, and now let me a little edge your resolution; you   20
see nothing is unready to this great work, but a great mind in you.
Call to your remembrance your disgraces, your loss of honour,
Hippolita's blood, and arm your courage in your own wrongs; so
shall you best right those wrongs in vengeance which you may
truly call your own.   25

SORANZO 'Tis well; the less I speak, the more I burn,
And blood shall quench that flame.

VASQUES Now you begin to turn Italian!° This beside; when my
young incest-monger comes, he will be sharp set on his old bit.°
Give him time enough, let him have your chamber and bed at   30

liberty; let my hot hare° have law° ere he be hunted to his death,
that if it be possible he may post to Hell in the very act of his
damnation.

Enter Giovanni

SORANZO It shall be so; and see, as we would wish,
He comes himself first.—Welcome, my much-loved brother,   35
Now I perceive you honour me; y'are welcome.
But where's my father?

GIOVANNI   With the other states,
Attending on the nuncio of the Pope
To wait upon him hither. How's my sister?

SORANZO Like a good housewife, scarcely ready yet;   40
Y'are best walk to her chamber.

GIOVANNI   If you will.

SORANZO I must expect my honourable friends;
Good brother, get her forth.

GIOVANNI   You are busy, sir.°

Exit Giovanni

VASQUES Even as the great devil himself would have it! Let him go
and glut himself in his own destruction.   45

Flourish

Hark, the nuncio is at hand; good sir, be ready to receive him.

Enter Cardinal, Florio, Donado, Richardetto, and attendants

SORANZO Most reverend lord, this grace hath made me proud
That you vouchsafe my house; I ever rest
Your humble servant for this noble favour.

CARDINAL You are our friend, my lord; his holiness   50
Shall understand how zealously you honour
Saint Peter's vicar in his substitute.°
Our special love to you.

SORANZO   Signiors, to you
My welcome, and my ever best of thanks
For this so memorable courtesy.   55
Pleaseth your grace to walk near?

CARDINAL   My lord, we come
To celebrate your feast with civil mirth,
As ancient custom teacheth; we will go.

SORANZO Attend his grace there! Signiors, keep your way.°

Exeunt

5.5

Enter Giovanni and Annabella [in her wedding dress] lying on a bed°

GIOVANNI What, changed so soon? Hath your new sprightly lord
    Found out a trick in night-games more than we
    Could know in our simplicity? Ha, is't so?
    Or does the fit come on you, to prove treacherous
    To your past vows and oaths?
ANNABELLA   Why should you jest   5
    At my calamity, without all sense
    Of the approaching dangers you are in?
GIOVANNI What danger's half so great as thy revolt?
    Thou art a faithless sister, else, thou know'st,
    Malice, or any treachery beside,   10
    Would stoop to my bent brows. Why, I hold fate°
    Clasped in my fist, and could command the course
    Of time's eternal motion, hadst thou been
    One thought more steady than an ebbing sea.
    And what? You'll now be honest, that's resolved?   15
ANNABELLA Brother, dear brother, know what I have been,
    And know that now there's but a dining-time
    'Twixt us and our confusion. Let's not waste
    These precious hours in vain and useless speech.
    Alas, these gay attires were not put on   20
    But to some end; this sudden solemn feast
    Was not ordained to riot in expense;
    I that have now been chambered here alone,
    Barred of my guardian, or of any else,
    Am not for nothing at an instant freed   25
    To fresh access. Be not deceived, my brother,°
    This banquet is an harbinger of death
    To you and me; resolve yourself it is,
    And be prepared to welcome it.
GIOVANNI   Well then,
    The schoolmen teach that all this globe of earth   30
    Shall be consumed to ashes in a minute.
ANNABELLA So I have read too.
GIOVANNI   But 'twere somewhat strange
    To see the waters burn; could I believe°

This might be true, I could believe as well
There might be Hell or Heaven.
ANNABELLA   That's most certain.   35
GIOVANNI A dream, a dream; else in this other world
We should know one another.
ANNABELLA   So we shall.
GIOVANNI Have you heard so?
ANNABELLA   For certain.
GIOVANNI   But d'ee think
That I shall see you there, you look on me?
May we kiss one another, prate or laugh,   40
Or do as we do here?
ANNABELLA   I know not that,°
But good, for the present, what d'ee mean°
To free yourself from danger? Some way, think
How to escape; I'm sure the guests are come.
GIOVANNI Look up, look here; what see you in my face?   45
ANNABELLA Distraction and a troubled countenance.
GIOVANNI Death, and a swift repining wrath—yet look,
What see you in mine eyes?
ANNABELLA   Methinks you weep.
GIOVANNI I do indeed. These are the funeral tears
Shed on your grave; these furrowed up my cheeks   50
When first I loved and knew not how to woo.
Fair Annabella, should I here repeat
The story of my life, we might lose time.
Be record, all the spirits of the air,
And all things else that are, that day and night,   55
Early and late, the tribute which my heart
Hath paid to Annabella's sacred love
Hath been these tears, which are her mourners now.
Never till now did Nature do her best
To show a matchless beauty to the world,   60
Which, in an instant, ere it scarce was seen,
The jealous Destinies required again.
Pray, Annabella, pray. Since we must part,
Go thou, white in thy soul, to fill a throne
Of innocence and sanctity in Heaven.   65
Pray, pray, my sister.
ANNABELLA   Then I see your drift;
Ye blessèd angels, guard me!

GIOVANNI   So say I.
    Kiss me. If ever after-times should hear
    Of our fast-knit affections, though perhaps
    The laws of conscience and of civil use   70
    May justly blame us, yet when they but know
    Our loves, that love will wipe away that rigour
    Which would in other incests be abhorred.
    Give me your hand. How sweetly life doth run
    In these well-coloured veins; how constantly   75
    These palms do promise health! But I could chide
    With Nature for this cunning flattery.
    Kiss me again—forgive me.
ANNABELLA   With my heart.
GIOVANNI Farewell.
ANNABELLA   Will you be gone?
GIOVANNI   Be dark, bright sun,
    And make this midday night, that thy gilt rays   80
    May not behold a deed will turn their splendour
    More sooty than the poets feign their Styx!°
    One other kiss, my sister.
ANNABELLA   What means this?
GIOVANNI To save thy fame, and kill thee in a kiss.
        Stabs her
    Thus die, and die by me, and by my hand.   85
    Revenge is mine; honour doth love command.
ANNABELLA O brother, by your hand?
GIOVANNI   When thou art dead
    I'll give my reasons for't; for to dispute
    With thy (even in thy death) most lovely beauty,
    Would make me stagger to perform this act   90
    Which I most glory in.
ANNABELLA Forgive him, Heaven—and me my sins; farewell,
    Brother unkind, unkind.—Mercy, great Heaven!—O!—O!—°
        Dies
GIOVANNI She's dead, alas, good soul; the hapless fruit
    That in her womb received its life from me,   95
    Hath had from me a cradle and a grave.
    I must not dally. This sad marriage-bed,
    In all her best, bore her alive and dead.°
    Soranzo, thou hast missed thy aim in this;
    I have prevented now thy reaching plots,°   100

And killed a love for whose each drop of blood
I would have pawned my heart. Fair Annabella,
How over-glorious art thou in thy wounds,°
Triumphing over infamy and hate!
Shrink not, courageous hand; stand up, my heart,   105
And boldly act my last and greater part!
     Exit with the body

5.6

A banquet. Enter Cardinal, Florio, Donado, Soranzo,
Richardetto, Vasques, and attendants; they take their places.

VASQUES [*aside to Soranzo*] Remember, sir, what you have to do; be
    wise and resolute.
SORANZO [*aside to Vasques*] Enough, my heart is fixed. [*To the*
    Cardinal] Pleaseth your grace
    To taste these coarse confections? Though the use
    Of such set entertainments more consists   5
    In custom than in cause, yet, reverend sir,
    I am still made your servant by your presence.
CARDINAL And we your friend.
SORANZO But where's my brother Giovanni?
    Enter Giovanni with a heart upon his dagger
GIOVANNI Here, here, Soranzo! trimmed in reeking blood   10
    That triumphs over death; proud in the spoil°
    Of love and vengeance! Fate, or all the powers
    That guide the motions of immortal souls,
    Could not prevent me.
CARDINAL   What means this?
FLORIO Son Giovanni!
SORANZO [*aside*]   Shall I be forestalled?   15
GIOVANNI Be not amazed. If your misgiving hearts
    Shrink at an idle sight, what bloodless fear°
    Of coward passion would have seized your senses
    Had you beheld the rape of life and beauty
    Which I have acted? My sister, O my sister!   20
FLORIO Ha! What of her?
GIOVANNI   The glory of my deed
    Darkened the midday sun, made noon as night.

You came to feast, my lords, with dainty fare.
I came to feast too, but I digged for food
In a much richer mine than gold or stone°   25
Of any value balanced; 'tis a heart,
A heart, my lords, in which is mine entombed.
Look well upon't; d'ee know't?

VASQUES What strange riddle's this?

GIOVANNI 'Tis Annabella's heart, 'tis; why d'ee startle?   30
I vow 'tis hers; this dagger's point ploughed up
Her fruitful womb, and left to me the fame
Of a most glorious executioner.

FLORIO Why, madman, art thyself?

GIOVANNI Yes, father, and that times to come may know   35
How as my fate I honoured my revenge,
List, father; to your ears I will yield up
How much I have deserved to be your son.

FLORIO What is't thou say'st?

GIOVANNI   Nine moons have had their changes
Since I first throughly viewed and truly loved   40
Your daughter and my sister.

FLORIO   How! Alas,
My lords, he's a frantic madman!

GIOVANNI   Father, no.
For nine months' space, in secret I enjoyed
Sweet Annabella's sheets; nine months I lived
A happy monarch of her heart and her.   45
Soranzo, thou know'st this; thy paler cheek
Bears the confounding print of thy disgrace,
For her too fruitful womb too soon bewrayed
The happy passage of our stol'n delights,
And made her mother to a child unborn.   50

CARDINAL Incestuous villain!

FLORIO   O, his rage belies him!

GIOVANNI It does not, 'tis the oracle of truth;
I vow it is so.

SORANZO   I shall burst with fury;
Bring the strumpet forth!

VASQUES I shall, sir.
          Exit Vasques

GIOVANNI   Do sir; have you all no faith   55
To credit yet my triumphs? Here I swear

By all that you call sacred, by the love
I bore my Annabella whilst she lived,
These hands have from her bosom ripped this heart.
  Enter Vasques
Is't true or no, sir?

VASQUES   'Tis most strangely true.   60

FLORIO Cursed man!—Have I lived to—
  Dies

CARDINAL   Hold up Florio;°
Monster of children, see what thou hast done,
Broke thy old father's heart! Is none of you
Dares venture on him?

GIOVANNI   Let 'em. O, my father,
How well his death becomes him in his griefs!   65
Why, this was done with courage; now survives
None of our house but I, gilt in the blood
Of a fair sister and a hapless father.

SORANZO Inhuman scorn of men, hast thou a thought
T'outlive thy murders?

GIOVANNI   Yes, I tell thee, yes;   70
For in my fists I bear the twists of life.°
Soranzo, see this heart which was thy wife's;
Thus I exchange it royally for thine,
  [Stabs him]
And thus, and thus; now brave revenge is mine.
  [Soranzo falls]

VASQUES I cannot hold any longer. You, sir, are you grown insolent 75
in your butcheries? Have at you!
  Fight

GIOVANNI Come, I am armed to meet thee.

VASQUES No, will it not be yet? *[Thrusting at him]* If this will not,
another shall. Not yet? I shall fit you anon.—Vengeance!°
  Enter Banditti

GIOVANNI Welcome! Come more of you, whate'er you be;   80
I dare your worst—
  [They surround and wound him]
O, I can stand no longer; feeble arms,
Have you so soon lost strength?
  [He falls]

VASQUES Now you are welcome, sir!—Away, my masters, all is done.
Shift for yourselves, your reward is your own; shift for yourselves. 85

BANDITTI Away, away!
  Exeunt Banditti
VASQUES How d'ee, my lord? See you this? How is't?
SORANZO Dead; but in death well pleased that I have lived
 To see my wrongs revenged on that black devil.
 O Vasques, to thy bosom let me give   90
 My last of breath; let not that lecher live—O!—
  Dies
VASQUES The reward of peace and rest be with him, my ever dearest
 lord and master.
GIOVANNI Whose hand gave me this wound?
VASQUES Mine, sir, I was your first man; have you enough? 95
GIOVANNI I thank thee; thou hast done for me but what
 I would have else done on myself. Art sure
 Thy lord is dead?
VASQUES O impudent slave! As sure as I am sure to see thee die.
CARDINAL Think on thy life and end, and call for mercy. 100
GIOVANNI Mercy? Why, I have found it in this justice.
CARDINAL Strive yet to cry to Heaven.
GIOVANNI   O, I bleed fast!
 Death, thou art a guest long looked-for; I embrace
 Thee and thy wounds. O, my last minute comes!
 Where'er I go, let me enjoy this grace,   105
 Freely to view my Annabella's face.
  Dies
DONADO Strange miracle of justice!
CARDINAL Raise up the city; we shall be murdered all!
VASQUES You need not fear, you shall not. This strange task being
 ended, I have paid the duty to the son which I have vowed to the 110
 father.
CARDINAL Speak, wretched villain, what incarnate fiend
 Hath led thee on to this?
VASQUES Honesty, and pity of my master's wrongs. For know, my
 lord, I am by birth a Spaniard,° brought forth my country in my 115
 youth by Lord Soranzo's father; whom, whilst he lived, I served
 faithfully; since whose death I have been to this man, as I was to
 him. What I have done was duty, and I repent nothing but that
 the loss of my life had not ransomed his.
CARDINAL Say, fellow, know'st thou any yet unnamed   120
 Of counsel in this incest?°
VASQUES Yes, an old woman, sometimes guardian to this murdered lady.

CARDINAL And what's become of her?

VASQUES Within this room° she is; whose eyes, after her confession,
I caused to be put out, but kept alive, to confirm what from   125
Giovanni's own mouth you have heard. Now, my lord, what I have
done you may judge of, and let your own wisdom be a judge in
your own reason.

CARDINAL Peace! First this woman, chief in these effects;°
My sentence is that forthwith she be ta'en   130
Out of the city, for example's sake,
There to be burnt to ashes.

DONADO   'Tis most just.

CARDINAL Be it your charge, Donado, see it done.

DONADO I shall.

VASQUES What for me? If death, 'tis welcome. I have been honest to   135
the son, as I was to the father.

CARDINAL Fellow, for thee, since what thou didst was done
Not for thyself, being no Italian,°
We banish thee for ever, to depart
Within three days; in this we do dispense   140
With grounds of reason, not of thine offence.°

VASQUES 'Tis well; this conquest is mine, and I rejoice that a
Spaniard outwent an Italian in revenge.
          Exit Vasques

CARDINAL Take up these slaughtered bodies; see them buried;
And all the gold and jewels, or whatsoever,   145
Confiscate by the canons of the Church,
We seize upon to the Pope's proper use.

RICHARDETTO [*discovers himself*] Your grace's pardon. Thus long I
    lived disguised,
To see the effect of pride and lust at once
Brought both to shameful ends.   150

CARDINAL What? Richardetto, whom we thought for dead?

DONADO Sir, was it you—

RICHARDETTO   Your friend.

CARDINAL   We shall have time
To talk at large of all; but never yet°
Incest and murder have so strangely met.
Of one so young, so rich in Nature's store,   155
Who could not say, *'Tis pity she's a whore?*
          Exeunt [with the bodies]

THE CHRONICLE HISTORY OF PERKIN WARBECK

A Strange Truth

To the rightly honourable William Cavendish,° Earl of
Newcastle, Viscount Mansfield, Lord Bolsover and Ogle

My Lord,
Out of the darkness of a former age (enlightened by a late, both
learned and an honourable pen)° I have endeavoured to personate a
great attempt, and in it, a greater danger. In *other* labours you may
read actions of antiquity discoursed. In this abridgement, find the
actors themselves discoursing; in some kind practised as well *what*   5
to speak, as speaking *why* to do. Your Lordship is a most competent
judge in expressions of such credit, commissioned by your known
ability in examining, and enabled by your knowledge in determining
the monuments of time. Eminent titles may indeed inform *who* their
owners are, not often *what*. To yours, the addition of that information   10
in both cannot in any application be observed flattery, the authority being
established by truth. I can only acknowledge the errors in writing,
mine own; the worthiness of the subject written, being a perfection
in the story, and of it. The custom of your Lordship's entertainments,°
even to strangers, is rather an example than a fashion, in which   15
consideration, I dare not profess a curiosity,° but am only studious
that your Lordship will please, amongst such as best honour your
goodness, to admit into your noble construction.

John Ford

To my own friend, Master John Ford, on his justifiable poem°
of Perkin Warbeck, this ode

    They, who do know me, know that I
       (Unskil'd to flatter)
    Dare speak this piece, in words, in matter,
    A work, without the danger of the lie.
    Believe me, friend, the name of this, and thee,   5
       Will live, your story.
    Books may want faith, or merit, glory;
    This, neither, without judgement's lethargy.
    When the arts dote, then some sick poet may
       Hope that his pen   10

In new-stained paper can find men
To roar, 'He is the wit's; his noise doth sway.'
But such an age cannot be known; for all,
 Ere that time be,
Must prove such truth, mortality.   15
So, friend, thy honour stands too fixed to fall.

        George Donne°

To his worthy friend, Master John Ford, upon his Perkin Warbeck

Let men, who are writ poets, lay a claim
To the Phoebean hill, I have no name,°
Nor art in verse. True, I have heard some tell
Of Aganippe, but ne'er knew the well;°
Therefore have no ambition with the times   5
To be in print for making of ill rhymes.
But love of thee, and justice to thy pen
Hath drawn me to this bar, with other men
To justify, though against double laws
(Waiving the subtle business of his cause),   10
The glorious Perkin, and thy poet's art
Equal with his, in playing the king's part.

     Ralph Eure, *Baronis primogenitus*°

To my faithful, no less deserving friend, the author, this indebted oblation

Perkin is redivived by thy strong hand,°
And crowned a king of new; the vengeful wand
Of greatness is forgot. His execution
May rest unmentioned, and his birth's collusion
Lie buried in the story, but his fame   5
Thou hast eternized; made a crown his game.
His lofty spirit soars yet. Had he been
Base in his enterprise, as was his sin
Conceived, his title (doubtless) proved unjust,
Had, but for thee, been silenced in his dust. 10

      George Crymes, *miles*°

To the author, his friend, upon his Chronicle History

These are not to express thy wit,
But to pronounce thy judgement fit;
In full-filed phrase those times to raise,°
When Perkin ran his wily ways.
Still let the method of thy brain   5
From Error's touch, and Envy's stain
Preserve thee free, that ever thy quill
Fair Truth may whet, and Fancy fill.
Thus Graces are with Muses met,
And practic critics on may fret;   10
For here thou hast produced a story
Which shall eclipse their future glory.

John Brograve, *Armiger*°

To my friend and kinsman, Master John Ford, the author

Dramatic poets (as the times go) now
Can hardly write what others will allow;
The cynic snarls, the critic howls and barks,
And ravens croak, to drown the voice of larks.
Scorn those stage-harpies! This I'll boldly say,   5
Many may imitate, few match thy play.

John Ford, *Graiensis*°

THE PERSONS OF THE PLAY

HENRY VII, King of England
LORD DAUBENEY
SIR WILLIAM STANLEY, king's chamberlain
EARL OF OXFORD [John de Vere]
EARL OF SURREY [Thomas Howard]
RICHARD FOX, Bishop of Durham
URSWICK, chaplain to King Henry
SIR ROBERT CLIFFORD
LAMBERT SIMNEL, a falconer
HIALAS [Don Pedro de Ayala], a Spanish agent
CONSTABLE, OFFICERS, SERVINGMEN, SOLDIERS, EXECUTIONER, POST, SHERIFF, CONFESSOR

JAMES IV, King of Scotland
EARL OF HUNTLY [George Gordon]
LADY KATHERINE GORDON, his daughter
JANE DOUGLAS, Lady Katherine's maid
EARL OF CRAWFORD
COUNTESS OF CRAWFORD
LORD DALIELL
MARCHMOUNT, a herald
ATTENDANTS, MASQUERS, HERALD, SERVANT TO LADY KATHERINE

PERKIN WARBECK
FRION, his secretary
JOHN A-WATER, Mayor of Cork
HERON, a mercer
SKETON, a tailor
ASTLEY, a scrivener

THE PROLOGUE

Studies have, of this nature, been of late
So out of fashion, so unfollowed, that°
It is become more justice to revive
The antic follies of the times than strive
To countenance wise industry. No want   5
Of art doth render wit, or lame, or scant,
Or slothful in the purchase of fresh bays,°
But want of truth in them who give the praise
To their self-love, presuming to out-do
The writer, or (for need) the actors too.   10
But such this author's silence best befits
Who bids them be in love with their own wits.
From him to clearer judgements we can say
He shows a history couched in a play.
A history of noble mention, known,   15
Famous, and true: most noble 'cause our own;
Not forged from Italy, from France, from Spain,
But chronicled at home; as rich in strain
Of brave attempts as ever fertile rage
In action could beget to grace the stage.   20
We cannot limit scenes, for the whole land
Itself, appeared too narrow to withstand
Competitors for kingdoms. Nor is here
Unnecessary mirth forced, to endear
A multitude. On these two rests the fate   25
Of worthy expectation: Truth and State.°

Perkin Warbeck

1.1

Enter King Henry, Durham, Oxford, Surrey, Sir William
Stanley (Lord Chamberlain),° Lord Daubeney. The King [is]
supported to his throne by Stanley and Durham. A guard

HENRY Still to be haunted, still to be pursued,
  Still to be frighted with false apparitions
  Of pageant majesty and new-coined greatness,
  As if we were a mockery king in state,
  Only ordained to lavish sweat and blood   5
  In scorn and laughter to the ghosts of York,°
  Is all below our merits; yet, my lords,
  My friends and counsellors, yet we sit fast
  In our own royal birthright. The rent face°
  And bleeding wounds of England's slaughtered people   10
  Have been by us, as by the best physician,
  At last both throughly cured and set in safety;
  And yet for all this glorious work of peace
  Ourself is scarce secure.
DURHAM   The rage of malice
  Conjures fresh spirits with the spells of York;   15
  For ninety years ten English kings and princes,°
  Threescore great dukes and earls, a thousand lords
  And valiant knights, two hundred fifty thousand
  Of English subjects have in civil wars
  Been sacrificed to an uncivil thirst   20
  Of discord and ambition. This hot vengeance
  Of the just powers above, to utter ruin
  And desolation had reigned on, but that
  Mercy did gently sheathe the sword of Justice
  In lending to this blood-shrunk commonwealth   25
  A new soul, new birth, in your sacred person.
DAUBENEY Edward the Fourth after a doubtful fortune
  Yielded to nature, leaving to his sons,
  Edward and Richard, the inheritance
  Of a most bloody purchase; these young princes°   30

Richard the tyrant, their unnatural uncle,
Forced to a violent grave, so just is Heaven.
Him hath your majesty by your own arm,
Divinely strengthened, pulled from his boar's sty°
And struck the black usurper to a carcass.   35
Nor doth the house of York decay in honours,
Though Lancaster doth repossess his right,
For Edward's daughter is King Henry's queen;°
A blessed union, and a lasting blessing
For this poor panting island, if some shreds,   40
Some useless remnant of the house of York,
Grudge not at this content.
OXFORD   Margaret of Burgundy°
Blows fresh coals of division.
SURREY   Painted fires,
Without or heat to scorch, or light to cherish.
DAUBENEY York's headless trunk (her father), Edward's fate°   45
  (Her brother king), the smothering of her nephews°
By tyrant Gloucester (brother to her nature),°
Nor Gloucester's own confusion—all decrees
Sacred in Heaven—can move this woman-monster,
But that she still from the unbottomed mine   50
Of devilish policies doth vent the ore
Of troubles and sedition.
OXFORD   In her age
(Great sir, observe the wonder) she grows fruitful,
Who in her strength of youth was always barren;
Nor are her births as other mothers' are,   55
At nine or ten months' end. She has been with child
Eight or seven years at least, whose twins being born°
(A prodigy in nature; even the youngest
Is fifteen years of age at his first entrance!)°
As soon as known i'th' world, tall striplings, strong   60
And able to give battle unto kings;
Idols of Yorkish malice.
SURREY°   And but idols;
A steely hammer crushes 'em to pieces.
HENRY Lambert, the eldest, lords, is in our service,
Preferred by an officious care of duty   65
From the scullery to a falc'ner (strange example!)
Which shows the difference between noble natures

And the base born. But for the upstart duke,°
The new revived York, Edward's second son,
Murdered long since i'th' Tower—he lives again,   70
And vows to be your king.
STANLEY   The throne is filled, sir.
HENRY True, Stanley, and the lawful heir sits on it;
    A guard of angels and the holy prayers
    Of loyal subjects are a sure defence
    Against all force and counsel of intrusion.°   75
    But now, my lords, put case some of our nobles,°
    Our great ones, should give countenance and courage
    To trim Duke Perkin, you will all confess
    Our bounties have unthriftily been scattered
    Amongst unthankful men.
DAUBENEY   Unthankful beasts,   80
    Dogs, villains, traitors!
HENRY   Daubeney, let the guilty
    Keep silence. I accuse none, though I know
    Foreign attempts against a state and kingdom
    Are seldom without some great friends at home.
STANLEY Sir, if no other abler reasons else   85
    Of duty or allegiance could divert
    A headstrong resolution, yet the dangers
    So lately passed by men of blood and fortunes
    In Lambert Simnel's party must command
    More than a fear, a terror to conspiracy.   90
    The high-born Lincoln, son to De la Pole,
    The Earl of Kildare, Lord Geraldine,
    Francis, Lord Lovell, and the German baron,
    Bold Martin Swart, with Broughton and the rest—°
    Most spectacles of ruin, some of mercy—   95
    Are precedents sufficient to forewarn
    The present times, or any that live in them,
    What folly, nay, what madness 'twere to lift
    A finger up in all defence but yours,
    Which can be but impostorous in a title.°   100
HENRY Stanley, we know thou lov'st us, and thy heart
    Is figured on thy tongue; nor think we less°
    Of any's here. How closely we have hunted
    This cub, since he unlodged, from hole to hole,
    Your knowledge is our chronicle. First Ireland,   105

The common stage of novelty, presented
This gewgaw to oppose us; there the Geraldines
And Butlers once again stood in support°
Of this colossic statue. Charles of France°
Thence called him unto his protection,   110
Dissembled him the lawful heir of England;
Yet this was all but French dissimulation,
Aiming at peace with us, which being granted
On honourable terms on our part, suddenly
This smoke of straw was packed from France again°   115
T'infect some grosser air. And now we learn,
Maugre the malice of the bastard Neville,
Sir Taylor, and a hundred English rebels,°
They're all retired to Flanders, to the dam
That nursed this eager whelp, Margaret of Burgundy.   120
But we will hunt him there too; we will hunt him,
Hunt him to death even in the beldam's closet,
Though the archduke were his buckler.

SURREY   She has styled him°
'The fair white rose of England'.

DAUBENEY   Jolly gentleman;
More fit to be a swabber to the Flemish   125
After a drunken surfeit.

     Enter Urswick [with a paper]

URSWICK   Gracious sovereign,
Please you peruse this paper.

     [Henry reads]

DURHAM   The king's countenance
Gathers a sprightly blood.

DAUBENEY   Good news, believe it.

HENRY Urswick, thine ear.—Th'ast lodged him?

URSWICK   Strongly safe, sir°

HENRY Enough. Is Barley come too?

URSWICK   No, my lord.°   130

HENRY No matter—phew, he's but a running weed,
At pleasure to be plucked up by the roots.
But more of this anon.—I have bethought me.—
My lords, for reasons which you shall partake,
It is our pleasure to remove our court   135
From Westminster to th'Tower. We will lodge
This very night there; give, Lord Chamberlain,

A present order for it.

STANLEY [*aside*]   The Tower! [*Aloud*] I shall sir.

HENRY Come, my true, best, fast friends, these clouds will vanish,
The sun will shine at full; the heavens are clearing.   140
   Exeunt. Flourish°

1.2

   Enter Huntly and Daliell

HUNTLY You trifle time, sir.

DALIELL   O my noble lord,
You construe my griefs to so hard a sense°
That where the text is argument of pity,
Matter of earnest love, your gloss corrupts it
With too much ill-placed mirth.

HUNTLY   Much mirth, Lord Daliell?   5
Not so, I vow. Observe me, sprightly gallant.
I know thou art a noble lad, a handsome,
Descended from an honourable ancestry,
Forward and active, dost resolve to wrestle°
And ruffle in the world by noble actions   10
For a brave mention to posterity.
I scorn not thy affection to my daughter,
Not I, by good St Andrew, but this bugbear,°
This whoreson tale of honour—honour, Daliell!—
So hourly chats and tattles in mine ear°   15
The piece of royalty that is stitched up
In my Kate's blood, that 'tis as dangerous
For thee, young lord, to perch so near an eaglet
As foolish for my gravity to admit it.
I have spoke all at once.

DALIELL   Sir, with this truth   20
You mix such wormwood that you leave no hope
For my disordered palate e'er to relish
A wholesome taste again. Alas, I know, sir,
What an unequal distance lies between
Great Huntly's daughter's birth and Daliell's fortunes.   25
She's the king's kinswoman, placed near the crown,
A princess of the blood, and I a subject.

HUNTLY Right, but a noble subject; put in that, too.
DALIELL I could add more; and in the rightest line
    Derive my pedigree from Adam Mure,   30
    A Scottish knight, whose daughter was the mother
    To him that first begot the race of Jameses,°
    That sway the sceptre to this very day.
    But kindreds are not ours when once the date°
    Of many years have swallowed up the memory   35
    Of their originals; so pasture fields,
    Neighbouring too near the ocean, are supped up°
    And known no more. For, stood I in my first
    And native greatness, if my princely mistress
    Vouchsafed me not her servant, 'twere as good°   40
    I were reduced to clownery, to nothing,°
    As to a throne of wonder.
HUNTLY [aside]   Now, by St Andrew,
    A spark of mettle; 'a has a brave fire in him.°
    I would 'a had my daughter, so I knew't not.
    But it must not be so, must not. [To him]—Well, young lord,°   45
    This will not do yet; if the girl be headstrong
    And will not hearken to good counsel, steal her
    And run away with her, dance galliards, do,
    And frisk about the world to learn the languages.
    'Twill be a thriving trade; you may set up by't.°   50
DALIELL With pardon, noble Gordon, this disdain°
    Suits not your daughter's virtue or my constancy.
HUNTLY You are angry. [Aside] Would a' would beat me; I
    deserve it.
    [To him] Daliell, thy hand, w'are friends; follow thy courtship,
    Take thine own time and speak. If thou prevail'st   55
    With passion more than I can with my counsel,
    She's thine; nay, she is thine, 'tis a fair match,
    Free and allowed. I'll only use my tongue,
    Without a father's power; use thou thine.
    Self do, self have; no more words, win and wear her.   60
DALIELL You bless me; I am now too poor in thanks
    To pay the debt I owe you.
HUNTLY   Nay, th'art poor
    Enough. [Aside] I love his spirit infinitely.
        Enter Katherine and Jane
    [To him] Look ye, she comes; to her now, to her, to her.

KATHERINE The king commands your presence, sir.

HUNTLY   The gallant—   65
　　This, this, this lord, this servant, Kate, of yours
　　Desires to be your master.

KATHERINE   I acknowledge him
　　A worthy friend of mine.

DALIELL   Your humblest creature.

HUNTLY [aside] So, so, the game's afoot. I'm in cold hunting;°
　　The hare and hounds are parties.

DALIELL   Princely lady,   70
　　How most unworthy I am to employ
　　My services in honour of your virtues,
　　How hopeless my desires are to enjoy
　　Your fair opinion, and much more your love,
　　Are only matter of despair, unless   75
　　Your goodness give large warrant to my boldness,
　　My feeble-winged ambition.

HUNTLY [aside]   This is scurvy.°

KATHERINE [to Daliell] My lord, I interrupt you not.

HUNTLY [aside]   Indeed?
　　Now, on my life, she'll court him.—Nay, nay, on sir.

DALIELL Oft have I tuned the lesson of my sorrows°   80
　　To sweeten discord, and enrich your pity;
　　But all in vain. Here had my comforts sunk
　　And never risen again to tell a story
　　Of the despairing lover, had not now,
　　Even now, the earl your father—

HUNTLY [aside]   'A means me, sure.   85

DALIELL After some fit disputes of your condition,°
　　Your highness and my lowness, given a licence
　　Which did not more embolden than encourage
　　My faulting tongue.

HUNTLY   How, how? How's that? Embolden?
　　Encourage? I encourage ye? D'ee hear, sir?   90
　　A subtle trick, a quaint one—will you hear, man?
　　What did I say to you? Come, come, to th'point.

KATHERINE It shall not need, my lord.

HUNTLY   Then hear me, Kate—
　　Keep you on that hand of her; I on this—
　　Thou stand'st between a father and a suitor,
　　Both striving for an interest in thy heart.   95

He courts thee for affection, I for duty;
He as a servant pleads, but by the privilege
Of nature, though I might command, my care
Shall only counsel what it shall not force.   100
Thou canst but make one choice; the ties of marriage
Are tenures not at will but during life.
Consider whose thou art, and who: a princess,
A princess of the royal blood of Scotland,
In the full spring of youth, and fresh in beauty.   105
The king that sits upon the throne is young
And yet unmarried, forward in attempts
On any least occasion to endanger
His person. Wherefore, Kate, as I am confident
Thou dar'st not wrong thy birth and education   110
By yielding to a common servile rage°
Of female wantonness, so I am confident
Thou wilt proportion all thy thoughts to side°
Thy equals, if not equal thy superiors.
My Lord of Daliell, young in years, is old   115
In honours, but nor eminent in titles
Or in estate that may support or add to
The expectation of thy fortunes. Settle
Thy will and reason by a strength of judgement;
For, in a word, I give thee freedom; take it.   120
If equal fates have not ordained to pitch°
Thy hopes above my height, let not thy passion
Lead thee to shrink mine honour in oblivion.
Thou art thine own; I have done.
DALIELL   O, y'are all oracle,
The living stock and root of truth and wisdom!   125
KATHERINE My worthiest lord and father, the indulgence
Of your sweet composition thus commands
The lowest of obedience; you have granted°
A liberty so large that I want skill
To choose without direction of example,   130
From which I daily learn, by how much more
You take off from the roughness of a father,
By so much more I am engaged to tender
The duty of a daughter. For respects
Of birth, degrees of title, and advancement,   135
I nor admire nor slight them; all my studies

Shall ever aim at this perfection only,
To live and die so, that you may not blush
In any course of mine to own me yours.

HUNTLY Kate, Kate, thou grow'st upon my heart like peace,   140
Creating every other hour a jubilee.

KATHERINE To you, my Lord of Daliell, I address
Some few remaining words. The general fame°
That speaks your merit, even in vulgar tongues
Proclaims it clear; but in the best, a precedent.   145

HUNTLY Good wench, good girl, i'faith!

KATHERINE   For my part, trust me,
I value mine own worth at higher rate
'Cause you are pleased to prize it. If the stream
Of your protested service, as you term it,
Run in a constancy more than a compliment,   150
It shall be my delight that worthy love
Leads you to worthy actions, and these guide ye
Richly to wed an honourable name;°
So every virtuous praise in after ages
Shall be your heir, and I, in your brave mention,°   155
Be chronicled the mother of that issue,
That glorious issue.

HUNTLY   O that I were young again!
She'd make me court proud danger, and suck spirit°
From reputation.

KATHERINE   To the present motion
Here's all that I dare answer. When a ripeness   160
Of more experience, and some use of time,
Resolves to treat the freedom of my youth
Upon exchange of troths, I shall desire
No surer credit of a match with virtue
Than such as lives in you. Meantime, my hopes are   165
Preserved secure, in having you a friend.

DALIELL You are a blessèd lady, and instruct
Ambition not to soar a farther flight
Than in the perfumed air of your soft voice.
My noble Lord of Huntly, you have lent   170
A full extent of bounty to this parley,
And for it shall command your humblest servant.

HUNTLY Enough; we are still friends, and will continue
A hearty love—O Kate, thou art mine own!—

Enter Crawford

No more: my Lord of Crawford.

CRAWFORD   From the king   175
I come, my Lord of Huntly, who in council
Requires your present aid.

HUNTLY   Some weighty business!

CRAWFORD A secretary from a Duke of York,
The second son to the late English Edward,
Concealed I know not where these fourteen years,   180
Craves audience from our master, and 'tis said
The duke himself is following to the court.

HUNTLY Duke upon duke! 'Tis well, 'tis well; here's bustling
For majesty. My lord, I will along with ye.

CRAWFORD My service, noble lady.

KATHERINE [*to Daliell*]   Please ye walk, sir?   185

DALIELL [*aside*] Times have their changes; sorrow makes men wise.
The sun itself must set as well as rise;
Then why not I?—Fair madam, I wait on ye.

          Exeunt

1.3

Enter Durham, Sir Robert Clifford, and Urswick [carrying]
lights°

DURHAM You find, Sir Robert Clifford, how securely
King Henry, our great master, doth commit
His person to your loyalty; you taste
His bounty and his mercy even in this,
That at a time of night so late, a place   5
So private as his closet, he is pleased
To admit you to his favour. Do not falter
In your discovery, but as you covet
A liberal grace and pardon for your follies,
So labour to deserve it, by laying open   10
All plots, all persons, that contrive against it.

URSWICK Remember not the witchcraft or the magic,
The charms and incantations, which the sorceress
Of Burgundy hath cast upon your reason!
Sir Robert, be your own friend now; discharge   15

Your conscience freely. All of such as love you
Stand sureties for your honesty and truth.
Take heed you do not dally with the king;
He is wise as he is gentle.
CLIFFORD   I am miserable
If Henry be not merciful.
            Enter King Henry [with a paper]
URSWICK   The king comes.   20
HENRY Clifford!
CLIFFORD [*kneels*] Let my weak knees rot on the earth
If I appear as leprous in my treacheries,
Before your royal eyes, as to mine own
I seem a monster by my breach of truth.
HENRY Clifford, stand up. For instance of thy safety°   25
I offer thee my hand.
CLIFFORD [*stands*]   A sovereign balm
For my bruised soul; I kiss it with a greediness.
Sir, you are a just master, but I—
HENRY   Tell me,
Is every circumstance thou hast set down
With thine own hand within this paper true?   30
Is it a sure intelligence of all
The progress of our enemies' intents
Without corruption?
CLIFFORD   True, as I wish Heaven,
Or my infected honour white again.
HENRY We know all, Clifford, fully, since this meteor,°   35
This airy apparition, first discradled
From Tournai into Portugal, and thence°
Advanced his fiery blaze for adoration
To th'superstitious Irish; since the beard°
Of this wild comet, conjured into France,   40
Sparkled in antic flames in Charles his court;°
But shrunk again from thence and, hid in darkness,
Stole into Flanders, flourishing the rags
Of painted power on the shore of Kent,
Whence he was beaten back with shame and scorn,°   45
Contempt, and slaughter of some naked outlaws.
But tell me, what new course now shapes Duke Perkin?
CLIFFORD For Ireland, mighty Henry; so instructed
By Stephen Frion, sometimes secretary°

In the French tongue unto your sacred excellence,   50
But Perkin's tutor now.
HENRY   A subtle villain,
That Frion! Frion—you, my Lord of Durham,
Knew well the man.
DURHAM   French both in heart and actions!°
HENRY Some Irish heads work in this mine of treason;
Speak 'em!
CLIFFORD   Not any of the best; your fortune°   55
Hath dulled their spleens. Never had counterfeit
Such a confused rabble of lost bankrupts
For counsellors; first Heron, a broken mercer,
Then John A-Water, sometimes Mayor of Cork,
Sketon, a tailor, and a scrivener   60
Called Astley; and whate'er these list to treat of°
Perkin must hearken to. But Frion, cunning
Above these dull capacities, still prompts him
To fly to Scotland to young James the Fourth,
And sue for aid to him; this is the latest   65
Of all their resolutions.
HENRY   Still more Frion!
Pestilent adder, he will hiss out poison
As dangerous as infectious. We must match 'em.
Clifford, thou hast spoke home; we give thee life.
But Clifford, there are people of our own   70
Remain behind untold; who are they, Clifford?
Name those and we are friends, and will to rest;
'Tis thy last task.
CLIFFORD   O sir, here I must break
A most unlawful oath to keep a just one.
HENRY Well, well, be brief, be brief.
CLIFFORD   The first in rank   75
Shall be John Ratcliffe, Lord Fitzwater, then
Sir Simon Mountford and Sir Thomas Thwaites,
With William Daubeney, Cressoner, Astwood,
Worsley the Dean of Paul's, two other friars,
And Robert Ratcliffe.
HENRY   Churchmen are turned devils.   80
These are the principal?
CLIFFORD   One more remains
Unnamed, whom I could willingly forget.

HENRY Ha, Clifford, one more?

CLIFFORD   Great sir, do not hear him;°
For when Sir William Stanley, your Lord Chamberlain,
Shall come into the list, as he is chief,   85
I shall lose credit with ye. Yet this lord,
Last named, is first against you.

HENRY   Urswick, the light!
View my face, sirs; is there blood left in it?

DURHAM You alter strangely, sir.

HENRY   Alter, lord bishop?
Why, Clifford stabbed me, or I dreamed 'a stabbed me.   90
Sirrah, it is a custom with the guilty
To think they set their own stains off by laying
Aspersions on some nobler than themselves.
Lies wait on treasons, as I find it here.
Thy life again is forfeit; I recall   95
My word of mercy, for I know thou dar'st
Repeat the name no more.

CLIFFORD   I dare, and once more,
Upon my knowledge, name Sir William Stanley,
Both in his counsel and his purse, the chief
Assistant to the feignèd Duke of York.   100

DURHAM Most strange!

URSWICK   Most wicked!

HENRY   Yet again, once more.

CLIFFORD Sir William Stanley is your secret enemy,
And, if time fit, will openly profess it.

HENRY Sir William Stanley? Who? Sir William Stanley,
My chamberlain, my counsellor, the love,   105
The pleasure of my court, my bosom friend,
The charge and the controlment of my person,°
The keys and secrets of my treasury,
The all of all I am! I am unhappy:
Misery of confidence! Let me turn traitor   110
To mine own person, yield my sceptre up
To Edward's sister, and her bastard duke!°

DURHAM You lose your constant temper.

HENRY   Sir William Stanley!
O do not blame me; he, 'twas only he,
Who having rescued me in Bosworth Field   115
From Richard's bloody sword, snatched from his head

The kingly crown, and placed it first on mine.
He never failed me; what, have I deserved°
To lose this good man's heart, or he his own?
URSWICK The night doth waste; this passion ill becomes ye;   120
Provide against your danger.
HENRY   Let it be so.
Urswick, command straight Stanley to his chamber.
'Tis well we are i'th' Tower; set a guard on him.
Clifford, to bed; you must lodge here tonight,
We'll talk with you tomorrow. My sad soul   125
Divines strange troubles.
DAUBENEY [*within*]   Ho, the king, the king!
I must have entrance.
HENRY   Daubeney's voice; admit him.
What new combustions huddle next to keep
Our eyes from rest?
          Enter Daubeney
                         The news?
DAUBENEY   Ten thousand Cornish,
Grudging to pay your subsidies, have gathered   130
A head, led by a blacksmith and a lawyer;°
They make for London, and to them is joined
Lord Audley; as they march, their number daily°
Increases; they are—
HENRY   Rascals! Talk no more;°
Such are not worthy of my thoughts tonight.   135
And if I cannot sleep, I'll wake:—to bed.
When councils fail, and there's in man no trust,
Even then, an arm from Heaven fights for the just.
          Exeunt

2.1

Enter above° [the] Countess of Crawford, Katherine, Jane,
with other ladies

COUNTESS Come ladies, here's a solemn preparation
For entertainment of this English prince.°
The king intends grace more than ordinary;
'Twere pity now if 'a should prove a counterfeit.

KATHERINE Bless the young man, our nation would be laughed at   5
For honest souls through Christendom. My father°
Hath a weak stomach to the business, madam,°
But that the king must not be crossed.

COUNTESS   'A brings
A goodly troop, they say, of gallants with him;
But very modest people, for they strive not   10
To fame their names too much. Their godfathers
May be beholding to them, but their fathers
Scarce owe them thanks. They are disguisèd princes,°
Brought up, it seems, to honest trades; no matter,
They will break forth in season.

JANE   Or break out,°   15
For most of 'em are broken by report.—
       Flourish
The king!

KATHERINE Let us observe 'em and be silent.
       Enter King James, Huntly, Crawford, and Daliell

JAMES The right of kings, my lords, extends not only
To the safe conservation of their own,
But also to the aid of such allies   20
As change of time and state hath oftentimes
Hurled down from careful crowns, to undergo
An exercise of sufferance in both fortunes.°
So English Richard, surnamed Coeur-de-Lion,
So Robert Bruce, our royal ancestor,   25
Forced by the trial of the wrongs they felt,°
Both sought, and found, supplies from foreign kings
To repossess their own. Then grudge not, lords,
A much distressèd prince; King Charles of France
And Maximilian of Bohemia both,   30

Have ratified his credit by their letters.
Shall we then be distrustful? No; compassion
Is one rich jewel that shines in our crown,
And we will have it shine there.
HUNTLY   Do your will, sir.
JAMES The young duke is at hand. Daliell, from us   35
First greet him, and conduct him on; then Crawford
Shall meet him next, and Huntly last of all
Present him to our arms. Sound sprightly music,°
Whilst majesty encounters majesty.

> *Hautboys. Daliell goes out, brings in Perkin [Warbeck] at the
> door where Crawford entertains him, and from Crawford,
> Huntly salutes him and presents him to the king. They
> embrace. Perkin in state retires some few paces back. During
> which ceremony the noblemen slightly salute Frion, Heron a
> mercer, Sketon a tailor, Astley a scrivener, with John
> A-Water, all Perkin's followers. Salutations ended: cease music*

WARBECK Most high, most mighty king! That now there stands   40
Before your eyes, in presence of your peers,
A subject of the rarest kind of pity
That hath in any age touched noble hearts,
The vulgar story of a prince's ruin°
Hath made it too apparent. Europe knows,   45
And all the western world, what persecution
Hath raged in malice against us, sole heir
To the great throne of old Plantagenets.
How from our nursery we have been hurried
Unto the sanctuary, from the sanctuary   50
Forced to the prison, from the prison haled
By cruel hands to the tormentor's fury,
Is registered already in the volume
Of all men's tongues, whose true relation draws
Compassion, melted into weeping eyes   55
And bleeding souls. But our misfortunes since
Have ranged a larger progress through strange lands,
Protected in our innocence by Heaven.
Edward the Fifth, our brother, in his tragedy
Quenched their hot thirst of blood, whose hire to murder   60
Paid them their wages of despair and horror;
The softness of my childhood smiled upon
The roughness of their task, and robbed them farther

Of hearts to dare, or hands to execute.
Great king, they spared my life, the butchers spared it;   65
Returned the tyrant, my unnatural uncle,°
A truth of my dispatch. I was conveyed°
With secrecy and speed to Tournai; fostered
By obscure means, taught to unlearn myself.°
But as I grew in years I grew in sense   70
Of fear, and of disdain; fear of the tyrant
Whose power swayed the throne then. When disdain
Of living so unknown, in such a servile
And abject lowness, prompted me to thoughts
Of recollecting who I was, I shook off   75
My bondage, and made haste to let my aunt
Of Burgundy acknowledge me her kinsman,
Heir to the crown of England snatched by Henry°
From Richard's head, a thing scarce known i'th' world.
JAMES My lord, it stands not with your counsel now°   80
To fly upon invectives; if you can°
Make this apparent what you have discoursed,
In every circumstance, we will not study
An answer, but are ready in your cause.
WARBECK You are a wise and just king, by the powers   85
Above, reserved beyond all other aids°
To plant me in mine own inheritance;
To marry these two kingdoms in a love
Never to be divorced while time is time.
As for the manner, first of my escape,   90
Of my conveyance next, of my life since,
The means and persons who were instruments,
Great sir, 'tis fit I overpass in silence;
Reserving the relation to the secrecy
Of your own princely ear, since it concerns   95
Some great ones living yet, and others dead,
Whose issue might be questioned. For your bounty,
Royal magnificence to him that seeks it,
We vow hereafter to demean ourself
As if we were your own and natural brother,   100
Omitting no occasion in our person
To express a gratitude beyond example.
JAMES He must be more than subject who can utter
The language of a king, and such is thine.

Take this for answer: be whate'er thou art,   105
Thou never shalt repent that thou hast put
Thy cause, and person, into my protection.
Cousin of York, thus once more we embrace thee;
Welcome to James of Scotland! For thy safety,
Know such as love thee not shall never wrong thee.   110
Come, we will taste a while our court delights,
Dream hence afflictions past, and then proceed
To high attempts of honour. On, lead on!
Both thou and thine are ours, and we will guard ye.
Lead on.—
     [Exeunt all but the ladies above]
COUNTESS   I have not seen a gentleman   115
Of a more brave aspect or goodlier carriage;
His fortunes move not him.—Madam, y'are passionate.
KATHERINE Beshrew me, but his words have touched me home,
As if his cause concerned me. I should pity him
If 'a should prove another than he seems.   120
     Enter Crawford [above]
CRAWFORD Ladies, the king commands your presence instantly,
For entertainment of the duke.
KATHERINE   The duke
Must then be entertained, the king obeyed;
It is our duty.
COUNTESS   We will all wait on him.
     Exeunt

2.2

     Flourish. Enter King Henry, Oxford, Durham, Surrey
HENRY Have ye condemned my chamberlain?
DURHAM   His treasons
Condemned him, sir, which were as clear and manifest
As foul and dangerous. Besides, the guilt
Of his conspiracy pressed him so nearly
That it drew from him free confession   5
Without an importunity.
HENRY   O lord bishop,
This argued shame and sorrow for his folly,

And must not stand in evidence against
Our mercy, and the softness of our nature;
The rigour and extremity of law   10
Is sometimes too, too bitter, but we carry
A chancery of pity in our bosom.
I hope we may reprieve him from the sentence
Of death; I hope we may.

DURHAM   You may, you may;
And so persuade your subjects that the title   15
Of York is better, nay, more just and lawful°
Than yours of Lancaster. So Stanley holds;
Which, if it be not treason in the highest,
Then we are traitors all, perjured and false,
Who have took oath to Henry and the justice   20
Of Henry's title; Oxford, Surrey, Daubeney,
With all your other peers of state and church,
Forsworn, and Stanley true alone to Heaven,
And England's lawful heir.

OXFORD   By Vere's old honours,°
I'll cut his throat dares speak it.

SURREY   'Tis a quarrel   25
T'engage a soul in.

HENRY   What a coil is here
To keep my gratitude sincere and perfect!
Stanley was once my friend, and came in time
To save my life; yet, to say truth, my lords,
The man stayed long enough t'endanger it.   30
But I could see no more into his heart
Than what his outward actions did present;
And for 'em have rewarded him so fully
As that there wanted nothing in our gift
To gratify his merit, as I thought,   35
Unless I should divide my crown with him
And give him half; though now I well perceive
'Twould scarce have served his turn without the whole.
But I am charitable, lords; let justice
Proceed in execution, whiles I mourn   40
The loss of one whom I esteemed a friend.

DURHAM Sir, he is coming this way.

HENRY   If 'a speak to me
I could deny him nothing; to prevent it,

I must withdraw. Pray, lords, commend my favours
To his last peace, which I, with him, will pray for.   45
That done, it doth concern us to consult
Of other following troubles.
   Exit [Henry]
OXFORD   I am glad
He's gone; upon my life, he would have pardoned
The traitor had 'a seen him.
SURREY   'Tis a king
Composed of gentleness.
DURHAM   Rare and unheard of;   50
But every man is nearest to himself,°
And that the king observes; 'tis fit 'a should.
  Enter Stanley, executioner, Urswick, and Daubeney
STANLEY May I not speak with Clifford ere I shake
This piece of frailty off?
DAUBENEY   You shall; he's sent for.°
STANLEY I must not see the king?
DURHAM   From him, Sir William,   55
These lords and I am sent. He bade us say
That he commends his mercy to your thoughts,
Wishing the laws of England could remit
The forfeit of your life as willingly
As he would, in the sweetness of his nature,   60
Forget your trespass; but, howe'er your body
Fall into dust, he vows—the king himself
Doth vow—to keep a requiem for your soul,
As for a friend close treasured in his bosom.
OXFORD Without remembrance of your errors past,   65
I come to take my leave, and wish you Heaven.
SURREY And I; good angels guard ye.
STANLEY   O, the king,
Next to my soul, shall be the nearest subject
Of my last prayers. My grave Lord of Durham,
My Lords of Oxford, Surrey, Daubeney, all,   70
Accept from a poor dying man, a farewell.
I was as you are once, great, and stood hopeful
Of many flourishing years; but fate and time
Have wheeled about, to turn me into nothing.°
  Enter Clifford
DAUBENEY Sir Robert Clifford comes—the man, Sir William,   75

You so desire to speak with.
DURHAM   Mark their meeting.
CLIFFORD Sir William Stanley, I am glad your conscience,
Before your end, hath emptied every burden
Which charged it, as that you can clearly witness°
How far I have proceeded in a duty   80
That both concerned my truth, and the state's safety.
STANLEY Mercy, how dear is life to such as hug it!
Come hither—by this token think on me—
      Makes a cross on Clifford's face with his finger [*-nail*]
CLIFFORD This token? What? I am abused!
STANLEY   You are not.
I wet upon your cheeks a holy sign,   85
The cross, the Christian's badge, the traitor's infamy.°
Wear, Clifford, to thy grave this painted emblem.
Water shall never wash it off, all eyes
That gaze upon thy face shall read there written
A state-informer's character, more ugly   90
Stamped on a noble name than on a base.
The Heavens forgive thee. Pray, my lords, no change°
Of words; this man and I have used too many.
CLIFFORD Shall I be disgraced
Without reply?
DURHAM   Give losers leave to talk;   95
His loss is irrecoverable.
STANLEY   Once more
To all a long farewell; the best of greatness°
Preserve the king. My next suit is, my lords,
To be remembered to my noble brother,
Derby, my much grieved brother. O, persuade him°   100
That I shall stand no blemish to his house°
In chronicles writ in another age.
My heart doth bleed for him, and for his sighs;
Tell him he must not think the style of Derby,
Nor being husband to King Henry's mother,   105
The league with peers, the smiles of fortune, can
Secure his peace above the state of man.°
I take my leave, to travel to my dust;
Subjects deserve their deaths whose kings are just.
Come, confessor; on with thy axe, friend, on.   110
      Exeunt [Stanley, Urswick, and executioner]

CLIFFORD Was I called hither by a traitor's breath
    To be upbraided? Lords, the king shall know it.
        Enter King Henry with a white staff°
HENRY The king doth know it, sir; the king hath heard
    What he or you could say. We have given credit
    To every point of Clifford's information,   115
    The only evidence 'gainst Stanley's head.
    'A dies for't; are you pleased?
CLIFFORD   I pleased, my lord?
HENRY No echoes. For your service, we dismiss
    Your more attendance on the court. Take ease
    And live at home; but, as you love your life,   120
    Stir not from London without leave from us.
    We'll think on your reward; away!
CLIFFORD   I go, sir.
        Exit Clifford
HENRY Die all our griefs with Stanley. Take this staff
    Of office, Daubeney; henceforth be our chamberlain.
DAUBENEY I am your humblest servant.
HENRY   We are followed   125
    By enemies at home that will not cease
    To seek their own confusion; 'tis most true
    The Cornish under Audley are marched on
    As far as Winchester. But let them come,
    Our forces are in readiness; we'll catch 'em   130
    In their own toils.
DAUBENEY   Your army, being mustered,
    Consist in all, of horse and foot, at least
    In number six and twenty thousand; men
    Daring and able, resolute to fight,
    And loyal in their truths.
HENRY   We know it, Daubeney.   135
    For them we order thus: Oxford, in chief,
    Assisted by bold Essex and the Earl
    Of Suffolk, shall lead on the first battalia;
    Be that your charge.
OXFORD   I humbly thank your majesty.
HENRY The next division we assign to Daubeney: 140
    These must be men of action, for on those°
    The fortune of our fortunes must rely.
    The last, and main, ourself commands in person,

As ready to restore the fight at all times
As to consummate an assured victory.   145
DAUBENEY The king is still oraculous.
HENRY   But, Surrey,
We have employment of more toil for thee!
For our intelligence comes swiftly to us
That James of Scotland late hath entertained
Perkin the counterfeit with more than common   150
Grace and respect; nay, courts him with rare favours.
The Scot is young and forward; we must look for°
A sudden storm to England from the north,
Which to withstand, Durham shall post to Norham,°
To fortify the castle and secure   155
The frontiers against an invasion there.
Surrey shall follow soon, with such an army
As may relieve the bishop and encounter
On all occasions, the death-daring Scots.
You know your charges all; 'tis now a time   160
To execute, not talk. Heaven is our guard still.
War must breed peace; such is the fate of kings.
     Exeunt

2.3

    Enter Crawford and Daliell
CRAWFORD 'Tis more than strange; my reason cannot answer
Such argument of fine imposture, couched
In witchcraft of persuasion, that it fashions
Impossibilities, as if appearance
Could cozen truth itself. This dukeling mushroom°   5
Hath doubtless charmed the king.
DALIELL   'A courts the ladies,
As if his strength of language chained attention
By power of prerogative.
CRAWFORD   It madded°
My very soul to hear our master's motion:
What surety both of amity and honour   10
Must of necessity ensue upon
A match betwixt some noble of our nation

And this brave prince, forsooth.

DALIELL   'Twill prove too fatal;
  Wise Huntly fears the threat'ning. Bless the lady
  From such a ruin!

CRAWFORD   How the council privy   15
  Of this young Phaethon do screw their faces°
  Into a gravity their trades, good people,
  Were never guilty of! The meanest of 'em
  Dreams of at least an office in the state.

DALIELL Sure, not the hangman's; 'tis bespoke already°   20
  For service to their rogueships.—Silence!
        Enter King James and Huntly

JAMES   Do not
  Argue against our will; we have descended
  Somewhat, as we may term it, too familiarly
  From justice of our birthright, to examine
  The force of your allegiance.—Sir, we have—   25
  But find it short of duty!

HUNTLY   Break my heart,
  Do, do king! Have my services, my loyalty—
  Heaven knows, untainted ever—drawn upon me
  Contempt now in mine age, when I but wanted
  A minute of a peace not to be troubled?   30
  My last, my long one? Let me be a dotard,°
  A bedlam, a poor sot, or what you please
  To have me, so you will not stain your blood,
  Your own blood, royal sir, though mixed with mine,
  By marriage of this girl to a straggler!   35
  Take, take my head, sir; whilst my tongue can wag
  It cannot name him other.

JAMES   Kings are counterfeits
  In your repute, grave oracle, not presently
  Set on their thrones with sceptres in their fists.
  But use your own detraction. 'Tis our pleasure°   40
  To give our cousin York for wife our kinswoman,
  The Lady Katherine. Instinct of sovereignty°
  Designs the honour, though her peevish father
  Usurps our resolution.

HUNTLY   O, 'tis well,°
  Exceeding well. I never was ambitious   45
  Of using congees to my daughter-queen.°

A queen; perhaps a queen? Forgive me, Daliell,
Thou honourable gentleman. None here
Dare speak one word of comfort?
DALIELL   Cruel misery!
CRAWFORD The lady, gracious prince, maybe hath settled   50
Affection on some former choice.
DALIELL   Enforcement
Would prove but tyranny.
HUNTLY   I thank 'ee heartily.
Let any yeoman of our nation challenge
An interest in the girl, then the king
May add a jointure of ascent in titles,   55
Worthy a free consent; now 'a pulls down
What old desert hath builded.
JAMES   Cease persuasions.°
I violate no pawns of faiths, intrude not°
On private loves; that I have played the orator
For kingly York to virtuous Kate, her grant   60
Can justify, referring her contents
To our provision. The Welsh Harry henceforth°
Shall therefore know, and tremble to acknowledge,
That not the painted idol of his policy
Shall fright the lawful owner from a kingdom.   65
We are resolved.
HUNTLY   Some of thy subjects' hearts,
King James, will bleed for this!
JAMES   Then shall their bloods
Be nobly spent. No more disputes; he is not
Our friend who contradicts us.
HUNTLY   Farewell, daughter!
My care by one is lessened; thank the king for't,   70
I and my griefs will dance now.
        Enter [Perkin] Warbeck leading Katherine, complimenting;°
        [*followed by the*] *Countess of Crawford, Jane, Frion,*
        [*John A-Water*] *Mayor of Cork, Astley, Heron, and*
        Sketon
                          —Look, lords, look,
Here's hand in hand already!
JAMES   Peace, old frenzy.—
How like a king 'a looks! Lords, but observe
The confidence of his aspect! Dross cannot

Cleave to so pure a metal; royal youth!   75
Plantagenet undoubted!
HUNTLY [*aside*]   Ho, brave youth!
But no Plantagenet, by'r Lady, yet,
By red rose or by white.
WARBECK   An union this way°
Settles possession in a monarchy
Established rightly, as is my inheritance.   80
Acknowledge me but sovereign of this kingdom,
Your heart, fair princess, and the hand of providence
Shall crown you queen of me and my best fortunes.
KATHERINE Where my obedience is, my lord, a duty,
Love owes true service.
WARBECK   Shall I?—
JAMES   Cousin, yes,   85
Enjoy her. From my hand accept your bride;
And may they live at enmity with comfort
Who grieve at such an equal pledge of troths.
Y'are the prince's wife now.
KATHERINE   By your gift, sir.°
WARBECK Thus I take seizure of mine own.
        [*They embrace*]
KATHERINE   I miss yet   90
A father's blessing. Let me find it. [*Kneels*] Humbly
Upon my knees I seek it.
HUNTLY   I am Huntly,
Old Alexander Gordon, a plain subject,°
Nor more nor less; and, lady, if you wish for
A blessing, you must bend your knees to Heaven,   95
For Heaven did give me you. Alas, alas,
What would you have me say? May all the happiness
My prayers ever sued to fall upon you
Preserve you in your virtues.—Prithee, Daliell,
Come with me, for I feel thy griefs as full   100
As mine; let's steal away and cry together.
DALIELL My hopes are in their ruins.
        Exeunt Huntly and Daliell
JAMES   Good kind Huntly
Is overjoyed; a fit solemnity
Shall perfect these delights. Crawford, attend
Our order for the preparation.   105

Exeunt all but Frion, [John A-Water], Astley, Heron, and
Sketon

FRION Now, worthy gentlemen, have I not followed
My undertakings with success? Here's entrance
Into a certainty above a hope.

HERON Hopes are but hopes; I was ever confident, when I traded but
in remnants, that my stars had reserved me to the title of a viscount 110
at least. Honour is honour, though cut out of any stuffs.

SKETON My brother Heron hath right wisely delivered his opinion;
for he that threads his needle with the sharp eyes of industry shall
in time go through-stitch° with the new suit of preferment.

ASTLEY Spoken to the purpose, my fine-witted brother Sketon; for 115
as no indenture° but has its counterpawn, no noverint but his
condition or defeasance,° so no right but may have claim, no claim
but may have possession, any act of parliament to the contrary
notwithstanding.

FRION You are all read in mysteries of state, 120
And quick of apprehension, deep in judgement,
Active in resolution; and 'tis pity
Such counsel should lie buried in obscurity.
But why in such a time and cause of triumph
Stands the judicious Mayor of Cork so silent? 125
Believe it, sir, as English Richard prospers,°
You must not miss employment of high nature.

A-WATER If men may be credited in their mortality,° which I dare
not peremptorily aver, but they may or not be, presumptions by
this marriage are then, in sooth, of fruitful expectation. Or else I 130
must not justify other men's belief more than other° should rely
on mine.

FRION Pith of experience! Those that have borne office
Weigh every word before it can drop from them.
But, noble counsellors, since now the present 135
Requires in point of honour (pray mistake not)
Some service to our lord, 'tis fit the Scots
Should not engross all glory to themselves
At this so grand and eminent solemnity.

SKETON The Scots? The motion is defied. I had rather, for my part, 140
without trial of my country, suffer persecution under the pressing-
iron° of reproach, or let my skin be punched full of eyelet-holes
with the bodkin of derision.

ASTLEY I will sooner lose both my ears° on the pillory of forgery.

HERON Let me first live a bankrupt, and die in the lousy hole of   145
    hunger,° without compounding for sixpence in the pound.°

A-WATER If men fail not in their expectations, there may be spirits,
    also, that digest no rude affronts, master secretary Frion, or I am
    cozened; which is possible, I grant.

FRION Resolved like men of knowledge. At this feast then,   150
    In honour of the bride, the Scots, I know,
    Will in some show, some masque, or some device,
    Prefer their duties. Now it were uncomely°
    That we be found less forward for our prince
    Than they are for their lady; and by how much   155
    We outshine them in persons of account,
    By so much more will our endeavours meet with
    A livelier applause. Great emperors
    Have, for their recreations, undertook
    Such kind of pastimes. As for the conceit,   160
    Refer it to my study; the performance
    You all shall share a thanks in. 'Twill be grateful.

HERON The motion is allowed. I have stole to a dancing-school when
    I was a prentice.

ASTLEY There have been Irish hubbubs, when I have made one° too.   165

SKETON For fashioning of shapes,° and cutting a cross-caper,° turn
    me off to my trade again.

A-WATER Surely there is, if I be not deceived, a kind of gravity in
    merriment; as there is, or perhaps ought to be, respect of persons in
    the quality of carriage,° which is, as it is construed, either so, or so.   170

FRION Still you come home to me; upon occasion
    I find you relish courtship with discretion,
    And such are fit for statesmen of your merits.
    Pray 'ee wait the prince, and in his ear acquaint him
    With this design; I'll follow and direct 'ee.   175
        Exeunt all but Frion
    O, the toil
    Of humouring this abject scum of mankind!
    Muddy-brained peasants! Princes feel a misery
    Beyond impartial sufferance, whose extremes
    Must yield to such abettors; yet our tide   180
    Runs smoothly, without adverse winds. Run on!
    Flow to a full sea! Time alone debates
    Quarrels forewritten in the book of fates.
        Exit

3.1

Enter King Henry, [with] his gorget on, his sword, plume of
feathers, [and] leading-staff, and [accompanied by] Urswick

HENRY How runs the time of day?

URSWICK   Past ten, my lord.

HENRY A bloody hour will it prove to some,
Whose disobedience, like the sons o'th' earth,°
Throw a defiance 'gainst the face of Heaven.
Oxford, with Essex and stout De la Pole,°   5
Have quieted the Londoners, I hope,
And set them safe from fear?

URSWICK   They are all silent.

HENRY From their own battlements they may behold
Saint George's Fields o'erspread with armèd men;°
Amongst whom our own royal standard threatens   10
Confusion to opposers. We must learn
To practise war again in time of peace,
Or lay our crown before our subjects' feet;
Ha, Urswick, must we not?

URSWICK   The powers who seated
King Henry on his lawful throne will ever   15
Rise up in his defence.

HENRY   Rage shall not fright
The bosom of our confidence. In Kent
Our Cornish rebels, cozened of their hopes,
Met brave resistance by that country's earl,°
George Aberg'enny, Cobham, Poynings, Guildford,   20
And other loyal hearts; now if Blackheath
Must be reserved the fatal tomb to swallow
Such stiff-necked abjects as with weary marches
Have travelled from their homes, their wives, and children,
To pay instead of subsidies, their lives—   25
We may continue sovereign. Yet, Urswick,
We'll not abate one penny what in parliament
Hath freely been contributed. We must not;
Money gives soul to action. Our competitor,
The Flemish counterfeit, with James of Scotland,   30
Will prove what courage, need and want can nourish°

Without the food of fit supplies; but, Urswick,
I have a charm in secret that shall loose
The witchcraft wherewith young King James is bound,
And free it at my pleasure without bloodshed.   35
URSWICK Your majesty's a wise king, sent from Heaven,
Protector of the just.
HENRY   Let dinner cheerfully
Be served in. This day of the week is ours,
Our day of providence, for Saturday°
Yet never failed in all my undertakings   40
To yield me rest at night.
    A flourish
                          What means this warning?
Good fate, speak peace to Henry!
    Enter Daubeney, Oxford, and attendants
DAUBENEY   Live the king,
Triumphant in the ruin of his enemies!
OXFORD The head of strong rebellion is cut off,
The body hewed in pieces.
HENRY   Daubeney, Oxford,   45
Minions to noblest fortunes, how yet stands
The comfort of your wishes?
DAUBENEY   Briefly thus:
The Cornish, under Audley, disappointed
Of flattered expectation from the Kentish,°
Your majesty's right-trusty liegemen, flew,   50
Feathered by rage and heartened by presumption,
To take the field even at your palace gates,
And face you in your chamber-royal. Arrogance
Improved their ignorance; for they, supposing,
Misled by rumour, that the day of battle   55
Should fall on Monday, rather braved your forces
Than doubted any onset. Yet, this morning,
When in the dawning I by your direction
Strove to get Deptford Strand Bridge, there I found°
Such a resistance as might show what strength   60
Could make; here arrows hailed in showers upon us
A full yard long at least; but we prevailed.
My Lord of Oxford with his fellow peers,
Environing the hill, fell fiercely on them
On the one side, I on the other, till, great sir—   65

Pardon the oversight—eager of doing
Some memorable act, I was engaged
Almost a prisoner, but was freed as soon°
As sensible of danger. Now the fight
Began in heat, which quenched in the blood of   70
Two thousand rebels, and as many more
Reserved to try your mercy, have returned°
A victory with safety.

HENRY   Have we lost
An equal number with them?

OXFORD   In the total
Scarcely four hundred. Audley, Flamank, Joseph,°   75
The ringleaders of this commotion,
Railed in ropes (fit ornaments for traitors),
Wait your determinations.

HENRY   We must pay
Our thanks where they are only due. O, lords,
Here is no victory, nor shall our people   80
Conceive that we can triumph in their falls.
Alas, poor souls! Let such as are escaped
Steal to the country back without pursuit.
There's not a drop of blood spilt but hath drawn
As much of mine; their swords could have wrought wonders   85
On their king's part, who faintly were unsheathed
Against their prince, but wounded their own breasts.
Lords, we are debtors to your care; our payment
Shall be both sure and fitting your deserts.

DAUBENEY Sir, will you please to see those rebels, heads   90
Of this wild monster-multitude?

HENRY   Dear friend,
My faithful Daubeney, no. On them our justice
Must frown in terror; I will not vouchsafe°
An eye of pity to them. Let false Audley
Be drawn upon an hurdle from the Newgate°   95
To Tower Hill in his own coat of arms
Painted on paper, with the arms reversed,
Defaced and torn. There let him lose his head.
The lawyer and the blacksmith shall be hanged,
Quartered, their quarters into Cornwall sent,   100
Examples to the rest, whom we are pleased
To pardon and dismiss from further quest.

My Lord of Oxford, see it done.
OXFORD   I shall, sir.
HENRY Urswick.
URSWICK   My lord?
HENRY   To Dinham, our high treasurer,
    Say we command commissions be new granted   105
    For the collection of our subsidies
    Through all the west, and that speedily.
    Lords, we acknowledge our engagements due
    For your most constant services.
DAUBENEY   Your soldiers
    Have manfully and faithfully acquitted   110
    Their several duties.
HENRY   For it we will throw
    A largess free amongst them, which shall hearten
    And cherish up their loyalties. More yet
    Remains of like employment; not a man
    Can be dismissed till enemies abroad,   115
    More dangerous than these at home, have felt
    The puissance of our arms. O, happy kings,
    Whose thrones are raisèd in their subjects' hearts!
        Exeunt

3.2

        Enter Huntly and Daliell
HUNTLY Now, sir, a modest word with you, sad gentleman.
    Is not this fine, I trow, to see the gambols,
    To hear the jigs, observe the frisks, b'enchanted
    With the rare discord of bells, pipes, and tabors,
    Hotch-potch of Scotch and Irish twingle-twangles,   5
    Like to so many choristers of Bedlam
    Trolling a catch? The feasts, the manly stomachs,°
    The healths in usquebaugh and bonny-clabber,°
    The ale in dishes never fetched from China,
    The hundred thousand knacks not to be spoken of,   10
    And all this for King Oberon and Queen Mab,°
    Should put a soul int'ee. Look'ee, good man,
    How youthful I am grown; but, by your leave,

This new queen-bride must henceforth be no more
My daughter. No, by'r Lady, 'tis unfit.   15
And yet you see how I do bear this change,
Methinks courageously; then shake off care
In such a time of jollity.
DALIELL   Alas, sir,
How can you cast a mist upon your griefs,
Which, howsoe'er you shadow, but present   20
To any judging eye the perfect substance
Of which mine are but counterfeits?
HUNTLY   Foh, Daliell,
Thou interrupts the part I bear in music
To this rare bridal feast; let us be merry,
Whilst flattering calms secure us against storms.   25
Tempests, when they begin to roar, put out
The light of peace, and cloud the sun's bright eye
In darkness of despair; yet we are safe.
DALIELL I wish you could as easily forget
The justice of your sorrows, as my hopes   30
Can yield to destiny.
HUNTLY   Pish, then I see
Thou dost not know the flexible condition
Of my apt nature. I can laugh, laugh heartily°
When the gout cramps my joints; let but the stone
Stop in my bladder, I am straight a-singing;   35
The quartan fever shrinking every limb°
Sets me a-cap'ring straight; do but betray me,
And bind me a friend ever. What! I trust
The losing of a daughter, though I doted
On every hair that grew to trim her head,   40
Admits not any pain like one of these.°
Come, th'art deceived in me. Give me a blow,
A sound blow on the face, I'll thank thee for't.
I love my wrongs; still th'art deceived in me.
DALIELL Deceived? O noble Huntly, my few years   45
Have learnt experience of too ripe an age
To forfeit fit credulity. Forgive°
My rudeness; I am bold.
HUNTLY   Forgive me first
A madness of ambition; by example
Teach me humility, for patience scorns   50

Lectures which schoolmen use to read to boys°
Uncapable of injuries. Though old,°
I could grow tough in fury, and disclaim
Allegiance to my king; could fall at odds
With all my fellow peers, that durst not stand   55
Defendants 'gainst the rape done on mine honour.
But kings are earthly gods, there is no meddling
With their anointed bodies; for their actions,
They only are accountable to Heaven.
Yet in the puzzle of my troubled brain   60
One antidote's reserved against the poison
Of my distractions; 'tis in thee t'apply it.

DALIELL Name it, O name it quickly, sir!

HUNTLY   A pardon
For my most foolish slighting thy deserts.
I have culled out this time to beg it: prithee   65
Be gentle; had I been so, thou hadst owned°
A happy bride, but now a castaway,
And never child of mine more.

DALIELL   Say not so, sir;
It is not fault in her.

HUNTLY   The world would prate
How she was handsome. Young I know she was,   70
Tender, and sweet in her obedience;
But lost now; what a bankrupt am I made
Of a full stock of blessings.—Must I hope
A mercy from thy heart?

DALIELL   A love, a service,
A friendship to posterity.

HUNTLY   Good angels°   75
Reward thy charity; I have no more
But prayers left me now.

DALIELL   I'll lend you mirth, sir,
If you will be in consort.

HUNTLY   Thank ye truly.°
I must; yes, yes, I must. Here's yet some ease,
A partner in affliction; look not angry.   80

DALIELL Good noble sir.
          Flourish

HUNTLY   O, hark! We may be quiet;°
The king and all the others come: a meeting

Of gaudy sights. This day's the last of revels;
Tomorrow sounds of war. Then new exchange:
Fiddles must turn to swords. Unhappy marriage!   85
    Enter King James, [Perkin] Warbeck leading Katherine,
    Crawford, Countess [of Crawford], and Jane. Huntly and
    Daliell fall among them

JAMES Cousin of York, you and your princely bride
Have liberally enjoyed such soft delights
As a new-married couple could forethink.
Nor has our bounty shortened expectation;
But after all those pleasures of repose,   90
Or amorous safety, we must rouse the ease
Of dalliance with achievements of more glory
Than sloth and sleep can furnish. Yet, for farewell,
Gladly we entertain a truce with time,
To grace the joint endeavours of our servants.   95
WARBECK My royal cousin, in your princely favour
The extent of bounty hath been so unlimited
As only an acknowledgement in words
Would breed suspicion in our state and quality.°
When we shall, in the fullness of our fate—   100
Whose minister, Necessity, will perfect—
Sit on our own throne, then our arms, laid open
To gratitude, in sacred memory
Of these large benefits, shall twine them close
Even to our thoughts and heart without distinction.   105
Then James and Richard, being in effect
One person, shall unite and rule one people,
Divisible in titles only.
JAMES   Seat ye.
Are the presenters ready?
CRAWFORD   All are ent'ring.
HUNTLY [*aside to Daliell*] Dainty sport toward, Daliell. Sit; come sit,   110
Sit and be quiet. Here are kingly bug's-words.°
    Enter at one door four Scotch Antics, accordingly habited;
    enter at another four wild Irish in trouses,° long-haired, and
    accordingly habited. Music.° The masquers dance
JAMES To all a general thanks!
WARBECK   In the next room
Take your own shapes again; you shall receive
Particular acknowledgement.

[Exeunt the masquers]

JAMES   Enough
  Of merriments. Crawford, how far's our army   115
  Upon the march?
CRAWFORD   At Heydonhall, great king;°
  Twelve thousand well prepared.
JAMES   Crawford, tonight
  Post thither. We in person with the prince,
  By four o'clock tomorrow after dinner,
  Will be wi'ee; speed away!
CRAWFORD   I fly, my lord.   120
    [Exit Crawford]
JAMES Our business grows to head now; where's your secretary,
  That he attends 'ee not to serve?
WARBECK   With Marchmount,
  Your herald.
JAMES   Good. The proclamation's ready;°
  By that it will appear how the English stand
  Affected to your title.—Huntly, comfort°   125
  Your daughter in her husband's absence; fight
  With prayers at home for us, who for your honours
  Must toil in fight abroad.
HUNTLY   Prayers are the weapons
  Which men, so near their graves as I, do use.
  I've little else to do.
JAMES   To rest, young beauties!   130
  We must be early stirring, quickly part;
  A kingdom's rescue craves both speed and art.
  Cousins, good-night.
    Flourish
WARBECK   Rest to our cousin king.
KATHERINE Your blessing, sir.
HUNTLY Fair blessings on your highness; sure, you need 'em.   135
    Exeunt all but [Perkin] Warbeck, Katherine, [and Jane]
WARBECK Jane, set the lights down, and from us return
  To those in the next room this little purse;
  Say we'll deserve their loves.
JANE   It shall be done, sir.
    [Exit Jane]
WARBECK Now, dearest, ere sweet sleep shall seal those eyes,
  Love's precious tapers, give me leave to use   140

A parting ceremony; for tomorrow
It would be sacrilege to intrude upon
The temple of thy peace. Swift as the morning
Must I break from the down of thy embraces,
To put on steel, and trace the paths which lead 145
Through various hazards to a careful throne.

KATHERINE My lord, I would fain go wi'ee; there's small fortune
In staying here behind.

WARBECK   The churlish brow
Of war, fair dearest, is a sight of horror
For ladies' entertainment. If thou hear'st 150
A truth of my sad ending by the hand°
Of some unnatural subject, thou withal°
Shalt hear how I died worthy of my right,
By falling like a king; and in the close°
Which my last breath shall sound, thy name, thou fairest, 155
Shall sing a requiem to my soul, unwilling
Only of greater glory 'cause divided
From such a heaven on earth as life with thee.
But these are chimes for funerals; my business
Attends on fortune of a sprightlier triumph; 160
For love and majesty are reconciled,
And vow to crown thee Empress of the West.

KATHERINE You have a noble language, sir; your right
In me is without question, and however
Events of time may shorten my deserts 165
In others' pity, yet it shall not stagger
Or constancy or duty in a wife.°
You must be king of me, and my poor heart
Is all I can call mine.

WARBECK   But we will live,
Live, beauteous virtue, by the lively test° 170
Of our own blood, to let the counterfeit
Be known the world's contempt.

KATHERINE   Pray do not use
That word; it carries fate in't. The first suit
I ever made I trust your love will grant?

WARBECK Without denial, dearest.

KATHERINE   That hereafter, 175
If you return with safety, no adventure
May sever us in tasting any fortune:

I ne'er can stay behind again.

WARBECK   Y'are lady
Of your desires, and shall command your will.
Yet 'tis too hard a promise.

KATHERINE   What our destinies   180
Have ruled out in their books we must not search,°
But kneel to.

WARBECK   Then to fear when hope is fruitless
Were to be desperately miserable;
Which poverty our greatness dares not dream of,°
And much more scorns to stoop to. Some few minutes   185
Remain yet; let's be thrifty in our hopes.
      Exeunt

3.3

      Enter King Henry, Hialas, and Urswick

HENRY   Your name is Pedro Hialas, a Spaniard?

HIALAS   Sir, a Castilian born.

HENRY   King Ferdinand,°
With wise Queen Isabel, his royal consort,
Write 'ee a man of worthy trust and candour.°
Princes are dear to Heaven who meet with subjects   5
Sincere in their employments; such I find
Your commendation, sir. Let me deliver
How joyful I repute the amity
With your most fortunate master, who almost
Comes near a miracle in his success   10
Against the Moors, who had devoured his country,°
Entire now to his sceptre. We, for our part,°
Will imitate his providence, in hope
Of partage in the use on't. We repute
The privacy of his advisement to us°   15
By you, intended an ambassador
To Scotland for a peace between our kingdoms,
A policy of love, which well becomes
His wisdom and our care.

HIALAS   Your majesty
Doth understand him rightly.

HENRY   Else,   20
   Your knowledge can instruct me; wherein, sir,
   To fall on ceremony would seem useless,
   Which shall not need, for I will be as studious
   Of your concealment in our conference
   As any counsel shall advise.
HIALAS   Then, sir,   25
   My chief request is that, on notice given
   At my dispatch in Scotland, you will send°
   Some learnèd man of power and experience
   To join in treaty with me.
HENRY   I shall do it,
   Being that way well provided by a servant°   30
   Which may attend 'ee ever.
HIALAS   If King James°
   By any indirection should perceive
   My coming near your court, I doubt the issue
   Of my employment.
HENRY   Be not your own herald;°
   I learn sometimes without a teacher.
HIALAS   Good days   35
   Guard all your princely thoughts.
HENRY   Urswick, no further
   Than the next open gallery attend him.—°
   [*To Hialas*] A hearty love go with you.
HIALAS   Your vowed beadsman.
     Exeunt Urswick and Hialas
HENRY King Ferdinand is not so much a fox
   But that a cunning huntsman may in time   40
   Fall on the scent; in honourable actions
   Safe imitation best deserves a praise.
     Enter Urswick
   What, the Castilian's passed away?
URSWICK   He is,°
   And undiscovered; the two hundred marks
   Your majesty conveyed 'a gently pursed,°   45
   With a right modest gravity.
HENRY   What was't
   'A muttered in the earnest of his wisdom,
   'A spoke not to be heard? 'Twas about—
URSWICK   Warbeck;

How, if King Henry were but sure of subjects,
Such a wild runagate might soon be caged,   50
No great ado withstanding.
HENRY   Nay, nay; something°
About my son Prince Arthur's match.
URSWICK   Right, right, sir.
'A hummed it out, how that King Ferdinand°
Swore that the marriage 'twixt the Lady Catherine
His daughter, and the Prince of Wales your son,   55
Should never be consummated as long
As any Earl of Warwick lived in England,
Except by new creation.
HENRY   I remember,°
'Twas so indeed. The king his master swore it?
URSWICK Directly, as he said.
HENRY   An Earl of Warwick!   60
Provide a messenger for letters instantly
To Bishop Fox. Our news from Scotland creeps,
It comes so slow. We must have airy spirits;
Our time requires dispatch.—The Earl of Warwick!
Let him be son to Clarence, younger brother   65
To Edward! Edward's daughter is, I think,
Mother to our Prince Arthur. Get a messenger.°
        Exeunt

3.4

        Enter King James, [Perkin] Warbeck, Crawford, Daliell,
        Heron, Astley, [John A-Water], Sketon, and soldiers
JAMES We trifle time against these castle walls;°
The English prelate will not yield. Once more
Give him a summons!
        [*A trumpet is sounded for a*] *parley. Enter above Durham*
        armed, a truncheon in his hand, and soldiers
WARBECK   See the jolly clerk
Appears, trimmed like a ruffian.
JAMES   Bishop yet°
Set ope the ports, and to your lawful sovereign,   5
Richard of York, surrender up this castle,

288

And he will take thee to his grace; else Tweed
Shall overflow his banks with English blood,
And wash the sand that cements those hard stones
From their foundation.
DURHAM   Warlike King of Scotland,   10
Vouchsafe a few words from a man enforced
To lay his book aside, and clap on arms
Unsuitable to my age or my profession.
Courageous prince, consider on what grounds
You rend the face of peace, and break a league   15
With a confederate king that courts your amity.
For whom too? For a vagabond, a straggler,
Not noted in the world by birth or name;
An obscure peasant, by the rage of Hell
Loosed from his chains, to set great kings at strife.   20
What nobleman, what common man of note,
What ordinary subject hath come in,°
Since first you footed on our territories,
To only feign a welcome? Children laugh at
Your proclamations, and the wiser pity   25
So great a potentate's abuse by one
Who juggles merely with the fawns and youth
Of an instructed compliment. Such spoils,°
Such slaughters as the rapine of your soldiers
Already have committed, is enough   30
To show your zeal in a conceited justice.°
Yet, great king, wake not yet my master's vengeance
But shake that viper off which gnaws your entrails!
I and my fellow subjects are resolved
If you persist, to stand your utmost fury,   35
Till our last blood drop from us.
WARBECK   O sir, lend
No ear to this traducer of my honour!
What shall I call thee, thou grey-bearded scandal,
That kick'st against the sovereignty to which
Thou owest allegiance? Treason is bold-faced   40
And eloquent in mischief; sacred king,
Be deaf to his known malice!
DURHAM   Rather yield
Unto those holy motions which inspire
The sacred heart of an anointed body!

It is the surest policy in princes   45
To govern well their own, than seek encroachment
Upon another's right.
CRAWFORD   The king is serious,
  Deep in his meditation.
DALIELL   Lift them up
  To Heaven, his better genius!
WARBECK   Can you study,
  While such a devil raves? O sir!
JAMES   Well—bishop,   50
  You'll not be drawn to mercy?
DURHAM   Construe me
  In like case by a subject of your own.°
  My resolution's fixed. King James, be counselled;
  A greater fate waits on thee.
        Exit Durham with his followers
JAMES   Forage through
  The country; spare no prey of life or goods.   55
WARBECK O sir, then give me leave to yield to nature.°
  I am most miserable; had I been
  Born what this clergyman would by defame
  Baffle belief with, I had never sought
  The truth of mine inheritance with rapes   60
  Of women, or of infants murdered, virgins
  Deflowered, old men butchered, dwellings fired,
  My land depopulated, and my people
  Afflicted with a kingdom's devastation.
  Show more remorse, great king, or I shall never   65
  Endure to see such havoc with dry eyes.
  Spare, spare, my dear, dear England.
JAMES   You fool your piety°
  Ridiculously, careful of an interest
  Another man possesseth! Where's your faction?°
  Shrewdly the bishop guessed of your adherents,   70
  When not a petty burgess of some town,
  No, not a villager hath yet appeared
  In your assistance. That should make 'ee whine,
  And not your country's sufferance, as you term it.
DALIELL The king is angry.
CRAWFORD   And the passionate duke   75
  Effeminately dolent.
WARBECK   The experience

In former trials, sir, both of mine own,
Or other princes cast out of their thrones,
Have so acquainted me how misery
Is destitute of friends or of relief,   80
That I can easily submit to taste
Lowest reproof, without contempt or words.°

JAMES An humble-minded man—
  Enter Frion

        Now, what intelligence
Speaks master secretary Frion?

FRION   Henry
Of England hath in open field o'erthrown   85
The armies who opposed him in the right
Of this young prince.

JAMES   His subsidies, you mean.
More, if you have it?

FRION   Howard, Earl of Surrey,°
Backed by twelve earls and barons of the north,
An hundred knights and gentlemen of name,
And twenty thousand soldiers, is at hand   90
To raise your siege. Broke, with a goodly navy,°
Is admiral at sea; and Daubeney follows
With an unbroken army for a second.°

WARBECK 'Tis false! They come to side with us.

JAMES   Retreat;   95
We shall not find them stones and walls to cope with.
Yet, Duke of York, for such thou sayest thou art,
I'll try thy fortune to the height. To Surrey,
By Marchmount, I will send a brave defiance
For single combat; once a king will venture°   100
His person to an earl, with condition
Of spilling lesser blood. Surrey is bold,°
And James resolved.

WARBECK   O rather, gracious sir,
Create me to this glory, since my cause°
Doth interest this fair quarrel; valued least,   105
I am his equal.

JAMES   I will be the man.
March softly off; where victory can reap
A harvest crowned with triumph, toil is cheap.
  Exeunt

4.1

Enter Surrey, Durham, soldiers, with drums and colours

SURREY Are all our braving enemies shrunk back,
    Hid in the fogs of their distempered climate,
    Not daring to behold our colours wave
    In spite of this infected air? Can they
    Look on the strength of Cundrestine defaced,   5
    The glory of Heydonhall devasted, that
    Of Edington cast down, the pile of Foulden
    O'erthrown, and this the strongest of their forts,
    Old Ayton Castle, yielded and demolished,°
    And yet not peep abroad? The Scots are bold,   10
    Hardy in battle; but it seems the cause
    They undertake, considerèd, appears
    Unjointed in the frame on't.
DURHAM   Noble Surrey,
    Our royal master's wisdom is at all times
    His fortune's harbinger; for when he draws   15
    His sword to threaten war, his providence
    Settles on peace, the crowning of an empire.
    Trumpet
SURREY Rank all in order; 'tis a herald's sound,
    Some message from King James. Keep a fixed station.
    Enter Marchmount and another herald in their coats°
MARCHMOUNT From Scotland's awful majesty we come   20
    Unto the English general.
SURREY   To me?
    Say on.
MARCHMOUNT Thus, then: the waste and prodigal
    Effusion of so much guiltless blood,
    As in two potent armies, of necessity
    Must glut the earth's dry womb, his sweet compassion   25
    Hath studied to prevent; for which, to thee,°
    Great Earl of Surrey, in a single fight
    He offers his own royal person, fairly
    Proposing these conditions only, that
    If victory conclude our master's right,°   30
    The earl shall deliver for his ransom

The town of Berwick to him, with the fishgarths.°
If Surrey shall prevail, the king will pay
A thousand pounds down present for his freedom
And silence further arms. So speaks King James.   35
SURREY So speaks King James; so like a king 'a speaks.
Heralds, the English general returns
A sensible devotion from his heart,
His very soul, to this unfellowed grace.
For let the king know, gentle heralds, truly,   40
How his descent from his great throne to honour
A stranger subject with so high a title
As his compeer in arms, hath conquered more
Than any sword could do. For which, my loyalty
Respected, I will serve his virtues ever°   45
In all humility. But Berwick, say,
Is none of mine to part with. In affairs
Of princes, subjects cannot traffic rights
Inherent to the crown. My life is mine,
That I dare freely hazard; and—with pardon   50
To some unbribed vainglory—if his majesty°
Shall taste a change of fate, his liberty
Shall meet no articles. If I fall, falling°
So bravely, I refer me to his pleasure
Without condition; and for this dear favour,   55
Say, if not countermanded, I will cease
Hostility, unless provoked.
MARCHMOUNT   This answer
We shall relate unpartially.
DURHAM   With favour,
Pray have a little patience—[aside to Surrey] Sir, you find
By these gay flourishes how wearied travail   60
Inclines to willing rest; here's but a prologue,
However confidently uttered, meant
For some ensuing acts of peace. Consider
The time of year, unseasonableness of weather,
Charge, barrenness of profit, and occasion   65
Presents itself for honourable treaty,
Which we may make good use of. I will back,
As sent from you in point of noble gratitude
Unto King James, with these his heralds. You
Shall shortly hear from me, my lord, for order   70

Of breathing or proceeding; and King Henry,°
Doubt not, will thank the service.

SURREY   To your wisdom
Lord bishop, I refer it.

DURHAM   Be it so then.

SURREY Heralds, accept this chain and these few crowns.°

MARCHMOUNT Our duty, noble general.

DURHAM   In part   75
Of retribution for such princely love,
My lord the general is pleased to show
The king your master his sincerest zeal
By further treaty, by no common man;
I will myself return with you.

SURREY   Y'oblige°   80
My faithfullest affections t'ee, lord bishop.

MARCHMOUNT All happiness attend your lordship.
      [*Exeunt Durham, Marchmount, and heralds*]

SURREY   Come friends
And fellow-soldiers; we, I doubt, shall meet
No enemies but woods and hills to fight with.
Then 'twere as good to feed and sleep at home;   85
We may be free from danger, not secure.°
      Exeunt

4.2

Enter [Perkin] Warbeck and Frion

WARBECK Frion, O Frion! All my hopes of glory
Are at a stand! The Scottish king grows dull,°
Frosty and wayward, since this Spanish agent
Hath mixed discourses with him. They are private;
I am not called to council now. Confusion   5
On all his crafty shrugs! I feel the fabric°
Of my designs are tottering.

FRION   Henry's policies°
Stir with too many engines.

WARBECK   Let his mines,°
Shaped in the bowels of the earth, blow up
Works raised for my defence, yet can they never   10

Toss into air the freedom of my birth,
Or disavow my blood, Plantagenet's!
I am my father's son still. But, O Frion,
When I bring into count with my disasters
My wife's compartnership, my Kate's, my life's,   15
Then, then my frailty feels an earthquake. Mischief
Damn Henry's plots, I will be England's king,
Or let my aunt of Burgundy report
My fall in the attempt deserved our ancestors!°
FRION You grow too wild in passion; if you will   20
  Appear a prince indeed, confine your will
  To moderation.
WARBECK   What a saucy rudeness
  Prompts this distrust! If, if I will appear?
  Appear a prince? Death throttle such deceits
  Even in their birth of utterance; cursed cozenage   25
  Of trust! Ye make me mad; 'twere best, it seems,
  That I should turn imposter to myself,
  Be mine own counterfeit, belie the truth
  Of my dear mother's womb, the sacred bed
  Of a prince murdered, and a living baffled!°   30
FRION Nay, if you have no ears to hear, I have
  No breath to spend in vain.
WARBECK   Sir, sir, take heed!
  Gold, and the promise of promotion, rarely
  Fail in temptation.
FRION   Why to me this?
WARBECK   Nothing.
  Speak what you will; we are not sunk so low   35
  But your advice may piece again the heart
  Which many cares have broken. You were wont
  In all extremities to talk of comfort;
  Have ye none left now? I'll not interrupt ye.
  Good, bear with my distractions! If King James   40
  Deny us dwelling here, next whither must I?
  I prithee be not angry.
FRION   Sir, I told ye
  Of letters, come from Ireland, how the Cornish
  Stomach their last defeat, and humbly sue
  That with such forces as you could partake,   45
  You would in person land in Cornwall, where

Thousands will entertain your title gladly.

WARBECK Let me embrace thee, hug thee! Thou'st revived
My comforts; if my cousin king will fail,
Our cause will never.

Enter [John A-Water,] Heron, Astley, [and] Sketon

          Welcome, my tried friends.   50
You keep your brains awake in our defence.
Frion, advise with them of these affairs,
In which be wondrous secret. I will listen
What else concerns us here; be quick and wary.

Exit Warbeck

ASTLEY Ah, sweet young prince! Secretary, my fellow counsellors 55
and I have consulted, and jump all in one opinion directly, that
if these Scotch garboils do not fadge to our minds,° we will
pell-mell run amongst the Cornish chuffs° presently, and in a
trice.

SKETON 'Tis but going to sea and leaping ashore, cut ten or twelve 60
thousand unnecessary throats, fire seven or eight towns, take
half-a-dozen cities, get into the market-place, crown him Richard
the Fourth, and the business is finished.

A-WATER I grant ye, quoth I, so far forth as men may do, no more
than men may do; for it is good to consider, when consideration 65
may be to the purpose. Otherwise still you shall pardon me; little
said is soon amended.°

FRION Then you conclude the Cornish action surest?

HERON We do so, and doubt not but to thrive abundantly. Ho, my
masters, had we known of the commotion when we set sail out of 70
Ireland, the land had been ours ere this time.

SKETON Pish, pish, 'tis but forbearing being an earl or a duke a
month or two longer; I say, and say it again, if the work go not on
apace, let me never see new fashion more. I warrant ye, I warrant
ye, we will have it so, and so it shall be. 75

ASTLEY This is but a cold phlegmatic country, not stirring enough
for men of spirit; give me the heart of England for my money.

SKETON A man may batten there in a week only with hot loaves and
butter, and a lusty cup of muscadine and sugar at breakfast, though
he make never a meal all the month after. 80

A-WATER Surely, when I bore office, I found by experience that to
be much troublesome was to be much wise and busy. I have
observed how filching and bragging has been the best service in
these last wars, and therefore conclude peremptorily on the design

in England. If things and things may fall out as who can tell what   85
or how, but° the end will show it.

FRION   Resolved like men of judgement! Here to linger
More time is but to lose it. Cheer the prince
And haste him on to this; on this depends
Fame in success, or glory in our ends.   90

    Exeunt

4.3

Enter King James; Durham and Hialas on either side

HIALAS   France, Spain, and Germany combine a league°
Of amity with England; nothing wants
For settling peace through Christendom but love
Between the British monarchs, James and Henry.

DURHAM   The English merchants, sir, have been received   5
With general procession into Antwerp;
The Emperor confirms the combination.°

HIALAS   The King of Spain resolves a marriage
For Catherine his daughter with Prince Arthur.

DURHAM   France courts this holy contract.

HIALAS   What can hinder   10
A quietness in England?

DURHAM   But your suffrage
To such a silly creature, mighty sir,
As is but in effect an apparition,
A shadow, a mere trifle!

HIALAS   To this union°
The good of both the church and commonwealth   15
Invite 'ee.

DURHAM   To this unity, a mystery
Of providence points out a greater blessing
For both these nations than our human reason
Can search into. King Henry hath a daughter,
The Princess Margaret. I need not urge   20
What honour, what felicity can follow
On such affinity 'twixt two Christian kings
Enleagued by ties of blood; but sure I am,
If you, sir, ratify the peace proposed,

I dare both motion and effect this marriage   25
For weal of both the kingdoms.
JAMES   Dar'st thou, lord bishop?
DURHAM Put it to trial, royal James, by sending
Some noble personage to the English court
By way of embassy.
HIALAS   Part of the business°
Shall suit my mediation.
JAMES   Well, what Heaven   30
Hath pointed out to be, must be; you two
Are ministers, I hope, of blessèd fate.
But herein only I will stand acquitted;
No blood of innocents shall buy my peace.
For Warbeck, as you nick him, came to me°   35
Commended by the states of Christendom.
A prince, though in distress; his fair demeanour,
Lovely behaviour, unappallèd spirit,°
Spoke him not base in blood, however clouded.
The brute beasts have both rocks and caves to fly to   40
And men the altars of the church. To us°
He came for refuge; kings come near in nature
Unto the gods in being touched with pity.
Yet, noble friends, his mixture with our blood,°
Even with our own, shall no way interrupt   45
A general peace; only I will dismiss him
From my protection, throughout my dominions
In safety, but not ever to return.
HIALAS You are a just king.
DURHAM   Wise, and herein happy.
JAMES Nor will we dally in affairs of weight.   50
Huntly, lord bishop, shall with you to England,
Ambassador from us; we will throw down
Our weapons; peace on all sides now! Repair
Unto our council; we will soon be with you.
HIALAS Delay shall question no dispatch; Heaven crown it.°   55
          Exeunt Durham and Hialas
JAMES A league with Ferdinand, a marriage
With English Margaret, a free release
From restitution for the late affronts!
Cessation from hostility! And all
For Warbeck not delivered, but dismissed!   60

We could not wish it better. Daliell—
    Enter Daliell
DALIELL   Here, sir.
JAMES Are Huntly and his daughter sent for?
DALIELL   Sent for
  And come, my lord.
JAMES   Say to the English prince,
  We want his company.
DALIELL   He is at hand, sir.
    Enter [Perkin] Warbeck, Katherine, Jane, Frion, Heron,
    Sketon, [John A-Water,] Astley
JAMES Cousin, our bounty, favours, gentleness,   65
  Our benefits, the hazard of our person,
  Our people's lives, our land, hath evidenced
  How much we have engaged on your behalf.
  How trivial and how dangerous our hopes
  Appear, how fruitless our attempts in war,   70
  How windy (rather smoky) your assurance°
  Of party shows, we might in vain repeat!°
  But now obedience to the mother church,°
  A father's care upon his country's weal,
  The dignity of state, directs our wisdom   75
  To seal an oath of peace through Christendom,
  To which we are sworn already. 'Tis you
  Must only seek new fortunes in the world,
  And find an harbour elsewhere. As I promised
  On your arrival, you have met no usage   80
  Deserves repentance in your being here;
  But yet I must live master of mine own.
  However, what is necessary for you
  At your departure, I am well content
  You be accommodated with, provided   85
  Delay prove not my enemy.
WARBECK   It shall not
  Most glorious prince. The fame of my designs
  Soars higher than report of ease and sloth
  Can aim at. I acknowledge all your favours,
  Boundless and singular; am only wretched   90
  In words as well as means to thank the grace
  That flowed so liberally. Two empires firmly
  You're lord of: Scotland and Duke Richard's heart.

My claim to mine inheritance shall sooner
Fail than my life to serve you, best of kings.   95
And witness Edward's blood in me, I am°
More loath to part with such a great example
Of virtue than all other mere respects.
But, sir, my last suit is, you will not force
From me what you have given: this chaste lady,   100
Resolved on all extremes.

KATHERINE   I am your wife;
No human power can or shall divorce
My faith from duty.

WARBECK   Such another treasure
The earth is bankrupt of.

JAMES   I gave her, cousin,
And must avow the gift; will add withal   105
A furniture becoming her high birth
And unsuspected constancy; provide°
For your attendance. We will part good friends.°
        Exeunt King [James] and Daliell

WARBECK The Tudor hath been cunning in his plots;
His Fox of Durham would not fail at last.   110
But what? Our cause and courage are our own.
Be men, my friends, and let our cousin king
See how we follow fate as willingly
As malice follows us. Y'are all resolved
For the west parts of England?

ALL   Cornwall, Cornwall!   115

FRION The inhabitants expect you daily.

WARBECK   Cheerfully
Draw all our ships out of the harbour, friends;
Our time of stay doth seem too long, we must
Prevent intelligence; about it suddenly.°

ALL A prince, a prince, a prince!   120
        Exeunt [Heron, Sketon, Astley, and John A-Water]

WARBECK Dearest, admit not into thy pure thoughts
The least of scruples, which may charge their softness
With burden of distrust. Should I prove wanting
To noblest courage now, here were the trial.
But I am perfect, sweet; I fear no change,   125
More than thy being partner in my sufferance.°

KATHERINE My fortunes, sir, have armed me to encounter

What chance soe'er they meet with.—Jane, 'tis fit
Thou stay behind, for whither wilt thou wander?
JANE Never till death will I forsake my mistress,   130
Nor then, in wishing to die with 'ee gladly.
KATHERINE Alas, good soul!
FRION   Sir, to your aunt of Burgundy
I will relate your present undertakings;
From her expect on all occasions welcome.
You cannot find me idle in your services.   135
WARBECK Go, Frion, go! Wise men know how to soothe
Adversity, not serve it. Thou hast waited
Too long on expectation; never yet
Was any nation read of, so besotted
In reason as to adore the setting sun.   140
Fly to the archduke's court; say to the duchess,
Her nephew, with fair Katherine his wife,
Are on their expectation to begin
The raising of an empire. If they fail,
Yet the report will never. Farewell, Frion.   145
     Exit Frion
This man, Kate, has been true, though now of late
I fear too much familiar with the Fox.°
     Enter Huntly and Daliell
HUNTLY I come to take my leave. You need not doubt
My interest in this sometime child of mine;
She's all yours now, good sir. [*To Katherine*] O poor lost creature,   150
Heaven guard thee with much patience! If thou canst°
Forget thy title to old Huntly's family,
As much of peace will settle in thy mind
As thou canst wish to taste, but in thy grave.
[*Weeps*] Accept my tears yet, prithee; they are tokens   155
Of charity, as true as of affection.
KATHERINE This is the cruell'st farewell!
HUNTLY   Love, young gentleman,
This model of my griefs. She calls you husband;°
Then be not jealous of a parting kiss,
It is a father's not a lover's off'ring.   160
Take it, my last—[*Kisses her*] I am too much a child.
Exchange of passion is to little use,
So I should grow too foolish. Goodness guide thee.
     Exit Huntly

KATHERINE [*weeping*] Most miserable daughter! Have you aught
  To add, sir, to our sorrows?
DALIELL   I resolve,   165
  Fair lady, with your leave, to wait on all
  Your fortunes in my person, if your lord
  Vouchsafe me entertainment.
WARBECK We will be bosom friends, most noble Daliell,
  For I accept this tender of your love   170
  Beyond ability of thanks to speak it.
  [*To Katherine*] Clear thy drowned eyes, my fairest; time and
    industry
  Will show us better days, or end the worst.
    Exeunt

4.4

    Enter Oxford and Daubeney
OXFORD No news from Scotland yet, my lord?
DAUBENEY   Not any
  But what King Henry knows himself. I thought
  Our armies should have marched that way; his mind,
  It seems, is altered.
OXFORD   Victory attends
  His standard everywhere.
DAUBENEY   Wise princes, Oxford,   5
  Fight not alone with forces. Providence
  Directs and tutors strength; else elephants
  And barbèd horses might as well prevail
  As the most subtle stratagems of war.
OXFORD The Scottish king showed more than common bravery 10
  In proffer of a combat hand to hand
  With Surrey.
DAUBENEY   And but showed it. Northern bloods
  Are gallant being fired, but the cold climate,
  Without good store of fuel, quickly freezeth
  The glowing flames.
OXFORD   Surrey, upon my life,   15
  Would not have shrunk an hair's-breadth.
DAUBENEY   May 'a forfeit

The honour of an English name and nature
Who would not have embraced it with a greediness
As violent as hunger runs to food.
'Twas an addition any worthy spirit°   20
Would covet next to immortality,
Above all joys of life. We all missed shares
In that great opportunity.

Enter King Henry and Urswick, whispering

OXFORD   The king—°
See, 'a comes smiling!

DAUBENEY   O, the game runs smooth
On his side, then, believe it; cards well shuffled   25
And dealt with cunning, bring some gamester thrift,
But others must rise losers.

HENRY   The train takes?

URSWICK Most prosperously.

HENRY   I knew it should not miss.
He fondly angles who will hurl his bait
Into the water 'cause the fish at first   30
Plays round about the line and dares not bite.
Lords, we may reign your king yet. Daubeney, Oxford,
Urswick, must Perkin wear the crown?

DAUBENEY   A slave!

OXFORD A vagabond!

URSWICK   A glow-worm!

HENRY   Now, if Frion,
His practised politician, wear a brain   35
Of proof, King Perkin will in progress ride°
Through all his large dominions. Let us meet him
And tender homage; ha, sirs? Liegemen ought
To pay their fealty.

DAUBENEY   Would the rascal were,
With all his rabble, within twenty miles   40
Of London.

HENRY   Farther off is near enough
To lodge him in his home. I'll wager odds°
Surrey and all his men are either idle
Or hasting back; they have not work, I doubt,
To keep them busy.

DAUBENEY   'Tis a strange conceit, sir.   45

HENRY Such voluntary favours as our people°

In duty aid us with, we never scattered
On cobweb parasites, or lavished out
In riot or a needless hospitality.
No undeserving favourite doth boast   50
His issues from our treasury; our charge
Flows through all Europe, proving us but steward
Of every contribution, which provides
Against the creeping canker of disturbance.
Is it not rare, then, in this toil of state   55
Wherein we are embarked, with breach of sleep,
Cares, and the noise of trouble, that our mercy
Returns nor thanks nor comfort? Still the west
Murmur and threaten innovation,
Whisper our government tyrannical,   60
Deny us what is ours, nay, spurn their lives,
Of which they are but owners by our gift.
It must not be.
OXFORD   It must not, should not.
          Enter a post
HENRY   So then.
    To whom?
POST   This packet to your sacred majesty.
HENRY Sirrah, attend without.   65
          [*Exit the post*]
OXFORD News from the north, upon my life.
DAUBENEY   Wise Henry
    Divines aforehand of events; with him
    Attempts and execution are one act.
HENRY Urswick, thine ear. Frion is caught, the man
    Of cunning is outreached; we must be safe.   70
    Should reverend Morton, our archbishop, move°
    To a translation higher yet, I tell thee°
    My Durham owns a brain deserves that see.°
    He's nimble in his industry, and mounting.
    Thou hear'st me?
URSWICK   And conceive your highness fitly.   75
HENRY Daubeney and Oxford, since our army stands
    Entire, it were a weakness to admit
    The rust of laziness to eat amongst them.
    Set forward toward Salisbury; the plains
    Are most commodious for their exercise.   80

Ourself will take a muster of them there,°
And or disband them with reward or else°
Dispose as best concerns us.
DAUBENEY   Salisbury?
Sir, all is peace at Salisbury.
HENRY   Dear friend,
The charge must be our own; we would a little   85
Partake the pleasure with our subjects' ease.
Shall I entreat your loves?
OXFORD   Command our lives.°
HENRY Y'are men know how to do, not to forethink.
My bishop is a jewel tried and perfect;
A jewel, lords. The post who brought these letters   90
Must speed another to the Mayor of Exeter.
Urswick, dismiss him not.
URSWICK   He waits your pleasure.
HENRY Perkin a king? A king!
URSWICK   My gracious lord.
HENRY Thoughts busied in the sphere of royalty
Fix not on creeping worms without their stings,   95
Mere excrements of earth. The use of time
Is thriving safety, and a wise prevention°
Of ills expected. W'are resolved for Salisbury.
    Exeunt

4.5

A general shout within. Enter [Perkin] Warbeck, Daliell,
Katherine, and Jane
WARBECK After so many storms as wind and seas
Have threatened to our weather-beaten ships,
At last, sweet fairest, we are safe arrived
On our dear mother earth, ingrateful only
To Heaven and us in yielding sustenance   5
To sly usurpers of our throne and right.
These general acclamations are an omen
Of happy process to their welcome lord.
They flock in troops, and from all parts with wings
Of duty fly, to lay their hearts before us.   10

Unequalled pattern of a matchless wife,
How fares my dearest yet?
KATHERINE   Confirmed in health:
  By which I may the better undergo
  The roughest face of change; but I shall learn
  Patience to hope (since silence courts affliction)°   15
  For comforts to this truly noble gentleman,
  Rare unexampled pattern of a friend!—
  And my beloved Jane, the willing follower
  Of all misfortunes.
DALIELL   Lady, I return
  But barren crops of early protestations,   20
  Frost-bitten in the spring of fruitless hopes.
JANE I wait but as the shadow to the body;
  For, madam, without you, let me be nothing.
WARBECK None talk of sadness; we are on the way
  Which leads to victory. Keep cowards thoughts   25
  With desperate sullenness! The lion faints not,°
  Locked in a grate but, loose, disdains all force
  Which bars his prey; and we are lion-hearted,
  Or else no king of beasts. (*Another shout*) Hark, how they shout
  Triumphant in our cause! Bold confidence   30
  Marches on bravely, cannot quake at danger.
        Enter Sketon
SKETON Save King Richard the Fourth; save thee, king° of hearts!
  The Cornish blades are men of mettle; have proclaimed through
  Bodmin and the whole country my sweet prince monarch of England.
  Four thousand tall yeomen, with bow and sword, already vow to   35
  live and die at the foot of King Richard.
        Enter Astley
ASTLEY The mayor, our fellow counsellor, is servant for an emperor.
  Exeter is appointed for the rendezvous, and nothing wants to
  victory but courage and resolution. *Sigillatum et datum decimo
  Septembris, anno regni regis primo, et cetera; confirmatum est.*° All's   40
  cock-sure.
WARBECK To Exeter, to Exeter, march on!
  Commend us to our people. We in person
  Will lend them double spirits; tell them so.
SKETON *and* ASTLEY King Richard, King Richard!   45
        [*Exeunt Sketon and Astley*]
WARBECK A thousand blessings guard our lawful arms!

A thousand horrors pierce our enemies' souls!
Pale fear unedge their weapons' sharpest points,
And when they draw their arrows to the head,
Numbness shall strike their sinews. Such advantage   50
Hath majesty in its pursuit of justice,
That on the proppers-up of Truth's old throne°
It both enlightens counsel and gives heart
To execution; whiles the throats of traitors
Lie bare before our mercy. O divinity   55
Of royal birth! How it strikes dumb the tongues
Whose prodigality of breath is bribed
By trains to greatness! Princes are but men,°
Distinguished by the fineness of their frailty,
Yet not so gross in beauty of the mind;   60
For there's a fire more sacred, purifies
The dross of mixture. Herein stands the odds:°
Subjects are men on earth; kings, men and gods.
    Exeunt

5.1

Enter Katherine and Jane in riding-suits, with one servant

KATHERINE It is decreed; and we must yield to fate,
Whose angry justice, though it threaten ruin,
Contempt, and poverty, is all but trial
Of a weak woman's constancy in suffering.
Here in a stranger's and an enemy's land,   5
Forsaken and unfurnished of all hopes
But such as wait on misery, I range
To meet affliction whereso'er I tread.
My train and pomp of servants is reduced
To one kind gentlewoman and this groom.   10
Sweet Jane, now whither must we?

JANE   To your ships,
Dear lady, and turn home.

KATHERINE   Home! I have none.
Fly thou to Scotland; thou hast friends will weep
For joy to bid thee welcome. But, O Jane,
My Jane, my friends are desperate of comfort,°   15
As I must be of them; the common charity,
Good people's alms, and prayers of the gentle
Is the revenue must support my state.
As for my native country, since it once
Saw me a princess in the height of greatness   20
My birth allowed me, here I make a vow
Scotland shall never see me, being fallen
Or lessened in my fortunes. Never, Jane;
Never to Scotland more will I return.
Could I be England's queen—a glory, Jane,   25
I never fawned on—yet the king who gave me,°
Hath sent me with my husband from his presence;
Delivered us suspected to his nation;
Rendered us spectacles to time and pity.
And is it fit I should return to such   30
As only listen after our descent°
From happiness enjoyed to misery
Expected, though uncertain? Never, never!
Alas, why dost thou weep, and that poor creature

Wipe his wet cheeks too? Let me feel alone°   35
Extremities, who know to give them harbour.
Nor thou nor he has cause. You may live safely.
JANE There is no safety whiles your dangers, madam,
    Are every way apparent.
SERVANT   Pardon, lady;
    I cannot choose but show my honest heart;   40
    You were ever my good lady.
KATHERINE   O dear souls,
    Your shares in grief are too, too much!
        Enter Daliell
DALIELL   I bring,
    Fair princess, news of further sadness yet
    Than your sweet youth hath been acquainted with.
KATHERINE Not more, my lord, than I can welcome. Speak it;   45
    The worst, the worst I look for.
DALIELL   All the Cornish
    At Exeter were by the citizens
    Repulsed, encountered by the Earl of Devonshire
    And other worthy gentlemen of the country.
    Your husband marched to Taunton, and was there   50
    Affronted by King Henry's chamberlain—
    The king himself in person, with his army,
    Advancing nearer to renew the fight
    On all occasions. But the night before
    The battles were to join, your husband, privately,   55
    Accompanied with some few horse, departed
    From out the camp, and posted none knows whither.
KATHERINE Fled without battle given?
DALIELL   Fled, but followed
    By Daubeney, all his parties left to taste
    King Henry's mercy—for to that they yielded—   60
    Victorious without bloodshed.
KATHERINE   O, my sorrows!
    If both our lives had proved the sacrifice
    To Henry's tyranny, we had fallen like princes,
    And robbed him of the glory of his pride.
DALIELL Impute it not to faintness or to weakness   65
    Of noble courage, lady, but foresight;
    For by some secret friend he had intelligence
    Of being bought and sold by his base followers.

Worse yet remains untold.

KATHERINE   No, no, it cannot.

DALIELL I fear y'are betrayed. The Earl of Oxford   70
Runs hot in your pursuit.

KATHERINE   'A shall not need;
We'll run as hot in resolution, gladly
To make the earl our jailor.

JANE   Madam, Madam,
They come, they come!
        Enter Oxford, with followers

DALIELL   Keep back, or he who dares
Rudely to violate the law of honour   75
Runs on my sword.

KATHERINE   Most noble sir, forbear!
What reason draws you hither, gentlemen?
Whom seek 'ee?

OXFORD   All stand off. With favour, lady,
From Henry, England's king, I would present
Unto the beauteous princess, Katherine Gordon,   80
The tender of a gracious entertainment.

KATHERINE We are that princess, whom your master king
Pursues with reaching arms to draw into
His power. Let him use his tyranny,
We shall not be his subjects.

OXFORD   My commission   85
Extends no further, excellentest lady,
Than to a service; 'tis King Henry's pleasure
That you, and all that have relation t'ee,
Be guarded as becomes your birth and greatness.
For rest assured, sweet princess, that not aught   90
Of what you do call yours shall find disturbance,
Or any welcome other than what suits
Your high condition.

KATHERINE   By what title, sir,°
May I acknowledge you?

OXFORD   Your servant, lady,
Descended from the line of Oxford's earls,   95
Inherits what his ancestors before him
Were owners of.

KATHERINE   Your king is herein royal
That, by a peer so ancient in desert

As well as blood, commands us to his presence.
OXFORD Invites 'ee, princess, not commands.
KATHERINE   Pray use   100
Your own phrase as you list; to your protection
Both I and mine submit.
OXFORD   There's in your number
A nobleman whom fame hath bravely spoken.°
To him the king my master bade me say
How willingly he courts his friendship; far   105
From an enforcement more than what in terms
Of courtesy so great a prince may hope for.
DALIELL My name is Daliell.
OXFORD   'Tis a name hath won
Both thanks and wonder from report. My lord,
The court of England emulates your merit,   110
And covets to embrace 'ee.
DALIELL   I must wait on
The princess in her fortunes.
OXFORD   Will you please
Great lady, to set forward?
KATHERINE   Being driven
By fate, it were in vain to strive with Heaven.°
        Exeunt

5.2

Enter King Henry, Surrey, Urswick, and a guard of soldiers
HENRY The counterfeit King Perkin is escaped;
Escape, so let him! He is hedged too fast
Within the circuit of our English pale
To steal out of our ports, or leap the walls
Which guard our land; the seas are rough, and wider   5
Than his weak arms can tug with. Surrey, henceforth
Your king may reign in quiet. Turmoils past,
Like some unquiet dream, have rather busied
Our fancy than affrighted rest of state.°
But Surrey, why, in articling a peace°   10
With James of Scotland, was not restitution
Of losses, which our subjects did sustain

By the Scotch inroads, questioned?
SURREY   Both demanded
　　And urged, my lord; to which the king replied,
　　In modest merriment but smiling earnest,   15
　　How that our master Henry was much abler
　　To bear the detriments than he repay them.
HENRY The young man, I believe, spake honest truth;°
　　'A studies to be wise betimes. Has, Urswick,°
　　Sir Rhys ap Thomas, and Lord Broke our steward   20
　　Returned the western gentlemen full thanks
　　From us for their tried loyalties?
URSWICK°   They have;
　　Which, as if health and life had reigned amongst 'em,
　　With open hearts they joyfully received.
HENRY Young Buckingham is a fair-natured prince,°   25
　　Lovely in hopes, and worthy of his father.°
　　Attended by an hundred knights and squires
　　Of special name, he tendered humble service,
　　Which we must ne'er forget. And Devonshire's wounds,
　　Though slight, shall find sound cure in our respect.   30
　　　　　　Enter Daubeney, with [Perkin] Warbeck, Heron, John
　　　　　　A-Water, Astley, Sketon
DAUBENEY Life to the king, and safety fix his throne!
　　I here present you, royal sir, a shadow
　　Of majesty, but in effect a substance
　　Of pity; a young man, in nothing grown°
　　To ripeness but th'ambition of your mercy:°   35
　　Perkin, the Christian world's strange wonder.
HENRY   Daubeney,
　　We observe no wonder. I behold, 'tis true,
　　An ornament of nature, fine and polished,
　　A handsome youth indeed, but not admire him.
　　How came he to thy hands?
DAUBENEY   From sanctuary   40
　　At Beaulieu, near Southampton, registered,°
　　With these few followers, for persons privileged.°
HENRY I must not thank you, sir! You were to blame
　　To infringe the liberty of houses sacred:
　　Dare we be irreligious?
DAUBENEY   Gracious lord,   45
　　They voluntarily resigned themselves

Without compulsion.

HENRY   So? 'Twas very well;
'Twas very, very well.—Turn now thine eyes,
Young man, upon thyself, and thy past actions!
What revels, in combustion through our kingdom,   50
A frenzy of aspiring youth hath danced,
Till, wanting breath, thy feet of pride have slipped
To break thy neck.

WARBECK   But not my heart; my heart
Will mount till every drop of blood be frozen
By death's perpetual winter. If the sun   55
Of majesty be darkened, let the sun
Of life be hid from me in an eclipse
Lasting and universal. Sir, remember
There was a shooting in of light when Richmond,°
Not aiming at a crown, retired, and gladly,   60
For comfort to the Duke of Bretagne's court.°
Richard, who swayed the sceptre, was reputed°
A tyrant then; yet then a dawning glimmered
To some few wand'ring remnants, promising day
When first they ventured on a frightful shore   65
At Milford Haven.

DAUBENEY   Whither speeds his boldness?°
Check his rude tongue, great sir!

HENRY   O, let him range.
The player's on the stage still, 'tis his part;
'A does but act. What followed?

WARBECK   Bosworth Field:°
Where, at an instant, to the world's amazement,   70
A morn to Richmond and a night to Richard
Appeared at once. The tale is soon applied.°
Fate, which crowned these attempts when least assured,
Might have befriended others, like resolved.

HENRY A pretty gallant! Thus your aunt of Burgundy,   75
Your duchess-aunt, informed her nephew; so,
The lesson, prompted and well conned, was moulded
Into familiar dialogue, oft rehearsed,
Till, learnt by heart, 'tis now received for truth.

WARBECK Truth in her pure simplicity wants art   80
To put a feigned blush on. Scorn wears only
Such fashion as commends to gazers' eyes

Sad ulcerated novelty, far beneath
The sphere of majesty. In such a court,
Wisdom and gravity are proper robes   85
By which the sovereign is best distinguished
From zanies to his greatness.
HENRY   Sirrah, shift°
Your antic pageantry, and now appear
In your own nature, or you'll taste the danger
Of fooling out of season.
WARBECK   I expect   90
No less than what severity calls justice,
And politicians, safety; let such beg
As feed on alms. But if there can be mercy
In a protested enemy, then may it
Descend to these poor creatures, whose engagements   95
To th'bettering of their fortunes have incurred
A loss of all; to them, if any charity
Flow from some noble orator, in death
I owe the fee of thankfulness.
HENRY   So brave!
What a bold knave is this! Which of these rebels   100
Has been the Mayor of Cork?
DAUBENEY   This wise formality.°
Kneel to the king, 'ee rascals!
HENRY   Canst thou hope°
A pardon, where thy guilt is so apparent?
A-WATER Under your good favours, as men are men, they may err.
For I confess, respectively, in taking great parts, the one side   105
prevailing, the other side must go down. Herein the point is clear,
if the proverb hold that hanging goes by destiny,° that it is to little
purpose to say this thing or that shall be thus or thus; for as the
fates will have it, so it must be, and who can help it?
DAUBENEY O blockhead! Thou a privy councillor?   110
Beg life, and cry aloud, 'Heaven save King Henry!'
A-WATER Every man knows what is best, as it happens. For my own
part, I believe it is true, if I be not deceived, that kings must be
kings, and subjects subjects. But which is which, you shall pardon
me for that. Whether we speak or hold our peace, all are mortal;   115
no man knows his end.
HENRY We trifle time with follies.
ALL [WARBECK'S FOLLOWERS]   Mercy, mercy!

HENRY Urswick, command the dukeling and these fellows
　　　To Digby, the Lieutenant of the Tower.
　　　With safety let them be conveyed to London.　　　　　　　120
　　　It is our pleasure no uncivil outrage,
　　　Taunts or abuse be suffered to their persons;
　　　They shall meet fairer law than they deserve.
　　　Time may restore their wits, whom vain ambition
　　　Hath many years distracted.
WARBECK　　　　　　　　　　　　Noble thoughts　　　　　125
　　　Meet freedom in captivity. The Tower?—
　　　Our childhood's dreadful nursery.
HENRY　　　　　　　　　　　　No more.
URSWICK Come, come, you shall have leisure to bethink 'ee.
　　　Exit Urswick with Perkin [Warbeck] and his [followers]
HENRY Was ever so much impudence in forgery?°
　　　The custom, sure, of being styled a king　　　　　　　130
　　　Hath fastened in his thought that he is such.
　　　But we shall teach the lad another language;
　　　'Tis good we have him fast.
DAUBENEY　　　　　　　　　The hangman's physic
　　　Will purge this saucy humour.
HENRY　　　　　　　　　　Very likely;
　　　Yet we could temper mercy with extremity,　　　　　　135
　　　Being not too far provoked.
　　　Enter Oxford, Katherine in her richest attire, [Daliell,] Jane,
　　　and attendants
OXFORD　　　　　　　　　　Great sir, be pleased
　　　With your accustomed grace to entertain
　　　The Princess Katherine Gordon.
HENRY　　　　　　　　　　Oxford, herein
　　　We must beshrew thy knowledge of our nature.
　　　A lady of her birth and virtues could not　　　　　　　140
　　　Have found us so unfurnished of good manners
　　　As not, on notice given, to have met her
　　　Half-way in point of love. Excuse, fair cousin,
　　　The oversight! *[Katherine begins to kneel]*°
　　　　　　　O fie, you may not kneel;°
　　　'Tis most unfitting. First, vouchsafe this welcome,　　145
　　　A welcome to your own, for you shall find us
　　　But guardian to your fortune and your honours.
KATHERINE My fortunes and mine honours are weak champions,

As both are now befriended, sir; however,
Both bow before your clemency.

HENRY   Our arms   150
Shall circle them from malice. [*Embraces Katherine*] A sweet lady!
Beauty incomparable! Here lives majesty
At league with love.

KATHERINE   O sir, I have a husband.

HENRY We'll prove your father, husband, friend, and servant;
Prove what you wish to grant us. Lords, be careful   155
A patent presently be drawn for issuing
A thousand pounds from our exchequer yearly
During our cousin's life. [*To Katherine*] Our queen shall be°
Your chief companion, our own court your home,
Our subjects all your servants.

KATHERINE   But my husband?   160

HENRY By all descriptions, you are noble Daliell,
Whose generous truth hath famed a rare observance!°
We thank 'ee; 'tis a goodness gives addition
To every title boasted from your ancestry,
In all most worthy.

DALIELL   Worthier than your praises,   165
Right princely sir, I need not glory in.

HENRY Embrace him, lords.
         [*To Katherine*]   Whoever calls you mistress
Is lifted in our charge; a goodlier beauty°
Mine eyes yet ne'er encountered.

KATHERINE   Cruel misery
Of fate, what rests to hope for?

HENRY   Forward, lords,   170
To London. [*To Katherine*]° Fair, ere long I shall present 'ee°
With a glad object: peace, and Huntly's blessing.
        Exeunt

5.3

Enter constable and officers, [Perkin] Warbeck, Urswick, and Lambert Simnel like a falconer° [with onlookers]. A pair of stocks [is set out]

CONSTABLE Make room there! Keep off, I require 'ee, and none
come within twelve foot of his majesty's° new stocks, upon pain of
displeasure. Bring forward the malefactor. [*To Warbeck*] Friend,
you must to this gear, no remedy. [*To officers*] Open the hole, and
in with his legs; just in the middle hole, there, that hole.   5
    [*Warbeck is put in the stocks*]
    Keep off, or I'll commit° you all. Shall not a man in authority be
obeyed? So, so there, 'tis as it should be. Put on the padlock, and
give me the key; off, I say, keep off!
URSWICK Yet, Warbeck, clear thy conscience. Thou hast tasted
    King Henry's mercy liberally. The law   10
    Has forfeited thy life; an equal jury°
    Have doomed thee to the gallows. Twice, most wickedly,°
    Most desperately, hast thou escaped the Tower,
    Inveigling to thy party with thy witchcraft°
    Young Edward, Earl of Warwick, son to Clarence,   15
    Whose head must pay the price of that attempt.
    Poor gentleman; unhappy in his fate,
    And ruined by thy cunning! So a mongrel
    May pluck the true stag down. Yet, yet, confess
    Thy parentage; for yet the king has mercy.   20
LAMBERT You would be Dick the Fourth; very likely!
    Your pedigree is published; you are known
    For Osbeck's son of Tournai, a loose runagate,
    A landloper. Your father was a Jew,
    Turned Christian merely to repair his miseries.   25
    Where's now your kingship?
WARBECK   Baited to my death?°
    Intolerable cruelty! I laugh at
    The Duke of Richmond's practice on my fortunes.°
    Possession of a crown ne'er wanted heralds.
LAMBERT You will not know who I am?
URSWICK   Lambert Simnel,°   30
    Your predecessor in a dangerous uproar;
    But, on submission, not alone received

To grace, but by the king vouchsafed his service.
LAMBERT I would be Earl of Warwick; toiled and ruffled
Against my master, leapt to catch the moon,   35
Vaunted my name Plantagenet, as you do.
An earl, forsooth! Whereas in truth I was,°
As you are, a mere rascal. Yet his majesty,
A prince composed of sweetness (Heaven protect him!)
Forgave me all my villainies, reprieved   40
The sentence of a shameful end, admitted
My surety of obedience to his service;
And I am now his falconer, live plenteously,
Eat from the king's purse, and enjoy the sweetness
Of liberty and favour, sleep securely.   45
And is not this now better than to buffet
The hangman's clutches, or to brave the cordage
Of a tough halter, which will break your neck?
So, then, the gallant totters. Prithee, Perkin,°
Let my example lead thee. Be no longer   50
A counterfeit; confess, and hope for pardon!
WARBECK For pardon! Hold, my heart-strings, whiles contempt
Of injuries, in scorn, may bid defiance
To this base man's foul language. Thou poor vermin!
How dar'st thou creep so near me? Thou an earl?   55
Why, thou enjoy'st as much of happiness
As all the swinge of slight ambition flew at.°
A dunghill was thy cradle. So a puddle,
By virtue of the sunbeams, breathes a vapour
To infect the purer air, which drops again   60
Into the muddy womb that first exhaled it.
Bread and a slavish ease, with some assurance
From the base beadle's whip, crowned all thy hopes.°
But sirrah, ran there in thy veins one drop
Of such a royal blood as flows in mine,   65
Thou wouldst not change condition to be second
In England's state, without the crown itself!
Coarse creatures are incapable of excellence.
But let the world, as all to whom I am
This day a spectacle, to time deliver,   70
And by tradition fix posterity,°
Without another chronicle than truth,
How constantly my resolution suffered

A martyrdom of majesty!

LAMBERT He's past

    Recovery; a Bedlam cannot cure him.   75

URSWICK Away, inform the king of his behaviour.

LAMBERT Perkin, beware the rope; the hangman's coming.

    Exit [Lambert] Simnel

URSWICK If yet thou hast no pity of thy body,

    Pity thy soul!

    Enter Katherine, Jane, Daliell, and Oxford

JANE   Dear lady!

OXFORD   Whither will 'ee,

    Without respect of shame?

KATHERINE   Forbear me, sir,°   80

    And trouble not the current of my duty!

    O my loved lord! Can any scorn be yours

    In which I have no interest? Some kind hand

    Lend me asistance, that I may partake

    Th'infliction of this penance. My life's dearest,   85

    Forgive me; I have stayed too long from tend'ring

    Attendance on reproach, yet bid me welcome.°

WARBECK Great miracle of constancy! My miseries

    Were never bankrupt of their confidence

    In worst afflictions, till this now, I feel them.°   90

    Report and thy deserts, thou best of creatures,

    Might to eternity have stood a pattern

    For every virtuous wife, without this conquest.

    Thou hast outdone belief; yet may their ruin

    In after-marriages be never pitied   95

    To whom thy story shall appear a fable.

    Why wouldst thou prove so much unkind to greatness

    To glorify thy vows by such a servitude?

    I cannot weep, but trust me, dear, my heart

    Is liberal of passion.—Harry Richmond!   100

    A woman's faith hath robbed thy fame of triumph.

OXFORD Sirrah, leave off your juggling, and tie up

    The devil that ranges in your tongue.

URSWICK   Thus witches,

    Possessed, even to their deaths deluded, say

    They have been wolves, and dogs, and sailed in egg-shells   105

    Over the sea, and rid on fiery dragons;

    Passed in the air more than a thousand miles

All in a night. The enemy of mankind°
Is powerful but false, and falsehood confident.

OXFORD Remember, lady, who you are; come from   110
   That impudent impostor.

KATHERINE   You abuse us:
   For when the holy churchman joined our hands,
   Our vows were real then; the ceremony
   Was not in apparition, but in act.°
      [*To Warbeck*]
   Be what these people term thee, I am certain°   115
   Thou art my husband. No divorce in Heaven
   Has been sued out between us; 'tis injustice
   For any earthly power to divide us.
   Or we will live, or let us die, together.
   There is a cruel mercy.

WARBECK   Spite of tyranny,   120
   We reign in our affections, blessed woman!
   Read in my destiny the wreck of honour;°
   Point out, in my contempt of death, to memory
   Some miserable happiness; since herein
   Even when I fell, I stood enthroned a monarch   125
   Of one chaste wife's troth, pure and uncorrupted.
   Fair angel of perfection, immortality
   Shall raise thy name up to an adoration;
   Court every rich opinion of true merit;
   And saint it in the calendar of virtue,   130
   When I am turned into the selfsame dust
   Of which I was first formed.

OXFORD   The lord ambassador,
   Huntly, your father, madam, should 'a look on
   Your strange subjection, in a gaze so public,
   Would blush on your behalf, and wish his country   135
   Unleft for entertainment to such sorrow.°

KATHERINE Why art thou angry, Oxford? I must be
   More peremptory in my duty. [*To Warbeck*] Sir,
   Impute it not unto immodesty
   That I presume to press you to a legacy,°   140
   Before we part for ever.

WARBECK   Let it be, then,
   My heart, the rich remains of all my fortunes.

KATHERINE Confirm it with a kiss, pray.

WARBECK O, with that
    I wish to breathe my last. Upon thy lips,
    Those equal twins of comeliness, I seal 145
    The testament of honourable vows.
       [Kisses her]
    Whoever be that man that shall unkiss°
    This sacred print next, may he prove more thrifty
    In this world's just applause, not more desertful.
KATHERINE By this sweet pledge of both our souls, I swear 150
    To die a faithful widow to thy bed,
    Not to be forced or won. O, never, never!
      Enter Surrey, Daubeney, Huntly, and Crawford
DAUBENEY Free the condemned person, quickly free him.
    What has 'a yet confessed?
URSWICK Nothing to purpose;
    But still 'a will be king.
SURREY Prepare your journey 155
    To a new kingdom, then. *[To Katherine]* Unhappy madam,
    Wilfully foolish! See, my lord ambassador,
    Your lady daughter will not leave the counterfeit
    In this disgrace of fate.
HUNTLY I never 'pointed°
    Thy marriage, girl, but yet, being married, 160
    Enjoy thy duty to a husband freely.
    The griefs are mine. I glory in thy constancy;
    And must not say I wish that I had missed
    Some partage in these trials of a patience.
KATHERINE You will forgive me, noble sir?
HUNTLY Yes, yes; 165
    In every duty of a wife, and daughter,
    I dare not disavow thee.—To your husband,
    For such you are, sir, I impart a farewell
    Of manly pity; what your life has passed through,
    The dangers of your end will make apparent. 170
    And I can add, for comfort to your sufferance,
    No cordial but the wonder of your frailty
    Which keeps so firm a station.—We are parted.
WARBECK We are. A crown of peace renew thy age,
    Most honourable Huntly. Worthy Crawford! 175
    We may embrace; I never thought thee injury.°
CRAWFORD Nor was I ever guilty of neglect

Which might procure such thought. I take my leave, sir.
WARBECK   To you, Lord Daliell—what? Accept a sigh;
  'Tis hearty and in earnest.
DALIELL   I want utterance;   180
  My silence is my farewell.
KATHERINE   Oh—Oh—
JANE   Sweet madam,
  What do you mean? My lord, your hand.
DALIELL   Dear lady,
  Be pleased that I may wait 'ee to your lodging.

> *Exit Katherine, [supported by] Daliell [and] Jane. Enter*
> *Sheriff and officers [with] Sketon, Astley, Heron,° and [John*
> *A-Water,] with halters about their necks*

OXFORD   Look 'ee; behold your followers, appointed
  To wait on 'ee in death.
WARBECK   Why, peers of England,   185
  We'll lead 'em on courageously. I read
  A triumph over tyranny upon
  Their several foreheads. Faint not in the moment
  Of victory! Our ends, and Warwick's head,
  Innocent Warwick's head—for we are prologue   190
  But to his tragedy—conclude the wonder°
  Of Henry's fears; and then the glorious race
  Of fourteen kings, Plantagenets, determines°
  In this last issue male. Heaven be obeyed.
  Impoverish time of its amazement, friends,   195
  And we will prove as trusty in our payments,°
  As prodigal to nature in our debts.°
  Death? Pish, 'tis but a sound, a name of air,
  A minute's storm, or not so much. To tumble
  From bed to bed, be massacred alive   200
  By some physicians for a month or two
  In hope of freedom from a fever's torments,
  Might stagger manhood; here, the pain is passed°
  Ere sensibly 'tis felt. Be men of spirit!
  Spurn coward passion! So illustrious mention   205
  Shall blaze our names, and style us Kings o'er Death.
DAUBENEY   Away—impostor beyond precedent!
  No chronicle records his fellow.

> *Exeunt [Sheriff], all officers and prisoners*

HUNTLY   I have

322

Not thoughts left; 'tis sufficient in such cases
Just laws ought to proceed.
     Enter King Henry, Durham, and Hialas
HENRY   We are resolved.   210
   Your business, noble lords, shall find success
   Such as your king importunes.
HUNTLY   You are gracious.
HENRY Perkin, we are informed, is armed to die;
   In that we'll honour him. Our lords shall follow
   To see the execution; and from hence   215
   We gather this fit use: that public states,
   As our particular bodies, taste most good
   In health, when purgèd of corrupted blood.
     Exeunt

THE EPILOGUE

Here has appeared, though in a several fashion,
The threats of majesty, the strength of passion,
Hopes of an empire, change of fortunes; all
What can to theatres of greatness fall,
Proving their weak foundations. Who will please,   5
Amongst such several sights, to censure these
No births abortive, nor a bastard brood—
Shame to a parentage, or fosterhood—
May warrant by their loves all just excuses,
And often find a welcome to the Muses.°   10

EXPLANATORY NOTES

ABBREVIATIONS

AM   Robert Burton, *The Anatomy of Melancholy* (1621)

Bawcutt   *'Tis Pity She's a Whore*, ed. N. W. Bawcutt (London, 1966)

Dodsley   *A Select Collection of Old Plays*, ed. Robert Dodsley (12 vols., 1744)

Dyce   *The Works of John Ford* with notes . . . by William Gifford . . . A New edition . . . revised by Alexander Dyce (3 vols., London, 1869)

Gainsford   *The True and Wonderfull History of Perkin Warbeck Proclaiming himself Richard the fourth* [by Thomas Gainsford] (London, 1618)

Gibson   *The Selected Plays of John Ford*, ed. Colin Gibson (Cambridge, 1986)

Gifford   *The Dramatic Works of John Ford*, ed. William Gifford (2 vols., 1827)

Hill   *The Lover's Melancholy*, ed. R. F. Hill (Manchester, 1985)

Lamb   Charles Lamb, *Specimens of English Dramatic Poets, Who Lived About the Time of Shakespeare: With Notes* (London, 1808)

OED   *The Oxford English Dictionary*

Oliphant   *Shakespeare and his Fellow Dramatists*, ed. E. H. C. Oliphant (New York, 1929)

Q   Quarto (British Library copies C. 12. g. 3/5, 1481. bb. 18, 644. b. 34, 644. b. 35, 644. b. 37, 644. b. 38, and Bodleian Library copies Malone 238 (3), 210 (2), and 214 (7) were consulted)

Roper   *'Tis Pity She's a Whore*, ed. Derek Roper (Manchester, 1975)

Spencer   *The Broken Heart*, ed. T. J. B. Spencer (Manchester and Baltimore, 1980)

Sturgess   *John Ford: Three Plays*, ed. Keith Sturgess (Harmondsworth, 1970)

Tilley   M. P. Tilley, *A Dictionary of the Proverbs in England in the Sixteenth and Seventeenth Centuries* (Ann Arbor, Mich., 1950)

Ure   *The Chronicle History of Perkin Warbeck: A Strange Truth*, ed. Peter Ure (Manchester, 1968)

Weber   *The Dramatic Works of John Ford*, ed. Henry Weber (2 vols., Edinburgh, 1811)

The Lover's Melancholy

To my worthily respected friends . . .

10 *first . . . courted reader*: *The Lover's Melancholy* was Ford's first play to be printed, although he had published poems and prose pamphlets previously.

To my Honoured Friend . . .

4 *bays*: the garland for literary merit formed from the leaves of the laurel (bay) tree.

9 *George Donne*: a son of John Donne.

To his worthy Friend . . .

13 *poet-apes*: those who imitate poets (an abusive term).

17 *William Singleton*: 'Friend and Kinsman' to Philip Massinger, according to his commendatory poem to Massinger's play *The Emperor of the East* (1632).

To the Author . . .

1 *Black choler*: in the Renaissance theory of bodily 'humours' (see note to 1.2.133), black choler or melancholy was one of the four cardinal humours which supposedly determined a person's physical and mental qualities.

9 *Phocion*: a virtuous Athenian who refused the generosity of patrons and disliked praise.

14 *jealousy*: anxiety (for the well-being of his work).

15 *Humfrey Howorth*: was admitted to the Middle Temple, 18 June 1624.

Of the Lover's Melancholy

5 ὁ Φιλος: (Greek) 'the friend'.

The Names of Such as Acted

T. W. Baldwin suggested a possible allocation of names to roles in *The Organization and Personnel of the Shakespearean Company* (Princeton, NJ, 1927), app. III, pp. 366–8. The last, central group probably indicates the actors who played the women's parts as there are four female characters and Grilla, a young man impersonating a female. 'Curteish Gr——' is Curteise Grivill who, like the others, was a member of The King's Men.

The Prologue

13 *quit his pains*: reward his efforts.

16 *the bye*: a secondary or side-issue.

1.1.14 *presents a feather-bed*: according to Pliny, dolphins were supposed to be willing to carry humans on their backs.

48 *funerals*: in the seventeenth century the word was used in the plural with the same sense as the singular.

66 *fawned upon*: was willing slave to.

78–9 *any . . . mentioned*: has seldom been mentioned in any story.

81 *Whereas*: 'Whenas' (*Q*).

89 *else*: on any other assumption.

95–6 *repute . . . are*: esteem him a god.

100 *Tempe*: a beautiful, temperate valley in Thessaly (north-eastern part of Greece) praised by poets and supposedly frequented by the gods.

109 *. . . at strife in*: *Q* has a marginal note here which refers to Book II, Exercise VI of the *Prolusiones Academicae, Oratoriae, Historicae, Poeticae* (1617) by Famiamus Strada; this describes a similar musical duel between a lute player and a nightingale.

123 *several strain*: separate melody.

124 *down*: a refrain.

125 *run division*: play or sing a rapid melodic passage—often a variation on a theme.

140 *voluntaries*: pieces played spontaneously.

143 *centre*: concentration.

154 *looked*: 'looks' (*Q*).

163 *truth*: true account.

178 *They . . . riotous*: they were neither meagre nor sufficient to support extravagent living.

183 *rare distractions*: unusual disturbances of mind.

188–9 *lose . . . For one part of my hopes*: miss . . . as one part of what I hope to enjoy. (The other part is Menaphon himself.)

1.2.17 *pursues . . . from*: looks for security in.

27 *guarded*: i.e. with ornate livery.

30 *entertained him*: employed him.

31 *waits . . . trencher*: serves at table.

33 *lackeys*: runs with.

37 *bare*: i.e. bare-headed.

42 *Agelastus*: surname of Crassus, grandfather of Marcus Licinius Crassus.

59 *A . . . instrument*: Grilla may mean a sow-gelder, as they blew horns to attract custom, but it is more likely to be merely a crude pun.

61 *dancer*: dancing master.

footcloth: rich drapery on a horse's back (here, to indicate the prosperity of a stylish 'dancer').

62 *muff and hood*: in the early 1600s muffs were fashionable and expensive, but hoods were worn by citizens' wives, not court women.

66 *head-piece*: either the brain itself or the whole skull.

67 *understanding*: a bawdy pun on his imagined dominance of her in the sexual act.

69 *big*: a pun on 'important' and 'pregnant'.

77 *sucked a brach*: was suckled by a bitch-hound.

80 *I'll . . . thee*: I'll buy you a banquet.

85 *woman-surgeon*: there were female surgeons at this time but Rhetias (ll. 90–1) implies that the term here refers to a cosmetic beautician.

96 *by proclamation*: i.e. his own foolish words are as good as a proclamation to identify him to others as a gull.

   S.D. *passing over*: crossing the stage.

106 *in spite . . . teeth*: despite your opposition (cf. *'Tis Pity* 2.4.25).

   gravity: serious status as a scholar (which the gown represents).

109–10 *suppositors*: those of lower rank (with a play on 'supporters' and 'suppositories', used for purging).

111 *horns*: horns supposedly grew on a cuckold's forehead.

133 *ill humours*: in Renaissance humour theory an imbalance of the body's main humours (blood, choler, melancholy, phlegm) was believed to produce a diseased state, often manifested as a personality disorder.

150 *make one*: take part.

158 *The melody . . . consort*: Rhetias is referring back, with a pun on keeping musical time.

1.3.23 *kindly*: according to kinship (with a play on 'kind', i.e. benevolent).

33 *sister*: she is Menaphon's cousin.

34 *innocent*: someone who is (1) pure; (2) guileless; (3) lacking intelligence.

49 S.D. *Enter . . . attire*: this edition follows *Q*, but most editors place the s.d. *after* Thamasta's aside; however, her words seem a response to Eroclea's appearance. Eroclea does not reveal that she is Parthenophill until 3.2.160, but an audience might begin to suspect as much from 2.1.187.

62 *call you servant*: acknowledge your suit as lover.

76 *relish . . . process*: promises a favourable consequence.

97 *Diamonds cut diamonds*: proverb (*Tilley*, D323).

2.1.3 *lost security*: vain confidence of safety.

36–7 *rear . . . head-piece*: praise me for my brains.

39 *citterns*: stringed instruments (often with grotesquely carved heads) frequently found in barbers' shops for customers' use.

45 *Mum, butterfly!*: be quiet you fop!

52 *balloon ball*: a game with a large, inflated leather ball.

53 *casting . . . sledge*: throwing the hammer.

72–3 *pretend . . . intermitted*: the Syrian king will reclaim an alleged ancient right (lately lapsed) to be paid a tribute.

81 *general voice*: view of the general population.

90 *affections*: (1) inclinations; (2) feelings.

111 *an't . . . highness*: if your highness pleases.

114 *golden days*: as in the classical Golden Age.

123 *Close*: keep close, i.e. out of sight.

153 *of proof*: impenetrable.

170 *rape*: abduction.

190 *merchant*: merchant vessel.

203 *these*: i.e. his hands.

207 *read*: understand.

210 *Open . . . bosom*: undo my clothing.

223 *be . . . secure*: either 'don't be too sure of your ability to keep my secret', or 'don't believe you will escape my wrath (should you prove disloyal)'.

228 *favour*: your favour.

244 *powers*: celestial or spiritual beings with a controlling influence.

248 *entrance*: words spoken on entering.

260–1 *old madman . . . girl*: i.e. Meleander . . . Cleophila.

281 *study ignorance*: be as if ignorant.

286–7 *much . . . belief*: prevailed on me to trust her.

311 *dishonest fame*: reputation for being unchaste.

313 *spoil . . . carriage*: put paid to your plans.

2.2.2–3 *hare . . . open*: proverb (*Tilley*, H153). Hares were thought to be timid and always fearfully alert.

7 S.D. *(within)*: presumably he is inside the discovery space at the back of the stage: this resembled an alcove behind a wide doorway or curtains.

13–14 *'has . . . years*: uncut hair was a sign of grief.

21 *is . . . yet?*: have you any appetite?

25 *no boot*: pointless.

30 *Trollia*: this may be an error for 'Trollio' or a deliberate echo of Cleophila's half-rhymes.

31 *implement*: instrument; servant.

34–5 *gall . . . with*: doves were not believed to have spleens (organs which supposedly produced melancholy and violent anger). See *'Tis Pity* 1.2.56.

39 *Agenor*: he betrothed his son, Palador, to Eroclea while having designs on her himself.

41 *too old in honour*: too used to old-fashioned honourable behaviour.

47–8 *whimsied . . . conundrumed*: full of perverse notions.

57 S.D. *Enter Amethus . . . Rhetias*: Q places this before Trollio's speech to allow time for them to move down a long stage. Later editors have placed it after l. 58, but this slightly reduces the impact of Trollio's rapid change in tone which is clearly linked to their appearance.

91 *make . . . plenty*: despite their abundance they do not satisfy.

111 *haled to the earth*: ceremoniously taken for burial.

112 *tilting day*: horses and riders were sumptuously attired for tilts (encounters between two mounted men, armed with weapons like lances, who each tried to knock the other from his horse).

113 *antique*: with a play on 'antique' and 'antic'.

   scorn . . . tears: such shows of pomp reduce to ridicule tears of genuine grief (which are ineffectual anyway).

115 *dropped*: i.e. let tears fall.

3.1.2 *cross-gartered*: crossed garters (bands worn below the knee, crossed behind it, then tied in a bow in front) were unfashionable after 1600.

   8 *creature . . . livery*: a servant fed and clothed for service. The connection with a stabled horse also suggests a kept woman.

26 *cod . . . cat*: bag of musk; perfume was extracted from the glands of the musk cat (civet).

36 *This . . . hear*: this will persuade, if I deign to listen. 'We' may be a royal plural, or it could be Grilla's joking reference to her multiple selves here.

50 *hear . . . not*: Q implies that Grilla speaks in the role of the haughty princess, i.e. 'I do not hear you, nor do I take any notice of you'.

54 *ac—count*: there is a sexual pun on 'cunt' and 'count' which were sometimes spelt and pronounced the same.

57 *—Look to yourself, housewife!*: perhaps this is a prompt because she is not listening, or he may be challenging her to summon her strength to answer in 'strong lines' (i.e. lines full of metaphysical conceits).

66 *cue*: disposition, with a bawdy pun on 'queue' or 'cue' (from the French) meaning 'tail'.

70 *no—thing*: i.e. the female genitals.

95 *humours*: see note to 1.2.133.

99–100 *scholar . . . Melancholy*: *Q* has a marginal note which refers to 'Democritus Junior', a pseudonym adopted by Robert Burton in *AM*.

3.2.6 *violent*: passionate.

8 *stand on points*: be concerned with niceties.

17 *green-sickness-livered*: suffering from an anaemia associated with young women (and so, ironically accurate), but it also implies a lack of virility in the apparent young man, as sexual passion was believed to lodge in the liver.

19 *mar her market*: spoil her trade, i.e. Thamasta's designs on Parthenophill.

45 *Walk . . . stairs*: Kala might lead him to one of the doors at the back (in the tiring-house wall) which has stairs to a gallery overlooking the stage, or he might simply exit from a door here and enter later through another to imply a new location.

50 S.D *Exit Menaphon*: positioned after l. 47 (*Q*).

51 *good turn*: i.e. a sexual opportunity.

63 *To . . . construction*: to the risk of being harshly judged.

85 *round*: encircle.

88 *these . . . creatures*: i.e. the plants.

106 *perfect friendship*: i.e. Thamasta's relationship with Menaphon.

121 *that glass*: i.e. Menaphon.

123 *idle*: out of his mind.

148 *entertainments*: relationships.

159 *his mother's doves*: the doves of Venus.

169–70 *printed . . . relation*: recording my genuine relating of events.

187 *servant*: lover.

197 *creep*: stoop.

205 *your jewel*: i.e. Parthenophill.

3.3 S.D. *paper plot*: an outline of the story (perhaps scene-by-scene).

7 *humorous*: affected by fluxes of his bodily humours.

19 *Nay . . . ceremony*: presumably they are bowing or curtseying to Palador.

21 *Since . . . wolf*: the character suffers from Lycanthropia (cited by Burton in *AM*) and imagines himself to be a wolf.

26 *Here . . . it*: i.e. in the plot he is reading.

34 *Hydrophobia*: a disease like rabies (associated with a hatred of water and looking-glasses by Burton in *AM*; the fear of cuckoldry is Ford's addition).

46 *not . . . course*: do not dislike the way the entertainment is proceeding.

S.D. *farthingale . . . ruff*: these were unfashionable at the time.

49 *pum*: lisping pronunciation of 'plum'.

51 *Phrenitis*: a madness accompanied by fever (not associated with women or pride by Burton).

53–4 *They . . . well*: attacks were made on tobacco by James I, Burton, and others.

58 *sup*: 'soope' (*Q*). He is still behaving as a wolf.

68 *Hypocondriacal*: according to Burton in *AM*, the third species of melancholy was 'Hypochondriacal or windy melancholy'.

76–84 *Hang . . . dance!*: the Nymph and Cuculus may sing their lines but *Q* does not specify apart from italicizing the lines.

86–8 *Wanton Melancholy . . . ceasing*: i.e. St Vitus's Dance.

91 *plot*: i.e. the written plot he has been reading.

4.1.4 *false fires*: fireworks.

11 *Jealous*: distrustful.

51 *pension*: tribute; or perhaps more sarcastically, 'wages'.

71 *childish plots*: weak excuses.

78 *must*: must do.

81 *wait ye*: wait on you.

4.2.3 *dog-leeches*: veterinaries (see also 5.2.19).

14–15 *a prince's . . . a prince's*: first, Palador's father's, then that of Palador himself or that of a prince(ss).

22 *play . . . rudeness*: act a role lacking courtesy.

28 *whoreson*: usually abusive, but here familiarity is implied.

36 *were . . . pageants*: an armed official cleared the way for pageants and public spectacles.

39 *. . . outstare him*: *Gifford* and *Hill* indicate that Corax puts on a Gorgon's mask here, but he may be creating the impression of a Gorgon merely by words, gestures, and the imaginative use of his cap (either headgear which indicates his physician's status or possibly the hood of a cloak).

41 *man of worship*: person of repute.

42 *firk . . . trangdido*: firk: to beat or whip (also 'to play the fiddle'). *OED* does not list 'trangdido' ('trangdillio' is the twanging of a musical instrument). 'Beat his backside' seems closest, with the suggestion of producing a twanging sound. Martin Wiggins suggests a pun on 'bumfiddle' (i.e. to beat).

43 *bounce and . . . mettle*: swagger courageously.

48–50 *dog . . . pieces*: Cerberus, the guard-dog of Hades, had three heads and was captured by Hercules who wore the skin of a slain lion.

51 *Gorgon's skull*: with his cap pulled down, Corax is pretending to be a Gorgon.

53 *Sisyphus*: in classical mythology his punishment in Hades was to push a stone up a hill, but it always rolled back from the summit, so the task was never-ending.

57–8 *the fates . . . thread*: the three Fates of classical mythology: Clotho spun the thread of a person's life, Lachesis drew it out, and Atropos cut it.

79 *To*: in comparison to.

98 *wild-fire*: highly inflammable substances used in warfare.

141 *sign*: sign of the zodiac.

149 *profession*: i.e. procuring for prostitution.

199 *with a witness*: with a vengeance, i.e. powerfully arouse him.

4.3.11 *bearded*: i.e. with a tail.

43–51 *As . . . strains*: perhaps the contrast is between the individual, opposing natures of created things which are, nevertheless, allied by kinship, and the specific example of man, considered Heaven's ideal creation, who contains a variety of passions within the individual, yet achieves harmony and perfection best when 'in consort' with the passions of another human.

55 *We . . . exercise*: we are, every one of us, heaven's gift, but fortune's sport.

58 *it*: this could refer to the process described in the previous clause, i.e. 'we watch helplessly as the span of time . . .', or, less likely, 'it' may refer back to the hourglass.

70 *figure stamped*: this implies false coinage—an image resembling Eroclea, not the woman herself.

81 *greatness*: state.

88 *are*: (*Q*) i.e. is.

89 *altar . . . proof*: place of sacrifice which proves me more constant (than you believe).

95 *boy*: Palador still believes that Eroclea is the boy, Parthenophill, disguised as a woman.

96 *shape*: assumed appearance, disguise.

101 *For . . . else*: or my thoughts will lead to violent action.

125 *perfumed*: i.e. with your sweet breath.

129 *in . . . bosom*: he keeps her portrait there.

130 S.D. *tablet*: i.e. a miniature portrait of Palador.

5.1.7 *wrecks*: 'wracks' (*Q*).

20 *big women*: important women; Thamasta is one but, as Eroclea is with Palador, the others are unidentified (unless he is mockingly referring to Pelias and Trollio).

20 *young old ape*: Cuculus.

21 *she-clog*: Grilla, his supposedly female page.

35 S.D. *to attendants within*: perhaps Cuculus and the rest (who enter at l. 118).

121 *linsey-woolsey*: a mixed weave of flax and wool spoken of contemptuously; figuratively, a confusion, 'neither one thing nor another' (*OED*).

139 *Whilst I'm in office . . .*: Cuculus switches to verse; this occurs at l. 137 (*Q*).

139–40 *the old . . . request*: the former fashion (i.e. male pages) will return.

159 *sanctuary*: holy place (hence the kneeling).

177 *the coach*: presumably a vehicle carried on two poles by bearers at front and back, or a kind of stage rickshaw.

5.2.23 *this tormenting noise*: i.e. Corax.

59 *grave familiar*: (1) evil spirit from the grave; (2) sombre demon.

71 S.D. *tablet*: i.e. the miniature portrait of Eroclea.

87 *Round*: encircle.

88 *cliffs*: i.e. eyelids.

124 *surfeit with*: feast.

171 *legend*: account.

183 *comfortable*: supporting, inspiriting.

186 *travelled*: 'trauayl'd' (*Q*): both 'travelled' and 'travailed' (i.e. 'studied' and 'laboured') make sense here.

205 *in the trim*: his hair and beard have been trimmed.

207 *noise*: often used to mean 'music'.

244 *they*: i.e. the gods.

Epilogue

6 *free*: (1) not obliged to you; (2) not bound to write for a living.

The Broken Heart

Dedication—To the most worthy deserver . . .

William, Lord Craven: the eldest son of a Lord Mayor of London and a distinguished soldier who had many works dedicated to him in 1633 and the years following.

3–4 even in youth: Craven was 27 in 1633.

22 *least respect*: merest sign of favour.

The Persons of the Play

Laconia: the south-eastern district of Peloponnesus of which Sparta (also called Lacedaemon) was the capital.

The Prologue

9 *virgin sisters*: the Muses.

bays: see note to *LM* dedicatory verse: 'To my Honoured Friend . . .'

14 *allow*: approve.

16 *A Truth*: see Introduction, p. xii

1.1.6 *Cynic, Stoic*: Greek philosophical schools. Cynics were contemptuous of leisure, wealth, and pleasure; Stoics were renowned for their harsh ethical doctrines.

7 *read . . . lecture*: study logic.

8 *Areopagite*: a member of the top Athenian judicial court.

26 *Hymenean bond*: marriage (from Hymen, god of matrimony).

32 *We had*: we would have.

37 *aconite*: monkshood or wolfsbane, a poisonous plant.

55 *savours . . . humanity*: does not smell of humanity (i.e. is hardly human).

91 *prefer . . . 'ee*: entreat you.

98 *Vesta's sacred fires*: Vesta, Roman goddess of the hearth, was attended by virgins and is associated with chastity here.

99 *Apollo*: the sun god.

104 *Preferment*: actions promoting a daughter's marriage.

112 *direct*: which direct.

118 *change . . . airs*: move to new surroundings.

1.2.7 *Apollo's locks*: he had long, golden hair.

13 *Laconia*: see note to The Persons of the Play.

a monarchy: under one rule.

15 *Messene*: the chief town of Messenia on the north-west border of Laconia. The name here may refer to the country as a whole.

20 *Pephnon*: Pephnus, the ancient border town between Laconia and Messenia.

42 *period . . . fate*: peak of my good fortune.

59 *in part of*: in part payment for.

66 *provincial*: honouring the acquisition of a new province.

72 *issue . . . mind*: results of merely serving willingly.

82 *Bacchus*: god of wine.

83 *leader-on*: i.e. the leading priest in the orgiastic rites.

89 *fit slights*: apt, self-deprecatory remarks.

99 *We . . . hand*: he may give Lemophil and Groneas his hand to kiss, or he may merely gesture to them.

100 *Observe . . . example*: note Ithocles's example with respect.

102 *are*: (*Q*) i.e. is.

105 *supporter*: someone to take her arm.

109 *mounting nature*: Groneas may kiss, or try to kiss Philema here, but any sexually suggestive gesture would fit the pun on 'mounting'—i.e. both 'aspiring' and 'sexually active'.

111 *you*: *Weber*'s substitution for *Q*'s 'yon'. The latter might fit if Philema addressed Chrystalla rather than Groneas and Lemophil, but where the same substitution occurs at l. 113 this could not be the case.

114 *You . . . peace*: a mocking echo of ll. 96–7.

116 *They . . . coming*: (*Q*) some editors believe the sentence should be spoken by Lemophil.

125 *put . . . use*: (1) loaned it for interest; (2) put it in action.

126 *Mars*: the god of war.

127 *Vulcan*: the god who was cuckolded by Venus with Mars.

132 *In forma pauperis*: as a pauper.

133 *aprons*: workmen's clothes.

137 *acorns*: i.e. pig food.

1.3.5 *their*: i.e. the stars'.

6 *thy aspect*: Tecnicus is reading the stars in relation to Orgilus.

20 *grudge*: 'grutch' (*Q*).

24 *frailty*: normal human weakness.

26 *Some . . . time*: for some little time.

27 *information*: matter formed by.

34 *hearken after*: seek to hear news of.

41 S.D. *passeth over*: crosses the stage.

S.D. *supporting*: taking her arm.

43 *amorous foldings*: physical closeness. Euphrania has taken Prophilus' arm and their heads are, presumably, close together.

47 S.D. *Enter . . . Euphrania*: l. 50 in *Q* (after '*reading*'). Orgilus's 'Again?' at l. 48 suggests the earlier placing.

49 *stand my privilege*: supply my right to be there.

57 *prompter—*: (*Gibson*); *Q* gives 'prompter;' and several editors since Weber have omitted punctuation here. The meaning is ambiguous:

Euphrania's eyes *may* be his prompter, *or* he may be arrested in the flow of his speech by her eyes and break off to gaze at them, or perhaps they admonish him—causing him to defend himself with his next words.

75 *law*: governing power.

86–7 *constant . . . opposition*: faithfully loving endurance in the event of our marriage being opposed.

90 *seal . . . like*: make a similar vow.

95 *pleasures*: pleasant grounds.

102 *Say it . . .*: Orgilus pretends to argue with himself.

104 *I come . . . sir*: this may be addressed to Prophilus, or he may pretend to hear Tecnicus call him. It could even be part of his pose of arguing with himself, i.e. 'now I've got you!'.

117 *speculations*: (1) opinions; (2) observations of astronomical phenomena.

123 *touch of writers*: test (touchstone) of written authority.

125 *taste the grammates*: acquire the rudiments.

134 *read to*: teach.

139 *modesty*: moderation.

177 *Mercury*: god of eloquence and feats of skill.

2.1.2 *prospect to temptation*: (1) a look-out on to temptation for Penthea; (2) a view of Penthea which will tempt other men.

5–6 *deformed . . . licked*: an old belief (found in Pliny) held that bear cubs were shaped at birth by their mothers licking them.

11 *close packets*: secret letters.

13 *earwig*: flatterer ('Eare-wrig' (*Q*); 'a wriggler into ears').

16 *maw*: (1) throat or gullet of a beast; (2) stomach.

21–2 *turn . . . eye*: the hundred-eyed Argus, commanded by Juno to guard Io (Jupiter's mistress, transformed into a heifer by the god), was usually depicted wearing robes covered with eyes.

23 *housewives*: with overtones of 'huswives' or 'hussies', meaning 'worthless or pert women'.

24 *chamber-merchandise*: bedroom products.

24–5 *set . . . wholesale*: sell all they have without discrimination.

27 *branched*: made to branch into cuckold's horns.

28 *rubs*: (1) a bowling term, meaning hindrances to the course of a ball, e.g. bumps; (2) reproofs.

31 *bias*: indirect course (bowling term); i.e. not the straight course of virtue.

32–3 *Their . . . incomes*: their illicit pleasures obtain promotion, status, and wealth for the cuckolded husband.

44 *up . . . me*: 'get on with it'.

54 *fled . . . dragon*: according to Ovid and Euripides, Medea fled to Athens in a chariot drawn by winged dragons.

58 *that's*: that his.

56–9 *'tis . . . divorced*: Phulas recalls Shakespeare's fools here: through jesting, he cuts to the heart of Bassanes' problem.

64 *horn of plenty*: a pun on the cornucopia and the horns of cuckoldry; i.e. 'may he be cuckolded many times, as he deserves'.

80 *brave it*: flount their finery.

81 *them*: themselves.

90 *Furies whip thee!*: ministers of vengeance of the gods, the Furies punished evil-doers in hell by continual whipping and repeated torments.

91 *handmaid*: female, personal attendant (i.e. how she regards her married role).

115 *stewed*: (1) be confined in close or ill-ventilated quarters; (2) be sent to a stew (brothel).

134 *tympany*: a swelling or tumour; i.e. his cuckold's horns.

136 *Wagtails and jays*: both are birds associated with wanton women: jays are also chatterers.

147–8 *better Railed*: 'if you had' is implied between these words.

155–6 *consideration . . . not*: 'a point I did not appreciate'.

2.2.1–2 *viper's . . . motion*: this is an emblem based on Pliny's report that young vipers gnawed their way out of their mothers' bodies.

3 *seeled*: with sewn eyelids (causing them to lose sense of direction and continue to fly upwards until they fall exhausted).

11 *form of books*: bookish theory.

64 *in*: with.

68 *mistress*: Calantha.

69 *brother's*: brother-in-law's.

104 *Argos*: a state north-east of Sparta.

114 S.D. *Exeunt . . . Bassanes*: in *Q* the s.d. reads '*Exeunt.*' at l. 114, followed by '*Bassanes.*' centred, which suggests that he may have left with the rest and re-entered for his soliloquy.

121 *dispatch a business*: make a sexual conquest.

125 *in request*: fashionable.

131 *presence lobby*: anteroom of a reception chamber.

2.3.9 *little skill*: (*Weber*); 'skill' (*Q*).

17 *account with*: consider.

19 *music of the spheres*: in Ptolemaic cosmology this divine sound (made by the heavenly spheres as they revolved) expressed perfect harmony.

21 *school terms*: pedantic jargon.

31 *The holiest altars*: (*Q*); Oliphant and subsequent editors emend to 'On Vesta's altars'.

32 *On Vesta's*: (*Q*); 'The holiest' (*Oliphant*). As these lines occur at the bottom and top of a *Q* page, respectively, a line which was once between them may now be lost. This could account for the awkwardness of 'like | On Vesta's odours'. Although probably incomplete, the lines make sense without transposing. Orgilus is urging Penthea to acknowledge the fire of their guiltless mutual passion by reminding her that their virgin tears fell to enhance the power of those first love vows, just as the virgin tears which fall on Vesta's perfumes (i.e. the incense on her altars) strengthen their fragrance.

56 *female change*: female inconstancy.

63 *My interest*: his right (through their former betrothal).

75 *change*: exchange.

79 *truth*: faithful love.

81 *tendering*: (1) offering; (2) cherishing.

95 *advise thee*: consider.

108 *wanton*: reckless.

117 *walks*: covered walks (such as cloisters).

124 *veil*: disguise.
   politic French: cunning dissimulation.

135 *in humours*: upset, in a bad mood.

3.1 S.D. *in his own shape*: i.e. undisguised.

8 *execution*: enterprise.

14 *state*: state business.

18 *disposed*: betrothed.

25 *growth . . . aspect*: developing change in your appearance.

33 *feeds content*: satisfies self-interest.

53 *in . . . thrifty*: 'may I always successfully follow your teachings'.

54 S.D. *Exit Orgilus*: after l. 53 (*Q*).

55 *Curiosity*: intellectual questing.

56 *rare attempts*: exceptional endeavours.

70 *Delphos*: the site of the oracle.

80 *Like*: the same.

3.2.16 S.D. *passing over the stage*: crossing the stage and exiting.

26 *chamber-combats*: bedroom encounters.

27 *heard*: 'hard' (*Q*).

29 *brother*: brother-in-law.

32 S.D. *discovered*: revealed (probably in a curtained 'discovery space' at the back of the stage).

41–2 *dead . . . being*: Thrasus, their father.

70 *spotted whore*: unchaste woman (with blemished character).

72 *friend*: Ithocles might mean Bassanes, Orgilus, or even himself.

87 *myrtle*: a plant held sacred to Venus and an emblem of love.

90 *Stygian banks*: in Greek mythology, souls crossed the River Styx on their way to the land of the dead.

93 *saint you serve*: woman you adore.

nearness: (*Lamb*); this is omitted from *Q*, and other editorial suggestions have been 'closeness', 'bond', and 'tie'.

95 *question as a secret, sister,*: (Spencer); 'question as a secret, Sister:' (*Q*).

102 *my injuries*: i.e. 'my injuries to you'.

117 *cheer . . . strain*: try to devise a plan of action.

120 *point*: i.e. point of his dagger.

123 *sloth to vengeance*: disinclination to revenge.

property: personal characteristic.

128–9 *popular . . . vanity*: vanity caused by public adulation.

130–1 *bestride . . . sun*: Bassanes is contemplating soaring ambition and perhaps hinting at a fall: when Phaethon, son of the sun god, drove his father's chariot recklessly, endangering the earth, Jupiter struck him with a thunderbolt and hurled him from heaven. There may also be a reference to Ixion (see 4.1.69, note).

133–4 *wait . . . doors*: wait outside the room until you have finished making love.

149 *franks*: a frank was an enclosure where boars (signifying animal lust) were fattened.

156 *touch-hole*: a term of abuse; literally, the ignition hole in the breech of a gun.

161 *studied*: deliberately contrived.

165 *preserve . . . fruition*: retain you in pleasurable possession.

167 *Pandora's box*: in Greek mythology, a box containing all human ills; these were released when Pandora opened it.

176 *by Juno's*: Juno was goddess of marriage and punished unvirtuous wives.

184 *your*: (*Gifford*); not in *Q*.

187 *approve it*: be certain of it.

200 *Diseases . . . alike*: proverb (*Tilley*, D357).

206 *cry*: perhaps a shortened form of 'decry', meaning 'suppress'.

3.3.28 —*Armostes . . .*: the focus moves from Nearchus and Calantha to Amyclas and his counsellors and back to the former at l. 42. Such shifts of focus continue throughout the scene.

40 *high attempts*: noble endeavours.

72 *Phoebus*: the sun god and, as Apollo, god of reason and patron of music and poetry.

3.4.2 *hold plea*: try a legal action.

10 *envy*: begrudge.

14 *maliced*: intended to harm.

19 *condition*: disposition.

28 *untoward*: declining.

34 *familiar*: witch's attendant spirit.

41 *general infection*: plague.

58 *smooth*: kindly.

65 *a greater ceremony*: i.e. legal marriage; here, they are betrothed.

96 *but*: only.

3.5.9 *glass*: hourglass.

12 *short*: imminent.

21 *inconstant*: 'unconstant' (*Q*).

24–5 *for . . . opinion*: merely to support commonplace opinions.

32 *fold of lead*: i.e. a lead coffin.

35 *enjoin*: (*Dyce*); 'enjoy' (*Q*).

52 *virgin wives*: faithful wives.

56 *married maids*: women who forgo the physical side of marriage.

62 *Time's . . . Truth*: proverbial (*Tilley*, T580).

99 *pursuit*: petition.

111 *My . . . even*: 'I have balanced with good any ills I may have done.'

4.1.12 *after-wit*: knowledge gained after the event.

46 *beauties*: beautiful women.

65 *it*: i.e. his hair.

69 *Ixion*: carried to heaven by Jupiter, Ixion attempted to seduce Juno but Jupiter substituted a cloud in her place and banished him to eternal punishment.

70 *bosomed*: embraced.

83 *Termed . . . 'spaniel'?*: see l. 35 above.

85 *doctor*: expert.

88 *less rash*: (*Gifford*); 'rash' (*Q*).

91 *presence*: royal presence.

98 *mushrooms . . . cedars*: upstarts . . . royal persons.

102 *Painted colts*: decorated young horses, symbolizing youthful folly.

112 *one dust on't*: one particle of its dust.

120 *What . . . here?*: 'What is he doing here?'
     mortal: destined to cause death.

123 *sealed up counsel*: i.e. his interpretation of the oracle.

132 *a greater prince*: Apollo.

136 *what I told thee*: i.e. in 3.1.

141 *I . . . Oedipus*: Oedipus solved the riddle of the Sphinx.

4.2.15 *garland . . . goodwill*: *The Garland of Goodwill* was a popular collection
     of ballads.

17 *mule*: 'moile' (*Q*).

18 *only . . . sense*: who only respond to their senses or instincts.

44 *words*: scandal.

57 *ken of*: sight of.
     S.D. *her . . . ears*: this was the conventional stage representation of the
     distracted woman.

69 *sirens*: beings, part woman and part bird, who sang to lure sailors to
     destruction.

70 *in parts*: taking different parts.

86 *antiquity*: Bassanes is an older man.

94 *I . . . child-bearing*: see the Introduction, p. xv

95 *Etna*: a volcano in north-east Sicily.

117 *he . . . home*: it affected him profoundly.

118 *cabinet*: (1) boudoir; (2) case for jewels and valuables.

119 *points and bride-laces*: needle-lace to adorn clothes, and pieces of gold,
     silk, or other lace used to bind up sprigs of rosemary at weddings.

133 *oracle*: something which instructs him—i.e. to take revenge.

151–3 *her blood . . . modesty*—: her abstinence from food is linked to the
     repression of her sexual feelings, a sexual self-starvation. See the
     Introduction, pp. xiv–xv.

153 *pleurisy*: excess.

161 *Enough*: 'Enow' (*Q*).

165 *Without . . . perfumes*: Sherman first cited a contemporary ballad (Shirburn collection) of a 'maide' who did not eat for sixteen years but sustained herself by smelling perfumes, and Burton, in *AM*, mentioned the issue of whether fumes could provide nourishment.

169 *leprous*: she means 'morally diseased' here because she considers herself to be adulterous with Bassanes, while truly bound to Orgilus.

177 *augury thing*: spirit of foreboding; editors since Weber have substituted 'angry' here.

192 *I honour 'ee*: presumably a gesture (bowing or kissing his hand) accompanies these words.

200 *or ever*: unless.

210 *jealous*: vigilant in scrutinizing.

4.3.24 *opening*: interpretation.

63 *maids . . . not*: (1) virgins know only that they lack sexual experience; (2) virgins know only that they do not know what experience it is that they lack.

65 *loose for strait*: loose for tight, i.e. after pregnancy.

67 *shrewd*: (1) cunning; (2) wicked.

89 *Rich fortunes guard the . . . princess*: 'rich fortuness guard to' (*Q*).

76–93 *Now . . . stumble*: there are ten people on stage, but these exchanges cannot be overheard by the others or there would be no explanation for Ithocles and Calantha keeping their betrothal a secret, or for Nearchus' surprise at 5.3.61 when Calantha talks of her 'neglected husband'.

112 *manage*: management.

141 S.D. *A Song*: according to 4.4.6 this was accompanied by a lute.

4.4 S.D. *an engine*: a trick device of ancient origin which trapped the seated person (a similar property appeared in Barnabe Barnes's play *The Devils Charter* (1606). The trick chair is to Penthea's right.

26 *Phaethon*: see 3.2.130, note.

55 *Determined*: elapsed.

76 S.D. *Exit Orgilus*: Orgilus may conceal the bodies in the discovery space before he exits or he may push the chairs off-stage.

5.1.1–8 *Athens . . . sure yet*: Bassanes is still seeking a cure for Penthea.

12 *doublers*: these are the sharp turns a hare makes to deceive hounds. If they crossed a person's path it was an unlucky omen.

43–4 *virgin . . . danger*: there was a superstition that lightning could not harm bay (laurel) trees.

48 *unheard moment*: unprecedented significance.

5.2 S.D. *supporting Calantha*: with Calantha on his arm.

   S.D. *Loud music ceases*: 'Cease loud music' (*Q*).

12 S.D. *the first change*: the first completed figure of the dance.

48 *habiliment*: 'abiliment' (*Q*).

54 *rend*: 'rent' (*Q*).

87 *frailty*: mortal life.

89 *make the reference*: pass on your request.

99 *bleed to death*: a form of suicide preferred by the Stoics.

102 *pipes . . . conduits*: veins . . . arteries.

109 *fillet*: bind with a narrow strip of cloth above the selected place to distend the vein (grasping a staff served the same purpose).

123 *Honourable infamy*: Gifford and subsequent editors attribute these words to Nearchus, but *Q*'s attribution to Orgilus makes sense as a retort which modifies Armostes' comment.

124 *loose*: free to leave.

136 *pair-royal*: three of a kind (card game), alluding to Amyclas, Penthea, and Ithocles.

143 *engage*: stake.

148 *mother*: mother earth.

150 *So . . . standards*: so fall the ensigns (flags). Orgilus may collapse here, dropping the staves which support him.

5.3.34 *consort*: (1) fellowship; (2) harmony.

40 *treat on*: negotiate (i.e. in relation to the marriage treaty).

42 *you*: this word should be emphasized.

51–3 *I . . . temple*: several editors reverse the women's names because Philema, meaning 'a kiss', seems more suited to marriage and Chrystalla, 'ice' or 'crystal', more fitted to being a vestal virgin. Yet the play as a whole suggests that a woman of ice is best suited to constancy, and one of passion might be safest in a convent.

74 *vow new pleasures*: marry again.

78 *Argos*: i.e. Nearchus.

80 S.D. *A Song*: this is omitted from some Quartos, e.g. B.L. 644. b 35.

96 *part*: role, as in a theatrical performance.

105 *counsels*: secret designs.

Epilogue

6 *mean*: appropriate moderation.

9 *'Twas . . . So*: ' 'twas *pretty*, *well* or *so*,' (*Q*).

13 *allowance . . . strain*: approval of this offspring.

'Tis Pity She's a Whore

To my Friend the Author

5 *Graces*: three daughters of Jupiter whose qualities were beauty, grace, and kindness: Venus was their mistress.

6 *Pallas*: goddess of the Liberal Arts.

11 *Thomas Ellice*: a Gray's Inn man, he was the brother of Robert Ellice, one of the dedicatees of *The Lover's Melancholy*.

To the . . . Baron of Turvey

John . . . Lord Mordaunt: a courtier of James and Charles I; later a general on the side of parliament in the Civil War.

5 *freedom*: distinction.

The Persons of the Play

Most of these names derive from literary sources. Bonaventura and Poggio are writers mentioned by Burton; characters called 'Soranso' (a witty Italian) and 'Bergetto' (an amorous, light-headed Frenchman) appear in Whetstone's *Heptameron of Civil Discourses*; John Florio compiled the Italian dictionary, *A World of Words* (1598), in which 'putana' is entered as 'a whore'; the name, Richardet appears in a story by François de Rosset (1615), which is a probable source for *'Tis Pity*, and Grimaldi is a character in Massinger's play *The Renegado* (1624).

Two names come from classical sources. Hippolita is associated with Hippolyte, the Amazon queen, and with Hipolyte, the wife of Acastus, who desired Peleus (in exile at her husband's court) and, when he did not requite her love, accused him of attempting to seduce her. Philotis may recall the faithful servant maid of that name who saved her Roman countrymen from destruction and protected the honour of their women. The word is from the Greek, meaning 'love, affection'.

Vasques's name indicates that he is the only Spaniard.

1.1.25 *A customary . . . to man*: a mere convention passed down from one generation to another; man-made, not divine.

49 *Bologna*: 'Bononia' (*Q*), which had a famous university.

58 *death*: (1) spiritual death (*see* 2.5.61); and (2) physical death—probably not intended by the friar, but ironically apt.

62 *'tis much less sin*: promiscuity is a lesser sin than incest.

66 *wilful flames*: there is a play on 'will', meaning 'desire', in conjunction with 'wilful'—'without regard to reason'.

73 *tears . . . blood*: tears of greatest sorrow were called 'tears of blood'.

1.2.1 *tackling*: weapons; i.e. 'stand and fight'.

3 *equal*: social equal. Grimaldi refuses to fight a servant.

7 *Wilt . . . gear?*: are you going to engage in this business (i.e. fight)?

17 *brave . . . fight*: some editors make this a question, but *Q* punctuates it as a statement. The dashes (in *Q*) may 'indicate intervals of provocative swordplay by Vasques' (*Gibson*, 350). Vasques is determined to provoke a fight: when Grimaldi presumably draws, or makes to draw his sword at 'for if thou dost—', Vasques has achieved his aim and starts the assault.

22 *spleen*: a violent fit. The ancients supposed the spleen to be the seat of anger, melancholy, or vexation.

28 s.d. *above*: on the upper stage or balcony. They hear the subsequent dialogue unobserved and descend between ll. 134 and 153.

41 *this tongue*: (*Q*); 'thy', *Sturgess*; 'his', *Dodsley*. Roper and Gibson follow Sturgess: this is reasonable if Soranzo is still addressing Grimaldi, but Vasques's speech at l. 43 implies that he is following his master's lead and that Soranzo may (at l. 40) have turned back to Florio and Donado, whom he had promised to satisfy with an explanation. *Q*'s 'this' implies more contempt than 'his'.

43–4 *let . . . gills*: anger has made Grimaldi red in the gills. Vasques likens himself to a doctor who might let blood to cure the condition, but jokes that *his* cure would have been to slit Grimaldi's throat.

45 *wormed*: the 'worm', a small ligament in the tongue, was removed from dogs as a precaution against rabies. See l. 41.

for running mad: (1) 'to prevent you becoming insane'; (2) 'because you were violently angry'.

47 *stay your stomach*: (1) 'satisfy your appetite for food'; and (2) 'check your pride and anger which caused you to fight'.

54 *Losers may talk . . .*: proverb (*Tilley*, L458) cf. *PW* 2.2.95

56 *unspleened dove*: see *LM*, 2.2.34–5, note.

60 *put up*: sheathe your sword.

74 *Monferrato*: 'Mount Ferratto' (*Q*).

77 *privy maim*: (1) secret injury; (2) mutilation of the private parts. The play on 'standing upright' at l. 78 implies that the wounds make them impotent.

78–9 *crinkles . . . hams*: (1) bends or bows obsequiously; (2) shrinks from his purpose.

79 *serve*: (1) suffice; (2) be useful for impregnation.

87 *wholesome*: healthy, with no venereal disease.

88 *liberal*: generous with his money (implying that he has paid Putana well for assisting his suit).

89 *good name*: high regard.

97–8 *ape . . . coat!*: proverb (*Tilley*, A262–3), cf. *LM* 2.2.109–10.

108–9 *wench, mine*: 'wench mine' (*Q*).

116 *golden calf*: (1) an idol (this suggests the worship of wealth, as in Exodus 32); (2) a wealthy simpleton.

118 *fool's bauble*: (1) jester's stick with carved head; (2) penis.

119–20 *you need . . . rate*: 'you need not consider taking someone like Bergetto: *you* have no shortage of potential lovers.'

123 *What man is he*: in François de Rosset's tale the brother has been away for some time. Annabella's failure to recognize Giovanni immediately would be more easily explainable if Ford followed this tack. Instead, he seems to stress their familiarity, with the exception of this instance where Annabella is off-guard.

133 s.d. *Exeunt*: Annabella and Putana descend as Giovanni speaks.

164 *office . . . credit*: (1) post of honour; (2) favour deserving reward.

187 *Promethean fire*: Prometheus formed man and woman from clay, bringing them to life with fire stolen from Heaven.

191 *change*: interchange.

204 *affliction . . . death*: suffering with fatal potential.

208 *rest*: (1) final peace; (2) earthly peace of mind.

217 *smoothed-cheek*: (1) inexperienced and beardless; (2) clean-shaven and sophisticated.

220 *in sadness*: in earnest, sincerely.

222–3 *brother Giovanni . . . sister Annabella*: *Q*'s lack of commas after 'brother' and 'sister' emphasizes their familiarity, while also drawing attention to their present need to see each other afresh.

226–8 *Wise . . . soul*: 'In Neoplatonic theory love results from a congenital affinity of souls which should ideally reveal itself in physical likeness' (*Roper*, 24).

231–2 *I have . . . love you*: either Giovanni is deliberately lying or he has convinced himself that the Church cannot provide an argument against his love.

239 *tear, shed*: 'tear shed' (*Q*).

1.3.27 *in good time*: just at the right time.

29 *How . . . fast?*: assigned to Poggio in *Q* but to Donado since *Weber* (1811). Martin Wiggins suggests the *Q* reading could be acceptable if Poggio was pursuing Bergetto, calling his name, but being ignored.

30–1 *news . . . mint*: proverb (*Tilley*, M985); up-to-the-minute news; the strangest ever heard.

34 *Why . . . uncle?*: (*Q*). Editors usually ignore the question-mark, as if it reads 'Why, look here . . .', but the phrase may refer to Donado's

expression. Answering a question with another also fits Bergetto's simple approach.

my barber: barbers were associated with gossip and false news.

35–6   *undertakes . . . sandbags*: probably a perpetual-motion machine.

38–9   *head . . . tail is*: a popular sideshow trick at fairs (the tail was tied to the manger).

45   *have more mind of*: care more about.

59   *parmesan*: 'parmasent' (*Q*); parmesan cheese.

72   *glory*: he means 'shame'.

75   *fit her*: answer her appropriately.

2.1   s.d.   *as from their chamber*: originally this may have been a balcony entrance, which would suggest a dialogue carried out on different levels at l. 52. Modern productions usually place it at stage level, sometimes implying a recent descent from above.

13–14   *music . . . playing*: i.e. 'A performer cannot create pleasure merely by playing; music must be heard to be appreciated.' It is a metaphor for love-making; the ear corresponds with the female sex organ.

15   *then*: (*Q*). Most editors give 'then?', but Giovanni does not seem to expect, nor to receive an answer.

16   *Jove . . . neck*: in the form of a swan, Jupiter seduced Leda (Ovid, *Metamorphoses*, vi), enacting an unnatural union which has been ennobled by art.

23   *have you*: (1) marry you; (2) possess you sexually.

24   *do not speak so without jesting*: 'so, without jesting' (*Q*); 'without jesting' makes more sense when not applied to 'you'll make me weep . . .'.

25   *What . . . not!*: i.e. 'Will you really refuse to marry?'

27   *live to me*: be solely mine in every sense.

40   *over*: through.

47   *for . . . people*: because that would cause gossip.

50   *work*: needlework.

54   *Padua*: Padua University's medical school was famous.

66   *make not strange*: i.e. do not stand on ceremony.

69   *bind . . . you*: i.e. with bonds of gratitude.

75   *touch . . . instrument*: cf. ll. 13–14; 'touch' can mean 'play', 'handle', or 'excite', and Florio unintentionally associates 'instrument' with 'penis' here.

2.2.4   *licentious*: Jacopo Sannazaro (*c.*1456–1530) had a reputation as an Italian love poet. He also wrote a famous work praising Venice, for which he was richly rewarded (see ll. 14–15).

9 *envy*: ill-will.

10 *the mean*: the golden mean; the true standard.

20 *taxed of*: blamed for.

26 *Do . . . now?*: perhaps she lifts her mourning veil. A parallel question and action occur at 4.1.38 when she, presumably, unmasks.

30 *foil . . . change*: background against which you can display your promiscuity (to heighten your new love with the contrast).

31 *modest fame*: reputation for decency.

40 *womanhood*: status as an honourable woman.

48 *Madam Merchant*: Annabella's family made its wealth through trade, so Hippolita considers herself of better social standing.

53 *habit*: her mourning clothes.

mourning weeds: black garments (including a veil).

56 *widow . . . widowhood*: i.e. he has not married her as promised.

74 *voyage . . . Leghorn*: 'Ligorne' (*Q*); a dangerous journey through mountains where brigands operated. The Italian name for Leghorn is 'Livorno'.

97 *a corse*: (*Roper*); 'a Coarse' (*Q corr*.); 'a Curse' (*Q uncorr*.). Some modern editors give 'accursed'.

101 *contemns his fate*: scorns approaching doom.

104 *his woe*: sorrow caused by him.

127 *So, perhaps too*: 'So perhaps too.' (*Q*).

136–7 *be private to*: keep secret.

2.3.4 *act*: (1) put on show; (2) bring about.

5 *borrowed shape*: disguise.

9 *Leghorn*: 'Ligorne' (*Q*).

13 *how . . . hereof*: how public opinion regards her.

24 *used you*: treated you.

27 s.d. *Enter Grimaldi*: after 'here?', l. 28 in *Q*.

30 *Monferrato*: 'Mount Ferratto' (*Q*).

40–1 *receipts . . . affection*: recipes to inspire love.

2.4.7 *fool's head*: (1) his own head; (2) a jester's stick (see 1.2.118).

22 *board*: (1) make amorous advances; (2) jest (a pun on 'bourd').

25 *in . . . teeth*: despite your opposition.

41 *you . . . no*: 'You will regret doing so.'

2.5.5 *cast away*: i.e. lost, damned.

6 *number*: company.

32 *of elder times*: i.e. before Christianity.

34 *Nature . . . blind*: 'Nature does not recognize Christian doctrine.'

44 *shrive her*: hear her confession.

54 *throne*: sovereign power and dignity. 'Thrones' were an order of angels (*Gibson*, 158).

55–6 *spheres . . . music*: in Ptolemaic cosmology, the sound made by the heavenly spheres as they revolved was divine music, expressing perfect harmony.

61 *second death*: damnation, following physical death.

64 *The . . . trespass*: 'God may treat your sin with mercy.'

2.6.13 *And*: if it.

21 *feeling . . . mind*: understanding of your interest in the match *and* of the rewards you will give for it.

45 *What say?*: what do you say?

46 *freedom*: (1) leave to speak freely; (2) free choice of husband. Without a question-mark (as in *Q*) Annabella appears forward; the alternative is a more hesitant, questioning approach.

48 *raise . . . fortunes*: improve his social position.

58 *What . . . make*: what is he up to.

64 s.d. *aside*: the line may be spoken to Bergetto but, given his simplicity in sexual matters, a bawdy aside to the audience is more likely.

70 *take the wall*: the cleanest place to walk—away from the 'kennel' or central gutter for drainage—was close to the wall. Quarrels (sometimes fatal) often ensued over this.

73 *hilts*: the plural may be an error or an unrecorded colloquialism.

98 *given . . . lie*: called him a liar (see Shakespeare, *As You Like It*, 5.4.77).

106 *half-a-crown*: this may have been a high price to pay for a prostitute: Antonia Fraser (*The Weaker Vessel* (London, 1984), 410–11) cites half-a-crown as double the usual rate in the 1640s.

113 *alone, alone still, still?*: (*Q*); 'alone, still, still?' (*Gifford*); *still, still*: on every occasion, ever more and more (*OED*, 3b).

121 *youth—*: (*Q*). Some modern editions give 'youth,' which implies that she is mischievously calling Donado 'a lusty youth', but a dash makes more sense dramatically (as *Gibson*), because the break indicates that she realizes she has teased Giovanni to the limit and can be followed by her placating him in a gentler tone.

3.1.3 *bob you off*: trick you.

5 *in despite of his nose*: notwithstanding his opposition.

12 *codpiece-point*: ornamental lace for tying the codpiece.

box: a small receptacle, perhaps a pot.

14 *clap up . . . in hugger mugger*: hastily settle a secret marriage.

16 *courage . . . rise*: my bravery increases (with a play on 'courage' as sexual desire which causes a physical erection).

21 *cart whores*: part of the traditional punishment of prostitutes was to parade them through the streets in carts or wagons.

21–2 *charges*: expense.

ere . . . myself: before I have finished breaking the peace myself.

3.2.5 *jointures*: offers of marriage.

9 *Come . . . [Putana]*: 'Come son and you, the rest let . . . alone;' (*Q*). Most modern editions follow *Weber*, with variations of 'son; and you the rest,' but 'you' could refer specifically to Putana who, like Giovanni, may be standing close to Annabella. Dismissively addressing the stranger, Vasques, as 'the rest' is not inappropriate.

11 s.d. *aside*: may be spoken to Annabella or to himself as he moves away.

all woman: i.e. inconstant (the stereotypical view of women).

14 *should tell*: may be about to tell.

16 *point of faith*: article of belief essential for salvation.

20 *woman's note*: standard female line or reply.

31 *Have*: (*Q*), i.e. has.

33 *Aqua-vitae*: water of life, i.e. here brandy or other spirits used medicinally to revive.

43 *taste*: knowledge of me (i.e. have been more welcoming).

64 *Look . . . Florio!*: this line is attributed to Giovanni in *Q*, but has been given to Soranzo since *Gifford*.

77–8 *maid's sickness*: green-sickness (chlorosis), teenage anaemia. Blood was considered to be the location of sexual passion and marriage is suggested here as a cure for a lack of 'blood', whereas at 3.4.8 Richardetto sees it as the cure for a 'fullness' of blood, i.e. sexual frustration, unfulfilled desire.

3.3.6 *quick*: (1) alive; (2) pregnant.

11 *water-pangs*: impulses to urinate.

12 *another thing*: menstruation has not occurred.

13 *credit's*: reputation's.

19 *take no care*: not worry.

22 *business*: matters to be dealt with.

3.4.6 *easy surfeit-water*: mild medicine for indigestion.

35 *dear impression*: (1) loving notion; (2) a reference to Annabella being a 'precious likeness' of himself which he would like to see marry and produce new likenesses.

3.5.5 *policy*: cunning.

7 *Play . . . hands*: is not working for both sides.

14–15 *'Tis . . . know all*: you only have a night; if you miss your chance the full calamity will be known to me tomorrow.

19 *speed*: despatch, kill.

31 *call . . . shrift*: summon . . . to confession.

37 *There's . . . yet*: this line is attributed to Philotis (*Q*); Poggio (*Bawcutt*); Richardetto (*Gifford*).

3.6 S.D. *in his study*: the location has been disputed. Editors often place the action in Annabella's chamber because of the direction 'below' at l. 44 (and Florio took the Friar there at 3.4.33), but the *Q* direction is so specific that authorial revisions elsewhere may have caused an inconsistency here. The 'study' may be the Friar's 'cell' of 3.5.12 where Richardetto told Grimaldi the affiancement would take place.

2 *unripped*: exposed.

6 *read a lecture*: deliver an admonitory speech.

36–7 *for your . . . soul*: the ranking here indicates that the Friar, like the Cardinal, puts worldly matters before spiritual.

42 *take the time*: seize this opportunity.

51 *Give me your hand . . .*: a formal, legally binding betrothal. The action is repeated in reverse by Hippolita at 4.1.46–54.

55 *More . . . sun*: a church ceremony will follow next day.

3.7 S.D. *dark lantern*: lantern with a slide or shutter to conceal the light.

2–3 *lie to listen*: i.e. with his ear to the ground.

3 S.D. *and after*: followed by.

8 *fallen*: burst.

9 *flesh-tailor*: surgeon.

31 *going . . . way*: i.e. dying.

3.8.16 *against . . . hopeful*: in comparison to so promising.

18 *my youth*: i.e. Soranzo.

3.9.14 *gate—that*: 'gate, that' (*Q*).

28 *saucy mates*: impudent fellows.

56 *Sir Florio*: (*Q*). The *Q* reading implies irony on the Cardinal's part in giving a merchant this title, but it may be a compositor's error.

62 *Justice . . . Heaven*: Astrea, goddess of justice, fled to Heaven when the earth's Golden Age ended, but Florio may be merely pointing to the gulf between true religion and its worldly representatives.

4.1 S.D. *A banquet*: there is a ceremonial quality to this feast; like the banquet in 5.6., it is planned as a formal occasion.

19 *wait*: serve the guests.

27 *offend*: (1) cause physical sickness; (2) displease.

29 *noise*: music (cf. *LM* 5.2.207).

32 *masque*: here, a dramatic entertainment (originally in dumbshow) at which masks were worn.

35 S.D. *willows*: the willow symbolized disappointed love.

37 *love*: kind act.

52 *Here . . . me*: most editors give 'Here take, Soranzo', which implies that Hippolita, having taken Annabella's hand, then gives it to Soranzo; but without the first comma (as in *Q*) it could be, rather, that she gives Soranzo to Annabella, which would be more galling for him. If she leads Annabella to Soranzo, takes his hand on her other side, and joins them, this will contrast Hippolita with Florio at 3.6.50–1, replacing father giving away daughter with mistress relinquishing lover, and it is in keeping with her return of Soranzo's vows at l. 58.

55 *engaged us*: bound us to each other and to you. Publically, he has to acknowledge an obligation; privately, this may be a tight-lipped rebuke.

56 *single charity*: sincere benevolence.

73 *Troppo . . . inganna*: 'Troppo sperar niganna,' (*Q*), 'To hope too much deceives'.

74 *but*: as good as.

77 *charity*: Christian love (cf. l. 56).

84 *yet—and*: (*Q*). The two dashes in *Q* may indicate missing or illegible text.

88 *minute*: moment of death.

95 *flame's*: i.e. the sensation of her body burning internally due to the poison. Sturgess suggests the compositor may have misread 'shame's'.

108 *event*: outcome.

4.2.10 *Debates*: 'Debate's' (*Q*).

20 *uneven*: (1) difficult; (2) unjust.

26 *beads*: rosary beads for prayer.

4.3 S.D. *unbraced*: with clothing (i.e. his doublet) unfastened.

5 *maintain'st*: (1) perseveres in; (2) defends.

8 *pleurisy*: excess.

11 *close*: (1) concealed; (2) physically close.

20 *would . . . doing*: pressing on with events—with a play on 'doing', meaning 'copulating'.

29 *stay*: appease.

34 *and*: if.

35 *A match*: a bargain, i.e. 'agreed!'

48 *that . . . creature*: that you existed.

48–9 *But . . . that*: 'And apart from the fact that I'm married to you, I still don't give your existence a thought.'

59 *più*: (*Weber*); 'pluis' (*Q*).

Che . . . amore?: 'What death is sweeter than to die for love?'

63 *a lui*: (*Roper*); 'Lei' (*Q*); 'Dei' (*Weber*).

morirei (*Bawcutt*); 'morirere' (*Q corr.*).

Morendo . . . dolore: 'Dying in favour with him, I would die without pain.'

98 *in any case*: by any means.

114–15 *Follow . . . passion*: i.e. 'Now that you have tempered your accusation, continue with a display of strong emotion.'

125 *humorous*: capricious.

139 *point*: an instance.

141–2 *make . . . alteration*: 'keep your feelings under control.'

146 *matter*: purpose.

151 *great woman*: (1) woman of rank; (2) pregnant woman.

stock: a pun on line of descent as well as a sexual image, i.e. (1) body; (2) stem in which a graft is inserted; (3) a rabbit burrow.

153 *cony-berry*: rabbit burrow (and by implication, female sexual organ).

157 *voluntary*: (1) improvised music; (2) free confession.

164–5 *proverb . . . houses*: *Tilley*, H778.

168 *quick*: (1) fast; (2) pregnant.

169 *whom. This*: (*Weber*); 'whom this' (*Q*).

200 *near and entire friend*: close, perfectly devoted lover.

201 *dear*: (1) beloved; (2) costly.

238 *Took . . . flesh*: she has (1) eaten too much meat; (2) over-indulged in sexual activity.

239 *hit it*: have the reason—with the hidden suggestion that he has shared in the sexual indulgence.

243 *liberality*: generosity to Vasques, but also licentiousness with Annabella.

245 *made a man*: am sure of success.

plied my cue: played my part.

257 *No . . . fear*: (1) 'I cannot conquer my fears'; (2) 'Whatever defeats I may suffer, the victor shall not have the glory of seeing me show fear' (*Roper*, 98).

5.1.9–10 *My . . . guilt*: as in a lawcourt, Conscience gives witness against Lust with testimony (depositions) written by Guilt (with a play on 'written in gilt lettering').

15 *Unmated*: mate-less.

17 *spoil*: (1) plunder, booty; (2) despoliation.

5.2.2 *horns*: cuckold's horns (see *LM* 1.2.111, note).

8 *great*: great with wrath.

17 *states*: dignitaries.

5.3.1 *opinion*: the common view of the people.

6–7 *But . . . sports*: 'although Annabella's sexual relations are now subject to the legal sanction of marriage, it has not altered my desire' (and perhaps, even, 'nor hers').

8 *one*: perfectly united.

17 *jubilee*: (1) exultant joy; (2) occasion for celebration.

26 *congealed coral*: in Ovid's *Metamorphoses* (iv. 740–52) coral is said to have been created when seaweed, placed under the severed head of Medusa by Perseus, absorbed her blood and hardened into stone.

30 *seared*: numbed (through cauterization, which cuts off the blood supply).

31 *stoop to*: obey (as the hawk is controlled by stooping to its lure).

52 *miss*: fail.

60 *blazing stars*: comets were believed to be (1) omens of disaster; and (2) dangerous in their own right because of their fiery tails.

69 *youngman*: (*Q*). This was in common use as one word.

71 *GIOVANNI*: Giovanni is not named as the speaker in *Q*.

72 *set up my rest*: am committed to hazarding all (from the card game primero; i.e. deciding to venture all on the cards in hand).

74–5 *curse . . . prescription*: biblical curse on incest (Deuteronomy 27: 22; also Leviticus 20: 17).

75 *gall*: (1) anger—supposedly produced by the bitter secretion of the human organ; (2) ink (produced by the gall of oak trees)—to write or enrol Giovanni's future courageous deed.

5.4.2 *undertake*: take responsibility.

4 *Liguria*: a district between Parma and Genoa (north-west Italy).

10 *free*: pardoned.

28 *turn Italian*: Italians were renowned for their capacity for and intensity in undertaking revenge.

29 *sharp . . . bit*: keen to taste his former morsel (i.e. Annabella).

31 *hot hare*: excessively lustful hare (the hare symbolized unnatural lust).

law: a start before the chase.

43 *get*: bring.

52 *Saint Peter's vicar*: the Pope.

59 *keep . . . way*: walk on.

5.5 s.d. *Enter . . . bed*: doors or curtains may have been opened to reveal the bed in the discovery space, or it may have been brought out on to the main stage, e.g. on wheels moving along runners.

11 *stoop . . . brows*: submit to my frown.

26 *fresh access*: newly allowed access to company.

30–3 *all . . . burn*: these are interpretations of Revelation 20 and 21.

41 *do*: (1) behave; (2) make love.

42 *mean*: i.e. intend to do.

82 *Styx*: the dark, poisonous river of the classical underworld.

93 *unkind*: (1) cruel; (2) not behaving like kin.

98 *her best*: this may indicate that she is wearing her bridal robes.

100 *reaching*: cunning.

103 *over-glorious*: beautiful beyond measure.

5.6.11 *spoil*: destruction and plunder.

17 *idle sight*: mere spectacle.

25 *stone*: precious stone, i.e. jewel.

61 *Hold up Florio*: this may be a command to Florio, but it is equally likely to be an order to others to go to his aid.

71 *twists*: threads (Giovanni claims the power of the Fates).

79 *Vengeance!*: the watchword for the banditti (see 5.4.13–14).

115 *Spaniard*: the Spanish were associated with cunning and hiding malice beneath a guise of friendship.

121 *of counsel*: involved.

124 *Within this room*: Vasques may point offstage at this point.

129 *this . . . effects*: the person chiefly involved. It seems more likely that he is referring to Putana (who has just been mentioned) than to Annabella, especially since there is no stage direction to suggest that Vasques returns with Annabella's body at l. 59. Vasques's speech at l. 135 also implies that one death sentence has just been meted out as punishment and he is expecting another for himself.

138 *no Italian*: cf. 5.4.28.

140–1 *dispense . . . reason*: grant a pardon because of your motives.
153 *at large*: fully.

Perkin Warbeck

To . . . Lord Bolsover and Ogle

William Cavendish: he was patron to a number of writers, including Ben Jonson, and wrote poetry and drama himself.

1–2 *late . . . pen*: Bacon wrote his *Henry VII* in 1622.
14 *entertainments*: patronage.
16 *curiosity*: skill.

To my own friend, Master John Ford . . .

justifiable poem: creation worthy to be called a poem (in the general sense of 'noble work').

17 *George Donne*: see *LM*, dedicatory verse 'To my Honoured Friend . . .'

To his worthy friend, Master John Ford . . .

2 *Phoebean hill*: the sacred Mount Helicon of the Muses.
4 *Aganippe*: a spring at the foot of Mount Helicon.
13 *Ralph Eure . . . primogenitus*: Ralph Eure was the son and heir to Lord Eure, but predeceased his father in 1640, aged about 34.

To my . . . friend, the author, this indebted oblation

1 *redivived*: brought back to life.
11 *George Crymes, miles*: Sir George Grimes of Peckham (he also spelt his name 'Crimes') was knighted in 1628; here, '*miles*' probably refers to his being a knight, rather than a soldier.

To the author . . . upon his Chronicle History

3 *full-filed*: perfectly polished.
13 *John Brograve, Armiger*: a son of the attorney to the duchy of Lancaster, Sir John Brograve (d. 1613). Like Ford, he was a member of Gray's Inn. 'Armiger' signifies that he was entitled to bear heraldic arms, because of the knighthood conferred on his father by James I.

To my friend . . . the author

7 *John Ford, Graiensis*: this John Ford of Gray's Inn was the dramatist's cousin and one of the dedicatees of *The Lover's Melancholy*.

The Prologue

2 *out . . . unfollowed*: few English history plays are recorded after Shakespeare's *Henry VIII* in 1613.

7 *bays*: see note to *LM*, dedicatory verse 'To my Honoured Friend . . .'

26 *State*: (1) matters of state; (2) stateliness, dignity.

1.1 S.D. *(Lord Chamberlain)*: naming this office may imply a special costume.

6 *the ghosts of York*: members of the rival House of York, including Richard, Duke of York, one of the princes in the Tower who, according to Bacon's *Henry VII*, haunted the king.

9 *royal birthright*: Henry's hereditary claim (through his mother) was not strong.

16 *for ninety years*: since the accession of Henry IV in 1399.

30 *purchase*: i.e. acquisition (Edward took the crown by force from Henry VI).

34 *boar's sty*: the boar was Richard's emblem.

38 *Edward's daughter*: Elizabeth of York.

42 *Margaret of Burgundy*: sister of Edward IV.

45 *York's headless trunk*: Richard, Duke of York, killed at the Battle of Wakefield, 1460.
Edward's fate: Edward IV had a reputation for sloth and self-indulgence; he sickened and died in 1483.

46 *nephews*: the princes in the Tower.

47 *Gloucester*: he became Richard III.

57 *twins*: Lambert Simnel and Perkin Warbeck.

59 *(A . . . entrance!)*: '(A Nature) even . . . entrance' (*Q*).

62 SURREY: 'Ox[ford]' (*Q*).

68 *But for*: as for.

75 *force . . . intrusion*: acts and plans of invasion.

76 *put case*: suppose.

91–4 *Lincoln . . . rest*: all were supporters of Simnel in his invasion from Ireland (defeated at Stoke, near Newark, in 1487).

100 *impostorous . . . title*: a cause based on a false claim.

102 *figured on*: represented by.

107–8 *Geraldines . . . Butlers*: rival Anglo-Norman families in Ireland.

109 *colossic statue*: a form outwardly heroic but inwardly phoney (cf. George Chapman, *Bussy d'Ambois* 1.1.15–17).

115 *smoke of straw*: i.e. Warbeck.

117–18 *bastard . . . Taylor*: according to Gainsford, Sir George Neville supported Warbeck in Paris, but this may not be historically accurate. John Taylor was not a knight: Henry mocks him with the title.

123 *archduke*: Maximilian I, the Holy Roman Emperor.

129 *him*: i.e. Sir Robert Clifford.

130 *Barley*: William Barley, a gentleman, supported Warbeck in Flanders and remained loyal for years afterwards.

s.d. *Flourish*: presumably sounded as Henry leaves (probably from the musicians' room in the tiring house).

1.2.2 *construe*: conster (*Q*).

9 *dost*: i.e. that thou dost.

13 *St Andrew*: patron saint of Scotland.

15 *So . . . ear*: i.e. So . . . ear of.

30–2 *Adam . . . Jameses*: Robert II of Scotland married Adam Mure's daughter, Elizabeth, and they produced the Stuart line of kings.

34 *kindreds . . . ours*: lineages are not recognized.

date: time period.

37 *supped*: 'sooped' (*Q*), i.e. swallowed.

40 *vouchsafed . . . servant*: did not accept me as her lover.

41 *clownery*: peasant's status.

43 *spark of mettle*: 'mettall' (*Q*). (1) sign of inherent spirit; (2) spark struck by high-friction impact on metal (coming from inside the metal).

45 *But it must*: 'But must' (*Q*).

50 *set up*: establish a home.

51 *Gordon*: Huntly's family name.

69 *cold hunting*: i.e. the scent is lost.

77 *scurvy*: contemptible, i.e. fawning does not become him.

80 *lesson*: musical exercise.

86 *fit . . . condition*: appropriate statements concerning your rank.

111 *servile rage*: slavish passion.

113 *side*: keep up with.

121 *equal*: impartial.

128 *lowest . . . obedience*: she may kneel to him here.

143 *general fame*: popular opinion.

153 *wed . . . name*: i.e. marry himself to honour and achieve an honourable name.

155 *brave mention*: record of brave deeds.

158 *suck spirit*: draw courage.

1.3 According to Henry's speech at 1.1.135–6, they are now at the Tower of London.

S.D. *lights*: these were probably pitch torches to symbolize that the scene takes place at night.

25 *For instance*: as proof.

35 *meteor*: i.e. Warbeck (implying a shooting star which quickly disappears).

36–7 *discradled . . . Portugal*: Warbeck was born in Tournai, Flanders (where Margaret of Burgundy was in exile), and later travelled to Portugal.

39 *since*: thereupon.

beard: tail.

41 *Charles*: Charles VIII of France.

45 *Whence . . . scorn*: Warbeck did not land on the Sandwich shore but his men who did so were routed and prisoners were executed.

49 *Frion*: he was listed by Bacon as Warbeck's principal counsellor.

53 *French*: i.e. treacherous (cf. 1.1.112).

55 *Speak*: name.

61 *list . . . of*: wish to plot.

83 *hear him*: i.e. hear his (Stanley's) name.

107 *charge . . . person*: one responsible for my movements and personal security.

112 *Edward's sister . . . duke!*: Margaret of Burgundy and Warbeck.

118 *what, have*: 'what have' (*Q*).

130–1 *gathered A head*: raised a military force.

131 *blacksmith . . . lawyer*: i.e. Michael Joseph and Thomas Flammock or Flamank.

133 *Audley*: James Touchet, 7th Baron Audley.

129–34 *Ten thousand . . . they are—*: there are no full stops in *Q*, which may indicate a breathless speech delivery.

2.1 S.D. *above*: on the upper stage or balcony.

2 *this . . . prince*: i.e. Warbeck.

6 *honest*: ingenuous, artless.

7 *Hath . . . to*: would rather have nothing to do with.

11–13 *godfathers . . . thanks*: their godfathers need not feel responsible for, nor tarnished by, their actions, but by denying their origins they displease their fathers.

15 *break . . . season*: show themselves in their true light (i.e. either as princes or as tradesmen).

15 *break out*: (1) erupt like a rash; (2) escape.

23 *both fortunes*: i.e. of time and state.

26 *trial*: experience.

38 *Sound sprightly music*: the women are 'above', where the musicians would usually be. The Phoenix may have had an additional music room in the balcony.

44 *vulgar*: well-known.

66 *tyrant . . . uncle*: i.e. Richard III.

67 *a truth*: an account represented as truth.

69 *unlearn myself*: i.e. of my former identity.

78 *Henry*: Henry VII.

80 *stands . . . counsel*: will not benefit you.

81 *fly . . . invectives*: resort to railing language.

86 *reserved*: appointed.

2.2.15–16 *title . . . York*: i.e. Warbeck's claim.

24 *Vere*: the family name of the earls of Oxford.

51 *nearest to himself*: puts self-interest first.

54 *piece of frailty*: mortal body.

74 *wheeled about*: revolved (as Fortune's wheel).

79 *charged it*: weighed it down.

    as: so.

86 *Christian . . . infamy*: to Christians the cross signifies Christ's suffering; to the Romans it was the punishment for thieves and other malefactors.

92 *change*: exchange.

97 *best of greatness*: i.e. God.

100 *Derby*: Thomas Stanley, 1st Earl of Derby and third husband of Henry VII's mother, Margaret Beaufort.

101 *stand*: be.

107 *state of man*: naturally insecure human condition.

112 s.d. *white staff*: all royal staffs of office were white. This one is for a Lord Chamberlain.

141 *action*: daring.

152 *look for*: expect.

154 *Norham*: border castle near Berwick.

2.3.5 *mushroom*: a common metaphor for an upstart.

8 *prerogative*: sovereign right.

16 *Phaethon*: see *BH* 3.2.130–1, note.

20 *not . . . hangman's*: the hangman's was the lowest-ranked lawful position available.

31 *My . . . one*: i.e. death.

40 *use . . . detraction*: make free with your slanders.

42 *Instinct of sovereignty*: the king's instinct that Warbeck is royal.

44 *our resolution*: the king's power to decide.

46 *using congees*: paying courtly tributes, e.g. bowing.

53–7 *Let . . . builded*: the king could give a yeoman titles prior to marriage with Katherine, but marrying her to one whose existing claims to nobility are false, destroys a future lineage rather than protects it.

58 *pawns of faiths*: existing vows of betrothal.

62 *Welsh Harry*: Henry VII was of Welsh descent.

71 S.D. *complimenting*: making ceremonial gestures of courtesy.

78 *red . . . white*: emblems of the Houses of Lancaster and York.

89 *Y'are . . . now*: apparently this is a spousal *de praesenti*, which was binding but had to be confirmed by a later church ceremony.

93 *Alexander*: Huntly's name was George; Ford repeated a mistake from his sources.

114 *go through-stitch with*: complete.

116 *indenture*: a deed agreed between parties, written on parchment which was then cut into counterparts (counterpawns): when fitted together again, these formed the agreement.

117 *defeasance*: clause defining how the bond may be made void.

126 *English Richard*: Richard, Duke of York (impersonated by Warbeck).

128 *men . . . mortality*: mere mortals may be believed.

131 *other*: others.

141–2 *pressing-iron*: (1) tailor's smoothing iron; (2) an allusion to pressing, a form of torture when the accused refused to make a plea: it could result in death.

144 *lose . . . ears*: slanderers had their ears nailed to the pillory.

145–6 *hole of hunger*: (1) dungeon, particularly the worst part of a debtors' prison; (2) a small, unpleasant living-place.

146 *compounding . . . pound*: settling to pay creditors in this proportion.

153 *prefer their duties*: offer their respects.

165 *made one*: taken part.

166 *shapes*: (1) costumes; (2) dance poses.

cutting a cross-caper: apart from the reference to the dance jump, tailors traditionally worked with crossed legs.

169–70 *perhaps . . . carriage*: perhaps people ought to take their deportment seriously and gain status from bearing themselves well.

3.1.3 *sons o'th' earth*: the Titans, giants defeated by Jupiter when they attacked Olympus.

5 *De la Pole*: Edmund, earl of Suffolk, a Yorkist claimant who later plotted against Henry VII.

9 *Saint George's Fields*: these are situated between Southwark and Lambeth.

19 *that . . . earl*: George Grey, 2nd Earl of Kent.

31 *courage, need and want*: 'courage neede, and want' (*Q*).

39 *Saturday*: according to Bacon, the victory of Bosworth was also on a Saturday: this is not historically accurate.

49 *flattered*: exaggerated. (They expected Kent would rise with them.)

59 *Deptford*: 'Dertford' (*Q*). Gainsford and others erroneously place the battle at Dartford.

67–8 *engaged . . . prisoner*: almost became a prisoner.

72 *have*: has (i.e. the fight).

75 *Flamank*: 'Flammock' (*Q*).

93 *in terror*: inspiring dread.

95 *the Newgate*: the city gate, Newgate, which was used as a prison.

3.2.7 *Trolling a catch*: bawling out a round (i.e. a song where parts are sung against each other).

manly stomachs: large appetites.

8 *usquebaugh and bonny-clabber*: whisky and coagulated sour milk.

11 *King . . . Mab*: the fairy king and queen, i.e. Warbeck and Katherine.

33 *apt*: 'ap't' (*Q*): ready to learn (*OED*, 5).

36 *quartan*: fever whose fits were believed to recur every fourth day.

41 *these*: i.e. the medical complaints.

47 *fit credulity*: capacity for proper belief or disbelief.

51 *use*: are accustomed to.

52 *injuries*: i.e. being injured.

66 *gentle*: generous.

75 *to*: lasting as long as.

78 *consort*: harmony (with me and with yourself).

81 *may*: must.

99 *in*: with regard to.

111 *bug's-words*: swaggering speech (a reference to Warbeck's language).

s.d. *trouses*: close-fitting drawers.

s.d. *Music*: as in Ben Jonson's *Irish Masque*, this was probably made by bagpipes and harps.

116 *Heydonhall*: 'Hedenhall' (*Q*), probably Hutton Hall.

123 *proclamation*: i.e. of Warbeck's claim to the English throne.

125 *affected to*: disposed towards.

151 *truth*: report.

152 *unnatural*: acting against the natural order, i.e. disloyal to the rightful king.

154 *close*: concluding cadence.

167 *Or . . . or*: Neither . . . nor.

170 *lively test*: living proof.

181 *ruled out*: set down.

search: examine.

184 *poverty*: i.e. of spirit.

3.3.2 *Castilian*: Aragon and Castile were united as the Kingdom of Spain in 1479.

4 *write 'ee*: write that you are.

10–11 *success . . . Moors*: Ferdinand captured Granada in 1492.

12 *Entire . . . sceptre*: completely under his rule.

15 *privacy . . . advisement*: private advice.

26–7 *given . . . dispatch*: sent by me.

30 *servant*: i.e. Bishop Fox.

31 *which*: who.

34 *Be . . . herald*: i.e. 'Don't broadcast your presence here.'

37 *open*: public.

43 *passed away*: gone on his way.

45 *pursed*: put in his purse.

51 *No . . . withstanding*: with no further ado.

53 *hummed*: as in 'to hum and haw', i.e. spoke in an embarrassed fashion.

58 *new creation*: i.e. the revival of the title after the present earl's death. (Warwick was the principal male heir of the House of York.)

65–7 *Let . . . Arthur*: Warwick was the son of George, Duke of Clarence (brother of Edward IV), but Henry's wife, Elizabeth, was Edward IV's daughter.

3.4.1 *these . . . walls*: the walls of Norham Castle on the River Tweed.

4 *trimmed*: dressed up.

22 *come in*: joined you.

28 *instructed compliment*: newly learnt civility.

31 *conceited justice*: imagined just cause.

51-2 *Construe . . . own*: 'Conster' (*Q*); understand me as though I were a subject of yours.

56 *nature*: natural feelings.

67 *fool*: make foolish.

69 *faction*: i.e. supporters.

82 *lowest reproof*: basest disgrace.

words: retort.

88 *More*: i.e. more news.

92 *Broke*: Sir Robert Willoughby, 1st Baron Willoughby de Broke.

94 *unbroken*: undefeated.

for . . . second: in support.

100 *once*: for once.

101-2 *with . . . blood*: on condition that the common soldiers will be spared the fight.

104 *Create me to*: give me the honour of.

4.1.5-9 *Cundrestine . . . Castle*: this is a catalogue of border castles.

19 S.D. *coats*: heraldic tabards (sleeveless coats).

26 *studied*: taken care.

30 *conclude*: prove.

32 *fishgarths*: enclosures for catching fish (salmon in Berwick).

44-5 *loyalty . . . Respected*: i.e. 'my loyalty to my own king (Henry) considered'.

51 *unbribed vainglory*: justified boasting.

53 *meet no articles*: not be subject to conditions.

71 *breathing*: pausing.

74 *chain*: a chain of gold or silver.

80 *oblige*: bind in obligation.

86 *not secure*: but not over-confident.

4.2.2 *dull*: blunted in purpose.

6 *crafty shrugs*: i.e. of Hialas.

fabric: building.

7 *are*: (*Q*), i.e. is.

8 *mines*: underground tunnels containing explosives.

19 *deserved*: was worthy of.

30 *prince murdered*: i.e. Edward, his putative brother.

a living baffled: a living prince (i.e. himself) affronted.

57 *fadge to our minds*: come off as we wish.

58 *chuffs*: 'choughs' (*Q*); rustics, boors, country fellows.

66–7 *little . . . amended*: proverb (*Tilley*, L. 358).

86 *but*: only.

4.3.1 *league*: i.e. the Holy League (organized by Ferdinand of Spain for the defence of Italy) which Henry joined in 1496—but, historically, this league was directed *against* France.

7 *combination*: treaty.

14 *trifle!*: 'trifle?' (*Q*). This may be taken as a continuation of a question begun by Hialas or, as here, it can be considered to be the conclusion of a question-and-answer, as question-marks are often used instead of exclamation-marks in *Q* punctuation.

29 *part of*: a share in.

35 *nick*: nickname.

38 *lovely*: loving.

41 *altars of the church*: i.e. places of sanctuary.

44 *our blood*: i.e. his marriage with Katherine, James's kin.

55 *question no dispatch*: not put the settlement in jeopardy.

71 *smoky*: insubstantial.

71–2 *assurance Of party*: political support.

73 *obedience . . . church*: Pope Alexander VI supported the Holy League.

96 *Edward's*: Edward IV's.

107 *unsuspected constancy*: faithfulness above suspicion.

108 *your attendance*: i.e. those who will attend you.

119 *prevent intelligence*: forestall news of our movements.

126 *More than*: other than.

147 *Fox*: 'Foxe' (*Q*). The capital implies that Warbeck is making a pun on the name of the Bishop of Durham, Richard Fox, and the sly nature of the fox.

151 *with*: by supplying you with.

158 *model*: image.

4.4.20 *addition*: mark of honour.

23 *king—*: 'King:' (*Q*).

36 *proof*: proven ability.

42 *lodge*: discover (a hunting metaphor).

46 *favours*: donations of money.

71 *Morton*: John Morton, Archbishop of Canterbury, 1486–1500 and Chancellor of the Exchequer from 1487.

72 *translation*: promotion (either to the papacy or to Heaven).

73 *My . . . see*: in fact, Fox became Bishop of Winchester in 1501.

81 *take . . . them*: assemble them for inspection.

82 *And or*: and either.

87 *Shall I*: do I need to? Must I?

96–7 *use . . . Is*: proper employment of time results in.

4.5.15 *hope (since . . . affliction)*: 'hope, since . . . affliction' (*Q*).

26 *desperate sullenness*: melancholy past hope.

32 *Save*: God save.

39–40 *Sigillatum . . . est*: sealed and dated on 10 September, in the first year of the king's reign, etc.; confirmed.

52 *on*: in.

58 *trains to*: the retinues which attend.

62 *dross*: worthless matter (ordinary humankind).

5.1.15 *desperate*: without hope.

26 *fawned on*: courted.

   gave me: i.e. in marriage.

31 *listen after*: listen to hear of.

35 *me feel alone*: i.e. me alone feel.

93 *high condition*: noble birth.

103 *whom . . . spoken*: with a splendid reputation.

114 *Heaven*: i.e. the power which commands her life.

5.2.9 *rest of state*: national tranquillity.

10 *articling*: arranging by treaty.

18 *young man*: James was 25.

19 *Has*: 'H'as' (*Q*); i.e. have.

22 URSWICK: (*Weber*); 'Sur[rey]' (*Q*).

25 *Young Buckingham*: Edward Stafford, 3rd Duke of Buckingham.

26 *his father*: he was executed by Richard III.

34 *young man*: Perkin Warbeck lived from *c*.1474 to 1499.

35 *ambition of*: great desire for (with a play on Warbeck's former ambitions).

41 *Beaulieu*: this was a Cistercian monastery at the time.

42 *for*: as.

59 *Richmond*: Henry VII's title before he was king.

61 *Bretagne's*: i.e. Brittany's (to Anglicize here would disrupt the metre).

62 *Richard*: Richard III.

66 *Milford Haven*: the Welsh harbour where Richmond landed in 1485.

69 *Bosworth Field*: the battle in which Richmond defeated Richard III.

72 *at once*: simultaneously.

87 *zanies to*: mimics of (Zanni was the comic servant in the commedia dell'arte).

shift: change (as in changing costume).

101 *wise formality*: i.e. 'pompous idiot' (*Ure*).

102 *Kneel to the king*: it is likely that they kneel as commanded, but this could occur at l. 102, 103, or 117.

107 *hanging . . . destiny*: proverb (*Tilley*, W232).

129 *forgery*: deceit.

144 s.d. *Katherine . . . kneel*: this edition.

may: must.

158 s.d. *To Katherine*: this edition.

162 *famed . . . observance!*: has made an incomparable example of devotion renowned.

168 *lifted . . . charge*: taken into our care.

171 s.d. *To Katherine*: this edition.

Fair: fair one.

5.3 s.d. *like a falconer*: he is presumably attired with gauntlet, satchel, and stave.

2 *his majesty's*: perhaps this is spoken ironically of Warbeck, but the appellation 'Friend' and the following tone suggest that he probably means Henry.

6 *commit*: i.e. to prison.

11 *equal*: impartial.

12 *Have*: i.e. Has.

14 *Inveigling*: enticing.

26 *Baited to*: tormented even up to the point of.

28 *practice on*: tricks against.

30 *will not*: do not want to.

37 *Whereas*: 'Whenas' (*Q*).

49 *totters*: (1) swings (i.e. is hanged); (2) wavers (with a view to giving up his claim).

57 *swinge*: driving power.

62–3 *assurance From*: protection against.

71 *tradition fix*: handing down my story make it known for.

80 *respect of*: regard for.

87 *reproach*: disgrace.

90 *now*: the present moment.

108 *enemy of mankind*: the devil.

114 *apparition*: semblance.

115 *Be what*: even if you are.

122 *wreck*: 'wrack' (*Q*).

135–6 *his . . . to*: he had not left his country to experience.

140 *to a legacy*: to make me a legacy.

147 *unkiss*: cancel with another kiss.

159 *'pointed*: appointed, arranged.

176 *thought thee injury*: intended you harm.

183 S.D. *Sketon, Astley, Heron*: 'In history, only a-Water and his son were executed with Warbeck' (*Ure*, 138).

191 *wonder*: extraordinary example of.

193 *determines*: comes to an end.

196 *our payments*: i.e. their lives.

197 *our debts*: i.e. life to be paid back to Nature.

203 *stagger manhood*: make courage fail.

Epilogue

10 *to*: to the company of.

GLOSSARY

'a he

abjects outcasts

abstract ideal (*LM*, 4.3.46)

accident unexpected event (*LM*,
  1.1.107); technical term for a
  non-substance, according to
  Aristotelian philosophy (*BH*, 1.3.118)

acquittance repayment of debt

admirable amazing (*BH*, 3.2.137)

admit imagine that (*LM*, 2.1.273;
  3.3.96); agree to, accept (*BH*, 1.1.44;
  2.2.58; *PW*, 5.3.41); tolerate, allow
  (*TP*, 1.1.4; *PW*, 1.2.19); entail (*PW*,
  3.2.41)

affect like

affections emotions (*BH*, 3.2.53)

affied betrothed

affronted confronted (*PW*, 5.1.51)

air song (*BH*, 4.3.155)

alone only (*PW*, 4.4.6; 5.3.32)

ambrosia the sweet, scented food of
  the gods which gave immortality

amity friendship

an if (*LM*, 2.1.111; 3.3.60)

anchorite a religious recluse

annoys (noun) troubles

antic (adj.) grotesque, clownish,
  theatrical, fantastic; (noun) a clown,
  a fool

apish fantastically foolish

apprehension understanding

aqua-vitae medicinal spirits

arms armorial bearings (*PW*, 3.1.97)

arrant notorious

arras curtain

art learning (*LM*, 3.3.8; *TP*, 1.1.6);
  practical skill or medical knowledge
  (*TP*, 1.2.144; 2.1.67; 2.3.40)

artist person skilled in intellectual
  arts

attempts (noun) enterprises,
  endeavours

attend await

auditor student (*BH*, 1.3.31)

available advantageous

avoid cure (*LM*, 1.2.116)

avow admit and justify

awful awe-inspiring

balk avoid, shun

ban-dog a fierce, chained dog

bandy band together

bane poison

barbed adorned (*PW*, 4.5.8)

battalia battalion

batten grow fat

battles battalions (*PW*, 5.1.55)

bawd brothel-keeper, pimp

beadsman servant; one paid to pray
  for souls

bear-leach bear doctor

bedlam a mental asylum (*LM*, 2.1.64;
  PW, 3.2.6; 5.3.75); a madman (*LM*,
  3.3.52; *PW*, 2.3.32)

beholding indebted

behoof benefit

beldam witch; furious raging woman
  (*PW*, 1.1.122)

belie slander, lie about

belike perhaps

benefit profit

bereaven bereft

beseeming suitable (*BH*, 3.5.65)

beshrew curse; blame greatly (*PW*,
  5.2.139)

bewray exhibit, reveal

big important

blade gallant; a daring fellow

blood sexual desire (*BH*, 3.5.55; *TP*,
  2.2.28); genetic affinity (*TP*, 1.1.32)

bodkin needle

bold convinced (*BH*, 2.1.39)

bolt (verb) sieve (*BH*, 3.1.63)

bootless futile, unworkable

Boreas the North Wind (a deity to the
  Greeks)

botchers tailors who repair clothes

bounce a heavy and noisy thump
(*LM*, 1.1.11)

bounty generosity

brave splendidly dressed (*TP*, 1.2.97);
fine, magnificent (*TP*, 4.3.45/208)

braved defied

braver finer (*TP*, 2.2.93)

braveries finery

broached pierced open, tapped (a
cask, a vein, etc.)

broken bankrupt (*PW*, 2.1.16)

buckler a small, round shield

buffet contend with, beat back (*PW*,
5.3.46)

bugbear imaginary object of terror

buss kiss

bustling contending (*PW*, 1.2.183)

buzz rumour, gossip

capital deadly (*BH*, 2.2.50)

careful full of care

carmen carters, carriers

carnation flesh-coloured

caroches luxury coaches or carriages

carriage behaviour (*LM*, 5.1.78)

case state, condition

cast devised (*LM*, 1.2.155)

cast-apothecaries discarded preparers
and sellers of medicinal drugs

cast-suit servant; someone wearing
cast-off clothing

censure judgement, opinion, views
(not necessarily hostile)

centaurs mythical creatures half-man,
half-horse

challenge claim (*PW*, 2.3.53)

chancery court of equity which dealt
with cases that could not be resolved
under the common law

chaplet garland for the head of the
victor

character sign (*PW*, 2.2.90)

charactered written

charge expense

charges duties, responsibilities (*PW*,
2.2.160; 4.4.85)

charm persuade (*LM*, 2.1.170)

check restrain (*BH*, 1.3.22)

checking putting a stop to

chimes tolling bells

chopping bouncing (*BH*, 2.1.123)

chops jaws (*BH*, 2.3.139)

ciphers noughts, nonentities

circumstance ceremony (*LM*, 5.1.160)

clapper-clawed struck

clefs signs on musical staves to
determine pitch

clew ball of thread

clipped embraced

clog (noun) a piece of wood to impede
motion or prevent escape (*BH*, 4.2.175)

close stool commode

closely secretly

closet box for keeping valuables (*LM*,
1.3.78); private room (*BH*, 2.3.140;
PW, 1.1.122)

cock-sure certain

codpiece an (often ornamented) piece
of apparel which exaggerated the
male genital area

coil uproar (*PW*, 2.2.26)

cokes simpleton

collect form (new) conclusions (*BH*,
2.2.53)

collops slices

combustion(s) commotion(s)

commend praise

commendation recommendation

commotion agitation, rising (*PW*,
4.2.70)

compeer equal

complaints laments of love (*LM*,
1.1.58)

complimentally courteously

con read and memorize

conceit judgement (*LM*, 2.1.96);
opinion (*LM*, 3.1.23); imaginative
idea (*BH*, 1.3.143; 2.3.84; 3.3.63;
4.2.8; *PW*, 2.3.160; 4.4.45)

conceive understand (*LM*, 2.1.282;
PW, 4.4.75)

concluded with come to an
arrangement with (*LM*, 2.1.20)

condolements lamentations

confirms assures (*BH*, 2.3.64)

confound destroy

confusion destruction, damnation

consort (noun) accord, harmony,
concert (*LM*, 4.3.51; *PW*, 3.2.78)

constantly confidently

construction interpretation

contemn despise

contents things which content or please

convinced disproved (*BH*, 5.2.54)

convoy funeral train (*LM*, 4.3.115)

cordial (noun) medicine, food, or drink which invigorates the heart

corn-cutters chiropodists

corse corpse

cot-quean a cottage wife; applied to a man—one who resembles a shrewish, vulgar woman

countenance patronage (*PW*, 1.1.77)

country county (*PW*, 3.1.19; 5.1.49)

courage lust, sexual vigour (*LM*, 3.2.60); spirit, vigour (*LM*, 5.2.132)

courtship court etiquette, courtly behaviour

cousin kinsman or kinswoman

coxcomb simpleton, fool; professional fool's head-dress

coz familiar term for cousin (applied to relatives generally)

cozen cheat

cozenage deception

craven a coward

creature instrument, devoted servant

credit high value (*TP*, 4.3.101); credibility (*PW*, 2.1.31)

crotchet whimsical fancy, perverse conceit (*LM*, 4.2.127)

cull embrace (*BH*, 2.1.26)

culled selected

cunning skill, wisdom

curiosity cleverness, ingenuity (*LM*, 1.1.141)

curious skilfully or beautifully wrought (*LM*, 1.3.50)

current acceptable currency (*BH*, 2.2.55)

dainties pleasures, delicacies

dainty fine, delightful (*LM*, 4.2.193)

dammed blocked (*BH*, 2.1.1)

debates quarrels (*TP*, 4.2.10)

declined debased (*LM*, 3.2.120)

d'ee do ye

defame false accusation

demean conduct

demur hesitation (*BH*, 2.2.80)

denier coin worth less than a farthing (approximately one-tenth of a new penny)

derived transmitted

descant sing, complain (*TP*, 5.1.16)

detriments losses (*PW*, 5.2.17)

devasted devastated

device dramatic device or masque

Diabolo devil

dial a watch or clock's face (*BH*, 3.2.4)

digest endure, stomach (*PW*, 2.3.148)

direction order (*PW*, 3.1.58)

directly absolutely, completely (*LM*, 5.2.28); exactly (*PW*, 3.3.60)

disavow deny, disown

discover reveal

discovery disclosure (*PW*, 1.3.8)

dissemble pretend

distaste (verb) dislike (*TP*, 2.2.42)

distinction discrimination (*PW*, 3.2.105)

distracted fickle, wavering (*TP*, 2.2.27; deranged in mind *LM*, 2.1.173)

dolent sorrowful

doodles silly fellows

dotage mental derangement (*LM*, 3.1.102)

dotard old fool

doubt fear; suspect

down a refrain (*LM*, 1.1.124), first feathers (*LM*, 2.2.34)

dreadful fearful

drenched drugged

drifts (noun) droves (like a moving herd) (*BH*, 2.1.130)

drill train in military fashion

drone(s) drone bee(s), sluggish and lazy creatures

dry severe (*TP*, 2.6.98)

durst past tense of dare

earnest introduction (*BH*, 3.5.48); payment (*BH*, 4.4.66); seriousness (*PW*, 3.3.47)

ecstasy state of trance (*LM*, 3.1.101)

edge (verb) sharpen

'ee ye

egregiously excellently

else at other times (*LM*, 3.2.162)

Elysium state of perfect happiness; the heaven of the ancient Greeks

empiric an untrained physician or surgeon

enamels (verb) adorns with colour

encomium a eulogy, work of praise

ends matters (*TP*, 1.2.66)

endued endowed (*LM*, 1.1.169)

engaged secured, pledged

engagements obligations

engine trick device (*BH*, 4.4.21 S.D.)

engines plots (*PW*, 4.2.8)

engross monopolize

engrossed acquired (*BH*, 3.3.59)

enjoin direct with authority or urgency (*BH*, 3.5.35)

entertain formally receive, welcome

entertainment reception, welcome, hospitality

equity justice (*BH*, 2.3.71)

except unless

excuse avoid (*BH*, 5.2.82)

execution operation, action (*PW*, 2.2.40; 4.5.54)

exercise (noun) discipline (*BH*, 2.3.153); (verb) try, test (*BH*, 4.2.44)

expect await (*BH*, 1.2.103)

extremes excesses (*TP*, 4.2.19); extreme needs (*PW*, 2.3.179); extremities (*PW*, 4.3.101)

extremities hardships (*TP*, 4.3.103)

extremity utmost severity or suffering

eyelet-holes holes for laces

factor agent

faintly weakly, weak-spiritedly (*PW*, 3.1.86)

fall to begin eating (*LM*, 3.3.23)

fame reputation

famous notorious

farthingale hooped petticoat to extend the skirt of a woman's dress

fashion manner (*BH*, 2.3.3)

faulting (adj.) that commits faults (*PW*, 1.2.89)

fawns flatteries (*PW*, 3.4.27)

fealty homage

feathered propelled (*PW*, 3.1.51)

feigned invented

fell (adj.) ruthless, cruel

fiddle-faddle fuss about petty trifles (*BH*, 1.3.110)

firks caprices

fit (noun) sudden inclination, impulse; (verb) supply a fitting punishment

for (*TP*, 5.6.79); (adj.) proper (*TP*, 2.5.13); apt (*PW*, 5.3.216)

fitted prepared (*BH*, 5.3.80)

fixed composed (*BH*, 2.3.137)

fleetings swift flowings (*BH*, 3.2.58)

flesh-tailor surgeon

floats fluxes or floods

Flourish S.D. fanfare to announce a distinguished person

fond foolish, weak in judgement

footposts foot messengers

fopperies follies

forage plunder (*PW*, 3.4.54)

forbear leave, keep away from

fore-dooming prejudging

forfeit loss

forfend forbid

frailty moral weakness (*TP*, 4.3.144); mortality (*PW*, 2.2.54; 4.5.59)

frantic violently mad or distracted

free noble, high-born

frightful terrifying

furniture trappings, necessaries

fustian pompous language (*BH*, 4.1.87)

gaffer good fellow (said respectfully of an older person)

gage stake (*TP*, 5.3.56)

'gainst in anticipation of

gallant a beau or lover; a man of fashion attentive to women

galliards lively dances

gallimaufry hodge-podge, an odd mixture

garboils tumults

gay fine

gelding eunuch (*LM*, 3.2.11)

generous noble, courageous, liberal

genius guiding or guardian spirit

gentlemen ushers gentlemen acting as ushers to a person of higher rank

ghostly spiritual (*TP*, 3.4.29)

gills flesh under the jaws and ears

gilt decorated with

Godamercy God have mercy on you—i.e. thank you (*TP*, 2.6.17)

good good friend, good man, good sir

good fellow an agreeable companion (*LM*, 4.2.163)

good sooth good faith, truth

goody goodwife, mistress, i.e. 'Mrs'
gorget throat armour
Gorgon female monster who could turn to stone anything she gazed upon
government prudence (*TP*, 1.1.51)
grant acknowledgement
grate (verb) intensify (*BH*, 2.1.62); (noun) cage (*PW*, 4.5.27)
grateful pleasing (*PW*, 2.3.162)
gratulate congratulate
grossly indelicately
ground cause (of quarrel) (*TP*, 1.2.28)
grudging (noun) an inward disquiet or vexation
gull (noun) credulous person, dupe; (verb) to cheat, to trick
habiliment ability (*BH*, 5.2.48)
habit clothing (*BH*, 1.3.3)
habited dressed
halberts spears with axe-heads, carried by the watch
haled dragged (*PW*, 2.1.51)
halter a rope with a noose for hanging someone (*LM*, 1.2.139)
hapless unlucky
haunted frequented (*TP*, 4.3.153)
hautboys ancestor of the oboe (shriller and usually played as a consort of instruments)
hearty heartfelt, genuine
Helicon Mount Helicon, sacred to the Muses
hereright immediately
hie go quickly
hit succeed (*TP*, 3.5.22)
hobby-horses performers dressed as horses in the morris dance and other entertainments
home directly, deeply (*PW*, 1.3.69; 2.1.118)
horribly exceedingly
hubbubs noisy entertainments
hucksters pedlars
hug cherish, cling to (*LM*, 1.2.14)
hurdle a frame on which condemned traitors were dragged through the streets to execution
Hydra a many-headed monster which grew two heads for every one cut off
Hymen god of marriage

idle futile (*TP*, 5.3.1)
idly deliriously (*BH*, 4.2.122)
illiterate unlearned
importune persistently insist
impostorous deceptive
impostumes abscesses
improved intensified (*PW*, 3.1.54)
index pointer in the margin of old books (*BH*, 5.1.36)
indifferent tolerably (*TP*, 3.4.1)
indirection roundabout means
indited written
infer determine (*TP*, 3.2.17)
inform guide (*BH*, 3.4.5)
ingeniously wittily
innocent simpleton
innovation revolt (*PW*, 4.4.79)
inroads invasions, forays (*PW*, 5.2.13)
instance reason, cause (*TP*, 1.2.224)
insulting arrogant
intelligence information, news
intermured walled in
intrenching infringing
inured accustomed
inurement habituation
inward private
issue descendants; outcome (*PW*, 3.3.33); proceeds (*PW*, 4.4.51)
jades horses
jealous suspicious (*BH*, 3.1.3)
jointure dowry
jolly fine, excellent (*LM*, 5.2.16)
jubilee time for rejoicing
juggler one who deceives by trickery
juggling (adj.) deceptive; (noun) pretence
Juno Jupiter's sister and his wife
keep dwell, be situated (*TP*, 1.2.150)
kennel central gutter in a street (i.e. sole drainage for mud and sanitation)
kind foolish (*BH*, 3.2.178)
kitling kitten
knacks choice dishes (*PW*, 3.2.10)
know acknowledge (*LM*, 3.2.103)
lackey serve (*BH*, 3.2.132)
landloper vagabond
largeness liberal bestowal of gifts (*BH*, 4.2.36)
largess liberal gift (*PW*, 3.1.112)
'las alas

leading-staff baton
league alliance
least (adj.) slightest
legerdemain sleight of hand, deception
licence authority (*BH*, 3.4.6)
liege-people faithful subjects
likes pleases
limn (fig.) paint (*LM*, 3.3.100)
list listen; wish (*PW*, 5.1.101)
livery clothes or other tokens worn to
  indicate service
lucre profit, gain (*BH*, 3.1.41)
luxury lechery, lustfulness (*BH*,
  3.2.23; *TP*, 4.3.9)
mad furious (*TP*, 4.3.171)
magnificence generosity (*PW*, 2.1.98)
magnifico any person in an exalted
  position
malice discouragement (*BH*, 1.3.21);
  wrongs suffered (*BH*, 4.2.109)
Marry (exclamation) ejaculation
  indicating indignation or surprise
  (originally an oath from the name of
  the Virgin Mary)
marts fairs
match encounter, combat (*PW*, 1.3.68)
maugre in spite of
May-game laughing-stock
mean the golden mean, the true
  standard (*TP*, 2.2.10)
meanings intentions (*BH*, 3.1.51)
measure a solemn dance with
  measured steps
meat food (in a general sense) (*TP*,
  1.2.6)
megrims whims
mercer dealer in textiles
mere pure
method arrangement
mettle courage
mew exclamation of contempt
mewed up imprisoned
mews (noun) seagulls
mewed moulted, shed (*BH*, 2.1.45)
mineralist a promoter of
  mineral-based medicines
minion darling, favourite
miscarry come to harm
mischief ill fortune (*TP*, 1.2.220;
  2.5.10)

misconceit misunderstanding
misdoubt distrust
miss lack (*PW*, 2.3.90)
mockery (adj.) counterfeit (*PW*, 1.1.4)
moods i.e. modes, the major and
  minor tonal systems (*LM*, 1.1.135)
moon-calves abnormal offspring
more further (*PW*, 2.2.119)
morion a visorless helmet
morning's draught early or
  mid-morning drink of ale, wine, or
  spirits
motion proposal (*LM*, 4.2.63; *BH*,
  1.1.95; 2.2.58; *PW*, 1.2.159; 2.3.9);
  puppet show (*LM*, 5.2.46; *TP*,
  2.4.40); puppet (*BH*, 4.2.105); life
  (*BH*, 2.2.2)
motion(s) violent stirring(s),
  impulse(s) (*LM*, 1.1.82; 2.1.89; *PW*,
  3.4.43)
mountebank an itinerant quack
mounting ambitious (*PW*, 4.4.74)
mumbled mauled (*LM*, 5.1.131)
muscadine muscatel wine
mystical secret, concealed (*BH*, 2.1.20)
naught worthless
nearly closely
nice fine, exact
niceness coyness
noddy simpleton
nonage immaturity, early stages (*BH*,
  4.3.106)
nonce time being
nor . . . nor neither . . . nor
noverint bond
number count
nuncio Papal representative
obedience authority (*LM*, 4.2.141)
observance courteous attention (*BH*,
  3.3.22)
occasions opportunities
odds difference (*PW*, 4.5.62)
once sometime (*TP*, 3.4.10)
only alone, exclusively
or now (*BH*, 2.1.105)
or . . . or either . . . or
oracle the place where a deity might
  be consulted; a prophet or wise
  person
oraculous divinely inspired

oratory place where oratorical arts are taught

orisons prayers

ouzel blackbird

overflux overflow

owing owning

painted false, pretended

pale domain (*PW*, 5.2.3)

pander a procurer of women

pand'ring procuring

pap breast

partage share

partake obtain (*PW*, 4.2.45); share (*PW*, 5.3.84)

particular private (*LM*, 2.1.14)

parties partners (*PW*, 1.2.70); supporters (*PW*, 5.1.59)

parts talents, qualities (*TP*, 2.1.64; 2.4.25)

pashing striking violently

passages interchanges (*LM*, 5.2.211)

passing (adv.) exceedingly (*LM*, 5.2.100)

patent licence (*LM*, 1.2.51); licence for monopolies (*LM*, 2.1.113); letters patent to convey a privilege or office (*LM*, 5.2.53)

pavan a stately dance

pawn'dst pledged

peevish foolish; spiteful (*TP*, 5.3.40)

pell-mell at close quarters, hand to hand (*PW*, 4.2.58)

pensioner hired man (*BH*, 2.1.14)

perfect (adj.) pure; (verb) complete

perfection accomplishments (*TP*, 2.1.60)

period (noun) stop

Periwinkle a playful term for a woman (*LM*, 1.2.92)

perstreperous noisy

persuade encourage

physic medical treatment, medicine, remedy

pieced to connected with (*LM*, 1.1.40)

pile large building (*PW*, 4.1.7)

pledge drink to (*TP*, 4.1.63)

politic cunning

politician shrewd schemer (*BH*, 2.1.150)

poniard dagger

portly stately

ports gates

post (verb) travel poste-haste; (noun) courier

pounded locked up (like a stray animal)

practic practising; artful (*PW*, Brograve comm. poem)

practice scheming (*LM*, 4.3.34)

prated chattered idly

precedent example to follow

preferred presented for favours; promoted

prejudice harm (*BH*, 5.2.76)

presence presence chamber or dais; place for royal ceremonial attendance (*LM*, 2.1.44)

present immediate, urgent

presenters performers

presently immediately; already (*PW*, 2.3.38)

presentment dramatic presentation (*BH*, Prol., 13)

pressed weighed on (*PW*, 2.2.4)

prettily fortunately (*TP*, 3.3.17)

pretty pleasing (*LM*, 2.1.185); excellent (*BH*, 1.3.164); ingenious (*BH*, 4.1.32)

prevent anticipate (*BH*, 4.1.148)

private alone (*LM*, 1.1.102)

prodigious monstrous

prodigy monster (*BH*, 4.1.73)

prognosticate betoken (*BH*, 1.1.10)

progress journey

proper personal (*TP*, 5.6.147)

proportion order (*BH*, 2.3.25)

protested declared, avowed

protests protestations (*TP*, 2.2.72)

prove put to the test

proves turns out (*TP*, 1.2.182)

providence foresight (*PW*, 4.1.16; 3.3.13)

provident fertile (*BH*, 4.1.11)

puddle (noun) confusion (*BH*, 4.3.108)

puff swagger (*LM*, 2.1.43)

puissance strength, power

pule whine

put up sheathe your sword

quab an imperfect thing

quacksalver a quack specializing in marvellous ointments quail (verb) wither

quaint cunning (*PW*, 1.2.91)

quaintest most unusual, most curious (*LM*, 1.1.148)

quaking trembling

qualify pacify (*LM*, 4.2.16)

qualities accomplishments (*TP*, 1.2.91)

quean promiscuous woman, whore

quest inquiry (*PW*, 3.1.102)

quick hasty (*LM*, 2.1.321)

quicken give life to (*BH*, 4.3.55)

quintessence purest manifestation

quit acquit (*BH*, 5.2.46)

quitted cleared (*LM*, 5.1.59)

race course of action (*BH*, 2.3.86)

railed fastened in a row (*PW*, 3.1.77)

range wander (*PW*, 5.1.7)

rapine plundering

rare incomparable, fine; unusual (*PW*, 4.4.55)

rated taxed

reach comprehend (*BH*, 1.3.180)

read (adj.) learned

recall withdraw, revoke (*PW*, 1.3.95)

recourse access (*TP*, 2.6.108)

reduce convert (*LM*, 1.2.38)

reel (verb) to wind wool or thread (*BH*, 1.2.134)

relation narration, telling (*PW*, 2.1.54)

relish flavour

remarked marked out

remember remind (*LM*, 2.1.158)

remit pardon

repining discontented

report fame, reputation

repute (verb) consider; (noun) opinion

reserved designated (*PW*, 3.1.22); preserved (*PW*, 3.1.72)

resolution interpretation (*BH*, 3.1.78)

resolve answer; assure

resolved decided (*TP*, 1.2.236)

resolves is determined on

respectively carefully (*LM*, 2.2.122); respectfully (*PW*, 5.2.105)

respects considerations (*BH*, 3.2.99)

rests remains (*LM*, 5.1.112)

retribution recompense (*PW*, 4.1.76)

riddle guess (*TP*, 2.6.66)

rigour offensive excess (*TP*, 5.5.72)

riot extravagent display, dissipated revels (*LM*, 1.2.2); wasteful living (*LM*, 4.3.61; *BH*, 2.1.31; *PW*, 4.4.49)

roaring roistering, blustering (as in 'roaring boys', i.e. riotous gallants) (*LM*, 3.1.64)

royalty authority (*BH*, 3.2.145); sovereignty (*BH*, 5.3.42)

ruffle do battle (*PW*, 1.2.10; 5.3.34)

rumour public opinion

runagate vagabond

sad sober (*BH*, 2.2.77)

sadly solemnly (*TP*, 5.1.35)

satire satirist (*LM*, 4.1.32)

save you! God save you! (a greeting)

savours smells of (*BH*, 1.1.55)

saw (noun) a traditional saying

school (verb) discipline (*LM*, 5.1.134)

school-points topics of academic debate

sconce head, brain

scrivener a scribe, a clerk

scruple doubt

seconding supporting, encouraging

secure immune, free from anxiety; unsuspecting

securely confidently (*PW*, 1.3.1)

sensible aware (*LM*, 2.1.278; *PW*, 3.1.69); strongly felt (*PW*, 4.1.38)

sensibly consciously (*PW*, 5.3.204)

sensuality sensuous pleasure (*BH*, 3.5.20)

several various (*LM*, 1.1.84); separate, individual (*LM*, 3.2.78; *BH*, 3.2.16 S.D.; 4.2.9)

'sfoot by God's foot

shag shaggy

shame (noun) modesty (*LM*, 1.3.81)

shape (verb) organize

shough a lap-dog

show look (*LM*, 1.3.1)

shrewd grievous (*LM*, 3.2.52); shrewish (*TP*, 2.2.114)

sift test

simples medicinal herbs

simplicity simpleton (*TP*, 2.6.96)

sir-reverence (1) respect, with a possible pun on (2) human excrement (*LM*, 5.1.25)

skimmed removed the surface matter

skirmishing weapon waving or flourishing

slack (verb) neglect (*LM*, 1.2.153); lessen, relax (*TP*, 4.3.76)

slightens slights, dismisses

slightly without much attention (*PW*, 2.1.39 S.D.)

sloth slowness (*LM*, 5.2.139)

slovenry slovenliness

solemn sumptuous (*TP*, 5.5.21)

sometimes formerly (*TP*, 5.6.122)

sooth truth (*TP*, 1.2.250)

sort apportion (*LM*, 2.1.254); turn out in a certain way (*BH*, 1.1.67)

sottish foolish

special leading (*TP*, 2.2.154)

speed prosper (*TP*, 2.3.50)

spleen impetuosity, eagerness (*PW*, 1.3.56)

splits (noun) splinters

spoon-meat food for babies or the infirm

springal (noun) a youth (*BH*, 2.1.12); (adj.) youthful (*BH*, 3.2.144)

squall a small or insignificant being (*LM*, 2.1.118)

square honest

stagger totter, waver

stand (verb) withstand; (noun) standstill (*PW*, 4.2.2)

stands (noun) positions

stark completely

staring frantic (*LM*, 2.2.46)

states dignitaries (*TP*, 5.2.17; 5.4.37)

stay (imperative) stop

stayed held back, delayed (*PW*, 2.2.30)

stays delays (*BH*, 1.2.105 S.D.)

still always; even so (*BH*, 4.3.123)

stout brave (*PW*, 3.1.5)

straggler vagabond, ragamuffin

strains tunes (*BH*, 3.2.21)

strangely exceedingly, surpassingly (*LM*, 5.2.120)

stranger foreign (*PW*, 4.1.42)

study consider at length (*PW*, 2.1.83)

stuffs fabrics

style (verb) title

styled called

subsidies taxes

succeeds follows (*BH*, 4.3.155)

sudden violent (*TP*, 1.2.20)

suddenly at once

sue beg

sufferance endurance; suffering (*PW*, 3.4.74; 5.3.171)

suit entreaty (*PW*, 3.2.173)

sullen gloomy

sumptuous splendidly dressed

superstitiously idolatrously, infatuatedly (*TP*, 4.3.118)

supplies reinforcements (*PW*, 2.1.27)

supplying assisting, healing (*BH*, 4.1.118)

supported formally escorted

suppositers supporters

surely certainly

surety guarantee

suspect suspicion, fear (*TP*, 5.1.50)

suspected regarded with suspicion (*PW*, 5.1.28)

swabber ship's cleaner

sways rules

table tablet (*BH*, 2.3.26)

tablet a flat, ornamental casing worn round the neck

tabors small drums

tall valiant (*PW*, 4.5.35)

tatterdemalion ragamuffin

t'ee to ye

temper (noun) disposition (*BH*, 4.1.79); (verb) mix (*PW*, 5.2.135)

tender (noun) offer

tent (verb) probe

tenters hooks for stretching cloth

terms circumstances (*TP*, 3.5.4)

testament will

tetchy irritable (*BH*, 1.3.113)

thou'lt thou wilt (will)

thrift prosperity, success

thriftless unprofitable

throughly thoroughly

thrum weave

tickled gratified (*TP*, 2.6.63)

tittle smallest detail

toils traps, snares (*LM*, 1.3.96; *PW*, 2.2.131)

toss-pot drunkard

tough violent (*PW*, 3.2.53)

toward about to begin (*PW*, 3.2.110)

trade course of action (*BH*, 2.1.154)

traduced slandered

train (verb) lure (*TP*, 5.3.57)

trained lured (*BH*, 4.4.28); seduced (*TP*, 4.3.230)

treat(ed) negotiated (*LM*, 2.1.160; *PW*, 1.2.162)

treaty negotiations

trial test (*PW*, 4.3.124)

tried proven, tested

trifle waste (*PW*, 5.2.117)

trim (noun) the latest fashions; (adj.) fine, prettily adorned

triumphs joys (*BH*, 1.1.34)

Trojan a merry or roystering fellow (*LM*, 4.2.166)

troth marriage vow; honesty, truth (*LM*, 1.1.65)

trow believe

trouses close-fitting drawers

trumperies trifling (*LM*, 3.1.76)

truncheon staff of office (*PW*, 3.4.3 S.D.)

try test

turtle turtle-dove

tutelage guardianship

twingle-twangles sounds of the Gaelic harp

Ud's God's

Uds sa'me God save me

uncompounded unalloyed, pure

uncouth desolate (*LM*, 4.2.49)

undone overthrown; ruined (*TP*, 1.2.205)

unedge (verb) blunt

unfellowed unequalled

unranged deranged, beyond all limits

unshook (adj.) unshaken

unskilful inexperienced, unwise

unsteady fickle (*LM*, 2.1.12)

untoward stubborn, stiff (*LM*, 5.2.235)

vapours boasts (*LM*, 4.2.44)

vent (noun) outlet, relief

venture presume (*LM*, 3.2.176)

very true; real

vizard mask

votaress a nun

vouchsafe bestow favour on; graciously accept (*PW*, 5.2.145)

wait accompany, attend, serve

waiter attendant (*BH*, 2.2.130)

wake (verb) continue unsleeping (*LM*, 4.2.116)

want lack

wanted lacked

w'are we are

watchword signal to begin an attack

wax-lights candles, tapers

wayward peverse (*PW*, 4.2.3)

weal prosperity

well-timbered well-built

whets sharpens

whiles while

whisk (noun) whipper-snapper

white boy fair-haired boy, i.e. favourite and heir

whoreson contemptible

widgeon fool

willing determined (*BH*, 2.3.8)

wink close eyes

wit intelligence (*TP*, 1.3.23); thought (*TP*, 1.3.72); common sense (*TP*, 3.9.59)

without outside

wonted customary, usual

woo entreat

woodcock a bird associated with foolishness

wood'st didst woo

wormwood medicinal herb with a bitter taste

y'are you are

	Women's Writing 1778–1838
WILLIAM BECKFORD	Vathek
JAMES BOSWELL	Life of Johnson
FRANCES BURNEY	Camilla
	Cecilia
	Evelina
	The Wanderer
LORD CHESTERFIELD	Lord Chesterfield's Letters
JOHN CLELAND	Memoirs of a Woman of Pleasure
DANIEL DEFOE	A Journal of the Plague Year
	Moll Flanders
	Robinson Crusoe
	Roxana
HENRY FIELDING	Joseph Andrews and Shamela
	A Journey from This World to the Next and
	The Journal of a Voyage to Lisbon
	Tom Jones
WILLIAM GODWIN	Caleb Williams
OLIVER GOLDSMITH	The Vicar of Wakefield
MARY HAYS	Memoirs of Emma Courtney
ELIZABETH HAYWOOD	The History of Miss Betsy Thoughtless
ELIZABETH INCHBALD	A Simple Story
SAMUEL JOHNSON	The History of Rasselas
	The Major Works
CHARLOTTE LENNOX	The Female Quixote
MATTHEW LEWIS	Journal of a West India Proprietor
	The Monk
HENRY MACKENZIE	The Man of Feeling
ALEXANDER POPE	Selected Poetry

*The
Oxford
World's
Classics
Website*

www.worldsclassics.co.uk

- Information about new titles
- Explore the full range of Oxford World's Classics
- Links to other literary sites and the main OUP webpage
- Imaginative competitions, with bookish prizes
- Peruse the Oxford World's Classics Magazine
- Articles by editors
- Extracts from Introductions
- A forum for discussion and feedback on the series
- Special information for teachers and lecturers

www.worldsclassics.co.uk

American Literature

British and Irish Literature

Children's Literature

Classics and Ancient Literature

Colonial Literature

Eastern Literature

European Literature

History

Medieval Literature

Oxford English Drama

Poetry

Philosophy

Politics

Religion

The Oxford Shakespeare

A complete list of Oxford Paperbacks, including Oxford World's Classics, Oxford Shakespeare, Oxford Drama, and Oxford Paperback Reference, is available in the UK from the Academic Division Publicity Department, Oxford University Press, Great Clarendon Street, Oxford OX2 6DP.

In the USA, complete lists are available from the Paperbacks Marketing Manager, Oxford University Press, 198 Madison Avenue, New York, NY 10016.

Oxford Paperbacks are available from all good bookshops. In case of difficulty, customers in the UK can order direct from Oxford University Press Bookshop, Freepost, 116 High Street, Oxford OX1 4BR, enclosing full payment. Please add 10 per cent of published price for postage and packing.